COMBATING TORTURE
– A MANUAL FOR ACTION

"No one shall be subjected to torture or to cruel, inhuman
or degrading treatment or punishment."
Universal Declaration of Human Rights, Article 5

Amnesty International is a worldwide voluntary activist movement working for human rights. It is independent of any government, political persuasion or religious creed. It does not support or oppose any government or political system, nor does it support or oppose the views of those whose rights it seeks to protect. It is concerned solely with the impartial protection of human rights.

Amnesty International's vision is of a world in which every person enjoys all the human rights enshrined in the Universal Declaration of Human Rights and other international human rights standards.

Amnesty International undertakes research and action focused on preventing and ending grave abuses of the rights to physical and mental integrity, freedom of conscience and expression, and freedom from discrimination. In this context, it:

- seeks the release of prisoners of conscience: these are people detained for their political, religious or other conscientiously held beliefs or because of their ethnic origin, sex, colour, language, national or social origin, economic status, birth or other status – who have not used or advocated violence;
- works for fair and prompt trials for all political prisoners;
- opposes without reservation the death penalty, torture and other cruel, inhuman or degrading treatment or punishment;
- campaigns for an end to political killings and "disappearances";
- calls on governments to refrain from unlawful killings in armed conflict;
- calls on armed political groups to end abuses such as the detention of prisoners of conscience, hostage-taking, torture and unlawful killings;
- opposes abuses by non-state actors where the state has failed to fulfil its obligations to provide effective protection;
- campaigns for perpetrators of human rights abuses to be brought to justice;
- seeks to assist asylum-seekers who are at risk of being returned to a country where they might suffer serious abuses of their human rights;
- opposes certain grave abuses of economic, social and cultural rights.
  Amnesty International also seeks to:
- cooperate with other non-governmental organizations, the United Nations and regional intergovernmental organizations;
- ensure control of international military, security and police relations to prevent human rights abuses;
- organize human rights education and awareness raising programs.

Amnesty International is a democratic, self-governing movement with more than a million members and supporters in over 140 countries and territories. It is funded largely by its worldwide membership and public donations.

Combating torture
– a manual for action

Amnesty International Publications

Update: The Optional Protocol to the UN Convention against Torture, providing for a global system of inspection visits by international experts to places of detention, working as a complement to national inspection institutions, as a safeguard against torture (see pages 141-142, 205), was adopted by the UN General Assembly voting in plenary session on 18 December 2002. Amnesty International is calling on all states parties to the Convention against Torture to become parties to the Optional Protocol as soon as possible.

First published in 2003 by
Amnesty International Publications
International Secretariat
Peter Benenson House
1 Easton Street
London WC1X 0DW
United Kingdom

www.amnesty.org

Printed by:
The Alden Press
Osney Mead
Oxford
United Kingdom

The information in this manual covers the period up to 31 December 2001.
Some details have been updated to October 2002.

The manual draws from the ideas and experiences of human rights defenders
around the world. Amnesty International particularly wishes to thank the
following experts for their valuable comments on the manuscript: Federico
Andreu Guzman, Roland Bank, Danielle Coquoz, Andrew Coyle, Ralph
Crawshaw, Malcolm D. Evans, Rod Morgan, Jelena Pejic, Sir Nigel Rodley and
Wilder Tayler.

Please note that readers may find some of the photographs and case histories
contained in this report disturbing.

Combating torture
– a manual for action

Contents

Endnotes   267

List of action examples

Abbreviations

Abbreviated titles of international and regional instruments and other abbreviations used in this manual are given below, along with their full titles. Further information on international and regional instruments can be found in Appendix 5.

Abbreviation	Full name
Additional Protocol I	Protocol Additional to the Geneva Conventions of 12 August 1949, and relating to the Protection of Victims of International Armed Conflicts
Additional Protocol II	Protocol Additional to the Geneva Conventions of 12 August 1949, and relating to the Protection of Victims of Non-International Armed Conflicts
Basic Principles on Force and Firearms	(UN) Basic Principles on the Use of Force and Firearms by Law Enforcement Officials
Beijing Rules	United Nations Standard Minimum Rules for the Administration of Juvenile Justice
Body of Principles on Detention	(UN) Body of Principles for the Protection of All Persons under Any Form of Detention or Imprisonment
CEDAW	(UN) Committee on the Elimination of Discrimination against Women
CINAT	Coalition of International NGOs against Torture
Convention against Torture	(UN) Convention against Torture and Other Cruel, Inhuman or Degrading Treatment or Punishment
CPT	(See European Committee for the Prevention of Torture)
Declaration against Torture	(UN) Declaration on the Protection of All Persons from Being Subjected to Torture and Other Cruel, Inhuman or Degrading Treatment or Punishment
Declaration on Enforced Disappearance	(UN) Declaration on the Protection of All Persons from Enforced Disappearance
Draft Basic Principles on Reparation	Draft Basic Principles and Guidelines on the Right to a Remedy and Reparation for Violations of International Human Rights and Humanitarian Law
ECOSOC	UN Economic and Social Council
European Committee for the Prevention of Torture (CPT)	European Committee for the Prevention of Torture and Inhuman or Degrading Treatment or Punishment
European Convention for the Prevention of Torture	(European) Convention for the Prevention of Torture and Inhuman or Degrading Treatment or Punishment

Abbreviation	Full name
European Convention on Human Rights	(European) Convention for the Protection of Human Rights and Fundamental Freedoms
First Geneva Convention	Geneva Convention for the Amelioration of the Condition of the Wounded and Sick in Armed Forces in the Field of August 12, 1949
(first) Optional Protocol to the ICCPR	Optional Protocol to the International Covenant on Civil and Political Rights
Fourth Geneva Convention	Geneva Convention relative to the Protection of Civilian Persons in Time of War of August 12, 1949
Geneva Convention	Convention on the Prevention and Punishment of the Crime of Genocide
Genocide Convention	Convention on the Prevention and Punishment of the Crime of Genocide
ICCPR	International Covenant on Civil and Political Rights
ICRC	International Committee of the Red Cross
NGO	non-governmental organization
PRI Handbook	*Making Standards Work: An International Handbook on Good Prison Practice,* published by Penal Reform International (cited in Appendix 1)
Principles on the Investigation of Torture	(UN) Principles on the Effective Investigation and Documentation of Torture and Other Cruel, Inhuman or Degrading Treatment or Punishment
Refugee Convention	(UN) Convention relating to the Status of Refugees
Rome Statute	Rome Statute of the International Criminal Court
Rwanda Tribunal	International Criminal Tribunal for Rwanda
Second Geneva Convention	Geneva Convention for the Amelioration of the Condition of Wounded, Sick and Shipwrecked Members of Armed Forces at Sea of August 12, 1949
Special Rapporteur on violence against women	(UN) Special Rapporteur on violence against women, its causes and consequences
Standard Minimum Rules	(UN) Standard Minimum Rules for the Treatment of Prisoners
Third Geneva Convention	Geneva Convention relative to the Treatment of Prisoners of War of August 12, 1949
Tokyo Rules	United Nations Standard Minimum Rules for Non-custodial Measures
UK	United Kingdom
UN	United Nations
UN Charter	Charter of the United Nations
USA	United States of America
Yugoslavia Tribunal	International Criminal Tribunal for the former Yugoslavia

List of cases

Short notes of cases cited in the manual are listed below, with page references.
Full case listings are given in Appendix 4.

Drawing by a former prisoner showing an interrogation technique used by the security forces in Casamance, Senegal, in the 1990s. The prisoner is beaten with ropes and clubs while suspended from an iron bar between two tables. (The captions *bar de fer, table* and *position pour interrogatoir* mean "iron bar", "table" and "position for interrogation".)

Foreword

"They started asking me questions from the first moment they put me into the minibus. When I did not answer, they started threatening me in the following manner. 'You don't talk now,' they would say; 'in a few minutes, when our hands will start roaming in between your legs, you will be singing like a nightingale'...

"[T]hey forced me to take off my skirt and stockings and laid me down on the ground and tied my hands and feet to pegs. A person by the name of Umit Erdal beat the soles of my feet for about half an hour. As he beat my soles he kept on saying, 'We made everybody talk here, you think we shall not succeed with you?' and insulting me...

"Umit Erdal attacked me and forced me to the ground. I fell on my face. He stood on my back and with the assistance of somebody else forced a truncheon into my anus. As I struggled to stand he kept on saying 'You whore! See what else we will do to you. First tell us how many people did you go to bed with? You won't be able to do it any more. We shall next destroy your womanhood'...

"They attached an electric wire to the small toe of my right foot and another to the end of a truncheon. They tried to penetrate my feminine organ with the truncheon. As I resisted they hit my body and legs with a large axe handle. They soon succeeded in penetrating my sexual organ with the truncheon with the electric wire on, and passed current. I fainted. A little later, the soldiers outside brought in a machine used for pumping air into people and said they would kill me..."

Statement of Ayse Semra Eker, arrested in Turkey in May 1972

This young woman's harrowing account of her treatment at the hands of the Turkish secret service opened Amnesty International's first major report on torture, published in 1973.[1] With minor changes, it could equally well describe a torture session at the beginning of the new millennium. The cruelty, the threats, the beatings, the use of electricity, the sexual attacks, the infliction of agonizing pain, the assault on the inner self in an attempt to attain the victim's total subjugation – all these techniques of torture are still with us today. Despite the redoubled efforts over the past half century to eliminate it, torture remains rife.

A survey of Amnesty International's research files from 1997 to mid-2000 found that the organization had received reports of torture or ill-treatment* by agents of the state in over 150 countries during the period. In more than 70 countries the victims included political prisoners,** but ordinary criminals and criminal suspects had reportedly been victims of torture or ill-treatment in over 130 countries. People had reportedly died as a result of torture in over 80 countries. These figures related only to actions by state agents and did not include abuses by armed political groups and private individuals that can be assimilated to the notion of torture or ill-treatment.[2]

In October 2000 Amnesty International launched a worldwide campaign against torture, the third in the organization's history. The slogan "Take a step to stamp out torture" was chosen to emphasize that people all over the world have important roles to play in combating torture and ill-treatment. The campaign was meant to rouse world opinion so as to ensure that the fight against torture remains high on the world agenda.

The Universal Declaration of Human Rights states that no one shall be subjected to torture or cruel, inhuman or degrading treatment or punishment. Since its adoption in 1948, much has happened in the fight against torture. The United Nations (UN) and regional intergovernmental organizations[3] have adopted detailed safeguards for the prevention of torture and have created mechanisms for tackling the problem. Governments have introduced legal reforms. National courts have adopted important decisions. Non-governmental organizations (NGOs) have been formed to combat torture and assist the victims. Lawyers, doctors and other professionals have acted courageously and expertly. Ordinary citizens have taken part in the effort, putting pressure on governments to act. Much has been accomplished, but the persistence of torture shows that there is still much to be done.

This manual for action is about the fight against torture. It brings together the ideas, the techniques, the achievements, the standards of governmental behaviour and the means of implementing those standards that have emerged from the efforts of anti-torture activists around the world over the past 25 years and more. The hope is that people and organizations around the world concerned about torture will benefit from learning what others have done, thus strengthening the fight against torture.

Chapter 1 of the manual outlines the development and principal achievements of the fight against torture since the Second World War. It gives an account of the evolving perceptions of the issue, offers a framework for action against torture based on the notion of political will, and provides brief descriptions of the main international and regional bodies and mechanisms established to combat torture – the UN Committee against Torture, the UN Special Rapporteur on torture and the European Committee for the Prevention of Torture (CPT).

Chapter 2 presents case studies illustrating the various routes that have been taken to combat torture in six countries, where achievements have often resulted from a combination of factors. Some factors may be unique to the country concerned, but others are of wider significance.

---

* The term "torture or ill-treatment" is used in this manual to stand for "torture or cruel, inhuman or degrading treatment or punishment". For ease of description, the term "torture" is often used for torture and ill-treatment together.

** The term "prisoners" is generally used in this manual to refer to people held under any form of detention or imprisonment. Where necessary, a distinction is made between convicted prisoners – people imprisoned bacause they have been convicted of an offence – and unconvicted prisoners or "detainees", including pre-trial detainees and people held in administrative detention.

Chapter 3 outlines the evolving international standards that provide a framework for action against torture. It describes the obligations of states under international law to prohibit and prevent torture and to bring those responsible to justice.

Chapters 4 and 5 are concerned with abuses inflicted on people who have been taken into custody by agents of the state. **Chapter 4** describes the safeguards which have been devised to protect prisoners, especially in the early stages of detention when the risk of torture is often greatest. **Chapter 5** deals with the conditions under which prisoners are held, some of which, singly or in combination, can constitute torture or ill-treatment.

Chapter 6 is on torture in other settings. It covers issues such as torture and ill-treatment in schools and mental institutions, corporal punishment, torture in armed conflict and violence in the community and the family.

Chapter 7 deals with prohibiting torture under national law, investigating complaints and reports of torture, bringing those responsible to justice and providing reparation to victims. It includes information on the exercise of universal jurisdiction and the work of the International Criminal Tribunals for the former Yugoslavia and Rwanda.

Chapter 8 describes additional measures to be taken by governments concerning the infliction of torture abroad, with recommendations on such matters as stopping the torture trade and preventing people being forcibly returned to a country where they risk being tortured. It also discusses the roles of the medical profession and other parts of civil society in eradicating torture.

Where possible, the manual cites the most important relevant international standards and gives ideas for practical implementation. Some sections are accompanied by **action examples** describing efforts which have brought results. Torture and ill-treatment may not have ended, but the achievements have all been significant in some way. These examples are not the only ones – many others could have been cited – but they have been chosen because they illustrate a broad variety of approaches to the challenge of fighting torture. Suggestions are also given for **further reading**.

Amnesty International's latest worldwide campaign against torture has sought to achieve progress in three interrelated areas – preventing torture, confronting discrimination and overcoming impunity. These three ideas are reflected throughout the manual. In particular, the relation between torture and discrimination is discussed in Chapter 1; preventive safeguards are described in Chapter 4, particularly in relation to people held in custody; and the measures needed to overcome impunity for torture by agents of the state are set out in Chapter 7.

Appended to the report are key texts, website addresses and other information which can help readers to stay abreast of developments. The developments will continue, but the basic information and ideas in this manual can serve to shape an agenda for the world anti-torture effort in the coming years.

© AI

Amnesty International Secretary General Pierre Sané (left) in December 1998 presenting UN Secretary-General Kofi Annan with millions of pledges of support for the Universal Declaration of Human Rights on the 50th anniversary of its adoption. The adoption of the Universal Declaration of Human Rights in 1948 signified a consensus among states that everyone has the right not to be tortured or ill-treated.

Chapter 1: The growth of the international response to torture

1.1 The rise of an international movement

Over the years, the horror of torture has incited people to take action against it. This chapter traces the growth of the anti-torture movement since the Second World War and outlines the changes in the way the issue has been seen.

Article 5 of the **Universal Declaration of Human Rights** states: "No one shall be subjected to torture or to cruel, inhuman or degrading treatment or punishment." The adoption of the Universal Declaration of Human Rights by the UN General Assembly in 1948 signified a consensus among states that everyone has a right not to be tortured or ill-treated. Under the International Covenant on Civil and Political Rights (ICCPR), adopted in 1966, this right must never be curtailed, even "[i]n time of public emergency which threatens the life of the nation" (Article 4). International humanitarian law, commonly referred to as the laws of war, also absolutely prohibits torture and ill-treatment.

Torture and ill-treatment are prohibited at all times and in all circumstances under international law. Most forms of torture and ill-treatment are also prohibited under national constitutions and laws. A public official who commits or tolerates torture is violating the laws which he or she is charged with upholding.

Much of the fight against torture involves establishing the rule of law – the principle which holds that the actions of public officials must be carried out strictly according to the law, and that public officials are not above the law but must be subject to it just like ordinary citizens.[1] At the international level, the fight against torture can be seen as involving the development of an international rule of law – entailing a capacity to deal on an international basis with breaches by all states, without distinction, of their obligation to respect and ensure the prohibition of torture and ill-treatment, and of a capacity internationally to ensure individual criminal responsibility for torture. Many of the achievements in the fight against torture since the Second World War have been in this realm.

The formation of the United Nations (UN) after the atrocities of the Second World War was a key step in the advancement of human rights. The UN was concerned with human rights from the outset. Article 1 of the Charter of the United Nations (UN Charter), adopted in 1945, establishes that one of the purposes of the UN is "[t]o achieve international co-operation... in promoting and encouraging respect for human rights". As described in a contemporaneous UN publication,

> "The promotion and protection of human rights, which was formerly vested in nation states, had been made an international responsibility. Nor was this responsibility limited merely to an international pledge set forth in general language. It became part of an international programme, sponsored by the major organs and agencies of the United Nations and articulated in the working programmes of appropriate commissions, committees, and sub-committees."[2]

The first major effort of the UN human rights program was the drafting of the Universal Declaration of Human Rights. By adopting it, the governments of the world, represented at the General Assembly, agreed that everyone is entitled to fundamental human rights. These rights apply everywhere, not just in those countries whose governments may choose to respect them. It follows from this principle that all governments must protect the rights of people under their jurisdiction, and that a person whose human rights are violated has a claim against the government which violates them. Furthermore, the fact that governments together adopted the Universal Declaration implies that violations of human rights are of concern to all governments. Freedom from torture and ill-treatment must be upheld everywhere.

The Universal Declaration of Human Rights has been followed over the years by the adoption of many other **international and regional human rights instruments** – normative texts concerned with human rights which are adopted by the UN or regional intergovernmental organizations such as the African Union (formerly the Organization of African Unity), the Organization of American States and the Council of Europe. These instruments incorporate **standards** of governmental behaviour and, indirectly, of private behaviour. The standards oblige governments and their officials to refrain from torturing or ill-treating anyone and to protect people against such abuses when these are carried out by private individuals. Depending on their origin, the standards either are legally **binding obligations**, or are **recommendations**, some of which are so strong that they can be considered to constitute obligations. Many of the instruments which set out these standards have been **adopted without a vote**, a sign of strong agreement in that no member state represented at the body which adopted them wished to go on record as opposing them.

The drafting of human rights instruments is always a matter of intense discussion over what should or should not be included. Non-governmental organizations (NGOs) over the years have often had a strong impact on the outcome of the discussions, even though they do not belong to intergovernmental organizations and cannot vote there. Amnesty International and other NGOs have persistently pressed governments to adopt instruments giving the strongest possible protection against human rights violations.

The Universal Declaration of Human Rights was followed in 1966 by the adoption of the **International Covenant on Civil and Political Rights**, under whose Article 7 torture and ill-treatment are prohibited.[3] On becoming a party to the ICCPR, a state is legally bound to respect the prohibition and to ensure to all individuals under its jurisdiction the right not to be subjected to torture or ill-treatment. Torture and ill-treatment are prohibited in similar terms in the general regional human rights treaties adopted since the Second World War – the **European Convention for the Protection of Human Rights and Fundamental Freedoms** (European Convention on Human Rights), adopted in 1950; the **American Convention on Human Rights**, adopted in 1969; the **African Charter on Human and Peoples' Rights**, adopted in 1981; and the **Arab Charter on Human Rights**, adopted in 1994 (not yet in force). In international humanitarian law, key treaties adopted since the Second World War – the **Geneva Conventions of 1949** and the 1977 **Protocols Additional to the Geneva Conventions of 1949** – also contain prohibitions of torture and ill-treatment.

In the 1960s and early 1970s, as an organization formed to campaign for the release of prisoners of conscience, Amnesty International was becoming increasingly aware of the problem of torture through the information it received from prisoners and other sources in different parts of the world. In 1972, on 10 December, Human Rights Day – a day established by the UN for the annual commemoration of the adoption of the Universal Declaration of Human Rights – Amnesty International launched its first worldwide Campaign for the Abolition of Torture. Its *Report on Torture*, published the following year, contained information on torture and ill-treatment in over 70 countries and territories in the period from 1970 to mid-1973. It was clear that many governments were flouting the prohibition of torture which they had espoused in 1948.

Exposure led to action. In 1975 the UN General Assembly adopted without a vote the **Declaration on the Protection of All Persons from Being Subjected to Torture and Other Cruel, Inhuman or Degrading Treatment or Punishment** (Declaration against Torture), setting out detailed measures which governments should take to prevent torture. It was followed by the adoption of UN instruments dealing with the prohibition of torture in relation to the police and medical professions.[4] In 1981 the General Assembly established the **United Nations Voluntary Fund for Victims of Torture**, an international fund for the provision of humanitarian assistance to torture victims and their families.

In the years following the Amnesty International campaign, new organizations were formed to fight torture, and the work of existing organizations developed. Amnesty International devised an Urgent Action network of members around the world who could launch immediate appeals on behalf of individuals under threat of torture. Among new NGOs, the organization known today as the Association for the Prevention of Torture was formed in 1977, initially to promote the establishment of an international system of visits to places of detention as a safeguard against torture (see section 5.8 of this manual).[5] The World Organization against Torture was formed in 1986 to facilitate international action by national NGOs. By the early 1980s, centres providing medical and psycho-social care for victims of torture had been established in countries where torture occurred, such as Argentina, Chile and Uruguay, as well as in countries receiving refugees, such as Belgium, Canada, Denmark, France, the Netherlands and Sweden (see section 8.6 of this manual).

While the number of international NGOs grew, national organizations increasingly took on the all-important task of combating torture in their own countries, often under extremely repressive conditions. These organizations carried out activities such as intervening urgently with the authorities when torture was feared; documenting cases; filing petitions in the courts on behalf of torture victims; and sending information to international NGOs and intergovernmental organizations which could take action from outside the country.

Despite the efforts and the achievements, torture persisted. Amnesty International launched its second Campaign for the Abolition of Torture in 1984 with the publication of *Torture in the Eighties*, documenting or referring to reports of torture and ill-treatment in 98 countries in the period from 1980 to mid-1983. Moving on from exposure and denunciation, the campaign focused on prevention. Amnesty International's 12-Point Program for the Prevention of Torture publicized the most important measures needed. Connected to this was the idea that stopping torture is primarily a matter of political will.

During the campaign Amnesty International urged governments to adopt a convention against torture and to establish a UN mechanism for intervention in urgent cases of torture. On 10 December 1984 the UN General Assembly adopted the **Convention against Torture and Other Cruel, Inhuman or Degrading Treatment or Punishment** (Convention against Torture) – an international treaty which obliges states parties to take specific steps to prevent and investigate torture and provides for **universal jurisdiction** in the prosecution of alleged torturers. The Convention also provides for the establishment of a **Committee against Torture** to oversee the implementation of its provisions. In 1985 the UN decided also to appoint a **Special Rapporteur on torture**, whose work now includes sending urgent appeals to governments in countries where a person is reportedly at risk of torture.

Over the next years the UN adopted many new instruments relating to the prevention of torture and the establishment of humane conditions of detention. One of the most important was the **Body of Principles for the Protection of All Persons under Any Form of Detention or Imprisonment** (Body of Principles on Detention), adopted by the General Assembly in 1988. Other important developments were the establishment of International Criminal Tribunals for the former Yugoslavia and Rwanda and the adoption in 1998 of the **Rome Statute of the International Criminal Court**, providing for international criminal trials of people accused of acts constituting war crimes, crimes against humanity or genocide, including torture (see Chapter 7).

At a regional level, the **European Convention for the Prevention of Torture and Inhuman or Degrading Treatment or Punishment** (European Convention for the Prevention of Torture), adopted by the Council of Europe in 1987, provides for the establishment of a Committee empowered to visit places of detention in Europe, while the **Inter-American Convention to Prevent and Punish Torture**, adopted by the Organization of American States in 1985, provides for a system of universal jurisdiction in the Americas.

The years following Amnesty International's second Campaign for the Abolition of Torture saw the creation of more national and international NGOs fighting torture as well as the wider availability of facilities for the treatment and care of victims. Yet the torture continued. In recent years Amnesty International has regularly received reports of torture or ill-treatment in over 100 countries each year.[6]

In 1993 the UN **World Conference on Human Rights** adopted the **Vienna Declaration and Programme of Action** stating that "one of the most atrocious violations against human dignity is the act of torture, the result of which destroys the dignity and impairs the capability of victims to continue their lives and their activities". The Conference urged "all States to put an immediate end to the practice of torture and eradicate this evil forever".[7]

In 1996 Amnesty International convened an **International Conference on Torture** in Stockholm, bringing together human rights defenders and experts from around the world. One of its tasks was to examine practical means of implementing the agreed standards. An important message emerging from the conference was that since governments had not fulfilled their obligation to stop torture, it was time for NGOs to join forces and hold governments accountable. The conference marked a new militancy and sense of common purpose among NGOs fighting torture.[8]

Amnesty International's third worldwide campaign against torture, launched in October 2000, took up this theme. Among other things, the campaign aimed at enhancing collaboration between local and international NGOs in combating torture.

The new campaign also provided an opportunity to look at the problem of torture in fresh ways.

Further reading

On the history of the use of torture and of its abolition as a legal method of investigation, see Peters, 1996, *Torture*.

On the development of international standards against torture, see Rodley, 1999, *The Treatment of Prisoners under International Law*, Chapters 1-2. On the history of the Convention against Torture, see Burgers and Danelius, 1988, *The United Nations Convention against Torture: A Handbook on the Convention against Torture and Other Cruel, Inhuman or Degrading Treatment or Punishment*; Boulesbaa, 1999, *The U.N. Convention on Torture and the Prospects for Enforcement*.

1.2 Changing understandings of torture

During the Second World War there were massive abuses of state power, committed against people deprived of their liberty and held by state agents. The international human rights instruments developed in the aftermath of the war were designed to forestall such abuses by stating absolute prohibitions and obligations, instituting safeguards and providing for effective remedies.

Amnesty International's first Campaign for the Abolition of Torture fitted easily into this vision. The victims whose cases were described in the *Report on Torture* were mainly prisoners held by the state for political reasons; the torture inflicted on them was a **method of political repression**. The preventive standards adopted in the aftermath of the campaign, such as those in the Declaration against Torture, were mainly for the protection of people in official custody. In pressing for the implementation of these standards, Amnesty International's second Campaign for the Abolition of Torture followed in the footsteps of the first.

The concept of torture and ill-treatment was broader than that, however. **Conditions of detention**, if sufficiently bad, could amount to cruel, inhuman or degrading treatment. Forced **medical or scientific experimentation** was recognized under Article 7 of the ICCPR as a form of torture or ill-treatment (see section 3.4 of this manual). **Corporal punishment** also came under the prohibition, according to the UN Human Rights Committee.[9]

Although the problem of torture was seen in the 1970s and 1980s mainly as having to do with political prisoners, the prohibition of torture and ill-treatment in the Universal Declaration of Human Rights applies to everyone without distinction. Many entries on individual countries in *Torture in the Eighties* acknowledged that the torture and ill-treatment of ordinary criminal suspects was widespread, but most of the information which reached Amnesty International concerned political prisoners and the report accordingly focused on them.

The 1980s saw a weakening of repressive regimes and the replacement of military dictatorships by elected civilian governments in various countries, followed by the ending of the Cold War. As the use of torture against political prisoners declined, various human rights groups began paying more attention to the torture and ill-treatment of **ordinary criminal suspects** and **members of other groups**. Along with this came a recognition of the importance of the links between torture and **discrimination** – discrimination against women, discrimination against the poor, discrimination against ethnic, racial and other groups, discrimination based on sexual identity – and of the need to provide special protection for the affected groups, including children, who are manifestly easier to hurt and abuse than adults.

Along with the end of the Cold War came new reports of the use of torture against civilians in **armed conflicts** – the rape of women and girls in the former Yugoslavia, cutting off of limbs in Sierra Leone and other atrocities elsewhere. Often the perpetrators were not governmental forces but members of opposition groups or non-state parties to armed conflicts.

As seen in the 1970s, torture typically took place in the interrogator's room, at the secret police headquarters or in police stations, prisons and other officially recognized establishments. But exposure of the practice of "disappearance" showed that people were also being held and tortured in secret places without their detention being acknowledged. The list of settings in which the problem of torture needed to be tackled, including non-custodial settings, was also expanding the work of intergovernmental organizations. The European Convention for the Prevention of Torture provided for the establishment of a Committee (referred to in this manual as the European Committee for the Prevention of Torture, CPT) empowered to visit "any place... where persons are deprived of their liberty by a public authority" (see section 5.8 of this manual), and the CPT soon began visiting and reporting on psychiatric institutions, orphanages and holding centres for immigration detainees as well as prisons and police stations. The Human Rights Committee stated in 1992 that the prohibition of torture and ill-treatment under Article 7 of the ICCPR "protects, in particular, children, pupils and patients in teaching and medical institutions".[10] And when members of the public are beaten by police while lying helplessly on the ground, this can also constitute ill-treatment or torture, even if the victims have not formally been taken into custody.

A further dimension in the developing understanding of the problem of torture and ill-treatment came through the efforts of the women's movement to address **violence in the community and the family**. The perpetrators in such cases were not state agents – they were private individuals – but the state was often negligent in providing protection, bringing perpetrators to justice and affording effective remedies, and the negligence was discriminatory.* The Human Rights Committee referred in 1992 to the duty of states parties to the ICCPR to afford everyone protection against torture or ill-treatment "inflicted by people acting... in a private capacity".[11] Measures which governments should take to eliminate violence against women, including torture and ill-treatment, were elaborated in General Recommendation 19 of the UN Committee on the Elimination of Discrimination against Women (CEDAW), adopted in 1992, and in the **Declaration on the Elimination of Violence against Women**, adopted by the UN General Assembly in 1993 (see section 6.6).

Other human rights issues also are closely connected with the problem of torture. Amnesty International has long held that the **death penalty** is the ultimate cruel, inhuman and degrading punishment and therefore violates Article 5 of the Universal Declaration of Human Rights as well as its Article 3 providing for the right to life – a view that is finding increasing acceptance.[12] **"Disappearances"** have been recognized as violations of the right not to be subjected to torture or ill-treatment, both for the victims and for their families (see section 3.4). Other abuses which have been deemed to constitute torture or ill-treatment include **corporal punishment, forcible house destruction**, and certain **gender-specific abuses** including **female genital mutilation.****

Much has changed over the years in the fight against torture. The formulation of Article 5 of the Universal Declaration of Human Rights as adopted in 1948 remains valid, but the interpretation and the applicable law have evolved. Torture is still with us, but the problem of torture is clearly vaster and more complex than it was then seen.

---

* As noted by the Human Rights Committee, "Inequality in the enjoyment of rights by women throughout the world is deeply embedded in tradition, history and culture, including religious attitudes" (General Comment 28 on Article 3 of the ICCPR, para. 5). The UN Declaration on the Elimination of Violence against Women affirms that "violence against women is a manifestation of historically unequal power relations between men and women" and "one of the crucial social mechanisms by which women are forced into a subordinate position compared with men" (preambular para. 4).

** See section 3.4 for a discussion of abuses which have been deemed to constitute torture or ill-treatment.

Amnesty International's third worldwide campaign against torture was designed to reflect these new ideas. It has sought to publicize the ways in which abuses by private individuals can constitute torture or ill-treatment and the need for states to exercise due diligence in protecting people against violence in the community and the family.

At the international level, much of the anti-torture effort has gone into the elaboration of standards for the prevention of torture, mainly of people who are held in official custody. There is also a considerable body of standards relating to conditions of detention. Drawing from the experiences of human rights defenders around the world in fighting torture, much of this report focuses on the task of implementing the standards. This effort can help to build a human rights culture in which torture will be universally seen as unacceptable.

A report written while the understanding of a problem is still evolving can only reflect the situation at the moment of writing. A new report published 10 years hence will doubtless convey new visions of the problem of torture, new insights and new solutions.

1.3 Torture and discrimination

One of the themes of Amnesty International's third campaign against torture has been the link between torture and discrimination, and the use of torture and ill-treatment against particularly vulnerable members of society, such as children.

Discrimination[13] is an assault on the very notion of human rights. It systematically denies certain people or groups their full human rights because of who they are or what they believe. It is an attack on the fundamental principle underlying the Universal Declaration of Human Rights: that human rights are everyone's birthright and apply to all without distinction.

Torture feeds on discrimination. Torture involves the dehumanization of the victim, the severing of all bonds of human sympathy between the torturer and the tortured.[14] This process of dehumanization is made easier if the victim is from a despised social, political or ethnic group. Discrimination paves the way for torture by allowing the victim to be seen not as human but as an object, who can, therefore, be treated inhumanely. As stated by the Committee against Torture, "discrimination of any kind can create a climate in which torture and ill-treatment of the 'other' group subjected to intolerance and discriminatory treatment can more easily be accepted, and... discrimination undercuts the realization of equality of all persons before the law".[15]

Discrimination against certain groups heightens their vulnerability to torture by state officials in a number of ways. Discrimination enshrined in law (for example, where the law criminalizes homosexuality or restricts women's fundamental freedoms) can act as a licence to torture. Discriminatory enforcement of laws may affect both a person's chances of coming into contact with the criminal justice system and their treatment once in its hands.

The victim's identity or status may also affect the nature and consequences of their ill-treatment. For example, children held in custody with adults are particularly vulnerable to rape and sexual violence. Victims from marginalized groups may also have less access to legal remedies. Discrimination reinforces impunity, lessening the likelihood of any official action in cases of torture or ill-treatment.

Discrimination also means that certain groups are denied equal protection of the law against violence inflicted on them in the community and the family, such as violence against women, attacks against street children, racist attacks and homophobic hate crimes. These violent manifestations of prejudice are often facilitated and encouraged by official inaction.

The ICCPR contains a clause stipulating that its provisions are to be observed "without distinction of any kind, such as race, colour, sex, language, religion, political or other opinion, national or social origin, property, birth or other status" (Article 2(1)). Other major international and regional human rights instruments which prohibit torture and ill-treatment contain similar provisions,[16] as do other instruments covering matters relevant to the prevention of torture, such as conditions of detention and the rights of detainees.[17] Under Article 1 of the Convention against Torture, the intentional infliction of severe pain or suffering "for any reason based on discrimination of any kind" is recognized as an act of torture. Conversely, international and regional instruments designed to combat discrimination or to protect particular groups contain explicit prohibitions of torture and ill-treatment, as well as prohibitions of the infliction of bodily or mental harm under which various acts of torture or ill-treatment would clearly be prohibited (see section 3.2.3 of this manual).

The Special Rapporteur on torture has discussed the torture of women[18], children[19] and members of sexual minorities[20] and the links between torture and poverty[21] in his reports to the UN General Assembly and the UN Commission on Human Rights. The links between torture and gender have been discussed by the UN Special Rapporteur on violence against women, its causes and consequences (Special Rapporteur on violence against women). The links between torture and racism have been discussed by the Committee against Torture.

The analysis of the torture of **women** by the Special Rapporteur on torture has focused particularly on rape and sexual abuse (see section 3.3.2). As the Special Rapporteur has pointed out:

> "In addition to being an especially traumatic form of torture for the victim, rape may have insidious correlative consequences. In many situations a woman may be reluctant to seek redress by reporting a rape because of the severe social repercussions that may flow therefrom. The stigma attached in many communities to a woman who has been raped may result in particularly dire consequences for the private and public life of the woman. In addition to social stigma, some victims may be subjected to direct reprisals from relatives. In a few countries, where severe legal sanctions have been adopted against adultery and where the evidentiary requirements to demonstrate rape are stringent, a woman reporting a rape may risk holding herself open to prosecution. Consequently, when rape or sexual assault against a woman constitutes a torture method, the chances of the torturer acting with impunity would appear disproportionately higher than with other torture methods."[22]

The Special Rapporteur has pointed out that "[p]regnant women are particularly vulnerable to torture", risking miscarriage and other health risks as well as damage to the foetus. Also, "women are sometimes tortured as surrogates for the real target, who may be the victim's spouse or family member or friend", and in some instances on which he received information, "the gender of an individual constituted at least part of the very motive for the torture itself, such as in those [instances] where women were raped allegedly for their participation in political and social activism".[23]

The Special Rapporteur on violence against women has stated:

"The most particularized element in custodial violence against women is the sexualization of torture. Although the sexual anatomy of men as well as women is targeted in the physical stages of torture, rape and the threat of rape, as well as other forms of sexual violence such as sexual harassment, forced impregnation, virginity testing, forced abortion, forced prostitution and forced miscarriage, are perpetrated more consistently against women detainees."[24]

The Committee on the Elimination of Discrimination against Women (CEDAW) established under the Convention on the Elimination of All Forms of Discrimination against Women, in its General Recommendation 19, has stated that gender-based violence against women, which may include torture or ill-treatment, constitutes discrimination within the meaning of that Convention (see section 6.6).*

On the torture and ill-treatment of **children**, concerns raised by the Special Rapporteur on torture have included the conditions and treatment of children in places of detention and non-penal institutions; the targeting of street children for torture and ill-treatment; the torture and ill-treatment of children "in a surrogate capacity, where the intended target is in fact the child's parents or other relatives or a friend";[25] the reported "lack of appropriate monitoring and complaints mechanisms for institutions dealing with children";[26] and the use of torture in armed conflict against child civilians and children recruited into the armed forces.**

In his analysis of the use of torture and ill-treatment against members of **sexual minorities**, the Special Rapporteur has noted that "they are often subjected to violence of a sexual nature, such as rape or sexual assault in order to 'punish' them for transgressing gender barriers or for challenging predominant conceptions of gender roles".[27] Issues raised by the Special Rapporteur include the forms which such torture and ill-treatment have taken, the effect of discriminatory attitudes on the part of law enforcement officials and the deprivation of means to claim and ensure the enforcement of victims' rights and to obtain legal remedies such as compensation.

---

* Extracts from General Recommendation 19 are reproduced in Appendix 12.

** The Special Rapporteur on torture has stated that "children are necessarily more vulnerable to the effects of torture and, because they are in the critical stages of physical and psychological development, may suffer graver consequences than similarly ill-treated adults" (E/CN.4/1996/35, para. 10). As Amnesty International has pointed out, one of the special considerations that mark out a difference between adults and children concerns the threshold of pain and suffering. Younger children, in particular, have a lower threshold of pain; and physical or mental abuse may have a much more profound impact on the body and mind of a child than on an adult. Treatment like prolonged solitary confinement, for instance, may be held to be ill-treatment in the case of an adult, but for a young child the experience may be so terrifying as to amount to torture. The age of the child is important; a five-year-old will probably be more terrified by a beating than a 17-year-old. Gender is also a factor: girls in custody may suffer more if they have a well-founded fear of rape or sexual abuse, whether or not such abuse takes place (see Amnesty International, *Hidden scandal, secret shame: Torture and ill-treatment of children*, pp. 15-22). The Human Rights Committee and the European Court of Human Rights have stated that the age of the victim is one of the factors to be considered in assessing claims of torture or ill-treatment (see section 3.3.1).

In his discussion of the links between torture and **poverty**, the Special Rapporteur has written:

> "[T]he overwhelming majority of those subjected to torture and ill-treatment are ordinary common criminals from the lowest strata of society. They are the ones who cannot afford good lawyers, or who may have access only to less-than-diligent lawyers provided, in some instances, by the State, or who may not have access to any lawyer at all; whose families do not have the connections to be taken seriously by the police, prosecutors or judges, or even the means of securing life-saving health care that may be obtained outside the place of detention, or of providing food fit to eat when the detaining authorities and institutions fail to make these available; and who do not have any idea of what their rights are, even the right not to be tortured, or how those rights may be secured. Indeed, they are often members of the lowest level of an underclass that is disconnected from all opportunity of leading decent lives as productive economic citizens."[28]

The Special Rapporteur has also drawn attention to the problem of the availability and use of **corporal punishment** as a penal sanction against particular groups – for gender-related crimes, as in the flogging of women for adultery or for the failure to observe strict Islamic dress laws, for conduct related to sexual orientation such as transgendered behaviour and consensual same-sex relationships, and against children reportedly as young as 12.[29]

Regarding the links between torture and **racism**, the Committee against Torture has recommended among other things that states "take all necessary steps to ensure that public officials, including law enforcement officers... do not manifest contempt, racial hatred or xenophobia which may lead them to commit acts amounting to torture or ill-treatment" against "ethnic, racial, religious, linguistic or national minorities, asylum-seekers or refugees, or on the basis of any other status". The Committee has emphasized "the vital importance of having transparent and effective official procedures through which individuals can raise complaints of ill-treatment and torture perpetrated on the basis of discrimination, unequal access to justice and related concerns". The Committee has also stated that states "must ensure that racism, racial discrimination, xenophobia or related intolerance do not result in decisions of deportation to another State where there are grounds for believing that the deportee would be in real danger of being subjected to torture".[30]

Specific standards and safeguards for the protection against torture and ill-treatment of women, children, lesbian, gay, bisexual and transgendered people and other groups are described in the following chapters of this manual. At a more general level, it is important to address underlying factors such as discrimination and poverty which can give rise to torture and ill-treatment. All countries should ratify international and regional treaties which seek to strengthen protection against the torture or ill-treatment of members of particular groups. Governments should bring their laws and policies into line with these treaties and repeal laws which breach the fundamental principle of non-discrimination. Governments must ensure equal treatment before the law and equal access to the mechanisms of justice regardless of such factors as age, gender, race, ethnic or national origin, sexual orientation or economic status.

Further reading

The use of torture and ill-treatment against particular groups and its relation to discrimination are examined in reports published by Amnesty International in 2000 and 2001 in connection with its third worldwide campaign against torture: *Broken bodies, shattered minds: Torture and ill-treatment of women*; *Hidden scandal, secret shame: Torture and ill-treatment of children*; *Crimes of hate, conspiracy of silence: Torture and ill-treatment based on sexual identity*; and *Racism and the administration of justice*. Reports by other NGOs include *Children, Torture and Power: The Torture of Children by States and Armed Opposition Groups*, produced by Save the Children (Man, 2000), and reports by Human Rights Watch on torture, ill-treatment and other violence directed against women, children and members of sexual minorities. See also Van Bueren, ed., 1998, *Childhood Abused: Protecting Children against Torture, Cruel, Inhuman and Degrading Treatment and Punishment*.

1.4 The importance of political will: Amnesty International's 12-Point Program

Amnesty International's 12-Point Program for the Prevention of Torture, produced for its second Campaign for the Abolition of Torture, was designed to promote the measures which governments should take to stop torture and ill-treatment. A revised version, prepared for Amnesty International's third worldwide campaign and entitled **12-Point Program for the Prevention of Torture by Agents of the State**, is reproduced in Appendix 16 of this manual.

The 12-Point Program starts by calling on the highest authorities of every country to demonstrate their opposition to torture by **condemning** it unreservedly whenever it occurs. This point has been placed first to emphasize the importance of the authorities exercising the **political will** to stop torture.[31] Condemnation must not be merely symbolic: the authorities should make clear to officials under their command that torture will not be tolerated.[32] All public officials should know that torture and ill-treatment are forbidden and that they will be punished for such abuses. The prohibition of torture should be conveyed to them through public statements, regulations and instructions, and through the authorities responding appropriately when allegations of torture are made.[33]

Related to the condemnation of torture, although not explicitly mentioned in the 12-Point Program, is the notion of **chain-of-command control**. The principle of chain-of-command control is set out in the UN Declaration on the Protection of All Persons from Enforced Disappearance (Declaration on Enforced Disappearance): "Each State shall... ensure strict supervision, including a clear chain of command, of all law enforcement officials responsible for apprehensions, arrests, detentions, custody, transfers and imprisonment, and of other officials authorized by law to use force and firearms" (Article 12(2)).[34] Chain-of-command control operates through a combination of measures, including issuing clear regulations, setting up clear operating procedures, exercising supervision through being regularly and accurately informed of the activities of those under one's command, and ensuring that there are effective procedures for investigating and punishing breaches of regulations.[35] These measures should be used to ensure that officers do not commit torture or ill-treatment.[36]

Points 2-4 of the 12-Point Program concern prisoners. Secret detention must be prohibited, and the authorities should institute safeguards against torture and ill-treatment, breaking down the isolation in which these abuses occur and establishing institutional responsibility for various aspects of the welfare of prisoners. The program also refers to the need to ensure humane conditions of detention.

Points 5, 6, 7 and 10 refer to the necessary official reaction when torture becomes known, and to the legal framework for its prevention and suppression. Governments must prohibit torture in law, conduct prompt and impartial investigations into complaints and reports of torture, bring those responsible to justice and afford reparation to the victims. Judicial and administrative corporal punishments should be abolished.

Point 8 states that statements and other evidence obtained through torture must not be invoked in any proceedings, except against a person accused of torture. Point 9 underlines the need for training.

Points 11 and 12 refer to governments' international responsibilities. All governments should ratify without reservations the relevant human rights treaties, including the Convention against Torture. Governments should work for the eradication of torture in other countries. No one should be forcibly returned to a country where he or she risks being tortured.

As stated in Point 5, the prohibition of torture and the essential safeguards for its prevention must not be suspended under any circumstances, including states of war or other public emergency. Essential safeguards for the prevention of torture include the availability at all times of effective judicial remedies to enable relatives and lawyers to find out immediately where a prisoner is held and under what authority, and to ensure the prisoner's safety (see section 4.8).

While many of the measures set out in the 12-Point Program are simply restatements of existing requirements under international human rights standards, some go beyond the standards on which the community of states has thus far been able to agree. The program serves at once to make the existing standards more understandable; to promote new standards which Amnesty International has found to be important; and as a yardstick of governmental behaviour. Above all, it is meant to be a coherent program of international action against torture, applicable in all countries.[37]

Although the program is particularly concerned with torture and ill-treatment in detention, the logic of the program (official condemnation, safeguards, repression, international action) can also be applied to other settings, such as torture in armed conflict (see section 6.5). Similarly, although the program is concerned with torture by agents of the state, many of the points can also be applied to the prevention of torture by non-state forces and armed political groups, and to the prevention of violence in the community and the family. Many of the action recommendations in this manual reflect the thinking behind the 12-Point Program.[38]

1.5 The international system for human rights protection

Over the years, the UN and regional intergovernmental organizations have set up bodies dealing with human rights. Foremost among them is the UN **Commission on Human Rights**, established under Article 68 of the UN Charter, which has adopted a resolution on "Torture and other cruel, inhuman or degrading treatment or punishment" annually since 1985.[39] **Treaty bodies**[40] have been created under international and regional human rights treaties, and the Commission on Human Rights has set up **mechanisms**[41] relating to particular countries or themes. Unlike intergovernmental bodies which consist of representatives of states, the treaty bodies and the mechanisms established by the Commission on Human Rights consist of individuals acting in their personal capacity (normally called "independent experts"). Whereas treaty bodies deal only with states which are parties to their respective treaties, intergovernmental bodies and human rights mechanisms are concerned with all states belonging to the intergovernmental organization in question.

Three treaty bodies and mechanisms are of special importance in the fight against torture.

- The **Committee against Torture** is the Committee established under Article 17 of the Convention against Torture. It consists of 10 individual experts elected at biennial meetings of states parties. Under Article 19 of the Convention, states parties are required to submit reports on "the measures they have taken to give effect to their undertakings under this Convention". An initial report is to be submitted within one year of the Convention entering into force for the state concerned, with supplementary periodic reports every four years.[42] Much of the time at the Committee's regular sessions[43] is devoted to the examination of these reports, in the presence of representatives of the governments concerned. After hearing the government representatives and putting questions to them, the Committee prepares conclusions and recommendations which include the Committee's assessment of the situation of torture and ill-treatment in the country and any recommendations for improvement.

  The Committee against Torture can hear complaints against a state party from another state party or from an individual subject to its jurisdiction, if the state or states concerned have made declarations under Articles 21[44] and 22[45] respectively, accepting the Committee's competence to do so.[46] There is also an inquiry procedure under Article 20 of the Convention which allows the Committee on its own initiative to look into allegations of the "systematic practice"[47] of torture in a state party, with the possibility of visiting the country, unless that state in the course of becoming a party to the Convention has formally declared that it does not recognize the Committee's competence to do so.[48]

- The **Special Rapporteur on torture** is an individual expert who reports annually to the UN Commission on Human Rights.[49] Unlike the Committee against Torture, whose work is concerned solely with states parties to the Convention against Torture, the Special Rapporteur can address the government of any state which is a member of the UN or has observer status there. The Special Rapporteur sends urgent appeals to governments concerning individuals feared to be undergoing or at risk of torture, and other messages to governments transmitting allegations of torture or concerning measures needed for its prevention. The Special Rapporteur also carries out visits to countries with the consent of the government concerned and makes detailed recommendations based on the findings of such visits.[50]

- The **European Committee for the Prevention of Torture and Inhuman or Degrading Treatment or Punishment** (European Committee for the Prevention of Torture, CPT) is the Committee established under Article 1 of the European Convention for the Prevention of Torture to visit places where people are deprived of their liberty with a view to strengthening, where necessary, the protection of such people from torture and ill-treatment. It is composed of one expert member from each state party to the Convention.

  The CPT makes periodic, scheduled visits to each state party to the Convention as well as *ad hoc* (unscheduled) visits (see section 5.8). After a visit, the CPT transmits its findings to the state, which is required to respond within a set time limit. The reports are confidential, but in practice most states have eventually agreed to their publication.[51] Meetings of the CPT are held in private, but its annual General Reports are public.[52]

Also of great importance is the **Human Rights Committee**, the committee of experts established under the ICCPR. Its main function is to monitor the implementation of the ICCPR on the basis of periodic reports submitted by states parties. A state party to the ICCPR which also becomes a party to the first **Optional Protocol** to the ICCPR recognizes the competence of the Committee to consider complaints from individuals that they are victims of a violation by that state of any of the rights set out in the ICCPR, including the prohibition of torture and ill-treatment under Article 7. The Human Rights Committee has made important statements about the obligations of states regarding torture and ill-treatment in the course of its examination of states parties' reports; in "General Comments", particularly its General Comment 20 on Article 7 of the ICCPR;* and in decisions (officially referred to as "views") on cases brought to it under the first Optional Protocol.

Allegations of torture can also be considered by bodies established under the regional human rights treaties – the **African Commission on Human and Peoples' Rights**, the **Inter-American Court of Human Rights** and the **European Court of Human Rights**. These bodies can consider complaints of violations of the human rights set out in the respective treaties.** The Inter-American and European courts have made important rulings in cases involving torture and ill-treatment.

---

* The text of General Comment 20 is reproduced in Appendix 11 of this manual.

** In the Americas, complaints are submitted first to the **Inter-American Commission on Human Rights**. Until 1998, European cases were heard first by the **European Commission of Human Rights**; since November 1998 cases have gone directly to the European Court of Human Rights. A Protocol to the African Charter on Human and Peoples' Rights on the Establishment of an African Court on Human and Peoples' Rights, adopted in 1998 but not yet in force, provides for cases to be submitted to that Court after consideration by the African Commission on Human and Peoples' Rights.

Other human rights bodies which may deal with practices of torture and ill-treatment in the course of their work include the **Committee on the Rights of the Child** established under the Convention on the Rights of the Child; the **Committee on the Elimination of Discrimination against Women** (CEDAW) established under the Convention on the Elimination of All Forms of Discrimination against Women; and the **Committee on the Elimination of Racial Discrimination** established under the International Convention on the Elimination of All Forms of Racial Discrimination. Like the Human Rights Committee and the Committee against Torture, these three committees examine periodic reports submitted by states parties on the measures they have adopted to give effect to the provisions of the respective treaties. The Committee on the Elimination of Racial Discrimination operates an individual complaints procedure, as does CEDAW under the Optional Protocol to the Convention on the Elimination of All Forms of Discrimination against Women.[53] There are also a **Special Rapporteur on violence against women, its causes and consequences** (Special Rapporteur on violence against women), a **Special Rapporteur on contemporary forms of racism, racial discrimination, xenophobia and related intolerance**, and a **Working Group on Arbitrary Detention**, all of which report annually to the UN Commission on Human Rights. Action against torture has also become an important part of human rights monitoring and promotion in international peace-keeping operations and other field presence of the UN and regional intergovernmental organizations.

NGOs play an important part in the work of human rights treaty bodies and mechanisms by supplying them with information, facilitating the submission of individual complaints, publicizing their findings and recommendations, and pressing for action.

Further reading

UN Human Rights Fact Sheets No. 17, *The Committee against Torture*, and No. 27, *Seventeen frequently asked questions about United Nations Special Rapporteurs*, provide concise descriptions of the work of the Committee against Torture and Special Rapporteurs respectively. Detailed information on the international and regional mechanisms dealing with torture can be found in the University of Essex *The Torture Reporting Handbook* (Giffard, 2000), with contact addresses and details on the procedures for submitting complaints and other information to them. Information on the Committee on the Elimination of Racial Discrimination and other bodies and mechanisms dealing with racial discrimination can be found in Amnesty International, 2001, *Using the international human rights system to combat racial discrimination: A Handbook*. On human rights monitoring in international field operations, see the UN *Training Manual on Human Rights Monitoring* (2001) and the handbook *Preventing Torture* published by the Organization for Security and Co-operation in Europe (1999). The UN publication *United Nations Action in the Field of Human Rights* (1994) gives details of the origins and work of UN bodies and mechanisms dealing with human rights.

An analysis of the work of the CPT can be found in Morgan and Evans, 2001, *Combating Torture in Europe: The work and standards of the European Committee for the Prevention of Torture (CPT)*. For additional details, see Evans and Morgan, 1998, *Preventing Torture: A Study of the European Convention for the Prevention of Torture and Inhuman or Degrading Treatment or Punishment*. On the development of the work of the Committee against Torture, see Ingelse, 2001, *The UN Committee against Torture: An Assessment*.

The annual reports and reports on visits to countries by the Committee against Torture, the Special Rapporteur on torture and the CPT contain a wealth of detail and many recommendations which are also applicable to other countries.

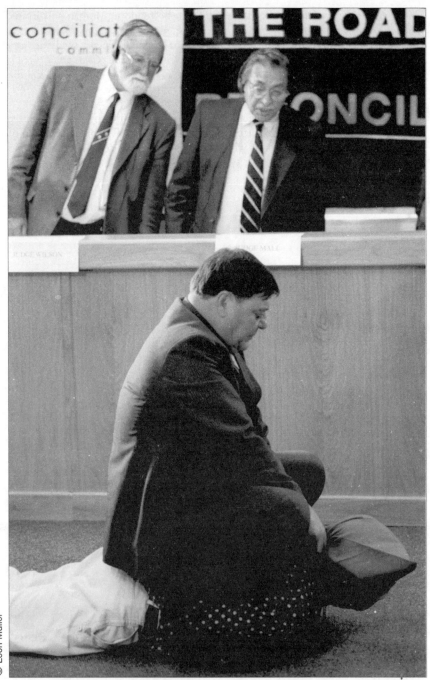

© Leon Muller

Former security police officer Jeffrey Benzien demonstrating the "wet bag" torture method on a volunteer at a 1997 hearing of the Amnesty Committee of the Truth and Reconciliation Commission, South Africa, as two committee members look on (see section 2.7).

Chapter 2: The fight against torture – case studies

2.1 Introduction

This chapter presents six case studies of action against torture and ill-treatment. The actions have led to reforms in areas such as the institution of safeguards for arrest and detention; the prohibition of particular interrogation methods and restraint techniques; the designation of torture as a specific crime; the improvement of conditions of detention; the establishment of systems of visits of inspection to places of detention; the prosecution of officials accused of torture; and the uncovering of the truth about torture practised under a former government. The measures have been taken by various branches of government – by the legislature, by the judiciary, or by particular units in the justice ministry. The changes have come in reaction to particular incidents, or against backgrounds of long-standing abuse. The impetus for action has come from various sectors of civil society, from international and regional human rights bodies, and from the pressure of international public opinion.

The six case studies illustrate some of the various paths that may lead to the elimination of torture and ill-treatment, or to a decline in their use.

2.2 Israeli Occupied Territories: Outlawing 'legal' torture

From 1967 the Israeli security services have routinely tortured Palestinian political suspects in the Occupied Territories – and from 1987 the use of torture was effectively legal. The effective legalization was possible because the Israeli government and the judiciary, along with the majority of Israeli society, accepted that the methods of physical and psychological pressure used by the General Security Service (GSS, also known as *shinbet* or *shabak*) were a legitimate means of combating "terrorism".

There has been a constant struggle with the government over the issue of torture. On one side, victims of torture, human rights lawyers and local and international human rights organizations searched for ways to challenge the system of legalized torture. On the other side, the Israeli government sought to defend and entrench the system.

In general, Israeli public opinion on the treatment of Palestinian detainees did not change. If anything, it hardened between 1993 (when the Oslo Agreement was signed by the Israeli government and the Palestine Liberation Organization, envisaging a gradual transfer of functions to a Palestinian self-governing authority to end in a final settlement within five years) and 1999, a period during which more than 120 civilians were killed in suicide bomb attacks carried out by militant Palestinian organizations *Hamas* and Islamic *Jihad*. Palestinians, Lebanese and other non-Israeli nationals were seen as "acceptable" victims of torture – and the torture methods were seen as "acceptable" because, among other things, the harshest methods were not used against Israeli Jews.[1]

Nevertheless, a powerful campaign against torture was mounted. On the national level, it included court cases and petitions to the Israeli High Court of Justice by human rights lawyers. At the international level, the campaign involved the mobilization of international public opinion. At the same time, the practice of torture was coming under increased scrutiny by UN bodies and mechanisms, including the Committee against Torture and the Human Rights Committee. As a result, pressure increased on the High Court of Justice, which until 1998 had largely accepted the pleas of the security services that certain interrogation methods were a "necessity" in their fight against "terrorism".

In September 1999 the High Court of Justice finally made a judgment banning torture. However, the judgment allowed torture to be used in so-called "ticking bomb" cases. This is among the reasons why torture has continued to be practised in Israel, especially since the beginning of the al-Aqsa *intifada* (uprising) in 2000.

Torture legalized – the Landau Commission

After the Israeli occupation of the West Bank and Gaza in 1967, Palestinians in those territories could be detained under military orders without access to lawyers and family for up to 90 days. Their detention had to be periodically renewed by military judges, but this was frequently a formality. Their interrogation was the responsibility of the GSS, directly under the control of the Prime Minister.

Political detainees were routinely subjected to methods of interrogation amounting to torture or ill-treatment by the GSS in order to obtain information and confessions that were used to convict them in military courts. At this time, GSS interrogators denied in court that they had used torture to obtain confessions.

The effective legalization of torture was the result of a report by a commission of inquiry headed by former Supreme Court Chief Justice Moshe Landau (the Landau Commission), which was set up in 1987 after a case involving extrajudicial executions by the GSS was exposed. In the public part of its report, published in October 1987 and endorsed by the government the following month, the Commission stated that in the previous two decades some 50 per cent of GSS interrogations led to trials, and that the "overwhelming majority of those tried were convicted on the basis of their confession in court". The Commission also noted that "among almost all those engaged in this subject the prevailing view is that recourse to some measure of physical pressure in the interrogation of HTA [hostile terrorist activity] suspects is unavoidable". GSS interrogators, faced with the "dilemma" of revealing methods of interrogation that could lead a court to reject confessions, or committing perjury in order to ensure the conviction of suspects they ostensibly believed to be guilty on the basis of other, classified, evidence, had routinely lied. The report stated: "False testimony in court soon became an unchallenged norm which was to be the rule for 16 years."

The Landau Commission recommended that the GSS should be authorized to use psychological pressure and "a moderate measure of physical pressure" in their interrogation of "security" detainees. The Commission relied on the concept of "the lesser evil" in stating that "actual torture... would perhaps be justified in order to uncover a bomb about to explode in a building full of people". Although the report stated that "the pressure must not reach the level of physical torture or maltreatment of the suspect or grievous harm to his honour which deprives him of his human dignity", the image of the "ticking bomb" was used repeatedly by the Israeli authorities to justify methods which constituted torture.

Part of the Landau Report was never made public – the part containing the guidelines on what treatment was allowed during interrogation. In the following years, human rights organizations documented a pattern of torture and ill-treatment of detainees during interrogation which included incommunicado detention; hooding; prolonged *shabeh* (sleep deprivation combined with position abuse, whereby the suspect is kept sitting or standing in a painful position); beating on various parts of the body; confinement to closet-size rooms; continuous exposure to loud music; exposure to extremes of heat or cold; and restrictions on time allowed for eating or going to the toilet.[2] Other methods used included squatting for prolonged periods like a frog and violent shaking.

The use of these torture methods was accompanied by a system of medical checks, presumably to try to ensure that detainees did not die or develop serious health problems in custody. In May 1993 a "medical fitness form" to be used in interrogation centres was made public by the *Davar* newspaper. The form required doctors to certify whether a detainee could withstand methods of inter-rogation including solitary confinement, tying up, hooding and prolonged standing. After protests, including by local human rights groups, the Israeli Medical Association instructed physicians not to use the form. The Israeli authorities suggested that the form had been a mistake. However, detainees continued to be checked by medical staff on arrival and torture was modified according to the state of their health.

The Landau Commission report recommended that a ministerial committee be set up to regularly review the secret guidelines on the use of "moderate pressure". The committee was established and was headed by the Prime Minister. Its members were normally the Minister of Defence, the Minister of Justice and the Minister of Internal Security.

The 'shaking' debate

In October 1994, after a suicide bombing in Dizengoff Street in Tel Aviv which killed 23 Israelis, the ministerial committee gave an "exceptional dispensation" to members of the GSS to use increased physical pressure for a period of three months. After the Beit Lid suicide bombing of January 1995, this dispensation was renewed at three-monthly intervals until the High Court of Justice judgment of 1999.

In April 1995 a death in custody highlighted the dangers of one of the methods – violent shaking – that appeared to have been sanctioned by the secret guidelines allowing "increased physical pressure". 'Abd al-Samad Harizat, a 30-year-old computer expert from Hebron, was arrested at about midnight on 21 April 1995 and fell into a coma soon after 4pm on 22 April. He died three days later without regaining consciousness. The US organization Physicians for Human Rights sent an expert, Professor Derrick Pounder, to observe the autopsy, carried out by two Israeli forensic pathologists. The autopsy found that 'Abd al-Samad Harizat had died from "violent shaking" which had caused a sub-dural haemorrhage within the skull. Pressure from the family's lawyer later obtained information about his inter-rogation: he had been shaken 12 times between 4.45am and 4.10pm, 10 times by holding his clothes and twice by holding his shoulders.

Although the interrogators who caused death or severe injury as usual escaped punishment[3], the death of 'Abd al-Samad Harizat brought torture and the use of shaking into public debate. The Minister of Justice, David Liba'i, and the Attorney General, Michael Ben Yair, were reported to be opposed to the continued use of shaking.

The Association for Civil Rights in Israel filed a suit with the High Court of Justice seeking an injunction against the practice of shaking. The Public Committee Against Torture in Israel and the Association of Israeli-Palestinian Physicians for Human Rights (now called Physicians for Human Rights – Israel) also sought an injunction against shaking from the High Court of Justice and asked that those officials it regarded as responsible for the death of 'Abd al-Samad Harizat be charged with manslaughter.

The public meanwhile was exposed to official reports suggesting that violent shaking was an effective means of gaining information. The GSS reported to the ministerial committee in August 1995 that 48 attacks had been foiled in the previous six months as a result of special interrogation methods. At the committee meeting later that month the "exceptional dispensation" to use "increased physical pressure" was renewed and shaking was effectively authorized – shaking would no longer be "regular" but would be used with the authorization of the head of the GSS or his deputy in each individual case.

National and international pressure

From the early 1990s Israeli non-governmental organizations (NGOs) and lawyers brought a number of cases to the Israeli Supreme Court, sitting as the High Court of Justice, through which they fought major battles on the meaning and legality of torture. (Under Israeli law, Palestinian lawyers from the Occupied Territories – except East Jerusalem annexed to Israel – do not have the right to make appeals to this court.) For example, in 1994 an Israeli lawyer started seeking injunctions from the High Court of Justice, requiring the GSS to allow his clients under interrogation to have six hours' sleep. However, this did not change the practice of sleep deprivation as a means of pressure: either the GSS responded by stating that they had completed their interrogation or – if the injunction was granted – the detainees would be granted the six hours' sleep and the interrogation would then resume.

At the same time, Israeli NGOs and individual lawyers brought petitions to the High Court of Justice to grant injunctions prohibiting the GSS from using "pressure" against individual detainees. However, the success of such injunctions was limited. In cases where the court issued the required injunction and the GSS returned to court to challenge it, the High Court consistently found in favour of the GSS.

For instance, on 24 December 1995 the High Court of Justice issued an injunction preventing the interrogators from using physical force on 'Abd al-Halim Belbaysi. The GSS ignored the injunction and continued to torture and ill-treat him physically, including by shackling his legs to a chair with his hands behind his back, blindfolding him, depriving him of sleep for three days and violently shaking him. 'Abd al-Halim Belbaysi then confessed to placing bombs. As a test case, his lawyer went back to the High Court to protest only against the use of violent shaking and asked that it should be forbidden. On 11 January 1996 not only was this request refused but the High Court also rescinded its injunction preventing physical force.

In response to an injunction sought in the case of Khader Mubarak, which came before the High Court of Justice in November 1996, the Court accepted the GSS argument that hooding was carried out in order to prevent the detainee from identifying other detainees and that the use of loud music was to prevent detainees from communicating with each other. They also accepted the "explanations of the Security Service... that the issue is not one of active sleep deprivation, but of periods of time during which the Appellant was held waiting for interrogation without being given a break designed especially for sleep". The Israeli human rights organization *B'Tselem*, having examined GSS documents on Khader Mubarak's sleep deprivation periods presented to the court, pointed out:

> "The periods of 'rest' which exceeded one day *invariably* included Friday and Saturday, i.e. the Israeli weekend. It seems highly unlikely that four times during three and a half weeks there was a 'pressing need' to deprive Mubarak of sleep only during mid-week, while, as the weekend approached, the 'pressing needs' mysteriously vanished, only to re-emerge come the next week."[4]

Criticisms of Israeli methods of interrogation by the UN Human Rights Committee and action by the UN Committee against Torture and the UN Special Rapporteur on torture increased the international pressure on the Israeli government. In 1991 Israel had become a party to three international human rights treaties that prohibit torture – the International Covenant on Civil and Political Rights (ICCPR), the Convention against Torture and the Convention on the Rights of the Child. None of these treaties was incorporated by statute into Israeli law, although Israel accepted the requirement under these treaties of submitting reports to the respective monitoring bodies (see section 1.5 of this manual).

Israeli, Palestinian and international NGOs had already been making use of UN human rights mechanisms by submitting many individual cases of torture to the Special Rapporteur on torture, and he had referred to them in his annual reports to the UN Commission on Human Rights.

The main answers of the Israeli government to criticisms of its use of torture (for instance, in thousands of letters from Amnesty International members) had been that detainees were "terrorists", that physical pressure saved lives from "terrorist" attacks, and that the interrogation methods used by the GSS did not constitute torture or ill-treatment.

In June 1994, after reviewing Israel's initial report under the Convention against Torture, the UN Committee against Torture recommended that "interrogation procedures be published in full so that they are both transparent and seen to be consistent with the standards of the Convention" and that "an immediate end be put to current interrogation practices that are in breach of Israel's obligations under the Convention".[5] However, the Committee stopped short of explicitly characterizing such practices as torture.

In 1997, however, the Committee took this step. After the High Court of Justice decisions which allowed and legitimized the use of torture in the Belbaysi, Hamdan[6] and Mubarak cases in 1996, the Committee, in response to an appeal from Amnesty International and *B'Tselem*, asked Israel to submit "as a matter of urgency" a special report – the first time such a request had been made to any country.[7] At its May 1997 meeting the Committee examined the special report submitted and, in an important statement, found that interrogation methods used by Israel – "restraining in very painful conditions", "hooding under special conditions", "sounding of loud music for prolonged periods", "sleep deprivation for prolonged periods", "threats, including death threats", "violent shaking", and "using cold air to chill" – constituted torture and should cease immediately. The Committee also emphasized the absolute nature of the prohibition of torture and the unacceptability of making any exceptions to this prohibition.[8]

In May 1998, after examining Israel's second periodic report under the Convention against Torture, the Committee against Torture reiterated its conclusions and recommendations of the previous year and expressed concern at "Israel's apparent failure to implement any of the recommendations of the Committee".[9]

National and international protests helped avert the threat posed by two bills put forward to parliament in 1995 and 1996. These would have put torture by the GSS on the statute books by permitting the use of "pressure" during interrogations and by offering impunity to GSS interrogators who used force. The proposed Amendment to the Penal Law – Prohibition on Torture 1995 was dropped altogether. It was supposed to bring Israel's law into conformity with the Convention against Torture, but would have excluded "pain or suffering inherent in interrogation procedures or punishment according to law". The proposed Law of the General Security Service (the "GSS Law"), debated in January 1996, was postponed. It would have accepted the use of "pressure" against those interrogated in certain defined circumstances "to prevent actual danger to the security of the state" and when "no other reasonable way exists to prevent said danger". In 2001 it was reintroduced but without reference to the use of "pressure".

As a result of the international campaigning and the injunctions incessantly sought by NGOs and individual lawyers (the Public Committee Against Torture in Israel alone submitted 67 such petitions between January and September 1999) as well as other local initiatives, the High Court of Justice eventually began to engage seriously with the issue of torture rather than, as before, simply accepting the "security" justifications of the GSS.

The September 1999 judgment

In January 1998 the High Court of Justice scheduled a rare nine-judge hearing to review the legality of GSS interrogation methods under Israeli law. There had at the same time been publicity surrounding the case of 'Abd al-Rahman Ghanimat, who had been arrested on 13 November 1997 and met his lawyer for the first time six weeks later, on 23 December. The High Court of Justice had three times refused to grant injunctions to stop the use of *shabeh* against 'Abd al-Rahman Ghanimat. In a sworn affidavit he stated that he had been forced for several five-day periods during those six weeks to sit on a small and low slanting chair to which his hands and legs were shackled, with a thick sack over his head. Loud music was played and he was deprived of sleep. His lawyer saw that her client's wrists were red and swollen because they had been so tightly shackled to the chair. 'Abd al-Rahman Ghanimat complained of dizziness and pain throughout his body, including his joints and back.

During the January 1998 hearing before the nine judges, the GSS admitted that methods such as hooding, *shabeh* and the playing of loud music were not only used between interrogations but were part of the interrogation. Long-standing petitions challenging torture, including individual petitions and two public petitions submitted by Israeli human rights organizations, were then joined to the case, which continued until final judgment was given in September 1999.

On 6 September 1999, in a unanimous ruling,[10] the High Court of Justice stated that the Minister of Justice had the authority to allow individuals to interrogate but that methods of interrogation had to be "reasonable". The Court noted that "a reasonable investigation is necessarily one free of torture, free of cruel, inhuman treatment of the subject and free of any degrading handling whatsoever... Human dignity includes the dignity of the suspect being interrogated." In this respect the judgment cited international human rights treaties ratified by Israel which prohibit torture and cruel, inhuman or degrading treatment.

The Court then considered in turn various methods of interrogation used by the GSS, including shaking; being forced to sit or stand in the *shabeh* position; being forced to squat on the tips of the toes (the "frog crouch"); excessive tightening of handcuffs; sleep deprivation; covering the head with a hood; and the playing of extremely loud music. The Court ruled that each method was not "reasonable" and should be prohibited.

Some leeway, however, was left for the interrogators. The judges said that prolonged sleep deprivation that was not necessary for the purposes of an investigation would not be reasonable, but they accepted that detainees might need to be interrogated for extended periods. They suggested that, if there was a need to use prohibited interrogation methods to save lives, GSS investigators "may avail themselves of the defence [of necessity]". Finally, they allowed a loophole for the legal reintroduction of torture by suggesting that parliament might legislate to allow "physical means" of interrogation:

> "If it will nonetheless be decided that it is appropriate for Israel, in light of its security difficulties, to sanction physical means in interrogation... this is an issue that must be decided by the legislative branch which represents the people."[11]

After the judgment

The High Court of Justice judgment was observed by the GSS, and the vast majority of reports received from Palestinian detainees in the months immediately after the judgment indicated that they were not being tortured under interrogation. Low chairs were not being used and there were no reports of violent shaking. But reports indicated that severe interrogation typically involved relays of interrogators who would continue the interrogation 20 hours a day.

There were strong protests against the judgment from the GSS and right-wing politicians. Bills were presented in parliament which proposed authorizing the GSS to use physical pressure during interrogation. Lobbying by Israeli, Palestinian and international organizations followed, and draft legislation which would have authorized torture was dropped in February 2000. A draft section allowing special interrogation methods was dropped from the law regulating the activities of the GSS that was adopted by the *Knesset* (the Israeli parliament) in February 2002. However, no bill has been introduced to fulfil Israel's obligations to give effect to the provisions of the Convention against Torture.

After the al-Aqsa *intifada* began in September 2000, reports of the use of previous methods of torture began to increase. For example, Jihad Latif Shuman, a United Kingdom (UK) citizen of Lebanese origin, was arrested on 5 January 2001 by the GSS, apparently on suspicion that he had been sent to Israel from Lebanon by *Hizbullah* to carry out an attack in Israel. During his interrogation, Jihad Shuman was made to sit on a low chair with his feet pulled behind him for hours on end. He was also forced to bend for prolonged periods, slapped until his nose bled and deprived of sleep. He suffered breathing problems following this treatment. According to his lawyer, the torture subsequently stopped and Jihad Shuman's health improved. The independent doctor who examined him reportedly said that his condition was consistent with his claims of physical maltreatment.

In November 2001, after reviewing Israel's third periodic report under the Convention against Torture, the UN Committee against Torture voiced regret that the 1999 High Court of Justice judgment did not "contain a definite prohibition of torture"; that it prohibited sleep deprivation for the purpose of breaking the detainee but not if it was merely incidental to the interrogation, whereas in practice "in cases of prolonged interrogation, it will be impossible to distinguish between the two conditions"; and that interrogators who used physical pressure in extreme circumstances might escape criminal liability by pleading the "defence of necessity". The Committee also expressed concern about continuing allegations of interrogation methods against Palestinian detainees that were prohibited by the 1999 judgment.[12]

Conclusion

The history of the struggle against legalized torture in Israel and the Occupied Territories shows the effectiveness of the campaign launched by Israeli and Palestinian organizations and lawyers, as well as by international NGOs, alongside scrutiny by UN human rights bodies. However, in a society which by and large continues to accept torture as a legitimate weapon against those whom it regards as "terrorists", the fragility of human rights victories at times of confrontation was exposed by the gradual return of torture after the al-Aqsa *intifada* began.

At the time of writing of this manual, many of the methods used in the past had been revived, and the torture of Palestinians held by the GSS was once again widespread. Letters from the State Attorney to the Public Committee Against Torture in Israel in February 2002 stated that in two cases where the committee had raised concerns about torture, there was a "heavy suspicion" that the detainees were "ticking bombs" and the "defence of necessity" therefore applied.

In the face of this challenge, Israeli lawyers and NGOs are continuing to bring petitions against incommunicado detention (increased in April 2002 to 18 days without access to lawyers or a judge, with the possibility of further extension of up to 90 days on a judge's order) and torture. In addition, coalitions of Israeli, Palestinian and international human rights organizations are continuing to encourage intergovernmental bodies to scrutinize Israel's interrogation methods and to demand that the practice of torture be stopped.

The continuing use of torture in Israel and the Occupied Territories shows the importance of leaving no loopholes in the law whereby torture can be revived.

2.3 Peru: Designating torture as a specific crime

Torture has been a long-standing problem in Peru. In 2001 the UN Committee against Torture stated that torture in Peru was "systematically" practised (see below). The torture of suspects detained under "anti-terrorism" legislation has diminished in recent years, but the torture of ordinary criminal suspects has remained widespread. Meanwhile, Peru's use of torture has increasingly come under scrutiny, both from human rights organizations in the country and from UN monitoring bodies – the Committee against Torture and the Human Rights Committee. This section gives an account of one of the government's recent reforms – the establishment of a specific crime of torture in Peruvian law – and of its initial impact on the punishment of torturers.

The campaign against torture

"Disappearances", extrajudicial executions and torture had been widespread in Peru since the early 1980s, and in 1992 "anti-terrorism" legislation came into effect that created a framework for the detention of prisoners of conscience and effectively made all "terrorism"-related trials unfair. It also allowed up to 10 days of total incommunicado detention, a practice which facilitated torture. Indeed, most of the cases documented by Amnesty International of prisoners detained on "terrorism"-related offences included complaints of torture and ill-treatment.

With the easing of the violent conflict between governmental forces and armed opposition groups in the early 1990s, the incidence of "disappearances" and extrajudicial executions decreased markedly. Until then the main focus of victims and their relatives as well as human rights organizations was on locating the "disappeared", stopping extrajudicial executions, and obtaining the release of people falsely imprisoned for "terrorism"-related offences; complaints of torture and ill-treatment were rarely pursued. However, the decline in "disappearances" and extrajudicial executions created the space for human rights defenders to pay increasing attention to the problem of torture and ill-treatment.

Peru had been a party to the International Covenant on Civil and Political Rights (ICCPR) since 1978, and in 1988 it ratified the Convention against Torture. By so doing, it took on a commitment under international law to fulfil the obligations regarding the prohibition of torture and ill-treatment set out in these two treaties. The treaties also obliged the country to submit periodic reports to the respective monitoring bodies – the Human Rights Committee and the Committee against Torture.

In November 1994 the Committee against Torture reviewed Peru's initial report under the Convention against Torture. National and international human rights organizations, including Amnesty International, seized the opportunity to ensure that Peru was made to answer for the widespread use of torture and ill-treatment in the country by submitting their own information to the Committee.

Having reviewed Peru's report, the Committee concluded that the legal and administrative measures adopted by Peru to comply with Article 2(1) of the Convention against Torture were not effective in preventing torture. It also stated that the authorities had failed to comply with Articles 12 and 13 of the Convention, which require prompt and impartial investigations of complaints and reports of torture. The Committee recommended to the Peruvian government a set of measures that included reviewing Peru's "anti-terrorism" legislation so as to eliminate incommunicado detention. The Committee also recommended "defining torture as an independent offence punishable by a penalty appropriate to its seriousness".[13] Peruvian law as it then stood contained no specific crime of torture by agents of the state, and torturers, if prosecuted, could be charged under the Penal Code only with "abuse of authority" or causing "injuries", with a maximum penalty of six years' imprisonment.

Two years later Peru had still not created a specific crime of torture, nor had the other recommendations of the Committee been implemented. In fact, Peru had gone a step backwards by effectively legalizing impunity. In 1995 Congress approved a law granting a general amnesty to all members of the security forces and civilian officials who were the subject of a complaint, investigation, indictment, trial or conviction, or who were serving prison sentences for human rights violations committed between May 1980 and 14 June 1995. This effectively meant that the thousands of cases of "disappearances", extrajudicial executions, torture and ill-treatment committed by the security forces during those 15 years would not be clarified, the perpetrators would not be brought to justice, and that none of the victims or their relatives would receive compensation. A further amnesty law passed at the end of June 1995 entrenched impunity by prohibiting the courts from deciding on the legality or applicability of the first law.

The amnesty laws provoked widespread international concern, and Peru became a focus of renewed international human rights campaigning. In July 1996 the UN Human Rights Committee reviewed Peru's third periodic report submitted under the ICCPR. The Committee expressed deep concern about the two amnesty laws and the "persistent reports of torture or cruel, inhuman or degrading treatment of persons detained under suspicion of involvement in terrorist activities or other criminal activities". The Committee called for repeal of the amnesty laws to the extent that they violated the right of victims of human rights violations to an effective remedy. It also recommended that "[p]rovisions should be made in the Penal Code to criminalize acts that are committed for the purpose of inflicting pain, without prejudice as to whether those acts result in permanent injury".[14] However, the Peruvian authorities took no action on most of the Human Rights Committee's recommendations.

By 1997 the human rights situation in Peru had deteriorated dramatically. A television station owner had been stripped of his Peruvian nationality and forced to flee the country because his station had reported grave human rights violations, including torture. Three judges of the Constitutional Tribunal had been removed from office for declaring that it would be unconstitutional for the then President, Alberto Fujimori, to stand as a presidential candidate for a third term, prompting the Inter-American Commission on Human Rights to express concern.[15]

By the end of 1997 Peru's authorities were aware that in May 1998 the Committee against Torture would review the country's second periodic report under the Convention against Torture. Local human rights organizations were already preparing for a national campaign against torture to be launched in 1999.

The 1998 law

Against this background, in February 1998 Congress approved unanimously a law in which the crimes of genocide, enforced disappearance and torture were incorporated into Peru's Penal Code. Law No. 26926 modified the Penal Code by introducing and criminalizing torture as a specific crime. The law provides for five to 10 years' imprisonment for any "civil servant or public official", as well as "any person acting with the consent or acquiescence of a public official", who is found guilty of inflicting torture as defined in the law. The penalty is increased to between eight and 20 years' imprisonment if the torture results in death.

At the time, a handful of congresspersons had drafted different bills which criminalized torture. Congress consulted several human rights lawyers over which draft bill was the most suitable. The lawyers decided to draft a new text that incorporated the positive aspects of all the draft bills that had already been presented to the Congressional Commission of Justice, and also added other key features that had been overlooked, such as extending the scope of the perpetrators to people who are not public officials but are acting at their behest. The Commission of Justice accepted the resulting draft bill and Congress unanimously passed the law on 18 February 1998 – an event which was welcomed by the Committee against Torture when it reviewed Peru's second periodic report in May 1998.[16]

The definition of torture under the new law incorporated elements from the Inter-American Convention to Prevent and Punish Torture, to which Peru was a party, as well as the UN Convention against Torture. The legislation also specifies that civil courts and not military courts should be in charge of investigating and trying cases of torture. Human rights defenders welcomed this, as the use of military courts to try members of the security forces for human rights violations had been seen as one of the main obstacles in the fight against impunity. In addition, the legislation states that forensic doctors have a duty immediately to attend to people who say they have been tortured or ill-treated, and that victims have the right to be seen by an independent doctor of their choice.

A case brought under the new law highlighted the impact of the legislation. In January 1999 an investigation was launched into the death of Pablo Pascual Espinoza Lome. A prisoner in Yanamilla prison, in the town of Ayacucho, Ayacucho department, he had been seized by two prison officers and accused of having consumed alcohol. He was taken to a cell where he was reportedly punched in the abdomen. He subsequently died. The autopsy report revealed that the cause of death was a ruptured spleen.

In August 1999 the High Court in Ayacucho sentenced one of the prison officers to 12 years' imprisonment and acquitted the other. On appeal, the Supreme Court, using the new legislation, increased the sentence to 15 years' imprisonment and ordered a new trial to investigate the involvement of the second officer. In August 2000 the criminal court in Ayacucho sentenced the second officer to four years' imprisonment for the crime of torture.

In November 1999, reviewing Peru's third periodic report, the Committee against Torture again welcomed the 1998 law but expressed concern over continuing numerous allegations of torture, the continuance of such practices as incommunicado detention and the use of military courts to try civilians, and "[t]he apparent lack of effective investigation and prosecution of those who are accused of having committed acts of torture". It recommended that "[a]mnesty laws should exclude torture from their reach".[17]

In November 2000, reviewing Peru's fourth periodic report under the ICCPR, the Human Rights Committee also welcomed the 1998 law but deplored the fact that the Committee's 1996 recommendation regarding the amnesty laws had not been followed, and again called for their repeal.[18]

In June 2001 the Committee against Torture published a summary account of an inquiry on Peru under Article 20 of the Convention against Torture (see section 1.5 of this manual). The Committee concluded that "torture is not an occasional occurrence but has been systematically used as a method of investigation". "Anti-terrorism" legislation was still in force, making detainees "particularly vulnerable to torture". The Committee made a series of recommendations for the eradication of torture, including legislative measures for reparation and compensation of the victims.[19]

Conclusion

The new law was a positive step towards eradicating torture in Peru. Unfortunately, however, torture and ill-treatment remained widespread at the time of writing of this manual.

Since the adoption of Law No. 26926 in February 1998 Amnesty International has documented scores of cases of torture or ill-treatment, and has remained concerned at the lack of effective investigations into complaints of torture under the legislation. For example, despite the law, cases were still being referred to military courts. In other instances, for crimes that appeared to fit the definition of torture, the legislation was not being invoked and lesser charges such as "abuse of authority" were being filed instead. In addition, victims and their relatives were still being intimidated, harassed and threatened and were consequently withdrawing accusations in fear of reprisals. This was reflected in the fact that by the end of 2001 only two cases brought against officials accused of torture under the February 1998 legislation had resulted in convictions.

The local and international campaign against torture in Peru helped to provide the legislation to back those trying to expose torturers and hold them to account. Pressure on the Peruvian authorities needs to be maintained, however, to ensure that the law is implemented in full and that the other recommendations of the Committee against Torture and the Human Rights Committee are followed.

2.4 USA: Federal action to combat local abuses

> "We saw them shock the [Haitian] detainee on his body with an electric shield, also with an electric gun... The Haitian detainee was shocked about three times. While being shocked, the Haitian detainee was handcuffed, his hands to his legs, laying on his side on the floor..."

This testimony was one of many disturbing allegations of torture or ill-treatment made by people detained by the US Immigration and Naturalization Service (INS) who were held at a local jail, the Jackson County Correctional Facility, in Marianna, Florida between August 1997 and July 1998. The allegations led to an investigation by the US government under the Civil Rights of Institutionalized Persons Act of 1980 (CRIPA). This law allows the federal (national) authorities to investigate and take appropriate action to enforce the constitutional rights of inmates against abuse in state and local detention facilities.

In the USA, most jails are under state or local jurisdiction. Under the US constitutional doctrine of states' rights, the federal government has only limited powers to intervene. Before the introduction of the CRIPA, the federal authorities could prosecute individuals for violations of federal criminal laws, including state or local officials acting under "color of law" (in their official capacity), but they had no authority to address systematic abuses or poor conditions in state facilities. The CRIPA provided the federal government with an important civil remedy, enabling the US (federal) Department of Justice to seek federal court orders or injunctions to eliminate patterns of abuse or unconstitutional conditions in state and local institutions.

Adopted by the US Congress in 1980, the CRIPA authorizes the Civil Rights Division of the Department of Justice to investigate conditions in state or local public facilities if it receives information that inmates are being systematically deprived of their rights under the US Constitution. The law covers state prisons and local jails as well as other public institutions such as psychiatric hospitals and care homes.

Allegations of abuse at the Jackson County jail

The detainees at the Jackson County Correctional Facility were people from different countries, including asylum-seekers, who were being held by the INS, a federal agency. The INS sends its detainees, including asylum-seekers, to county jails when its own facilities are full. In June 1998 allegations of abuse began reaching the INS. The INS was sufficiently concerned by the allegations that it transferred all 34 of its detainees out of the jail the following month.

Affidavits from 17 of the INS detainees, taken by lawyers at the non-governmental Florida Immigrant Advocacy Center in Miami, described abuses the prisoners said they had suffered in the Jackson County jail between August 1997 and July 1998. The 17 were from the Bahamas, Bangladesh, Cuba and Honduras. The alleged abuses included shocks from electro-shock stun shields (see section 6.3.1 of this manual), including while shackled in four-point restraint to concrete beds; beatings and other physical ill-treatment; denial of medical care; excessive periods of punitive solitary confinement; and verbal – including racist – abuse. According to the inmates, such treatment was meted out arbitrarily or as punishment for intervening in a fight, for example, or for complaining about racist insults by prison personnel.

The Florida Immigrant Advocacy Center sent its findings to the US government for investigation. It also informed Amnesty International of its findings and requested assistance from the organization in bringing attention to them.

In October 1998 Amnesty International wrote to local and federal authorities calling for an investigation into the allegations. A prompt but superficial reply from the head of the jail merely gave general assurances that all inmates in the facility were protected from abuse. In December the Department of Justice wrote to Amnesty International thanking the organization for bringing the concerns to its attention, and stating that the Special Litigation Section of the Civil Rights Division was collecting and reviewing information about the Jackson County jail to determine whether a CRIPA investigation was warranted.

In May 1999, in response to apparent delays in the federal investigation, Amnesty International activists worldwide sent letters of concern to the Department of Justice, copying them to the head of the Jackson County jail. This led to renewed media attention to the jail and the investigations into the alleged abuses.

The investigation

On 30 March 2000 the Department of Justice's Civil Rights Division issued a "letter of findings" concerning the Jackson County Correctional Facility. These findings largely confirmed, and expanded upon, the sorts of concerns raised in the affidavits obtained by the Florida Immigrant Advocacy Center. Among the numerous findings was that medical treatment in the jail was inadequate, including in the care and supervision of isolated or restrained inmates. The letter of findings cited the case of a prisoner who appeared to have been placed in segregation as punishment for having lodged a complaint about lack of care for a medical problem he was experiencing. He was confined in a medical observation cell for five days, without being evaluated by medical staff, and then returned to the general prison population after apologizing for filing the grievance. The letter also revealed that juvenile inmates had been placed in administrative segregation "for the convenience of the facility", citing the case of a juvenile who had been placed in a medical cell for three months despite not having a medical condition that warranted such placement.

The letter stated that staff at the jail "engage in excessive and unwarranted use of restraints to control inmates, causing serious risk of bodily harm". It expressed particular concern at the frequency and haste with which the jail resorted to four-point restraint of inmates, securing their wrists and ankles to eye-bolts attached to cement-block beds with mattresses removed, sometimes for prolonged periods and without proper monitoring and supervision. On the specific question of electro-shock stun shields, it found that the shield had been

> "... overused for inmate control purposes... The facility's use of force reports indicate that in a number of instances activation of the shield was the first resort after verbal counselling failed to gain compliance. In many of these instances such use of force was unreasonable, as lesser types of force would have achieved compliance."

The Civil Rights Division also found that the jail's inadequate screening for inmate illness or consideration of other relevant conditions rendered the use of the shield potentially dangerous. In one incident, an electro-shock shield had been "brought into the room for possible use on an inmate who was nine months pregnant". The letter stated, however, that "[t]here appears to have been a decrease in activations of the shield since January 1999", suggesting that the revelations of the Florida Immigrant Advocacy Center and Amnesty International's actions may have had some effect in reducing the use of this particular type of restraint in the jail.

The letter of findings made a series of recommendations to improve policy and practice in the jail, including a recommendation that the remedial measures, which should be seen as a minimum response to the violations uncovered, be instigated by cooperation rather than through a lawsuit. As of mid-2001, it appeared that the jail's authorities were cooperating.

The CRIPA experience

The CRIPA has been used extensively in recent years, with more than 300 institutions across the USA and its territories made to improve conditions or under ongoing review. The institutions have included local jails in Alabama, California, Georgia, Mississippi, New York and Virginia, and juvenile correctional facilities in Georgia, Kentucky, Louisiana and the territory of Puerto Rico. In 1999 the states of Arizona and Michigan were forced to institute safeguards in their women's prisons following lengthy CRIPA investigations into alleged widespread sexual abuse and retaliation against inmates by male guards.

The problems meriting a CRIPA investigation cover a broad range of issues including fire safety, sanitation and health care, abuse by guards and failure to protect inmates from abuses by other inmates. Information leading to an investigation may come from a variety of sources, including individuals, the media, NGOs and advocacy groups. Federal investigators then seek access to the institution to conduct on-site inspections and interview staff and inmates, often using independent expert consultants. This results in a detailed letter of findings from the Department of Justice to the institution, listing any violations found, with recommendations.

The legislation requires that, before filing a lawsuit, the Department of Justice must wait 49 days after issuing a letter of findings to allow the institution an opportunity to make voluntary changes without going to court (the time taken to negotiate a settlement can extend beyond this period). Most cases are eventually settled without full-scale litigation – sometimes informally at an early stage, more often as the result of a court-endorsed agreement between the parties that has the effect of a court order, known as a "consent decree". Once the changes are ordered and accepted, there is usually a period of oversight by the Department of Justice, in which investigators conduct periodic follow-up visits, and the institution is required to issue status reports.

The CRIPA did not create any new rights or standards, but it does enable the Department of Justice to litigate on the basis of previously established constitutional or statutory rights. There are, however, some limitations to the process. Usually, an investigation focuses on an individual facility and settlements do not have a wider application outside that jurisdiction. For example, a ban on the use of a restraint chair in Iberia Parish Jail, Louisiana, following a CRIPA investigation into egregious abuses, did not lead to a ban in other facilities where there were complaints of similar abuse.

The greatest limitation is one of resources: demands for CRIPA investigations far outweigh the capacity of the Department of Justice to respond. However, the Department of Justice attempted to maximize its resources in the 1990s by securing state-wide relief in a number of cases. For example, it conducted investigations into 18 jails in Mississippi in 1993, finding hazardous conditions, squalor and overcrowding as well as grossly deficient medical and suicide prevention care. It ordered four jails to be closed and improvements to be made in others. Similar "cluster" investigations have been conducted into 11 jails in Georgia and all four state-operated mental retardation facilities in Tennessee.

The Department of Justice paid particular attention to addressing abuses in juvenile facilities after being criticized for under-using its resources in this area. During the mid-1990s it addressed state-wide problems in all 13 juvenile treatment facilities in Kentucky and eight juvenile detention facilities in Puerto Rico.

In 1997 the Department of Justice opened a lengthy investigation into a range of juvenile facilities in Georgia, assisted by 10 expert consultants. Its letter of findings in February 1998 documented widespread abuses including inadequate mental health care; overcrowded and unsafe conditions; abusive disciplinary practices, especially in "boot camps" (juvenile prison camps run along military lines); and the abusive use of mechanical and chemical restraints on mentally ill juveniles.

In 2000 the Department of Justice concluded a similar investigation into secure juvenile facilities in Louisiana, including two privately run institutions: the Tallulah Correctional Center for Youth and the Jena Juvenile Justice Center. Their findings included children being subjected to excessive force by staff; prolonged isolation; inadequate health care, education and nutrition; and, in the Jena centre, deprivation of shoes and blankets.

In both Georgia and Louisiana, the Department of Justice stepped in after abuses had been highlighted by NGOs.[20] Settlements were reached mandating substantial improvements to juvenile detention conditions in all of the above states and Puerto Rico. In Louisiana this resulted in the two privately run facilities being taken under state control.

Litigation is one of the most effective means of securing redress for human rights violations in US prisons and detention facilities – although this does not reduce the need for the authorities to ensure adequate standards of treatment in the first place. Most such litigation is conducted by NGOs or private law firms, often working under difficult conditions. Under the CRIPA the Department of Justice has a vital role to play because of the special authority it has to conduct such litigation, the resources allocated to it by Congress, and its ability to draw upon a wide range of expert and technical advisers.

Under separate legislation introduced in 1994 to deal with police misconduct (the Violent Crime Control and Law Enforcement Act of 1994), the Department of Justice has also obtained consent decrees with respect to several US police agencies, including the Los Angeles Police Department, California, covering such issues as excessive use of force, false arrest and racism. The consent decrees negotiated thus far have mandated a series of measures, including reforms to training, investigation of complaints, and monitoring of the race or ethnicity of people stopped by the police. These have provided useful models for other law enforcement agencies.

Conclusion

Since the CRIPA was passed, the federal authorities have been able to take effective action to stop patterns of torture, ill-treatment and other abuses in a number of state and local facilities. However, there are limitations to the procedure as regards its resources and capacity to respond. Funding for the Special Litigation Section, which handles CRIPA investigations, depends on the political will of the executive and the US Congress. Although the CRIPA is extremely valuable as a mechanism for addressing systematic abuses in state and local facilities, there is still a need for effective ongoing monitoring and oversight bodies for all prisons and detention facilities at the state and local levels.

2.5 India: Landmark judgment establishes safeguards

Torture of ordinary criminal suspects and political prisoners by police has long been widespread in India. Torture and ill-treatment are used to extract confessions, to extort money and to punish detainees. Methods of torture and ill-treatment include electric shocks, suspension from ceilings, severe beating with *lathis* (long wooden sticks) and kicking. Most torture occurs during periods of illegal detention following arrests that are unrecorded.

Torture persists despite official acknowledgement of the problem and a series of positive judicial and administrative initiatives in recent years.[21] There is a long tradition of judicial activism in India, with courts liberally interpreting the scope of fundamental rights set out in the Indian Constitution. Access by individuals to claim these rights has been assured through the development of Public Interest Litigation: since the late 1970s individuals and organizations have been permitted under Articles 32 and 226 of the Constitution to approach the Supreme Court and High Courts "in the public interest" on issues of fundamental rights on behalf of those unable to do so themselves.

In September 1996 the Supreme Court of India made a landmark judgment condemning custodial violence and making several recommendations (see below). This allowed the development of practical mechanisms for preventing torture during arrest and detention and has had a significant impact on the manner in which individuals can be arrested and detained. Although levels of custodial violence have continued to be high, the judgment has forced police to rethink their widespread use of illegal detention and torture, and has provided human rights activists with a stronger legal position from which to challenge such practices. Crucially, the Supreme Court has treated custodial violence as an ongoing concern and continues to monitor implementation of its recommended safeguards and to issue further orders to protect detainees.

Background to the 1996 judgment

The origins of the 1996 judgment lie in the state of West Bengal 10 years earlier. On 26 August 1986 the Executive Chairman of the Legal Aid Services, D.K. Basu, wrote to the Chief Justice of the Supreme Court of India highlighting concerns about custodial violence in the state and reported deaths in custody.[22] He argued that it was vital to examine the issues, develop "custody jurisprudence", formulate steps for awarding compensation to the victims or their relatives, and ensure accountability of police officers found responsible for torture.

The Supreme Court accepted D.K. Basu's request that his letter be treated as a Public Interest Litigation and asked the respondents – the State of West Bengal –

to reply to the charges made in the petition. The state government of West Bengal replied that the police were not covering up deaths in custody and that wherever police personnel were found to be responsible, action was being taken against them.

On 14 August 1987 the Supreme Court stated that there were increasing allegations of custodial violence in almost every state and a rising number of reported deaths in custody. The Court noted that there appeared to be no machinery to deal effectively with such allegations. It issued an order requesting all state governments to provide their response to the allegations, and further requesting the Law Commission of India to make suitable suggestions in relation to the question of custodial violence.

In response to this order, affidavits were filed by several state governments, by the central government and by the Law Commission of India concerning custodial violence. The Court appointed a Supreme Court lawyer, Dr A.M. Singhvi, to act as *amicus curiae* (friend of the court) to help it gather information on custodial violence.

In 1992 D.K. Basu – by this time a judge with the West Bengal High Court – gave a comprehensive judgment in his court on the issue of custodial violence. He set out in full the processes he thought should be followed to prevent custodial violence, to ensure independent investigations leading to prosecution of those responsible, and to provide compensation for victims.

In the meantime, between 1986 and 1996, newspapers reported cases of torture and deaths in custody, human rights organizations raised such cases and pursued them in the courts, and Amnesty International conducted a major international campaign on human rights violations in India, putting forward detailed recommendations on arrest and custody procedures to combat torture and other abuses of human rights.

The 1996 judgment

In 1996 the Supreme Court finally issued its judgment in the case of *Basu v. State of West Bengal*.[23] The judgment expressed the Supreme Court's concern that "torture is more widespread now than ever before". It stated that "'[c]ustodial torture' is a naked violation of human dignity and degradation which destroys, to a very large extent, the individual personality. It is a calculated assault on human dignity and whenever human dignity is wounded, civilization takes a step backward."

The judgment referred to international human rights standards and to the fact that Article 21 of the Constitution of India protects the right to life, a provision that has been held by the Indian courts to include a guarantee against torture. It also made general recommendations relating to amendments to the law on burden of proof and the need for police training, and put forward arguments against the right to sovereign immunity for agents of the state responsible for torture and in favour of compensation.

The judgment's most far-reaching legacy is its 11 "requirements" to be followed in all cases of arrest and detention (para. 35). The "requirements" would, the Court hoped, "help to curb, if not totally eliminate, the use of questionable methods during interrogation and investigation" (para. 39).

Briefly (and paraphrased), the requirements set out by the Supreme Court are as follows:

1.   Police arresting and interrogating suspects should wear "accurate, visible and clear" identification and name tags, and details of interrogating police officers should be recorded in a register.[24]

2.   Police making an arrest should prepare a memo of arrest to be signed by a witness and countersigned by the arrested person, giving the time and date of arrest.

3.   Anyone arrested should be entitled to have a friend or relative informed of their arrest and place of detention "as soon as practicable".[25]

4.   If such a friend or relative lives outside the district, the time and place of arrest and place of detention should be notified to them by police through the Legal Aid Organization within eight to 12 hours.

5   Anyone arrested should be informed of their right to inform someone of their arrest and detention "as soon as" they are arrested.

6.   Information about the arrest and the details of the person informed of the arrest should be kept in a diary at the place of detention along with names of police officers supervising custody.[26]

7.   On request, anyone arrested should be examined at the time of arrest and any injuries recorded. This "inspection memo" should be signed by the arrested person and the arresting police officer, and a copy given to the arrested person.[27]

8.   Anyone arrested should be medically examined by a doctor every 48 hours during detention.[28]

9.   Copies of all the documents referred to above should be sent to the magistrate.[29]

10.   Anyone arrested should be permitted to meet their lawyer during interrogation "though not throughout the interrogation".

11.   A police control room should be established at all district and state headquarters with information regarding details of those arrested and their place of custody displayed on a notice board.

Although the Supreme Court commented that these requirements should be followed until "legal provisions are made in that behalf" (para. 35), it was no doubt aware of previous judicial directions along similar lines which had still not led to amendments in law. The Court could not direct the government to enact legislation, but stated that in its opinion it was clearly desirable that existing legislation should be amended to incorporate the "requirements". This view was supported in November 2000 by the Law Commission of India, which in its Consultation Paper on Law Relating to Arrest recommended incorporation of the "requirements" into law. As of June 2002 the Indian government had not given any commitment that it intended to do so.

To reinforce the "requirements", the judgment stated that "Failure to comply with the requirements herein above-mentioned shall, apart from rendering the concerned official liable for departmental action, also render him liable to be punished for contempt of court and the proceedings for contempt of court may be instituted in any High Court of the country having territorial jurisdiction over the matter" (para. 36). The judgment further ordered that the requirements be issued to the Director Generals of Police and Home Secretaries of all states who in turn are obliged to circulate them to every police station under their jurisdiction and to have them posted in a conspicuous place in every police station. It also recommended that the requirements be broadcast on radio and television and distributed in pamphlets in local languages "creating awareness... transparency and accountability" (para. 39).

Implementation of the judgment

In a visit to West Bengal in June 1999, Amnesty International delegates were told that arrest memos were issued in the majority of cases. The delegates saw copies of arrest memos and "inspection memos" as well as government orders instructing police to incorporate the guidelines into their working practices. The guidelines had also appeared on websites set up by some state police forces. However, there were continuing concerns about non-implementation of the requirements in many areas of the country where police were failing to issue arrest or inspection memos or to publicize the requirements, or were failing to implement the requirements, in full.

For example, human rights activists in West Bengal told Amnesty International that arrest memos rarely had the signature of witnesses to the arrest or, where witnesses were specified, police were accused of inserting the names of individuals well known to them as "stock" witnesses. Moreover, the use of inspection memos had not become widespread.

Although acknowledging that the documents specified by the requirements would provide additional evidence in cases of illegal detention, human rights activists have pointed out that it is still possible for police to manipulate the memo of arrest (as above). Given that the detainee is not required to be provided with a copy of the memo of arrest, if information is filled in falsely there is no opportunity to challenge it or for the magistrate to verify its accuracy. Human rights activists have also pointed out that magistrates often fail to challenge police when the custody records are incomplete. These issues highlight the need for extreme vigilance within the judiciary to ensure proper implementation of the safeguards.

The requirement to give detainees a medical examination every 48 hours was not being fulfilled; there was no established system for doctors to visit police stations to medically examine or treat detainees, who therefore remained at the mercy of police officers to take them to hospital for treatment.

There were also problems with the implementation of the requirement allowing detainees to have their lawyer with them during interrogation. The Supreme Court had previously interpreted the right of detainees to legal counsel (provided by Article 21 of the Constitution) to mean that detainees had a right to consult a lawyer of their choice and a right to the presence of a lawyer during interrogation. However, this right was rarely being granted in India even after the

Supreme Court's 1996 judgment. A list of "Rights regarding arrest" on the website of the Uttar Pradesh police, reflecting the 11 requirements of the Supreme Court, stated: "As per provisions of law, persons under detention have the right to have the services of an advocate. However, during interrogation the advocate is not allowed to be present."

Implementation of the court's directions nationwide has been monitored by the Supreme Court through its *amicus curiae*. Almost every six weeks the Supreme Court hears the *amicus curiae* on the progress of states in achieving implementation of its order – in relation to the 11 requirements and its general directions on investigation, prosecution and granting of compensation in cases of death in custody. As of June 2001, Amnesty International understood that the Supreme Court had received affidavits from every state government asserting that they were complying with the 11 requirements. The fact that such affidavits were on record ensures that evidence of non-compliance can promptly lead to contempt proceedings.

The *amicus curiae* can highlight major violations and individual grievances, and in this role Dr Singhvi filed several applications recommending that the court issue further directions concerning custodial violence. On the basis of such applications, the Supreme Court in 1998 expressed concern about "deficient" information furnished by states on compliance with its 1996 judgment. It ordered all states to file affidavits indicating the status of all inquiries into custodial deaths and provide copies of all reports of inquiries.

Dr Singhvi also made an application in which he urged the Supreme Court to issue a range of further directions relating to inquiries and post-mortems in particular. The application pointed to continuing failures to carry out impartial investigations into deaths in custody and drew on findings by the National Human Rights Commission on torture. In response, in January 2001 the Supreme Court issued a further notice to the central and state governments asking them to demonstrate why the Court should not issue further directions for adopting measures to prevent custodial deaths.

Conclusion

In following up its original order in this way, the Supreme Court has indicated its continuing concern and willingness to tackle the problem of custodial violence. However, there is still much work to be done to raise awareness of the Supreme Court's guidelines among police and judicial officers as well as the public at large, and to monitor implementation of the 11 "requirements". Nevertheless, the fact that the guidelines exist and that their non-implementation can lead to contempt proceedings and departmental action has strengthened the hand of human rights activists. Numerous petitions have been filed by lawyers and human rights activists challenging incidents of illegal detention, which carefully cite violations by police of the Supreme Court's orders in the case of *Basu v. State of West Bengal*. Growing awareness among the public of their rights under this judgment through legal literacy training has been encouraged by human rights activists and judicial officers. Although torture and ill-treatment remain widespread in India, the Supreme Court's 1996 judgment and the efforts being made to implement it are encouraging signs that serious attempts are being made to get to the heart of the problem.

2.6 Austria: Death of deportee triggers human rights reforms

Long-standing calls for an independent watchdog of police activities and human rights in Austria were finally acted upon in 1999 after the death of a gagged deportee sparked widespread outrage. The section below looks at the tragedy that was the catalyst for the creation of the Human Rights Advisory Council, and assesses the functions and early record of the Council.

Death of Marcus Omofuma

On 1 May 1999 Marcus Omofuma died while being forcibly deported on a flight from Vienna Schwechat airport to Nigeria via Sofia, Bulgaria. At the time of his forced deportation, the 25-year-old Nigerian national was gagged and his hands and feet were bound. He had resisted the attempt to deport him and as a result police officers reportedly took the decision to restrain him.

On the aircraft he was put in an empty row of seats at the back. Witnesses stated that police officers had already gagged him with several pieces of adhesive tape before bringing him onto the aircraft, and then strapped him to the seat using adhesive tape. One witness stated: "He was like a slaughtered animal with his hands and feet bound." Another reportedly said: "They wrapped the entire upper part of his body and arms with adhesive tape like a mummy stuck to the seat." When Marcus Omofuma continued to protest, the police officers allegedly applied more adhesive tape to his chin and used a plastic belt to further secure him to the seat. A crewman on the flight was quoted in an Austrian weekly magazine to have said: "The black man was thrashing around wildly and trying over and over to get air. But the officials did nothing... The man appeared to be really fighting for his life."

Witnesses said that some time into the two-and-a-half-hour journey to Sofia, Marcus Omofuma calmed down. When the officers untied him and removed the adhesive tape from his mouth, they reportedly realized that he had lost consciousness. By the time a doctor arrived, Marcus Omofuma was dead.

There was some controversy about the exact cause of death. An autopsy conducted in Bulgaria shortly after the incident pointed to death by asphyxia. However, an autopsy concluded in November 1999 in Austria suggested that an undetected respiratory-related heart defect meant that it could not be said with the required certainty that there was a causative link between the gagging of Marcus Omofuma and his death. A third autopsy conducted by a German specialist and made public in early May 2001 appeared to reinforce the findings of the first autopsy – that Marcus Omofuma had indeed died of asphyxia.

Three police officers were charged in the case with ill-treating a detainee resulting in death. On 15 April 2002 Korneuburg Regional Court found them guilty of the lesser charge of "negligent manslaughter in particularly dangerous conditions" and sentenced them to eight months' imprisonment, which was suspended. At the time of writing, the police officers were appealing against the sentences.

Marcus Omofuma's death was a catalyst for two positive developments concerning the protection of human rights in Austria – the explicit banning of the use of gags during deportations, and the creation of an independent human rights advisory body.

Legacy of Marcus Omofuma's death

The death of Marcus Omofuma caused a major political scandal in Austria. It was reportedly the first death in police custody in the recent history of the Republic of Austria and to many observers it was brutal and could have been avoided. There were calls for the resignation of the government figures deemed responsible for the tragedy, and peaceful demonstrations were held in Vienna to express concern about the treatment of Marcus Omofuma.

An immediate consequence of such pressure was that, despite the disputed findings of the autopsies, the use of gags during deportations was explicitly banned on 28 May 1999 with the introduction of guidelines regulating deportations. In a letter dated 30 August 1999, the then Minister of the Interior, Karl Schlögl, informed Amnesty International: "I prohibited without exception the use of adhesive tapes or similar materials." Prior to these swift changes no guidelines existed regulating deportations and police officers received no special training in this respect.

The inquiry into Marcus Omofuma's death revealed a considerable degree of ambiguity about whether gags could have been permissibly used during the expulsion of a deportee. At a press conference on 16 August 1999, Karl Schlögl stated: "Gagging of the mouth was neither permitted nor prohibited, it was a failure in the system." He and several senior police officials maintained they knew nothing of the practice of gagging during forced expulsions. It also emerged that the Head of Vienna's Alien Police Branch, Stefan Stortetcky, had banned the use of gagging in September 1998 after the death of Nigerian national Semira Adamu by asphyxia during her forced deportation from Belgium. He told subordinates during a meeting in September 1998: "... deportees are to be returned to the police jail if expulsion is only possible through the gagging of the mouth". However, the position of these senior officials directly contradicted statements made by the police officers involved in the deportation of Marcus Omofuma. On 7 May 1999 one of the accused officers reportedly stated before a court in Korneuburg: "I take the position that everyone at our department knew about these practices."

The second positive development was the establishment on 5 July 1999 of the Human Rights Advisory Council (HRAC) which, according to a member of the Council, "would never have happened without the death of Marcus Omofuma". This sentiment is echoed by the HRAC's official website: "After the death of the Nigerian deportee Marcus Omofuma... efforts to create an advisory council of this type were intensified." It was also no coincidence that the first report and recommendations issued by the HRAC dealt with human rights issues related to "problematic deportations".

The formation of an independent human rights body concerned with police practices had originally been recommended by the European Committee for the Prevention of Torture (CPT) in its initial and second periodic reports on Austria. In the initial report, after a visit to Austria in 1990, the CPT recommended that the Austrian authorities "explore the possibility of empowering an independent body to inspect on a regular basis the conditions of detention in police jails".[30] In the second report, based on a 1994 visit, the CPT repeated this recommendation. Responding to the second report, the Austrian government stated: "In principle, creating such a body appears worth considering, but the idea requires closer examination. It is safe to say from the outset that any such institution must be possessed of the necessary legal and practical instruments if it is able to work efficiently. Such a project will require some long-term planning before it can be launched."[31] However, while there were tentative discussions in Austria's parliament, the *Nationalrat*, on the possibility of establishing such a body, no concrete steps were taken until Marcus Omofuma's death rocked the political establishment.

The Human Rights Advisory Council

The legislative basis of the HRAC is found in Article 15 of the Security Police Law (*Sicherheitspolizeigesetz*). The provisions of this law outline the Council's composition, functions and powers, and are supplemented by regulations found in several accompanying ordinances.

    The HRAC comprises 11 members who are appointed for three-year periods of service by the Minister of the Interior. The chairperson is nominated by the President of the Constitutional Court, five of the members are nominated by Austrian NGOs, two are nominated by the Federal Ministry of Justice and Chancellor's Office, and three are staff of the Federal Ministry of the Interior. In addition, 11 substitute members are nominated who stand in for permanent members when the latter are unavailable.[32]

    The HRAC has two broad functions. First, it can examine all aspects of human rights relating to activities of the Ministry of the Interior and on this basis offer advice to the Minister of the Interior. A main focus of the HRAC's activities is to reveal possible structural shortcomings that give rise to human rights violations and suggest improvements to facilitate greater future protection.

    Secondly, the HRAC, like the CPT, may actively check police activities, such as by visiting places of detention under the jurisdiction of the Ministry of the Interior or observing the policing of demonstrations. For this purpose, six human rights commissions were created in July 2000 to act as "the eyes and ears of the Human Rights Advisory Council on the ground", as described by a member of the HRAC. The same HRAC member told Amnesty International that the decision to create a system of visits, whereby empirical research could be conducted, was a serious breakthrough to avoid the "debating club syndrome".

Working groups and reports of the HRAC

Since its inception the HRAC has embraced a number of different human rights topics and in some instances has produced reports for public use. Topics are usually discussed and adopted during the meetings of the HRAC, which take place every six weeks. Initially, the adoption of new topics reportedly took place on an *ad hoc* basis, although a working group on planning was formed in the latter part of 2001 to select criteria for the adoption of future topics. This working group acts as a kind of steering group for the HRAC.

    When embarking upon a human rights topic, a working group is usually formed from the members of the HRAC and its commissions, NGOs and experts from the ministries to discuss how the research will be conducted and written up. The working group then presents the HRAC with a draft report which is com- mented on by the HRAC's members. After any necessary amendments have been made, the report is officially adopted by the HRAC for presentation to the Minister of the Interior. According to the regulations, adoption is by majority vote, but to date consensus has reportedly been reached through discussion. Obtaining the consensus of the members nominated by the ministries of justice and interior is said to make a report "stronger" and increases the likelihood that the recommendations will be implemented.

In its short history the HRAC has looked at a wide range of human rights topics, the findings of several of which have been published as official reports. The first report, *Problematical Deportations*, adopted in October 1999, contained 32 recommendations about how such deportations can be facilitated while safeguarding human rights. Other issues studied include: minors in pre-deportation detention; the medical and psychological treatment of people in police detention or prior to their deportation; women in detention; information given to detainees; and the use of discriminatory language by police officers. An annual report of the activities of the HRAC and its commissions is published.

One challenge facing the HRAC is to see whether its recommendations are implemented. A working group was set up to examine the action taken by the Ministry of the Interior in response to the first report on problematic deportations. In the future, this process of evaluation will reportedly be conducted by a working group after the Minister of the Interior has been presented with the HRAC's recommendations.

Visits of the commissions

The HRAC's "eyes and ears on the ground" – the commissions – comprise a wide range of individuals, including lawyers, academics, organizational consultants, doctors, psychologists, social workers, a theologian and a journalist. The leader of each commission is directly appointed by the HRAC on the strength of his or her human rights expertise, while the remaining members are chosen by the leader of the commission and approved by the HRAC. Three of the commissions cover the regions in and around Vienna; the other three are responsible for the rest of Austria and are based in the cities of Graz, Innsbruck and Linz. These locations coincide with the seats of Austria's high courts.

The six commissions – which each consist of six members – have access to any police establishment under the jurisdiction of the Ministry of the Interior in their respective regions. The police authorities in such establishments are obliged to cooperate with the commission members, support their activities and permit them access to both police buildings and documents. Commission members also have the right to meet detainees in private in the absence of third parties, namely the police. Visits can be conducted in a routine manner or according to the dictates of circumstances, and do not have to be announced.

The main task of the commissions is to oversee the conditions of detention under the jurisdiction of the Ministry of the Interior and the exercise of force by the police authorities. When visiting places of detention the commissions use a checklist of standards to determine whether basic safeguards are in place. Their findings are passed on to the HRAC, which decides how the information should be used. The sheer number of reports and the need to attain greater uniformity between the reports of the different commissions has not always made this task straightforward. In the first year of their existence, the six commissions conducted around 120 visits. At the time of writing, the HRAC was in the process of enhancing the training of the commissions' members in order to attain greater uniformity and consistency in their work.

Successes and limitations of the HRAC

A major success of the HRAC is the breadth of its mandate, which allows it to take up any human rights issue relating to the activities of the Ministry of the Interior in Austria. This is reflected in the relatively diverse topics on which the HRAC has created working groups to conduct research.

A further success has been the cooperation experienced by the HRAC and the commissions when visiting institutions under the jurisdiction of the Ministry of the Interior. Amnesty International has been informed that there exists a high degree of awareness among police officers about the work of the HRAC and its right of access to a wide range of establishments. Moreover, members of the HRAC and the commissions have reportedly been cordially received by police officials during their visits. This positive picture stands in contrast to the experiences of the CPT during its initial visit to Austria in 1990, which referred in its report to the "reticence on the part of authorities" at the establishments it visited. The CPT believed that this reaction might have been explained to some extent "by a lack of information on the part of officials directly concerned, especially in the case of the police, who were only vaguely, or not at all, aware of the CPT's visit and its role".[33]

One of the main limitations on the investigatory powers currently bestowed on the HRAC is that its powers of investigation relate only to the institutions under the jurisdiction of the Ministry of the Interior. Prisons are therefore beyond its scope as they fall under the jurisdiction of the Ministry of Justice. Consequently, there is no independent body in Austria that oversees conditions of detention in penal institutions. It remains to be seen whether the HRAC can expand its mandate in the coming phases of its development.

The inability of the HRAC to oversee investigations into allegations of police ill-treatment of detainees might also be regarded as a major limitation. Such a supervisory function might have acted as a powerful deterrent against police ill-treatment, particularly in the light of Amnesty International's concerns about investigations into alleged police ill-treatment in Austria. In recent years Amnesty International has expressed concern about the impartiality and thoroughness of such investigations, a concern that has been echoed by human rights lawyers within Austria. The CPT has also expressed concern about such investigations in the past. Following its 1990 visit to Austria, the CPT said the question should be addressed of whether an independent person should take part in the disciplinary procedure relating to allegations of police ill-treatment in order to improve the intrinsic quality of the procedure and enhance public confidence in its fairness.[34] In its second periodic report, the CPT asked for comments from the authorities on the apparently lenient attitude of the Ministry of the Interior with regard to disciplining police officers for behaviour which constituted a serious infringement of a person's fundamental rights and – in the light of these concerns – on the desirability of having complaints of police ill-treatment investigated by people with appropriate qualifications and skills from outside the police service.[35]

Conclusion

The death of Marcus Omofuma and the subsequent creation of the HRAC have contributed to an increased awareness and protection of human rights in Austria. Although practical difficulties and a restricted mandate limited the HRAC's effectiveness in its first year or so, there were nevertheless many encouraging signs that the HRAC will make a considerable impact on the protection of human rights in relation to police activities. The CPT also expressed its satisfaction about the creation of the HRAC, stating in its report on its third periodic visit to Austria: "If it works effectively, the Human Rights Advisory Council will represent an important guarantee against ill-treatment".[36] However, the key questions – whether and how the government will implement the recommendations of the HRAC and its commissions – have yet to be answered.

2.7 South Africa: Exposing torture under apartheid

"**Peter Jacobs** [torture victim]: [Y]ou would undress me, tie my blue belt around my feet, throw me on the ground... at some point, I think it is about the fourth time, when I thought I am dying, you woke me up and said, 'Peter, I will take you to the verge [of] death as many times as I want to. But here you are going to talk and if it means that then you will die, that is okay.' Do you remember that?

"**Jeffrey Benzien** [former member of the Terrorist Tracing Unit]: I concede that I may have said that, Sir.

"**Peter Jacobs**: I want to know, I want you to tell me, because this is important for me. The Truth Commission can amnesty, but this is important for me, did you say that?

"**Jeffrey Benzien**: Yes, I did say that.

. . .

"**Jeffrey Benzien**: [T]hese orders would not be for a specific person, go in now and torture that person... This was the order of the day, when interrogating a terrorist, you got your information as soon as possible, by using any methods [at] your disposal. And in my case, it was torture... we [had] been giving evidence in numerous trials and... especially when it came to things like torture... you lied about it, you did not concede.

"**Gary Kruser** [torture victim]: [U]nder whose orders did you lie? You said you were given instructions to lie, so under whose orders did you lie?

"**Jeffrey Benzien**: I could say it was under the orders of Lieutenant Liebenberg [his commander]... It was a known fact, under certain circumstances you had to lie, and under those circumstances when it was my testimony that could put a bad light on the Security Branch, I lied. It was an accepted method."[37]

These remarkable exchanges took place in Cape Town, South Africa, in July 1997 at a public hearing by the autonomous Amnesty Committee of the Truth and Reconciliation Commission.

The Truth and Reconciliation Commission

The Truth and Reconciliation Commission was established in South Africa by the Promotion of National Unity and Reconciliation Act No. 34 of 1995. It had extensive and unusual powers in comparison to "truth commissions" set up to examine past human rights violations in other countries.[38] Reflecting the delicate political and power balance at the time of the country's transition from white minority (apartheid) rule in 1994, the legislation establishing the Commission equipped it with:

* investigation and subpoena powers;

* a wide mandate to inquire into patterns of human rights abuses by public officials and members of opposition organizations over a 34-year period;

* the power to make recommendations, including for reparations for victims of abuses; and

* the quasi-judicial power to grant amnesty, under certain conditions, to perpetrators of human rights abuses.[39]

Adopted during the period of the Government of National Unity, which included members of the former government, the legislation had been intensely debated in the Cabinet, in the national parliament and among NGOs. The roots of the decision to include the power to grant amnesties lay in the difficult political negotiations leading to the agreement on an interim Constitution in 1993 and the holding of universal franchise elections in 1994. Members of the then government, and possibly members of opposition organizations, feared the possibility of criminal prosecutions and civil liability for crimes that had been committed in the name of apartheid or in opposition to it.[40] During the negotiations, opposition parties resisted the government's push for a blanket amnesty. The compromise reached was reflected in a postscript to the interim Constitution, referred to as the post-amble, which stated that there would be amnesty for politically motivated offences and that future legislation would provide the criteria and procedures to regulate the process.[41] On this basis the new government under President Nelson Mandela drafted legislation for a wide-ranging commission of inquiry, with powers to grant amnesties.

During the drafting there were fears that Cabinet-level compromises would lead to a decision that the proposed inquiry body could only consider applications for amnesty behind closed doors. However, the pressures within the Cabinet were counter-balanced by open debate in parliament and intense lobbying by NGOs.[42] The final outcome was a provision in Section 20 of the 1995 Promotion of National Unity and Reconciliation Act that where "gross human rights violations" were acknowledged by a perpetrator in an application for amnesty there had to be an open hearing. The victim or relative had to be informed about the date and location of the hearing and would have the right to "testify, adduce evidence and submit any article to be taken into consideration". An applicant had to make "full disclosure of all relevant facts" and demonstrate that the act for which amnesty was sought "was an act associated with a political objective committed in the course of the conflicts of the past".

The result was likely to be drastic from the point of view of the rights of the victims, as a successful applicant would be permanently protected from any criminal or civil liability in relation to the offence acknowledged. There was no requirement in the Act that the perpetrator should show remorse or make individual reparations to the survivor or their family. Relatives of some prominent anti-apartheid activists who were victims of police brutality challenged these provisions in the Constitutional Court. The Court, while acknowledging that the provisions had an impact on fundamental rights protected under the new Constitution, ruled that the post-amble effectively limited those rights and that victims would have to look to a broader state program of post-apartheid reparations to obtain compensation.[43] In sum, it was a balancing act between the perceived "national interest" and the claims of victims. Only time would tell if the fruits of "full disclosure" from the amnesty process, implemented by the Truth and Reconciliation Commission's Amnesty Committee (see below), and the reconciliation that it was assumed to evoke would satisfy the needs and claims of victims and the country's international human rights obligations.[44]

Under the apartheid state victims of human rights violations, including torture, or their relatives had faced years of denial from officials that the violations had taken place. The evidence of widespread and routine torture and ill-treatment accumulated by health and legal practitioners and human rights monitoring organizations was simply denied. The statements of victims brought to trial after months of often incommunicado detention about their treatment at the hands of the security police were mostly ignored by the courts. At best, victims might receive an out-of-court settlement in a civil case, but with police denying any liability. The Truth and Reconciliation Commission and the public hearings held in particular by one of its three sub-committees, the Human Rights Violations Committee, finally gave survivors or their relatives an opportunity to tell publicly their painful accounts.

The hearings

The Human Rights Violations Committee held a number of public hearings around the country to investigate and make findings on the claims of victims. These hearings gave some survivors or their family members an opportunity to describe what happened to them and to tell the committee what they hoped would come out of its work on their case. The hearings were held in major urban centres, small towns and rural areas and were attended by members of local communities. Often highly emotionally charged, and sometimes dogged by legal complexities owing to court rulings constraining the naming of alleged perpetrators without prior notice to them,[45] the hearings were broadcast nationally on television and radio and widely reported in the print media.

Among the numerous testimonies heard, Gladys Ntsizakalo from the Northern Karoo town of Noupoort told the Human Rights Violations Committee that her 15-year-old son, Siphiwo Ntsizakalo, became mentally disturbed after his detention and torture in the 1980s. She had been denied access to her son for up to three months. She testified that when she was finally given access to him at the police station,

> "[I found him] alone in the cell. Both his hands and his legs were tied. When I looked at him as a parent, I realised that he was mentally disturbed. When he saw me, he just cried. I could see that my son had changed. When I asked, he said that they kept on beating him up... that is why he was deranged. They would take a sack – a wet sack – and then they would cover him with that sack. They would put him in the boot

[of a car], drive him to a place that he did not know, and then... they would beat him up... Now he cannot do anything for himself."[46]

Over the 18-month period of these public hearings, hundreds of witnesses gave searing accounts of torture and ill-treatment by police and other agents of the apartheid state.[47] There were some accounts also of torture and ill-treatment inflicted by opposition organizations, including the African National Congress (ANC) in exile in camps they controlled outside South Africa. The Truth and Reconciliation Commission regarded these hearings as vital to achieve one of its statutory objectives – "restoring the human and civil dignity of such victims by granting them an opportunity to relate their own accounts of the violations of which they are the victims". It also stated that "they revealed the extent of gross violations of human rights and made it impossible for South Africans ever again to deny that such violations had indeed taken place".[48]

In a severely divided society in which many beneficiaries of the apartheid system had ignored widespread and systematic human rights violations, it was the chilling testimony of the perpetrators that breached the wall of denial. The Commission concluded: "[I]n reviewing its efforts to uncover the deeper truth behind the violations of the apartheid era, [it] frankly acknowledges that much of its success is due to the fact that large numbers of security police members grasped at the possibility of amnesty in exchange for full disclosure." It also acknowledged that what drove these security officials to speak was the extent of the disclosures made by one of them, Eugene de Kock, "who broke the code of silence".[49] This former head of a covert police unit based at Vlakplaas had been prosecuted in the Pretoria High Court for multiple counts of murder and other crimes. Availing himself of the provisions of the 1995 Act, he launched an application for amnesty from C-MAX maximum security prison in Pretoria where he had been serving multiple life sentences. The hearings on his lengthy application threatened to expose the role of others in his crimes. It was in part the fear of likely prosecution that drove other members of the security police to apply for amnesty. Perpetrators from other sectors, such as the military, did not feel similarly threatened and were conspicuously absent as applicants for amnesty.[50]

Amnesties

The Truth and Reconciliation Commission received just over 7,000 applications for amnesty, the majority of them from prisoners serving sentences. Another of the Commission's sub-committees – the autonomous Amnesty Committee, which was chaired by a High Court judge – was responsible for considering and deciding on these applications. Many of them were disposed of, on the basis of papers submitted, without a hearing. However, in at least 1,000 cases the decisions on the applications were reached after public hearings before the Amnesty Committee. Of these, some 50 cases involved applicants who disclosed that they or other police officers had used torture or other severe ill-treatment against detainees, or against individuals whom they had abducted and later murdered.

The record of the hearings indicate that in a number of cases survivors of torture, their relatives or their legal representatives were present to challenge the versions presented by the applicants. In the majority of the 50 cases, the Amnesty Committee granted amnesty on the grounds that the applicant had complied with the requirements of Section 20 of the Act, in that he had made "full disclosure of all the relevant facts"; that the act disclosed was "associated with a political objective committed in the course of the conflicts of the past", and had been committed, ordered or planned by an employee of the state acting within the course and scope of his duties, or by a member or supporter of a publicly known political organization or liberation movement in furtherance of that organization's objectives.

Gerhardus Johannes Nieuwoudt,[51] who had been one of the most notorious members of the police Security Branch in Port Elizabeth, sought amnesty in relation to a number of prominent cases, including the assault of political activist Mkhuseli Jack in August 1985. Gerhardus Johannes Nieuwoudt claimed in his testimony that under the terms of the then State of Emergency law he was obliged in the "national interest" and was under pressure from the highest political authorities to stabilize "the unrest". This included detaining and interrogating Mkhuseli Jack in a bid to break a consumer boycott of local businesses. Gerhardus Johannes Nieuwoudt claimed that when the detainee proved "very hard-headed", he "took a black plastic *sjambok* [whip] and... gave him several lashes over his body and legs... It was one way to diminish his resistance." He stated that he took advantage of the emergency regulations which "gave [him] wide protection... against prosecution and civil claims". He said that if a case had emerged against him or other members of the Security Branch, "we would have tried to cover it up whatever the case may be to ensure that we would not get to court".

His carefully phrased admissions, however, were taken apart during the public hearing in September 1997 by Mkhuseli Jack and his lawyer. The lawyer challenged Gerhardus Johannes Nieuwoudt, alleging that he had not just assaulted the detainee with a *sjambok* but had actively along with other police officers inflicted the "so-called helicopter torture" on him.

Gerhardus Johannes Nieuwoudt denied this. Mkhuseli Jack, who was at the hearing, was able to confront him:

> "I'm going to read from an affidavit which was the basis for the civil claims which... [the police had] settled on the basis of the information that is in this document...

> "[Warrant-Officer Coetzee] took out a towel and tied it nicely around each of my wrists and placed the handcuffs over the towelling. He screwed the handcuffs tight. I was told to sit on the floor and place my handcuffed arms over my legs. A stick was then inserted below my knees and above my forearms, locking me into a permanent crouch. Nieuwoudt entered the room... Both men then lifted me up by means of the stick and suspended me between two tables...

> "About 60 other applicants who were the basis of the civil claim... were subjected to that. On 80 per cent of them, he [Nieuwoudt] was involved... I am not going into the discomfort, because everybody knows what this thing [helicopter torture] is about... I find it strange that he doesn't remember this, because he [then] was bragging about how he has assaulted all the other people... How... Nieuwoudt can deny this, I really don't understand. How does he hope to get amnesty? [T]his platform of amnesty should be used with the dignity it deserve[s] and mustn't be turned into a mockery with the aim of insulting the families... [my] family and myself and the families of

many other people who would not be having an opportunity to come and speak in front of this [committee]..."

Gerhardus Johannes Nieuwoudt's lawyer replied that it was highly unlikely that he would have commented about his responsibility for assaults "to a person who would eventually one day be able to give evidence against him". Mkhuseli Jack replied: "[Nieuwoudt] never believed that he [would] be facing these people here and sitting here... [He] feared no claims from detainees." Indeed, in the end it was the long-practised arrogance of the Security Branch, reflected in Gerhardus Johannes Nieuwoudt's testimony, which undermined his application. The Amnesty Committee rejected his application on the grounds that he had failed to make a "full disclosure" and that the limited assault he had admitted to was not an act associated with a political objective.

In another case the Amnesty Committee's decision to grant amnesty to a former Durban Security Branch officer, Christo Nel,[52] for his role in the torture of a detainee, Yunis Shaik, in July 1985 was supported by the victim. Christo Nel testified that he had held down the detainee while he was being tortured by other police officers. He said that one of the torturers was a medical doctor, who had in fact "administered" the "very unusual" method of (anal) torture on Yunis Shaik. The victim, who had been held in solitary confinement for 11 months, told the Amnesty Committee that he substantially agreed with the version given by the applicant. He said, "[A]s I've listened... it's almost as if... I was reliving a rather traumatic memory." He went on to state, generously, that Christo Nel's disclosures had provided "an opportunity for [Yunis] and [his] family to bring closure" on a period when his father and three brothers had also been detained and his mother had suffered a heart attack and died. He himself had suffered an enormous amount of rage after his release. He reflected that the applicant had shown some courage in presenting himself before the Committee, when "many other police officers" had failed to do so.

In contrast, the hearing on the application of Jeffrey Benzien,[53] a former member of the police Security Branch, revealed a profound ambivalence on the part of his former victims, who ultimately doubted the extent to which he had fully disclosed the relevant information in defence of his claim to amnesty. At one level Jeffrey Benzien's statements to the Amnesty Committee represented an astonishingly frank acknowledgment of his routine infliction of torture on anyone suspected of "terrorist" activities on behalf of the ANC in the late 1980s. His testimony and that of his supporting witness, retired Major General Johannes Griebenauw, a former senior officer of the police Security Branch, confirmed that this conduct was condoned at the highest level politically. At one stage in the hearing, on the request of one of his former victims, Tony Yengeni, Jeffrey Benzien demonstrated on a volunteer in front of the panel, the audience and television cameras his notorious "wet bag" method of suffocation torture, which observers saw as a form of "public shaming". Despite this, his victims' persistent questioning in the hearing frequently exposed his failure to admit to other forms of ill-treatment and to name other police officers who participated in the torture sessions.

In reaching its decision on Jeffrey Benzien's application, the Amnesty Committee did not, as it did routinely in other rulings, reflect on the extent to which the applicant had made a full disclosure. Nonetheless, he was granted amnesty for assault with intent to inflict grievous bodily harm on seven named detainees. The Committee simply commented that on the evidence before them, "the offences for which the applicant seeks amnesty were committed during and arose out of the conflicts of the past between the State and Liberation Movement".

In the case of Stanza Bopape, whose "disappearance" in June 1988 had been vigorously investigated by his family, the Amnesty Committee accepted, with some uneasiness, the claims of 10 former Security Branch officers, including the then head of the Security Branch, that they had unlawfully killed him (as a result of inflicting electric shocks), disposed of the body and concocted an elaborate cover-up to conceal the crime. In a worrying reflection on the issue of "proportionality", the Committee commented that

> "The methods used in the interrogation of the Deceased were both odious and unlawful. We are, however, after careful consideration, of the view that their use of the electric shock device in the interrogation was not disproportionate to the objective they were pursuing. According to them the use of electric shock devices in interrogation was common practice... They perceived it as being an effective and convenient method of forcing the victim to co-operate and they did not anticipate or suspect that its use would have fatal consequences."[54]

The Amnesty Committee completed its hearings and delivered its final rulings by June 2001. The remaining task for the Truth and Reconciliation Commission was to compile its concluding report, which would incorporate the factual findings of the Amnesty Committee into the Commission's earlier findings published in October 1998 and make additional recommendations on reparations for victims of human rights violations who had been identified by the Amnesty Committee. That report, which has to be handed to the President of South Africa, was still pending in early 2002.

Conclusion

The work of the Truth and Reconciliation Commission ended years of denial by state officials and political parties that torture occurred systematically and with impunity during the period of apartheid rule. It also gave many victims the opportunity to recount their experiences in public hearings and gave some the chance to challenge their torturers face to face.

However, not all were comfortable with the results of the Commission, and the price they paid in the name of the perceived national interest has been underlined by the government's failure to implement swiftly or with any grace the recommended reparations for named victims. Moreover, little interest has been displayed by the government and other political parties in parliament in considering the Commission's recommendations, made in its 1998 report, for preventing a repetition of the kinds of human rights violations it had helped to expose.

Since 1996, when the Commission began its work, the political mood in the country has changed considerably. Attention has shifted away from the rights and claims of the victims of torture and other human rights violations under apartheid to the rights of victims of violent crime, the levels of which are causing increasing public concern.

South Africa is still a country where torture occurs, primarily in the context of the "war against crime".[55] Despite the achievements of the Truth and Reconciliation Commission, the justifications given by the torturers who applied for amnesty and the acceptance of these by the Amnesty Committee under the terms of the Act may prove to be a dangerous legacy in terms of the continuing fight to end torture.

© AP

Nazli Top, one of several defendants on trial in Turkey for "insulting" the army and police after denouncing sexual torture at a conference in 2000. Nazli Top was allegedly raped with a truncheon in 1992 while pregnant, but seven police officers accused of torturing her were acquitted in 1994. Amnesty International believes that the rape of a prisoner by a prison, security or military official always constitutes torture.

Chapter 3: International law and the obligations of states

3.1 Introduction

The prohibition of torture and ill-treatment was proclaimed in 1948 in the Universal Declaration of Human Rights. As shown in Chapter 1, developments since then have included:

- the incorporation of the prohibition in binding international and regional treaties, other international and regional human rights instruments* and many national constitutions;

- the designation of the prohibition in leading international and regional treaties as a *non-derogable right* – a right which must never be suspended, even in time of public emergency;

- the recognition of the prohibition of torture and other ill-treatment as a rule of *customary international law*, and the recognition of the prohibition of torture as a *peremptory norm of general international law*, binding on all states whether or not they are parties to treaties which contain the prohibition (see section 3.2.6 below);

- the elaboration of standards on the prevention of torture and ill-treatment, on their investigation, on bringing perpetrators to justice and affording reparation to victims;

---

* International treaties are *binding* on states parties: on becoming a party to a treaty, a state formally agrees to be bound by its provisions. Other human rights instruments adopted by intergovernmental bodies may include recommendations to states but are *non-binding* in the sense that states have not formally agreed to be bound by them. The term "international standards" refers both to international human rights instruments and to the standards set out in them.

- the progressive recognition of these standards as constituting not merely recommendations, but *obligations* of states;

- the development of international standards and practice relating to *individual criminal responsibility* for torture and ill-treatment;

- the expansion of the forms of abuse which are recognized as included in the prohibition (see section 3.4);

- an increasing awareness of the obligation of states to protect people from *abuses by private individuals* which are contrary to the prohibition of torture and ill-treatment.

These developments have come about by various means, including:

- the adoption of human rights treaties and other standards by international and regional intergovernmental organizations;

- judgments, decisions and statements by the regional human rights courts and commissions, other international human rights bodies and mechanisms, and the International Criminal Tribunals for the former Yugoslavia and Rwanda;

- the efforts of non-governmental organizations (NGOs) to ensure that governments honour their international human rights obligations.

This chapter sets out the relevant international standards and examines how the prohibition of torture and ill-treatment is currently treated under international law.*

3.2 A conjunction of international standards

Torture and ill-treatment are prohibited under international human rights law, under the laws of war (international humanitarian law) and under general international law. In addition, individual acts of torture or ill-treatment are proscribed as crimes under international law if committed as war crimes, as crimes against humanity or as genocide. International human rights standards also prescribe measures which governments should take to prevent torture and ill-treatment, to investigate alleged cases, to bring to justice those responsible and to afford reparation to victims.[1]

3.2.1 General human rights instruments**

The **Universal Declaration of Human Rights** is a highly authoritative instrument which applies to all states. Article 5 states:

> "No one shall be subjected to torture or to cruel, inhuman or degrading treatment or punishment."

---

* A checklist of international and regional instruments relevant to the prohibition of torture can be found in Appendix 5 of this manual.

** The texts of prohibitions of torture and ill-treatment in general international and regional human rights instruments are reproduced in Appendix 6 of this manual.

The **International Covenant on Civil and Political Rights** (ICCPR) is the pre-eminent worldwide treaty on civil and political rights. It is binding on states parties, of which there were 148 as of 1 October 2002.* Article 7 states:

> "No one shall be subjected to torture or to cruel, inhuman or degrading treatment or punishment. In particular, no one shall be subjected without his free consent to medical or scientific experimentation."**

Other articles of the ICCPR which are relevant to the elimination of torture include Article 2 on the obligation to respect and ensure human rights, Article 6 on the right to life, Article 9 on the right to liberty and security of person, Article 10 on the right of persons deprived of liberty to be treated with humanity and respect for human dignity, and Article 14 on the right to a fair trial.

Torture and ill-treatment are also prohibited under the four general regional human rights treaties adopted to date – the **African Charter on Human and Peoples' Rights** (Article 5), the **American Convention on Human Rights** (Article 5), the **European Convention on Human Rights** (Article 3) and the **Arab Charter on Human Rights** (not yet in force, Article 13).[2]

3.2.2 Specialized instruments on the prohibition and prevention of torture

The UN **Convention against Torture and Other Cruel, Inhuman or Degrading Treatment or Punishment** (Convention against Torture) is binding on states parties, of which there were 130 as of 30 June 2002. It sets out a series of measures regarding prevention, investigation, bringing those responsible to justice both domestically and across borders, and affording reparation to victims. Certain provisions of the Convention apply to both torture and other ill-treatment, while others, such as those referring to criminalization, prosecution and the exercise of universal jurisdiction, apply only to torture.***

The UN **Declaration on the Protection of All Persons from Being Subjected to Torture and Other Cruel, Inhuman or Degrading Treatment or Punishment** (Declaration against Torture) is an older instrument, many of whose provisions are similar to those in the Convention against Torture. The application of its provisions to ill-treatment other than torture is generally wider than in the Convention. It is a non-binding but authoritative set of standards which applies to all states.[3]

There are also two regional treaties concerned specifically with torture:

- The **Inter-American Convention to Prevent and Punish Torture** provides for universal jurisdiction over torture among states parties in the Americas region and sets out other measures regarding prevention, investigation, bringing those responsible to justice and affording reparation. Sixteen states were parties as of 1 October 2002.[4]

---

* The number of *states parties* refers to the number of states which formally agree to be bound by the provisions of a treaty. States normally become parties to a treaty by signature followed by *ratification,* or by *accession.* (Up-to-date lists of states parties to international treaties can be found on the websites listed in Appendix 5 of this manual.)

** For historical reasons, the English-language versions of some international human rights instruments employ gender-specific language, such as the pronoun "his", referring to people who may be of either sex.

*** Part I of the Convention against Torture is reproduced in Appendix 7 of this manual. Parts II-III deal with the functioning of the Committee against Torture and with the procedures whereby states may become parties to the Convention.

- The **European Convention for the Prevention of Torture and Inhuman or Degrading Treatment or Punishment** (European Convention for the Prevention of Torture) provides for the establishment of a Committee (European Committee for the Prevention of Torture, CPT) empowered to visit places where people are deprived of their liberty in states parties, of which there were 44 as of 1 October 2002.[5] Under Protocol No. 1 to the Convention, there is a possibility for non-member states of the Council of Europe to be invited to become parties.

3.2.3 Other specialized human rights treaties

Torture and ill-treatment are explicitly prohibited under a number of specialized human rights treaties which apply to specific groups of people or in specific circumstances. Thus, Article 37 of the **Convention on the Rights of the Child** states: "No child shall be subjected to torture or other cruel, inhuman or degrading treatment or punishment." As of 1 October 2002, 191 states were parties to the Convention on the Rights of the Child. The **International Convention on the Protection of the Rights of All Migrant Workers and Members of Their Families** (not yet in force) and the **African Charter on the Rights and Welfare of the Child** also contain explicit prohibitions of torture and ill-treatment.[6]

International and regional instruments designed to combat *discrimination* contain explicit prohibitions of torture and ill-treatment or prohibitions of the infliction of bodily or mental harm under which various acts of torture or ill-treatment would clearly be prohibited. Article 5 of the **International Convention on the Elimination of All Forms of Racial Discrimination** obliges states parties "to guarantee the right of everyone, without distinction as to race, colour, or national or ethnic origin, to equality before the law, notably in the enjoyment of the following rights: ... (b) The right to security of person and protection by the State against violence or bodily harm, whether inflicted by government officials or by any individual group or institution". Article 4 of the **Inter-American Convention on the Prevention, Punishment and Eradication of Violence against Women** states: "Every woman has the right to the recognition, enjoyment, exercise and protection of all human rights and freedoms embodied in regional and international human rights instruments", including "[t]he right not to be subjected to torture". Also, the Committee on the Elimination of Discrimination against Women (CEDAW) established under the **Convention on the Elimination of All Forms of Discrimination against Women**, in its General Recommendation 19 on violence against women, has enumerated the right not to be subjected to torture or ill-treatment among the rights impaired or nullified by gender-based violence, constituting discrimination within the meaning of that Convention (see section 6.6).

Other international treaties also contain similar prohibitions. Article II of the **Convention on the Prevention and Punishment of the Crime of Genocide** (Genocide Convention) prohibits "[c]ausing serious bodily or mental harm" to members of a national, ethnical, racial or religious group with intent to destroy the group as such in whole or in part. Article 5 of the **Supplementary Convention on the Abolition of Slavery, the Slave Trade, and Institutions and Practices**

Similar to Slavery prohibits "mutilating, branding or otherwise marking a slave or a person of servile status" in countries where slavery still exists. Torture or ill-treatment is also included as a component of the crime of apartheid in Article II of the **International Convention on the Suppression and Punishment of the Crime of** *Apartheid.*

3.2.4 International humanitarian law

Torture and ill-treatment are prohibited in all circumstances under *international humanitarian law* – the body of international law which regulates the behaviour of parties to armed conflicts, also known as the laws of war. The four **Geneva Conventions of August 12, 1949**[7] prohibit the "torture or inhuman treatment, including biological experiments" and "wilfully causing great suffering or serious injury to body or health" of persons protected by these Conventions; they identify such acts as "grave breaches" of the Conventions if committed against *"protected persons "*[*] and provide for universal jurisdiction over grave breaches (see section 7.5). Rape of women is also proscribed under Article 27 of the Fourth Geneva Convention. These provisions are applicable to international armed conflicts – wars between states. In addition, Article 3, a text common to all four Conventions, extends to "armed conflict not of an international character"[8] a list of fundamental rules for the protection of persons who have not taken, or are no longer taking, "active part in the hostilities", which each party to the conflict is "bound to apply, as a minimum". Under common Article 3, "violence to life and person, in particular murder of all kinds, mutilation, cruel treatment and torture" and "outrages upon personal dignity, in particular humiliating and degrading treatment" "are and shall remain prohibited at any time and in any place whatsoever" with respect to these persons.[**]

The two **Protocols Additional to the Geneva Conventions of 1949**, adopted in 1977, expand the list of specific prohibited acts. **Additional Protocol I**, relating to international armed conflicts, expands the list of grave breaches (Articles 11, 85). It reaffirms the prohibition of "violence to the life, health, or physical or mental well-being of persons", in particular "torture of all kinds, whether physical or mental", corporal punishment and mutilation, and "enforced prostitution and any form of indecent assault", committed against "persons who are in the power of a Party to the conflict" (Article 75); it also requires the protection of women against rape, forced prostitution and any other form of indecent assault (Article 76) and of children against indecent assault (Article 77). **Additional Protocol II**, relating to non-international armed conflicts, prohibits "violence to the life, health and physical or mental well-being of persons, in particular murder as well as cruel treatment such as torture, mutilation or any form of corporal punishment" and "rape, enforced prostitution and any form of indecent assault" committed against "persons who do not take a direct part or who have ceased to take part in hostilities, whether or not their liberty has been restricted" (Article 4). The Geneva Conventions and the Additional

---

[*] Persons protected by the Geneva Conventions in international armed conflicts are, chiefly, wounded and sick members of armed forces in the field (First Geneva Convention); wounded, sick and shipwrecked members of armed forces at sea (Second Geneva Convention); prisoners of war (Third Geneva Convention); and civilians in occupied territories or elsewhere who "find themselves, in case of a conflict or occupation, in the hands of a Party to the conflict or Occupying Power of which they are not nationals" (Fourth Geneva Convention, Article 4). Common Article 3, applicable in non-international armed conflicts, protects "[p]ersons taking no active part in the hostilities, including members of armed forces who have laid down their arms and those placed *hors de combat* by sickness, wounds, detention, or any other cause".

[**] Extracts from common Article 3 are reproduced in Appendix 8 of this manual.

Protocols also establish safeguards (Article 4) and standards for detention[9] and measures for the protection of women and children,[10] many of which are similar to those found in international human rights standards.

The obligations set out in the Geneva Conventions and the Additional Protocols are binding on states parties to these instruments. Virtually all states are parties to the Geneva Conventions, and the majority are parties to the Additional Protocols. Furthermore, not only states but other parties to an armed conflict are bound to apply the provisions of common Article 3 and, where applicable, of Additional Protocol II.[11]

The International Court of Justice has held that under the "fundamental general principles of international humanitarian law", the rules set out in common Article 3 constitute a "minimum yardstick" which applies to international as well as non-international armed conflicts.[12] In accordance with this ruling, torture and other ill-treatment prohibited under common Article 3 would, if inflicted in any armed conflict, be a violation of general international law. Rules of general international law apply to all states, whether or not they are parties to a treaty expressly containing the rule (see section 3.2.6 below).

3.2.5 Crimes under international law: war crimes, crimes against humanity and genocide

Crimes under international law are crimes by individuals which are defined by international law itself and which international law permits or requires states to punish. The notion that certain especially serious crimes by public officials constitute crimes under international law was first put into practice with the International Military Tribunal (the Nuremberg Tribunal) which convicted political and military Nazi leaders in Germany for grave crimes committed during the Second World War. The Charter of the Nuremberg Tribunal gave the Tribunal jurisdiction over crimes against peace, over *war crimes* (described as "violations of the laws or customs of war", including "ill-treatment" of prisoners of war and civilian populations in occupied territories) and over *crimes against humanity* (including "inhumane acts" against a civilian population).[13] Article 7 of the Charter provided that "[t]he official position of defendants, whether as Heads of States or responsible officials in Government Departments, shall not be considered as freeing them from responsibility or mitigating punishment". The Charter also provided that there was to be no defence of superior orders.[14]

The Nuremberg Principles, a formulation adopted by the International Law Commission[15] of the principles of international law recognized in the Charter and the Judgment of the Nuremberg Tribunal, state that war crimes and crimes against humanity are punishable as crimes under international law. Under the Nuremberg Principles, "Any person who commits an act which constitutes a crime under international law is responsible therefore and liable to punishment", even if the crime is not punishable under national law.[16]

As noted above, the Geneva Conventions of 1949 specify certain acts as "grave breaches" of the Conventions if committed against "protected persons". The rules set out in the Geneva Conventions entail individual criminal responsibility for grave breaches of the Conventions, including torture and inhuman treatment, and provide for mandatory universal jurisdiction over these crimes among states parties to the Conventions (see section 7.5 of this manual). Grave breaches of the Geneva Conventions or of Additional Protocol I are war crimes.[17] According to a ruling of the International Criminal Tribunal for the former Yugoslavia, customary international law also imposes criminal liability for serious violations of common Article 3 to the Geneva Conventions, and such acts can constitute war crimes regardless of whether they are committed in an international or a non-international armed conflict.[18]

Other developments since the Second World War have included the recognition of *genocide* as a crime under international law and the adoption of a convention on that crime, and the adoption by the UN General Assembly of instruments which preclude the application of statutes of limitations to war crimes, crimes against humanity and genocide and provide for international cooperation in bringing to justice perpetrators of war crimes and crimes against humanity.[19] Under the Convention on the Non-Applicability of Statutory Limitations to War Crimes and Crimes against Humanity (Article I), war crimes include those defined as such in the Charter of the Nuremberg Tribunal and grave breaches of the Geneva Conventions. Genocide is defined in Article II of the Genocide Convention as any of a series of specified acts "committed with intent to destroy, in whole or in part, a national, ethnical, racial or religious group, as such". As mentioned above (section 3.2.3), the specified acts include "causing serious bodily or mental harm to members of the group".

One of the most important recent developments has been the establishment of *ad hoc* International Criminal Tribunals to try people accused of extremely serious crimes in connection with specific events. Two such tribunals are currently in existence: the International Criminal Tribunal for the former Yugoslavia (Yugoslavia Tribunal), established by the UN Security Council in 1993 in connection with the armed conflicts which began in the former Yugoslavia in 1991,[20] and the International Criminal Tribunal for Rwanda (Rwanda Tribunal), established by the Security Council in 1994 in connection with the genocide which began in April of the same year.[21]

The crimes set out in the Statutes of the two Tribunals are drawn from the provisions of the Geneva Conventions and other instruments cited above.

- The **Yugoslavia Tribunal** has jurisdiction over the following crimes committed in the territory of the former Yugoslavia since 1 January 1991: *grave breaches of the Geneva Conventions of 1949*, including "wilful killing", "torture or inhuman treatment" and "wilfully causing great suffering or serious injury to body or health"; *violations of the laws or customs of war*;[22] *crimes against humanity*, with "torture", "enslavement", "rape" and "other inhumane acts" included among the possible constituent crimes, committed in armed conflict and "directed against any civilian population"; and *genocide*, with "causing serious bodily or mental harm to members of the group" as a possible constituent crime.[23]

- The **Rwanda Tribunal** has jurisdiction over the following crimes committed in Rwanda, or committed by Rwandan citizens in neighbouring states, during 1994: *violations of common Article 3 to the Geneva Conventions of 1949*; *violations of Additional Protocol II of 1977 to the Geneva Conventions*; *crimes against humanity*, with "torture", "enslavement", "rape" and "other inhumane acts" included among the possible constituent crimes, committed as "part of a widespread or systematic attack against any civilian population on national, political, ethnic, racial or religious grounds"; and *genocide*, with "causing serious bodily or mental harm to members of the group" as a possible constituent crime.[24]

As noted in section 7.6, torture, rape (both as a form of torture and as a separate crime) and other ill-treatment have been among the acts for which defendants have been convicted by the Yugoslavia and Rwanda Tribunals under the headings of one or another of the crimes listed above.

A further key step was taken in 1998 with the adoption of the **Rome Statute of the International Criminal Court** (Rome Statute), a treaty providing for the establishment of a permanent international court to try war crimes, crimes against humanity, genocide and the crime of aggression.[25] The Court is able to try cases of people accused of these crimes committed on or after 1 July 2002, the date of entry into force of the Rome Statute, if the conditions for the exercise of its jurisdiction set out in Articles 12 and 13 of the Rome Statute have been met.[26]

Under the Rome Statute, the jurisdiction of the Court extends to the following crimes, many of which may involve torture or ill-treatment.*

- **War crimes** under the Rome Statute (Article 8) include torture, "inhuman treatment" as a grave breach of the Geneva Conventions, "cruel treatment" as a violation of common Article 3 to the Geneva Conventions, "wilfully causing great suffering, or serious injury to body or health", mutilation, "outrages upon personal dignity, in particular humiliating and degrading treatment", rape, sexual slavery, enforced prostitution, forced pregnancy, enforced sterilization and "any other form of sexual violence".

- **Crimes against humanity** are defined as any of a series of acts specified in Article 7(1) of the Rome Statute "when committed as part of a widespread or systematic attack directed against any civilian population, with knowledge of the attack".[27] The acts specified in Article 7(1) include torture, enslavement, rape, sexual slavery, enforced prostitution, forced pregnancy, enforced sterilization, "any other form of sexual violence of comparable gravity" and "other inhumane acts of a similar character intentionally causing great suffering, or serious injury to body or to mental or physical health".

- **Genocide** is defined in Article 6 as any of a series of specified acts "committed with intent to destroy, in whole or in part, a national, ethnical, racial or religious group, as such". As in the Genocide Convention, the list of specified acts includes "causing serious bodily or mental harm to members of the group".[28]

An act of torture or ill-treatment conforming to the list of prohibited acts in Article 8 of the Rome Statute could be tried by the International Criminal Court as a war crime if committed in an international or non-international armed conflict. An act of torture or ill-treatment conforming to the list of acts specified

---

* Extracts from the Rome Statute are reproduced in Appendix 9 of this manual.

in Article 7 could be tried as a crime against humanity if "committed as part of a widespread or systematic attack directed against any civilian population, with knowledge of the attack". Acts of torture or ill-treatment causing "serious bodily or mental harm" to members of a "national, ethnical, racial or religious group" could be tried as genocide if "committed with intent to destroy" the group "in whole or in part".

Criminal responsibility extends to a person who commits or attempts to commit a crime within the jurisdiction of the Court or who orders, solicits or induces, aids, abets or otherwise assists in or contributes to the commission or attempted commission of such a crime (Article 25). The Rome Statute also has provisions concerning the non-admissibility of the defence of superior orders (Article 33), the criminal responsibility of commanders and other superiors for acts committed by subordinates or people under their command (Article 28) and the lack of exemption of a person from criminal responsibility on grounds of official capacity even if the person has immunity under national law (Article 27). No crime within the jurisdiction of the Court is subject to any statute of limitations (Article 29). The death penalty is excluded from the penalties which the Court may impose (Article 77).

There were 81 states parties to the Rome Statute as of 1 October 2002.

3.2.6 General international law

The agreements between states formalized in international treaties are not the only sources of international law. Under Article 38 of the Statute of the International Court of Justice,[29] that Court, whose function is "to decide in accordance with international law such disputes as are submitted to it", shall apply, in addition to international treaties, "international custom, as evidence of a general practice accepted as law" (customary international law) and "the general principles of law recognized by civilized nations", with "judicial decisions and the teachings of the most highly qualified publicists of the various nations" as subsidiary sources. The term *general international law* refers to the law which may be derived from the non-treaty sources specified in Article 38: customary international law and "general principles of law", with judicial decisions and the writings of eminent international lawyers as additional sources of clarification. Rules of general international law apply to all states, whether or not they are parties to a treaty expressly containing the rule.

Customary international law (also known as "customary law"), the principal source of general international law, comprises international rules derived from state practice and regarded as law *(opinio juris)*.[30]

Certain rules of general international law are of such importance that they are accepted as "peremptory norms" from which states may not derogate – they may not withdraw from their obligation to respect them under any circumstances. A **peremptory norm of general international law,** also known as a norm of *jus cogens*, is defined in the Vienna Convention on the Law of Treaties (Article 53) as "a norm accepted and recognized by the international community of States as a whole as a norm from which no derogation is permitted and which can be modified only by a subsequent norm of general international law having the same character".

The UN Human Rights Committee has stated that the obligation not to subject people to torture or ill-treatment is a *rule of customary international law* and that the prohibition of torture is a *peremptory norm*.[31] These points can be considered to be firmly established: they have never been seriously challenged, and they are supported by important judicial decisions.[32]

The International Court of Justice has identified certain international obligations as *obligations erga omnes*, that is, obligations which a state has towards the international community as a whole and in the fulfilment of which every state has a legal interest. Such obligations derive from, among other things, "the principles and rules concerning the basic rights of the human person".[33] According to the UN Special Rapporteur on torture, the right not to be subjected to torture belongs to these basic rights "beyond any doubt"; the obligation to respect this right is an obligation *erga omnes*.[34]

The prohibition of torture and ill-treatment under customary international law, the prohibition of torture as a peremptory norm and the obligation *erga omnes* to prohibit torture have important consequences regarding the obligations of states.

- All states are bound to respect the prohibition of torture and ill-treatment as a matter of customary international law, whether or not they are parties to treaties which expressly contain the prohibition.

- All states are obliged to prevent torture and to punish acts of torture, whether or not they are parties to treaties which expressly require them to do so.[35]

- As stated by the Yugoslavia Tribunal, the prohibition of torture as a peremptory norm implies that any state is entitled to "investigate, prosecute and punish or extradite" an alleged torturer who is present in a territory under its jurisdiction.[36] Its prohibition as a peremptory norm also suggests that there should be no statute of limitations for the crime of torture.[37]

- The obligation *erga omnes* implies that the failure by a state to respect the prohibition of torture is not merely a matter of domestic law: it is a breach of the state's obligations towards all other states. Other states are entitled to become involved in the matter and to demand satisfaction. One way for states to enforce the obligation could be through the exercise of universal jurisdiction over alleged torturers found in territory under their jurisdiction.

3.2.7 Non-binding standards

There are also a great many non-binding international instruments which are relevant to the prohibition of torture. Some contain explicit prohibitions of torture and ill-treatment;[38] others set out standards, safeguards and other measures contributing to prevention.

Most of the instruments are in the form of resolutions adopted by the UN General Assembly or other UN bodies. Although not binding under international law, these "soft law" instruments should not be regarded as mere sets of recommendations which governments are free to follow or not as they choose. The adoption of these instruments has often involved a scrutiny as intense as that applied to the drafting of treaties. Many of them have been adopted without a vote, a sign of strong agreement by states that the standards set out in them should be implemented. These "soft law" standards may subsequently be adopted as legally binding obligations, as happened when various provisions of the Declaration against Torture were incorporated in the Convention against Torture. Some "soft law" standards may reflect actual or emergent rules of general international law. The standards may be used by national and international judicial bodies to elaborate the scope of established rules of law and to interpret and develop the rules set out in international human rights treaties.[39]

Two of the most important instruments are the UN **Body of Principles for the Protection of All Persons under Any Form of Detention or Imprisonment** (Body of Principles on Detention) and the UN **Standard Minimum Rules for the Treatment of Prisoners** (Standard Minimum Rules). These and other instruments are cited frequently in this manual.

At the regional level, several European intergovernmental organizations have adopted non-binding instruments relevant to the prohibition of torture, in addition to the treaties cited above. Thus, the **Council of Europe** has adopted a number of instruments,[40] while the **Organization for Security and Co-operation in Europe** (formerly the Conference on Security and Co-operation in Europe) has reaffirmed the prohibition of torture and the need to eliminate it.[41] The **European Union** (EU) has adopted guidelines for a policy to promote the elimination of torture outside the EU (see section 8.2).

3.3 What is prohibited?

The prohibition of torture and ill-treatment appears in Article 5 of the Universal Declaration of Human Rights as follows:

> **"No one shall be subjected to torture or to cruel, inhuman or degrading treatment or punishment."**

"Torture" and "cruel, inhuman or degrading treatment or punishment" should not be seen as separate categories in this formulation. It should, rather, be understood that certain acts of cruel, inhuman or degrading treatment or punishment can constitute torture. This relationship has been underlined by the use of the word "other" in the full title of the Convention against Torture ("Convention against Torture and Other Cruel, Inhuman or Degrading Treatment or Punishment") and elsewhere.[42]

Since its adoption in 1948, the Universal Declaration of Human Rights has served as an inspiration and a model for other human rights instruments. The prohibition of torture and ill-treatment and its expression with the aid of the terms "cruel", "inhuman", "degrading", "treatment" and "punishment" have been incorporated in international and regional instruments and in many national constitutions. All these elements of the formula in the Universal Declaration of

Human Rights have been carried over into the ICCPR and the regional human rights treaties with the exception of the European Convention on Human Rights, where the word "cruel" is omitted – an omission of little significance.[43]

Article 7 of the ICCPR states:

> "No one shall be subjected to torture or to cruel, inhuman or degrading treatment or punishment. In particular, no one shall be subjected without his free consent to medical or scientific experimentation."

The formulations in Article 5 of the Universal Declaration of Human Rights and Article 7 of the ICCPR can be seen as encompassing a class of prohibited behaviour. Often it is not necessary to distinguish among the different elements of the formulation, since the entire class of behaviour – torture and other ill-treatment – is prohibited. All the obligations of states parties with regard to Article 7 of the ICCPR apply to all of the behaviour described in Article 7, and all of these obligations are absolute, non-derogable and unqualified. (Under the Convention against Torture and the Inter-American Convention to Prevent and Punish Torture, however, certain obligations apply only to torture, as noted in section 3.2.2.)

At face value, the formulation in the first sentence of Article 7 of the ICCPR would appear to comprise as many as seven modes of prohibited behaviour: torture, cruel treatment or punishment, inhuman treatment or punishment, degrading treatment or punishment. Indeed some of these will sometimes need to be distinguished from others, but they cannot and should not be thought of as seven distinct subclasses of the prohibition. Some may overlap with others: torture is a form of ill-treatment; treatment which is "cruel" may also be "degrading"; a "punishment" may also be thought of as a form of "treatment". Assessments of allegations of prohibited behaviour will usually have to be made on a case-by-case basis, and the details of cases can vary enormously. The obligation to prevent torture and ill-treatment applies to everything described in Article 7. Moreover, an attempt to establish rigid definitions of each of the elements of Article 7 could preclude later developments which might enlarge or enrich the understanding of what it includes, in line with evolving notions of human rights.

In applying the prohibition of torture and ill-treatment to cases brought before it under the first Optional Protocol to the ICCPR, the Human Rights Committee has sometimes stated that the abuses inflicted on the complainant amounted to "torture" or to other elements of the formulation such as "degrading" treatment; in other cases it has not referred to particular elements of the formulation but has simply stated that there has been a violation of Article 7, engaging responsibility on the part of the state.[44] In its General Comment 20 on Article 7 of the ICCPR (para. 4), the Human Rights Committee has stated: "The Covenant does not contain any definition of the concepts covered by article 7, nor does the Committee consider it necessary to draw up a list of prohibited acts or to establish sharp distinctions between the different kinds of punishment or treatment; the distinctions depend on the nature, purpose and severity of the treatment applied." The European Commission and Court of Human Rights, however, have gone further in ascribing specific meanings to the terms "torture" and "inhuman" or "degrading" treatment or punishment (see below).

Like the ICCPR, most other international and regional instruments which prohibit torture and ill-treatment do not define these abuses. The seeming lack of precision in the absence of a definition has not impeded the work done by inter-governmental bodies and human rights defenders under the standards set out in these instruments; on the contrary, the very lack of a definition may have helped the work to develop.[45]

There are, however, several international definitions of "torture".

3.3.1 Defining torture

The Convention against Torture

Article 1 of the Convention against Torture states:

> "1. For the purposes of this Convention, the term 'torture' means any act by which severe pain or suffering, whether physical or mental, is intentionally inflicted on a person for such purposes as obtaining from him or a third person information or a confession, punishing him for an act he or a third person has committed or is suspected of having committed, or intimidating or coercing him or a third person, or for any reason based on discrimination of any kind, when such pain or suffering is inflicted by or at the instigation of or with the consent or acquiescence of a public official or other person acting in an official capacity. It does not include pain or suffering arising only from, inherent in or incidental to lawful sanctions.

> "2. This article is without prejudice to any international instrument or national legislation which does or may contain provisions of wider application."

Article 4 requires each state party to the Convention to ensure that "all acts of torture are offences under its criminal law". Article 8 requires states parties to deem offences of torture to be extraditable offences between them, while Articles 5-7 deal with the application of the criminal justice system and the exercise of universal jurisdiction over torture. In relation to these articles, Article 1 serves to define the elements of the crime of torture for the purpose of bringing torturers to justice in accordance with the provisions of the Convention.

The definition in Article 1 has assumed ever greater importance with the increasing number of states parties to the Convention, the increasing number of states which incorporate the elements of the definition in national laws prohibiting torture (see section 7.2), the increasing tendency of the regional human rights courts and the Yugoslavia and Rwanda Tribunals to draw from it in making findings of torture, and authoritative references to key elements of the definition as matters of customary international law.[46]

The definition in Article 1 has five elements:

- Torture involves the infliction of *"pain or suffering, whether physical or mental"*. The inclusion of the notion of "mental" suffering is important: torture is not restricted to the infliction of physical pain.

- The pain or suffering is "*severe*". If it is not, the act does not amount to torture under the Convention, although it may constitute ill-treatment.*

- It is inflicted *intentionally*. Pain or suffering inflicted accidentally cannot constitute torture.

- It is inflicted for a *purpose* such as those listed in Article 1, or "for any reason based on discrimination of any kind".

- It is inflicted "by or at the instigation of or with the consent or acquiescence of a *public official* or other person acting in an official capacity".[47] [Emphases added]

The second sentence of Article 1 states that the definition does not include "pain or suffering arising only from, inherent in or incidental to lawful sanctions". The Special Rapporteur on torture has stated that this exclusion (commonly known as the "lawful sanctions" exclusion) "must necessarily refer to those sanctions that constitute practices widely accepted as legitimate by the international community, such as deprivation of liberty through imprisonment, which is common to almost all penal systems". With reference to judicial corporal punishments (see section 6.4), he has pointed out that "cruel, inhuman or degrading punishments are... by definition unlawful; so they can hardly qualify as 'lawful sanctions' within the meaning of Article 1 of the Convention against Torture".[48]

The Inter-American Convention to Prevent and Punish Torture

Article 2 of the Inter-American Convention to Prevent and Punish Torture states:

"For the purposes of this Convention, torture shall be understood to be any act intentionally performed whereby physical or mental pain or suffering is inflicted on a person for purposes of criminal investigation, as a means of intimidation, as personal punishment, as a preventive measure, as a penalty, or for any other purpose. Torture shall also be understood to be the use of methods upon a person intended to obliterate the personality of the victim or to diminish his physical or mental capacities, even if they do not cause physical pain or mental anguish.

"The concept of torture shall not include physical or mental pain or suffering that is inherent in or solely the consequence of lawful measures, provided that they do not include the performance of the acts or use of the methods referred to in this article."

Unlike the definition in Article 1 of the UN Convention against Torture, this definition does not mention the perpetrator. However, Article 3 states:

"The following shall be held guilty of the crime of torture:

"a. A public servant or employee who acting in that capacity orders, instigates or induces the use of torture, or who directly commits it or who, being able to prevent it, fails to do so.

---

* See below on the approach taken by the European Court of Human Rights to the notion of severity.

"b. A person who at the instigation of a public servant or employee mentioned in subparagraph (a) orders, instigates or induces the use of torture, directly commits it or is an accomplice thereto."

As with the UN Convention against Torture, the definition in the Inter-American Convention serves mainly to establish the elements of the crime of torture for the purpose of addressing criminal acts, where necessary through the exercise of extradition or universal jurisdiction. It differs from the definition in the UN Convention against Torture in the specific purposes cited, in the inclusion of "any other purpose" and in the reference to torture "intended to obliterate the personality of the victim or to diminish his physical or mental capacities".

As of 1 October 2002, 14 states parties to the UN Convention against Torture were also parties to the Inter-American Convention and had thus accepted the definitions of torture in both instruments.

Judgments of the European Court of Human Rights

The European Convention on Human Rights, as amended by its Protocol No. 11, provides a possibility for individuals to submit formal complaints that their rights under that Convention have been violated.[49] Until November 1998, complaints were submitted to the European Commission of Human Rights; the Commission could not issue binding judgments, but its "opinions" could be referred to the European Court of Human Rights, which makes rulings that are binding on states parties.[50] Since November 1998, complaints have gone directly to the Court.[51] The opinions of the Commission and the rulings of the Court have considerably developed the meaning and application of the prohibition of torture and inhuman or degrading treatment or punishment under Article 3 of the European Convention on Human Rights.

The first important set of findings, in the *Greek Case*, concerned political prisoners held in Greece after the military coup of April 1967.[52] After examining the findings of its Sub-Commission which had travelled to Greece to investigate allegations of torture and ill-treatment, and materials including statements by witnesses and alleged victims, medical reports, reports by members of foreign parliaments, journalists and private investigators and documents furnished by the Greek government,[53] the European Commission of Human Rights found that there had been "a practice of torture and ill-treatment" by the Athens Security Police, consisting most often of the application of *falanga* (beatings on the soles of the feet) or other severe beatings for the purpose of extracting confessions and other information.[54] In its report on the *Greek Case*, the Commission examined the terms **torture** and **inhuman** or **degrading** treatment or punishment* and stated: "It is plain that there may be treatment to which all these descriptions apply, for all torture must be inhuman and degrading treatment, and inhuman treatment also degrading."[55]

In subsequent judgments, the European Court of Human Rights has continued to attach specific meanings to the terms "torture", "inhuman" and "degrading" treatment under the European Convention on Human Rights and has developed the notion of thresholds of severity** and other criteria for passing from one category to another, or from acts which are not prohibited as torture or ill-treatment to those which are.

---

* Article 3 of the European Convention on Human Rights states: "No one shall be subjected to torture or to inhuman or degrading treatment or punishment."
** See section 1.3 of this manual for a discussion of thresholds of severity in relation to children.

- In the case of *Ireland v. UK*, the Court introduced the notion that "torture" involves the infliction of "very serious and cruel suffering".[56] In a 1977 ruling, which has been criticized by one authority as involving "unsatisfactory reasoning from an authoritative judicial body",[57] the Court held that five techniques of sensory deprivation, applied together in the interrogation of prisoners held under emergency legislation in Northern Ireland, amounted to inhuman and degrading treatment but "did not occasion suffering of the particular intensity and cruelty implied by the word torture as so understood".[58] But in the case of *Selmouni v. France*, in which the victim was subjected to humiliation, threats, sexual abuse and repeated beatings over several days of questioning in police custody, the Court held in 1999 that the violence against the victim "caused 'severe' pain and suffering" under the terms of the UN Convention against Torture and constituted torture.[59] Citing its established doctrine that the European Convention is a "living instrument which must be interpreted in the light of present-day conditions",[60] the Court stated that "certain acts which were classified in the past as 'inhuman and degrading treatment' as opposed to 'torture' could be classified differently in future... the increasingly high standard being required in the area of the protection of human rights and fundamental liberties correspondingly and inevitably requires greater firmness in assessing breaches of the fundamental values of democratic societies".[61]

- In the case of *Tyrer v. UK*, which involved the infliction of judicial corporal punishment on a 15-year-old schoolboy, the Court found in 1978 that "the applicant was subjected to a punishment in which the element of humiliation attained the level inherent in the notion of 'degrading punishment'" under Article 3 of the Convention.[62] The Court held that "in order for a punishment to be 'degrading' and in breach of Article 3, the humiliation or debasement involved must attain a particular level and must in any event be other than that usual element of humiliation" in judicial punishments.[63]

The current approach of the European Court of Human Rights to the definition of torture and ill-treatment under Article 3 of the European Convention on Human Rights may be summarized as follows:*

- "The Court recalls that ill-treatment must attain a **minimum level of severity** if it is to fall within the scope of Article 3. The assessment of this minimum is relative: it *depends on all the circumstances of the case*, such as the duration of the treatment, its physical and/or mental effects and, in some cases, the sex, age and state of health of the victim".[64]

- **Torture** involves "*deliberate inhuman treatment causing very serious and cruel suffering*".[65] Under the UN Convention against Torture, as the Court has noted, torture involves the infliction of "severe" physical or mental pain or suffering. "The Court considers that this 'severity' is, like the 'minimum severity' required for the application of Article 3 of the European Convention, in the nature of things, relative; it depends on all the circumstances of the case, such as the duration of the treatment, its

---

* Certain words or phrases as quoted here have been placed in boldface type or italics to emphasize key elements in the Court's definitions.

physical or mental effects and, in some cases, the sex, age and state of health of the victim, etc."[66] The Court has also stated that "[i]n addition to the severity of the treatment, there is a *purposive* element" as recognized in the UN Convention against Torture.[67]

- "The Court has considered treatment to be '**inhuman**' because, *inter alia*, it was *premeditated, was applied for hours at a stretch* and caused either *actual bodily injury or intense physical or mental suffering*. It has deemed treatment to be '**degrading**' because it was such as to arouse in the victims feelings of *fear, anguish and inferiority* capable of *humiliating and debasing* them. On the other hand, the Court has consistently stressed that the suffering and humiliation involved must in any event go *beyond that inevitable element of suffering or humiliation* connected with a given form of legitimate treatment or punishment".[68]

- "In considering whether a punishment or treatment is '**degrading**' within the meaning of Article 3, the Court will also have regard to whether its *object* is to humiliate and debase the person concerned and whether, as far as the consequences are concerned, it adversely affected his or her personality in a manner incompatible with Article 3".[69] However, the absence of a positive intention of humiliating or debasing the victim "cannot conclusively rule out a finding of violation of Article 3" in relation to conditions of detention.[70] The "*public nature* of the punishment or treatment may be a relevant factor", but "the absence of publicity will not necessarily prevent a given treatment from falling into that category: it may well suffice that the victim is humiliated in his or her own eyes, even if not in the eyes of others".[71]

- Severity of suffering is a significant consideration, but "there are circumstances where proof of the **actual effect on the person** may not be a major factor".[72]

While the judgments of the European Court of Human Rights have developed the notion of torture and ill-treatment as prohibited under human rights law, the approach taken and the criteria developed in them will not necessarily be the most appropriate ones for the work of other bodies where these are dealing with different legal aspects of the general prohibition of torture, such as the prevention of torture or the application of criminal law. Certain criteria will be needed if torture is to be defined as a crime, as in the Convention against Torture, but it is not necessary to ascribe specific meanings to the various elements of the phrase "torture or cruel, inhuman or degrading treatment or punishment" or to establish overlapping categories among the elements in order to make findings of violations of the right not to be subjected to torture or ill-treatment for the purpose of establishing state responsibility or individual civil responsibility.[73]

Torture as a war crime

Torture is a war crime under international humanitarian law and is designated as a war crime in the Rome Statute of the International Criminal Court (see section 3.2.5 above).

The Preparatory Commission for the International Criminal Court has drawn up draft Elements of Crimes which under Article 9 of the Rome Statute are to assist the Court in the interpretation and application of the articles of that Statute defining war crimes, crimes against humanity and genocide.[74] The draft Elements of Crimes will be submitted for adoption to the first session of the Assembly of States Parties to the Rome Statute in September 2002.

Under the draft Elements of Crimes, the war crime of torture under the Rome Statute must include the following elements:

"1. The perpetrator inflicted severe physical or mental pain or suffering upon one or more persons.

"2. The perpetrator inflicted the pain or suffering for such purposes as: obtaining information or a confession, punishment, intimidation or coercion or for any reason based on discrimination of any kind."

Other required elements of the crime include the protected status of the victim,[75] the connection of the act of torture to an international or non-international armed conflict and the perpetrator's knowledge of these factors.[76]

The draft Elements of Crimes also provides definitions of a number of other acts of ill-treatment as war crimes.[77]

Torture as a crime against humanity

For the purpose of the definition of *crimes against humanity* under the Rome Statute, Article 7(2)(e) of the Statute states:

"'Torture' means the intentional infliction of severe pain or suffering, whether physical or mental, upon a person in the custody or under the control of the accused; except that torture shall not include pain or suffering arising only from, inherent in or incidental to, lawful sanctions."

In contrast to the definition in the Convention against Torture, this definition of torture as a crime against humanity does not include a specific purposive element: as noted in the draft Elements of Crimes for the International Criminal Court, "[i]t is understood that no specific purpose need be proved for this crime". However, under the Rome Statute torture as a crime against humanity must be committed "as part of a widespread or systematic attack directed against any civilian population, with knowledge of the attack", and the draft Elements of Crimes stipulates that the perpetrator "knew that the conduct was part of or intended the conduct to be part of" such an attack.

3.3.2 Rape as torture

Amnesty International believes that the rape of a prisoner by a prison, security or military official always constitutes torture. Other sexual abuse of prisoners by such officials always constitutes torture or ill-treatment.[78] Inter-prisoner sexual violence may also constitute torture or ill-treatment if the authorities have failed to ensure compliance with rules such as those requiring the separation of male and female prisoners or otherwise failed to take appropriate action (see sections 1.3, 5.7.1).

Under the draft Elements of Crimes for the International Criminal Court, the war crime of rape under the Rome Statute and the crime of rape as a crime against humanity under the same Statute include the following elements:[79]

"1. The perpetrator invaded the body of a person by conduct resulting in penetration, however slight, of any part of the body of the victim or of the perpetrator with a sexual organ, or of the anal or genital opening of the victim with any object or any other part of the body.[80]

"2. The invasion was committed by force, or by threat of force or coercion, such as that caused by fear of violence, duress, detention, psychological oppression or abuse of power, against such person or another person, or by taking advantage of a coercive environment, or the invasion was committed against a person incapable of giving genuine consent."[81]

The draft Elements of Crimes also provide definitions of a number of other sex-related acts as war crimes or crimes against humanity.[82]

As the Special Rapporteur on torture has stated, rape is "an especially traumatic form of torture" and it "may have insidious correlative consequences". Women may be reluctant to seek reparation by reporting a rape because of the severe social repercussions which may ensue. There may be "dire consequences for the private and public life of the woman".[83] The Special Rapporteur on torture has stated that "[s]ince it was clear that rape or other forms of sexual assault against women in detention were a particularly ignominious violation of the inherent dignity and the right to physical integrity of the human being, they accordingly constituted an act of torture".[84]

In the case of *Mejía v. Peru*, the Inter-American Commission on Human Rights found that the rape of the victim by a member of the security forces constituted torture in violation of Article 5 of the American Convention on Human Rights.[85] In the case of *Aydın v. Turkey*, the European Court of Human Rights ruled that the rape and other physical and mental violence inflicted on a 17-year-old girl detained by the Turkish security forces amounted to torture.[86]

As noted in section 7.6 below, the Yugoslavia Tribunal has convicted several defendants of torture as a war crime for the rape of women who were under inter-rogation.[87] The Yugoslavia and Rwanda Tribunals have convicted defendants of rape as a war crime,[88] as a crime against humanity and as genocide.[89]

As noted by the Yugoslavia Tribunal, there is "a momentum towards addressing, through legal process, the use of rape in the course of detention and interrogation as a means of torture and, therefore, as a violation of interna-tional law";[90] but "[d]epending upon the circumstances, under international criminal law rape may acquire the status of a crime distinct from torture".[91] Thus, both torture and rape are proscribed under international humanitarian law, and both are explicitly proscribed as crimes against humanity under the Statutes of the Yugoslavia and Rwanda Tribunals and as war crimes and crimes against humanity under the Rome Statute of the International Criminal Court (see sections 3.2.4, 3.2.5).

Amnesty International further considers that rape of women by private individuals constitutes torture for which the state may be held responsible when the state has failed to act with due diligence to prevent, punish or redress the crime. For example, laws governing rape are often inadequate and many countries do not recognize and prohibit marital rape. In some countries a woman who alleges that she has been raped may herself be prosecuted for illicit sexual relations. Frequently, the rules of evidence make it very difficult for a woman to raise her complaint appropriately and fairly in court as the rules specify that the testimony of a woman who alleges she has been raped is inherently unreliable. Restrictions on women's movement and legal rights may further hamper access to justice. In many parts of the world, the police routinely fail to investigate abuses reported by women and the courts appear biased against women victims.

Amnesty International holds states responsible when they fail to take measures to protect and ensure enjoyment of the fundamental human rights of women. States have a duty under international law to take positive measures to prohibit and prevent rape and sexual assault and to respond adequately to these crimes, regardless of where they take place and whether the perpetrator is an agent of the state, a violent husband or a total stranger.

Rape and sexual abuse are inflicted on men as well as women,[92] on children as well as adults.[93] Appropriate measures of protection are needed for both sexes and all ages.

3.4 The expanding understanding of the scope of torture

The general understanding of the scope of torture and ill-treatment has expanded greatly since the adoption of the Universal Declaration of Human Rights in 1948. This section gives examples of forms of abuse that have been deemed to constitute torture or ill-treatment by international human rights bodies and mechanisms, regional human rights courts and commissions, and the Yugoslavia and Rwanda Tribunals, in addition to the "classic" use of torture as a method of interrogation.

- **Intimidation:** As noted in section 3.3.1, the notion of mental suffering is a component of the definition of torture under Article 1 of the Convention against Torture and other international definitions, and intimidation is one of the possible purposes of torture under that Convention.[94] The Special Rapporteur on torture has pointed out that "the fear of physical torture may itself constitute mental torture".[95] He has noted that "the absence of marks on the body that would be consistent with allegation[s] of torture should not necessarily be treated by prosecutors and judges as proof that such allegations are false" and has called for "the judiciary to be made more aware of other forms of torture, such as intimidation and other threats".[96] The UN General Assembly also has referred to intimidation as a means of torture.[97] The UN Commission on Human Rights has stated that "intimidation and coercion, as described in article 1 of the Convention [against Torture], including serious and credible threats, as well as death threats, to the physical integrity of the victim or of a third person, can amount to cruel, inhuman or degrading treatment or to torture".[98]

- **Sensory deprivation:** As noted in section 3.3.1, the European Court of Human Rights in the case of *Ireland v. UK* held that five techniques of sensory deprivation, applied together in the interrogation of prisoners held under emergency legislation in Northern Ireland, amounted to inhuman and degrading treatment; earlier, the European Commission of Human Rights had found that they amounted to torture.[99] More recently, the Committee against Torture found that the regime of sensory deprivation and "almost total prohibition of communication" under which prisoners at a maximum security detention centre in Peru were held caused "persistent and unjustified suffering which amounts to torture".[100]

- **Conditions of detention:** In the *Greek Case* (see section 3.3.1), citing "gross overcrowding" and other factors, the European Commission of Human Rights found conditions in several places of detention to amount to inhuman or degrading treatment in violation of the European Convention on Human Rights.[101] The European Court of Human Rights also has found conditions of detention to amount to inhuman or degrading treatment in several recent cases.[102] The Committee against Torture has found certain conditions of detention to amount to "inhuman and degrading treatment" and some conditions to amount to torture.[103] The Human Rights Committee has found violations of Article 7 or Article 10 of the ICCPR in a number of cases involving conditions of detention.[104] The Special Rapporteur on torture has referred to conditions of detention as cruel, inhuman or degrading[105] and – in one instance – as "torturous".[106] The CPT has found inhuman or degrading conditions of detention in a number of European countries.[107] The Yugoslavia Tribunal has convicted defendants of "wilfully causing great suffering or serious injury to body or health" for subjecting inmates of a prison camp to inhumane conditions of detention (see section 7.6).[108]

  Specific aspects of the treatment of prisoners, such as overcrowding, lack of access to food and water, lack of medical attention, lack of provision of basic hygiene needs for women, and prolonged solitary confinement have also been the subject of findings of ill-treatment or have been characterized as possibly constituting ill-treatment by international human rights bodies and mechanisms and regional human rights courts (see sections 5.3.1, 5.4.1, 5.4.2, 5.5.5).

- **"Disappearances":**[109] As stated in Article 1 of the UN Declaration on the Protection of All Persons from Enforced Disappearance (Declaration on Enforced Disappearance),

  "Any act of enforced disappearance places the persons subjected thereto outside the protection of the law and inflicts severe suffering on them and their families. It constitutes a violation of the rules of international law guaranteeing, *inter alia,* the right to recognition as a person before the law, the right to liberty and security of the person and the right not to be subjected to torture and other cruel, inhuman or degrading treatment or punishment. It also violates or constitutes a grave threat to the right to life."

In the case of *Celis Laureano v. Peru*, concerning a 17-year-old girl who had "disappeared" after being abducted by the security forces, the Human Rights Committee concluded that "the abduction and disappearance of the victim and prevention of contact with her family and with the outside world constitute cruel and inhuman treatment", in violation of Article 7 read together with Article 2(1) of the ICCPR.[110] Similarly, in the case of *Velásquez Rodríguez v. Honduras*, concerning a student who "disappeared" after being abducted by men connected with the armed forces, the Inter-American Court of Human Rights held that "the mere subjection of an individual to prolonged isolation and deprivation of communication is in itself cruel and inhuman treatment" in violation of Article 5 of the American Convention on Human Rights.[111] The Special Rapporteur on torture has stated that "prolonged incommunicado detention in a secret place may amount to torture as described in article 1 of the Convention against Torture".[112]

The suffering of relatives of the "disappeared" has also been held to amount to torture or ill-treatment. In the case of *Quinteros v. Uruguay*, the Human Rights Committee, noting "the anguish and stress caused to the mother by the disappearance of her daughter and by the continuing uncertainty concerning her fate and whereabouts", found that the mother of a woman who "disappeared" after being arrested by the security services was herself a victim of a violation of Article 7 of the ICCPR.[113] In the case of *Kurt v. Turkey*, the European Court of Human Rights held that a woman who had witnessed her son's detention and was thereafter denied any official information on his fate was "herself the victim of the authorities' complacency in the face of her anguish and distress" and had suffered a violation of Article 3 of the European Convention on Human Rights.[114] The Inter-American Court of Human Rights has made a similar ruling in the case of *Blake v. Guatemala*.[115]

- **Forcible house destruction:** In the case of *Selçuk and Asker v. Turkey*, where the security forces had deliberately burned the homes and most of the property of two villagers, depriving them of their livelihoods and forcing them to leave their village, the European Court of Human Rights held that the two victims "must have been caused suffering of sufficient severity for the acts of the security forces to be categorised as inhuman treatment within the meaning of Article 3 [of the European Convention on Human Rights]".[116] The Committee against Torture has stated that Israeli policies on house demolition and "closures" "may, in certain instances, amount to cruel, inhuman or degrading treatment or punishment".[117]

- **Non-consensual medical or scientific experiments:** Article 7 of the ICCPR states that "no one shall be subjected without his free consent to medical or scientific experimentation". The inclusion of a specific reference to this form of torture or ill-treatment was a reaction to atrocities perpetrated by Germany under Nazi rule, where prisoners had been subjected to infection, surgical operations, anatomical research and other experiments, usually ending in death.[118] In keeping with this notion, "biological experiments" are specified as a form of torture or inhuman treatment in the four Geneva Conventions of 1949, punishable as grave breaches of those Conventions, and unwarranted medical or scientific experiments are also prohibited.[119]

- **Corporal punishment:** The Human Rights Committee has stated that the prohibition of torture and ill-treatment under Article 7 of the ICCPR "must extend to corporal punishment, including excessive chastisement ordered as punishment for a crime or as an educative or disciplinary measure" and, in this regard, that "article 7 protects, in particular, children, pupils and patients in teaching and medical institutions".[120] The European Court of Human Rights has found specific instances of judicial corporal punishment and corporal punishment in the home to constitute degrading punishment contrary to Article 3 of the European Convention on Human Rights.[121] (For additional references, see section 6.4.)

- **Excessive use of force in law enforcement:** The European Court of Human Rights has held that "in respect of a person deprived of his liberty, any recourse to physical force which has not been made strictly necessary by his own conduct diminishes human dignity and is in principle an infringement of the right set forth in Article 3 of the [European] Convention [on Human Rights]".[122] (See section 6.3.)

- **Use of the death penalty:** In the case of *Soering v. UK*, the European Court of Human Rights held that "The manner in which it [a death sentence] is imposed or executed, the personal circumstances of the condemned person and a disproportionality to the gravity of the crime committed, as well as the conditions of detention awaiting execution, are examples of factors capable of bringing the treatment or punishment received by the condemned person within the proscription under Article 3 [of the European Convention on Human Rights]".[123] The Committee against Torture, in examining the reports of states parties to the Convention against Torture, has referred to the continuing use of the death penalty as a subject of concern[124] and has stated that the uncertainty of many people under sentence of death amounts to "cruel and inhuman treatment in breach of article 16 of the Convention" and that the death penalty should therefore be abolished as soon as possible.[125] (As stated in section 1.2, Amnesty International regards the death penalty as the ultimate cruel, inhuman and degrading punishment.)

- **Racial discrimination:** In the case of *East African Asians v. UK*, the European Commission of Human Rights held in 1973 that "discrimination based on race could, in certain circumstances, of itself amount to degrading treatment within the meaning of Article 3 of the [European] Convention [on Human Rights]".[126] In a more recent case, the European Court of Human Rights found in view of their living conditions that

Greek Cypriots living in the Turkish Cypriot-administered area of northern Cyprus had been subjected to "discrimination amounting to degrading treatment".[127]

- **Abuses in armed conflict:** The Yugoslavia Tribunal has convicted a defendant of "inhuman treatment" and "cruel treatment" for his responsibility in using civilians as "human shields" and forcing civilians to dig trenches under dangerous conditions at the battlefront.[128]

- **Gender-specific forms of torture or ill-treatment:** The Special Rapporteur on torture has referred to acts of rape, sexual abuse and harassment, virginity testing, forced abortion and forced miscarriage as "gender-specific forms of torture".[129] The UN Special Rapporteur on violence against women, its causes and consequences (Special Rapporteur on violence against women) has referred to cultural practices such as female genital mutilation[130,] honour killings, bride-burning and "any other form of cultural practice that brutalizes the female body" as practices which "involve 'severe pain and suffering' and may be considered 'torture like' in their manifestation".[131] The Human Rights Committee has implied that forced abortion, forced sterilization, female genital mutilation, domestic violence against women and a lack of access to safe abortion for women who have become pregnant as a result of rape can give rise to violations of the right not to be subjected to torture or ill-treatment under Article 7 of the ICCPR.[132] In addition to convictions for rape, male defendants who raped women have been convicted of torture as a war crime and a crime against humanity by the Yugoslavia Tribunal, while a defendant who committed acts of sexual violence against women was convicted by the Rwanda Tribunal of "inhumane acts" as crimes against humanity and of "causing serious bodily or mental harm to members of the group" as acts of genocide (see sections 3.3.2, 7.6).

3.5 When is torture prohibited?

Torture and ill-treatment are prohibited at all times, in all circumstances. Attempts to justify the use of torture in certain situations cannot be accepted.

The prohibition of torture and ill-treatment in Article 7 of the ICCPR is formulated in absolute terms, envisaging no exception to the rule. Furthermore, under the ICCPR freedom from torture and ill-treatment is a **non-derogable right** – a right entailing obligations from which no derogation is permitted. Article 4(1) of the ICCPR permits states parties to derogate from some of their obligations "[i]n time of public emergency which threatens the life of the nation and the existence of which is officially proclaimed", but under Article 4(2) no derogation is permitted from Article 7. Other treaties which permit derogation from some of their provisions in time of public emergency likewise make no such allowance for the prohibition of torture and ill-treatment.[133]

Under Article 2(2) of the Convention against Torture, "No exceptional circumstances whatsoever, whether a state of war or a threat of war, internal political instability or any other public emergency, may be invoked as a justification of torture." Article 3 of the Declaration against Torture contains the same principle with regard to torture and ill-treatment, as does Article 5 of the UN Code of Conduct for Law Enforcement Officials. The Inter-American Convention to Prevent and Punish Torture (Article 5) precludes invoking exceptional circumstances as a justification for torture. Under the Rome Statute, there are also no exceptions to the prohibition of torture as a war crime or a crime against humanity. The UN Commission on Human Rights has condemned "all forms of torture and other cruel, inhuman or degrading treatment or punishment, which are and shall remain prohibited at any time and in any place whatsoever and can thus never be justified".[134]

In a case in which the government tried to justify the police officers' physical assault of a prisoner by citing "the fact that he had been suspected of participating in a terrorist attack which had resulted in the death of one man and grave injuries to another", the European Court of Human Rights stated: "The requirements of the investigation and the undeniable difficulties inherent in the fight against crime, particularly with regard to terrorism, cannot result in limits being placed on the protection to be afforded in respect of the physical integrity of individuals." The Court found that the prisoner had been subjected to inhuman and degrading treatment in violation of the European Convention on Human Rights.[135]

The universal character of the prohibition of torture and ill-treatment is reinforced by the prohibition of torture in the laws of war and reflected by the status of the prohibition as a rule of customary international law.

The argument is sometimes advanced that torture should be used as a method of interrogation in certain circumstances in the interest of some "greater good".[136] Such arguments must be rejected. Under international law, there are no circumstances in which torture can legally be inflicted.

Further reading

On the arguments sometimes advanced in favour of torture, see Rodley, 1999, *The Treatment of Prisoners under International Law*, pp. 78-84, "Justifiability?"; and Amnesty International, 1975, *Report on Torture* (2nd edition), pp. 23-27; 1984, *Torture in the Eighties*, pp. 6-8, "The moral argument"; 1996, *Report of the Stockholm Conference on Torture*, pp. 33-34, "General moral rejection" and "Effectiveness".

3.6 Relation to other human rights norms

The Human Rights Committee has stated that the aim of the prohibition of torture and ill-treatment under Article 7 of the ICCPR "is to protect both the dignity and the physical and mental integrity of the individual".[137] The Human Rights Committee has thus linked the prohibition of torture and ill-treatment to two important human rights norms: the principle of *human dignity* and the right to *physical and mental integrity.*

- The principle of **human dignity** is cited in the preamble of the Charter of the United Nations and the preamble of the Universal Declaration of Human Rights. Article 1 of the Universal Declaration of Human Rights states that all human beings are born "equal in dignity and rights". The preambles of the ICCPR and the International Covenant on Economic, Social and Cultural Rights state, in identical language, that "recognition of the inherent dignity and of the equal and inalienable rights of all members of the human family is the foundation of freedom, justice and peace in the world" and that "these rights derive from the inherent dignity of the human person". A similar statement appears in the preamble of the Convention against Torture.[138]

  The UN General Assembly has stated: "Any act of torture or other cruel, inhuman or degrading treatment or punishment is an offence to human dignity and shall be condemned as a denial of the purposes of the Charter of the United Nations and as a violation of the human rights and fundamental freedoms proclaimed in the Universal Declaration of Human Rights."[139]

  In the African Charter on Human and Peoples' Rights, the prohibition of torture and ill-treatment is contained in Article 5. Article 5 begins: "Every individual shall have the right to the respect of the dignity inherent in a human being..."

  Under Article 10 of the ICCPR, all persons deprived of their liberty must be treated "with humanity and with respect for the inherent dignity of the human person" (see section 5.1).

- The right to **physical, mental and moral integrity** is explicitly recognized in the American Convention on Human Rights under Article 5, "Right to Humane Treatment". Article 5, in paragraphs 1 and 2, states:

  "1. Every person has the right to have his physical, mental, and moral integrity respected.

  2. No one shall be subjected to torture or to cruel, inhuman, or degrading punishment or treatment. All persons deprived of their liberty shall be treated with respect for the inherent dignity of the human person."[140]

Additional Protocol I to the Geneva Conventions of 1949 (Article 11) qualifies certain acts which seriously endanger the "physical or mental health or integrity" of persons in the hands of a foreign power in an international armed conflict as grave breaches of the Protocol, punishable as war crimes.

In finding that complainants have been subjected to torture or cruel, inhuman or degrading treatment or punishment, the regional human rights courts and commissions have stated on several occasions that the victims' dignity[141] and/or physical or mental integrity was violated.[142]

The Inter-American Commission on Human Rights has also treated torture as a violation of the right to **security of person** under Article 1 of the American Declaration on the Rights and Duties of Man.[143]

Other human rights also may be violated in cases of torture and ill-treatment:

- The **right to freedom from discrimination**, if torture or ill-treatment is inflicted in a discriminatory way or for a discriminatory purpose, for example in gender-based torture.[144]

- The **right to personal liberty**, if the victim has been arbitrarily detained.

- The **right to a fair trial**, if torture or ill-treatment is used to extract information or a confession which is used in the course of a judicial procedure.

- The **right to life**, if torture or ill-treatment leads to the victim's death.

Torture is also frequent in cases of "disappearance". Torture, "disappearances" and extrajudicial executions often go hand in hand.

3.7 Obligations of the state: prevention, investigation, punishment, reparation

International law establishes the right of everyone not to be subjected to torture or cruel, inhuman or degrading treatment or punishment. What are the consequent obligations of states?

Article 2 of the ICCPR sets out the basic obligations of states concerning the human rights recognized therein, including the right not to be subjected to torture or ill-treatment. Under Article 2, each state party undertakes "to respect and to ensure to all individuals within its territory and subject to its jurisdiction the rights recognized in the present Covenant". There are similar provisions in the African Charter on Human and Peoples' Rights (Article 1), the American Convention on Human Rights (Article 1), the European Convention on Human Rights (Article 1) and the Arab Charter on Human Rights (Article 2).

In its judgment in the case of *Velásquez Rodríguez v. Honduras*, the Inter-American Court of Human Rights has interpreted the responsibility of states parties under Article 1 of the American Convention on Human Rights to "respect" and "ensure" the rights set out in that Convention. According to the Court, the obligation to **respect** human rights implies that officials must not violate them, while the obligation to **ensure** human rights implies duties of prevention, investigation, punishment and reparation. "Whenever a State organ, official or public entity violates one of those rights, this constitutes a failure of the duty to respect the rights and freedoms set forth in the Convention."[145] And as a consequence of the obligation to ensure the free and full exercise of human rights, "the States must prevent, investigate and punish any violation of the rights recognized by the Convention and, moreover, if possible attempt to restore the right violated and provide compensation as warranted for damages resulting from the violation".[146]

Article 2(2) of the ICCPR obliges states parties "to adopt such laws or other measures as may be necessary to give effect to the rights recognized in the present Covenant". Article 2(3) obliges states parties to ensure that people whose rights are violated have an effective remedy.

In its General Comment 20 on Article 7 of the ICCPR, the Human Rights Committee has stated that "it is not sufficient for the implementation of article 7 to prohibit such treatment or punishment or to make it a crime" (para. 8). The General Comment refers to the need for prevention, investigation, punishment and reparation (see Appendix 11 of this manual).

The Convention against Torture requires states parties to take "effective legislative, administrative, judicial or other measures" to prevent acts of torture or ill-treatment in any territory under their jurisdiction (Articles 2, 16). The Convention specifies preventive measures regarding training public officials (Articles 10, 16) and keeping arrangements for interrogation and custody under systematic review (Articles 11, 16). States parties must conduct prompt and impartial investigations into all complaints and credible reports of torture or ill-treatment (Articles 12, 13, 16). These obligations apply both to torture and to other acts of cruel, inhuman or degrading treatment or punishment. States parties must also ensure that all acts of torture are offences under their criminal law (Article 4) and that those alleged to have committed offences of torture are brought before the courts, where necessary through the exercise of extradition or universal jurisdiction (Articles 5-9). Victims of torture must have an enforceable right to compensation (Article 14). Statements made as a result of torture must not be invoked as evidence in any proceedings, except against a person accused of torture as evidence that the statement was made (Article 15). States parties must not forcibly return a person to another state where there are substantial grounds for believing that he or she would be in danger of being subjected to torture (Article 3).

The Inter-American Convention to Prevent and Punish Torture contains obligations regarding torture similar to those in Articles 4-10 and 12-15 of the Convention against Torture as well as a general obligation to prevent other cruel, inhuman or degrading treatment or punishment (Article 7).

In so far as these bodies are applying norms that are grounded in general international law, it can be concluded that the above obligations are not limited to states parties to the Convention against Torture or the Inter-American Convention to Prevent and Punish Torture. The Human Rights Committee and the regional human rights courts and commissions have issued opinions and judgments setting out specific obligations under the prohibition of torture and ill-treatment in the respective regional treaties, particularly the obligation to investigate complaints and reports of torture or ill-treatment (see section 7.3). Similar findings have been made by the Human Rights Committee in cases brought under the first Optional Protocol to the ICCPR. The European Court of Human Rights has also held that the prohibition of torture and ill-treatment under the European Convention on Human Rights entails an obligation not to extradite or expel a person to a country where they would be at risk of torture or ill-treatment (see section 8.3).

These obligations of states are discussed in greater detail in the following chapters.

3.8 Protection against abuses by private individuals

The prohibition of torture and other fundamental human rights provisions in the Universal Declaration of Human Rights and the ICCPR were conceived as bulwarks to protect human beings against egregious violent abuses of state power of the sort seen under the Nazi regime in Germany.[147] But in human rights discussions in recent years, especially in the fields of women's and children's rights, much attention has been focused on the need to protect people also against abuses by private individuals. To what extent do such abuses come under the prohibition of torture and ill-treatment? What are the attendant obligations of states?[148]

The Human Rights Committee has linked the right not to be subjected to torture or ill-treatment under Article 7 of the ICCPR to an obligation to provide protection, through "legislative and other measures", against torture or ill-treatment inflicted by private individuals:

> "The aim of the provisions of article 7 of the International Covenant on Civil and Political Rights is to protect both the dignity and the physical and mental integrity of the individual. It is the duty of the State party to afford everyone protection through legislative and other measures as may be necessary against the acts prohibited by article 7, whether inflicted by people acting in their official capacity, outside their official capacity or in a private capacity."[149]

In the case of *A v. UK*, the European Court of Human Rights considered a complaint concerning a nine-year-old boy whose stepfather had repeatedly beaten him with a garden cane as a punishment. The stepfather had been brought to trial but was acquitted under the defence of "moderate and reasonable chastisement" as provided under English law. The Court, referring to the beatings, found that "treatment of this kind reaches the level of severity prohibited by Article 3" of the European Convention on Human Rights.[150] It considered that "the obligation on the High Contracting Parties under Article 1 of the Convention to secure to everyone within their jurisdiction the rights and freedoms defined in the Convention, taken together with Article 3, requires States to take measures designed to ensure that individuals within their jurisdiction are not subjected to torture or inhuman or degrading treatment or punishment, including such ill-treatment administered by private individuals".[151] In this case, however, "the law did not provide adequate protection to the applicant against treatment or punishment contrary to Article 3... In the circumstances of the present case, the failure to provide adequate protection constitutes a violation of Article 3 of the Convention."[152]

In subsequent decisions, the European Court of Human Rights has distinguished two types of measures to be taken to protect people against torture or ill-treatment by private individuals: protection through the "framework of the law", which the Court had found lacking in the case of *A v. UK*,[153] and practical measures of protection to be taken in the face of a risk of ill-treatment. As stated by the Court, "State responsibility may... be engaged where the framework of law fails to provide adequate protection... or where the authorities fail to take reasonable steps to avoid a risk of ill-treatment which they knew or ought to have known".[154]

In the case of *Velásquez Rodríguez v. Honduras* cited above (section 3.7), which involved among other things the right not to be subjected to torture or ill-treatment, the Inter-American Court of Human Rights held that the obligation of states parties to the American Convention on Human Rights to ensure the exercise of rights recognized by that Convention "implies the duty of States Parties to organize the governmental apparatus and, in general, all the structures through which public power is exercised, so that they are capable of juridically ensuring the free and full enjoyment of human rights" and that "[a]n illegal act which violates human rights and which is initially not directly imputable to a State (for example, because it is the act of a private person or because the person responsible has not been identified) can lead to international responsibility of the State, not because of the act itself, but because of the lack of due diligence to prevent the violation or to respond to it as required by the Convention".[155]

The approaches of the Human Rights Committee and the European and Inter-American Courts of Human Rights have several implications:

- An act committed by a private individual can constitute torture or ill-treatment within the meaning of international and regional human rights standards.

- The criteria by which particular acts by private individuals are deemed to constitute torture or ill-treatment may include their having attained a particular "level of severity" as in the usage of the European Court of Human Rights.

- Inasmuch as the prohibition of torture and ill-treatment is conceived as a human right ("no one shall be subjected to..."),[156] and inasmuch as human rights are seen as "inherent" and "inalienable",[157] it can be said that everyone has a right not to be subjected to torture or ill-treatment whether at the hands of a public official or of a private individual.

- The obligation of states parties to international human rights treaties to respect and ensure (under the European Convention on Human Rights, to "secure") the prohibition of torture and ill-treatment entails not only an obligation to prevent the commission of torture or ill-treatment by public officials, but an obligation to take measures to protect people under their jurisdiction against acts of torture or ill-treatment committed by private individuals. These measures include ensuring that the framework of the law provides adequate protection, and taking reasonable steps to avoid a risk of torture or ill-treatment of which the authorities know or should know.

---

* As used in this manual, the term "human rights violation" refers to the violation by a state of its obligations concerning the human rights of a person.

- The right of any person under international human rights law not to be subjected to torture or ill-treatment can be violated if he or she becomes the victim of an act of torture or ill-treatment committed by a private individual and the state has failed to fulfil its obligations as described above.*

- As a result of such a violation, the state may be required to provide reparation to the victim.

Amnesty International considers that acts of violence by private individuals can constitute torture or ill-treatment when they are of the nature and severity envisaged by the concept of torture or cruel, inhuman or degrading treatment or punishment in international standards and when the state has failed to fulfil its obligation to provide effective protection.

This reasoning opens the way to addressing various forms of violence in the family and the community as forms of torture or ill-treatment. How this can be done is discussed in section 6.6.

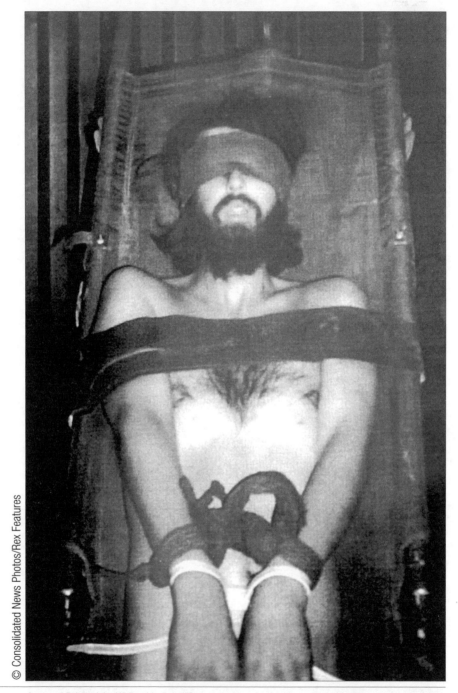

© Consolidated News Photos/Rex Features

Captured fighter John Walker Lindh in US custody, bound naked in a metal shipping container at Camp Rhino, near Kandahar, Afghanistan, December 2001. John Walker Lindh later alleged that he had been held in this way without light or heating for two or three days and that he was threatened with death and torture during transport to the military camp (see Amnesty International, 2002, "Memorandum on the rights of people in US custody in Afghanistan and Guantanamo Bay", p. 4). Safeguards are needed at all stages of arrest and custody to ensure that prisoners are treated humanely (see Chapter 4).

Chapter 4: Safeguards in custody

4.1 Introduction

Most of the torture and ill-treatment recorded by human rights organizations is inflicted on people who have been taken into custody by agents of the state. The safeguards set out in this chapter are meant to protect the potential victims, reducing to a minimum the opportunities for torture.

Law enforcement officials are endowed by the state with coercive powers. A person taken into custody is vulnerable to the risk of abuse of these powers through violent and unlawful behaviour. Isolation from the outside increases the risk.

The safeguards described below are meant to reduce the isolation of prisoners, maximizing the opportunities to monitor the actions of state agents and intervene if torture is threatened. The safeguards also aim to preserve the evidence of torture so that a proper investigation can be made and sanctions imposed on the perpetrators. If state agents know that they are watched and will be punished if caught, the incidence of torture should decline.

Many of the safeguards consist of establishing proper procedures concerning arrest and detention and ensuring that these procedures are followed. The task of ensuring that they are followed should be assigned to the law enforcement agencies and to other state institutions, including the judiciary. Clearly, there is sometimes a wilful failure to follow proper procedures on the part of the agencies in question, countenanced by higher authorities. Other individuals and organs of civil society therefore need to be vigilant, pressing for the safeguards to be observed.

If the authorities are prepared to commit such a serious crime as torture, there is a risk that they will resort to further abuses to keep their deeds secret: arbitrary arrests, secret detention, "disappearances" or extrajudicial executions. These practices increase the risk to prisoners by depriving them of the protection of the law and making it difficult or impossible for relatives and others to intervene on their behalf. Many of the safeguards against torture are also safeguards against these abuses.[1]

The obligation of states under international law to respect the prohibition of torture and ill-treatment entails an obligation to prevent their agents from inflicting torture or ill-treatment (see section 3.7 of this manual). The UN Human Rights Committee has set out a series of custodial safeguards and other measures to be taken to this end.[2] Detailed safeguards have been set out in UN human rights instruments, notably the **Body of Principles for the Protection of All Persons under Any Form of Detention or Imprisonment** (Body of Principles on Detention), the **Standard Minimum Rules for the Treatment of Prisoners** (Standard Minimum Rules) and the **Declaration on the Protection of All Persons from Enforced Disappearance** (Declaration on Enforced Disappearance).[3] Other important findings and recommendations have been made by the UN Committee against Torture, by the UN Special Rapporteur on torture* and in judgments of the Inter-American Court of Human Rights and the European Court of Human Rights.

The European Committee for the Prevention of Torture (CPT) has developed three "fundamental safeguards" against ill-treatment which it regularly includes in its recommendations to states. They have been formulated as follows:

> "The CPT wishes to recall the particular importance which it attaches to three rights for persons detained by the police:
>
> • the right of those concerned to have the fact of their detention notified to a close relative or third party of their choice,
>
> • the right of access to a lawyer,
>
> • the right to a medical examination by a doctor of their choice (in addition to any medical examination carried out by a doctor called by the police authorities).
>
> "The CPT considers that these three rights are fundamental safeguards against the ill-treatment of persons in detention, which should apply from the very outset of custody (i.e. from the moment when those concerned are obliged to remain with the police).
>
> "Moreover, it considers it equally fundamental that detained persons be informed without delay of all their rights, including those mentioned above."[4]

Because torture and ill-treatment can begin very quickly after arrest, or even while an arrest is being effected, it is important that the key safeguards take effect as soon as possible. The phrase "without delay" is used in certain international standards to express this notion. What it means is that if the act in question cannot be done immediately, there must be no unreasonable cause for delay. If there is a delay, it is important that other safeguards are in operation to protect detainees against any risks occasioned by the delay. It is also very important that – like the prohibition of torture itself – the essential safeguards for the prevention of torture, including the availability of habeas corpus or other key judicial remedies for protecting prisoners, are never suspended, even in time of emergency.

---

* The Special Rapporteur's consolidated recommendations are reproduced in Appendix 14 of this manual.

Articles 11 and 16 of the Convention against Torture provide that each state party to the Convention "shall keep under systematic review... arrangements for the custody and treatment of persons subjected to any form of arrest, detention or imprisonment in any territory under its jurisdiction" with a view to preventing any cases of torture or ill-treatment. Article 6 of the UN Declaration against Torture, a non-binding instrument which applies to all states, contains a similar provision. Citing these provisions, individuals and organizations can press their governments to disclose what arrangements are in place and what is being done to keep them under systematic review.[5]

One important aspect of a systematic review is to monitor incidents of torture, deaths in custody and other violent incidents and to make statistics and other information on them publicly available.[6] Surprise checks and "early warning systems" to alert the authorities to emerging patterns of impermissible behaviour should be features of a system of review.

Article 10(1) of the International Covenant on Civil and Political Rights (ICCPR) states: "All persons deprived of their liberty shall be treated with humanity and with respect for the inherent dignity of the human person." This provision must be observed as soon as a person is arrested or otherwise deprived of their liberty. Similarly, the measures concerning conditions of detention set out in Chapter 5 of this manual, which are designed to prevent conditions or practices amounting to torture or ill-treatment, apply to the custodial situations discussed in this chapter. Particularly important are measures relating to the **separation of categories of prisoners** (see section 5.3.2), **accommodation and basic needs** (sections 5.3, 5.4), and for proper **records** to be kept and made available to prisoners and their lawyers (see sections 4.2.5, 4.9, 4.11, 5.6). Also, international standards on the **use of force** and **instruments of restraint** (sections 5.5, 6.3) must be observed both during arrest and in custody.

Further reading

The UN manual *Human Rights and Pre-trial Detention* (1994) provides a compendium of international standards relating to arrest and detention. The UN manual *Human Rights and Law Enforcement* (1997) and the police training manual published by the International Committee of the Red Cross (ICRC), *To Serve and to Protect: Human Rights and Humanitarian Law for Police and Security Forces* (de Rover, 1998), describe the international standards on arrest and detention from a law enforcement official's point of view. International safeguards relating to arrest and detention are discussed in Rodley, 1999, Chapter 11. Standards developed by the CPT are analysed in Morgan and Evans, 2001, Chapter 4 and Evans and Morgan, 1998, Chapter 7. Additional detailed references to safeguards can be found in Amnesty International's *Fair Trials Manual* (1998).

4.2 Safeguards at arrest

4.2.1 Grounds and procedures for arrest

Arbitrary arrest* – deprivation of liberty on improper grounds or with improper procedures – opens the way to torture, "disappearances" and other abuses. An important means of preventing these abuses is to ensure that proper **grounds** and **procedures** for arrest are adhered to.

The Universal Declaration of Human Rights provides for the right to liberty and prohibits arbitrary arrest and detention (Articles 3, 9). There are similar provisions in other major international and regional human rights instruments and in many national constitutions.

Article 9(1) of the ICCPR states:

> "Everyone has the right to liberty and security of person. No one shall be subjected to arbitrary arrest or detention. No one shall be deprived of his liberty except on such grounds and in accordance with such procedure as are established by law."[7]

The Human Rights Committee has stated that Article 9(1) of the ICCPR "is applicable to all deprivations of liberty, whether in criminal cases or in other cases such as, for example, mental illness, vagrancy, drug addiction, educational purposes, immigration control, etc."[8]

Principle 2 of the Body of Principles on Detention states: "Arrest, detention or imprisonment shall only be carried out strictly in accordance with the provisions of the law and by competent officials or persons authorized for that purpose." Article 12 of the Declaration on Enforced Disappearance provides that states shall establish rules under their national law "indicating those officials authorized to order deprivation of liberty" and "establishing the conditions under which such orders may be given". It also provides that states shall "ensure strict supervision, including a clear chain of command, of all law enforcement officials responsible for apprehensions, arrests, detentions, custody, transfers and imprisonment".

Under Article 37(b) of the Convention on the Rights of the Child, "The arrest, detention or imprisonment of a child... shall be used only as a matter of last resort and for the shortest appropriate period of time." The detention of asylum-seekers and refugees also is to be avoided (see sections 5.2, 5.7 of this manual).

To prevent arbitrary arrests and "disappearances", Amnesty International regularly recommends to governments that officials carrying out an arrest should identify themselves to the person arrested and, on demand, to others witnessing the event. Police officers and other officials who make arrests should wear name tags or numbers so that they can be clearly identified. Other identifying markings such as the insignia of soldiers' battalions or detachments are also to be recommended. Police and military vehicles should be clearly identified as such. They should carry number plates at all times.[9]

---

*   In the Body of Principles on Detention, "arrest" means "the act of apprehending a person for the alleged commission of an offence or by the action of an authority". The term is used in a similar way in this manual.

Proper arrest procedures need to be backed up by proper record-keeping. Records should include the reasons for the arrest, the time of the arrest and the identity of the law enforcement officials concerned.

4.2.2 Informing prisoners of the reasons for their arrest, and of their rights

Article 9(2) of the ICCPR states:

> "Anyone who is arrested shall be informed, at the time of arrest, of the reasons for his arrest and shall be promptly informed of any charges against him."[10]

Principle 10 of the Body of Principles on Detention contains the same provision. Principle 13 requires that information also be given on prisoners' rights:

> "Any person shall, at the moment of arrest and at the commencement of detention or imprisonment, or promptly thereafter, be provided by the authority responsible for his arrest, detention or imprisonment, respectively with information on and an explanation of his rights and how to avail himself of such rights."[11]

Principle 14 of the Body of Principles on Detention states that a person who does not adequately understand the language used by the authorities is entitled to receive the information referred to in Principles 10 and 13 in a language which he or she understands "and to have the assistance, free of charge, if necessary, of an interpreter in connection with legal proceedings subsequent to his arrest".[12]

As implied in Principle 13, it may not be possible to give a comprehensive **explanation** of prisoners' rights at the moment of arrest (see section 5.9.1), but arrested people do need to be **informed** without delay in simple, non-technical language of the rights which are of immediate operational importance, including the key safeguards protecting them against torture or ill-treatment. These include the right to notify relatives and others of their arrest, the right to legal counsel, provisions for bringing prisoners before a judicial authority without delay and the right to medical assistance. To forestall attempts to coerce statements under torture or ill-treatment, it is also important to inform them of their rights under interrogation (see section 4.9), as such attempts can begin very shortly after arrest.

Information on prisoners' rights should also be made available to the public.[13]

4.2.3 Notifying relatives and others

Principle 16(1) of the Body of Principles on Detention states:

> "Promptly after arrest and after each transfer from one place of detention or imprisonment to another, a detained or imprisoned person shall be entitled to notify or to require the competent authority to notify members of his family or other appropriate persons of his choice of his arrest, detention or imprisonment or of the transfer and of the place where he is kept in custody."[14]

Other standards, monitoring bodies and mechanisms have stated that relatives should be notified immediately or very quickly. The Human Rights Committee has stated that people arrested or detained on a criminal charge must be permitted to contact their families "from the moment of apprehension"[15] and has called for "the mandatory notification of relatives of detainees without delay".[16] Similarly, Rule 92 of the Standard Minimum Rules states that "[a]n untried prisoner shall be allowed to inform immediately his family of his detention". The CPT has stated that the right of people detained by the police "to have the fact of their detention notified to a close relative or third party of their choice" is one of the "fundamental safeguards" against ill-treatment which "should apply from the very outset of custody (i.e. from the moment when those concerned are obliged to remain with the police)" (see section 4.1).[17] The Special Rapporteur on torture has in some instances called for immediate notification of relatives[18] and has stated: "In all circumstances, a relative of the detainee should be informed of the arrest and place of detention within 18 hours."[19]

The right of prisoners to notify relatives of their detention is complemented by the right of people outside to obtain information about them. Article 10 of the Declaration on Enforced Disappearance provides that accurate information on the detention of all persons deprived of liberty "and their place or places of detention, including transfers, shall be made promptly available to their family members, their counsel or to any other persons having a legitimate interest in the information unless a wish to the contrary has been manifested by the persons concerned". This safeguard is particularly important for the prevention of "disappearances" and other unacknowledged detentions, during which those detained are often tortured or ill-treated.

Additional safeguards apply to the notification of relatives of detained children and to the right of foreign prisoners to communicate with their country's consular representatives (see section 4.10).

4.2.4 Safeguards during transport to a place of detention

Prisoners are often ill-treated or tortured while in transit to an initial place of detention or during subsequent transfers. Often the victims are beaten or otherwise ill-treated in a police vehicle; sometimes they are taken to a lonely place and tortured there. While such practices are forbidden under the general prohibition of torture and ill-treatment, there is no international standard which addresses the problem of torture in transit specifically.

To prevent torture in transit, the authorities should:

- Ensure that prisoners are taken directly to the initial place of detention without delay.

- Require the authorities responsible for the place of detention to certify that the prisoners arrived in good condition.

- Institute proper means of surveillance and supervision of the actions of officials during transport.

- Ensure that prisoners are not transported under dangerous or life-threatening conditions, for instance in overcrowded or dangerous vehicles.

Rule 45(2) of the Standard Minimum Rules states: "The transport of prisoners in conveyances with inadequate ventilation or light, or in any way which would subject them to unnecessary physical hardship, shall be prohibited."

- Ensure that procedures for the safe transport of prisoners are backed up by proper record-keeping, including records of the time of arrest and the subsequent time of arrival at a place of detention.

Similar precautions should be taken to avoid ill-treatment during transfers from one place of detention to another, or between a place of detention and the court.

A further safeguard is for transfers from one detaining agency to another to be the subject of a judicial order. In Pakistan, where the Special Rapporteur on torture found that the use of torture was facilitated by detainees being transferred from agency to agency and from place to place, some of which were not officially recognized places of detention, the Special Rapporteur recommended: "It should not be possible for persons to be handed over from one police or security agency to another police or security agency without a judicial order. Where this happens, the officials responsible for the transfers should be held accountable under the criminal law."[20]

4.2.5 Record-keeping

Accurate record-keeping is an essential element of the conduct of law enforcement functions, including arrest and detention. The existence of official records that are open to review helps to ensure that proper procedures are followed and that law enforcement officials engaged in their functions can be held accountable for their actions. (See also section 5.6.)

Principle 12 of the Body of Principles on Detention states:

"1. There shall be duly recorded:

(a) The reasons for the arrest;

(b) The time of the arrest and the taking of the arrested person to a place of custody as well as that of his first appearance before a judicial or other authority;

(c) The identity of the law enforcement officials concerned;

(d) Precise information concerning the place of custody.

"2. Such records shall be communicated to the detained person, or his counsel, if any, in the form prescribed by law."

The CPT has proposed that details relating to arrest be included in a single comprehensive custody record which should be kept for each prisoner:

"The CPT considers that the fundamental safeguards granted to persons in police custody would be reinforced (and the work of police officers quite possibly facilitated) if a single and comprehensive custody record were to exist for each person detained, on which would be recorded all aspects of his custody and action taken regarding them (when deprived of liberty and reasons for that measure; when told of rights; signs of injury, mental illness, etc; when next of kin/consulate and lawyer contacted and when visited by them; when offered food; when interrogated; when transferred or released, etc.). For various matters (for example, items in the person's possession, the fact of being told of one's rights and of invoking or waiving them), the signature of the detainee should be obtained and, if necessary, the absence of a signature explained. Further, the detainee's lawyer should have access to such a custody record."[21]

The requirement of keeping and preserving accurate and complete records of arrest and custody and making the information available when required should be incorporated in national laws and regulations. Any breach of these requirements should be punished by appropriate sanctions.

4.3 No secret detention

In some countries the practice of torture is accompanied by a practice of holding prisoners secretly in private homes or apartments, military camps or other locations which are not officially recognized as places of detention, where they can be tortured at will. Secret detention also facilitates "disappearances" by enabling the authorities to conceal the whereabouts of the victims. Secret detention should be absolutely prohibited.

Article 10 of the Declaration on Enforced Disappearance states: "Any person deprived of liberty shall be held in an officially recognized place of detention". Similarly, the Human Rights Committee has stated that "provisions should be made for detainees to be held in places officially recognized as places of detention".[22]

The Special Rapporteur on torture has stated:

"[T]he maintenance of secret places of detention should be abolished under law. It should be a punishable offence for any official to hold a person in a secret and/or unofficial place of detention. Any evidence obtained from a detainee in an unofficial place of detention and not confirmed by the detainee during interrogation at official locations should not be admitted as evidence in court."[23]

Up-to-date lists of all officially recognized places of detention should be published in a form that is readily accessible to lawyers and members of the public.

4.4 Bringing prisoners before a judicial authority

The requirement to bring detainees before a judicial or other competent authority after arrest is a key safeguard for the human rights of prisoners. It is a means of ensuring that detentions are lawful and necessary. It is a safeguard against torture: a judge can see if there are any noticeable signs of ill-treatment and can hear any allegations by the prisoner. It is a means of providing supervision of detention through judicial control, removing the absolute power over a prisoner which officials might otherwise wield.

Article 9(3) of the ICCPR states:

"Anyone arrested or detained on a criminal charge shall be brought promptly before a judge or other officer authorized by law to exercise judicial power and shall be entitled to trial within a reasonable time or to release."

Under Article 10 of the Declaration on Enforced Disappearance, the requirement to bring prisoners before a judicial authority covers not just those detained on criminal charges but anyone deprived of their liberty. Article 10(1) states: "Any person deprived of liberty shall... in conformity with national law, be brought before a judicial authority promptly after detention." Similarly, Principle 11 of the Body of Principles on Detention states:

"1. A person shall not be kept in detention without being given an effective opportunity to be heard promptly by a judicial or other authority. A detained person shall have the right to defend himself or to be assisted by counsel as prescribed by law...

"3. A judicial or other authority shall be empowered to review as appropriate the continuance of detention."

Principle 37 of the Body of Principles on Detention states:

"A person detained on a criminal charge shall be brought before a judicial or other authority provided by law promptly after his arrest. Such authority shall decide without delay upon the lawfulness and necessity of detention. No person may be kept under detention pending investigation or trial except upon the written order of such an authority. A detained person shall, when brought before such an authority, have the right to make a statement on the treatment received by him while in custody."

Amnesty International holds that detainees should be brought before a judicial or other competent authority **without delay**,[24] and preferably before a judge. Any "other authority" exercising this function should be one who exercises judicial power established by law and should be equivalent to a judge in independence, powers and professional competence.

Principle 37 of the Body of Principles on Detention specifies two roles for a judicial or other authority when a person is brought before them after arrest:

- to decide on the lawfulness and necessity of the detention, and

- to hear any statement from the detainee on his or her treatment while in custody.

Although Principle 37 refers only to people detained on criminal charges, these two judicial roles should apply, as a safeguard against torture, to anyone deprived of their liberty. The prisoner should be brought before the judge in person; the judge should not decide on the lawfulness and necessity of the detention without having seen and heard the prisoner. The prisoner should be able to address the judge in an atmosphere free from intimidation. If there is any sign of torture or ill-treatment, the judge should inquire into it without delay, even if the prisoner has not volunteered any statement.[25] If the inquiry, or the prisoner's own statement, gives reason to believe that torture or ill-treatment was committed, the judge should initiate an investigation and take effective steps to protect the prisoner against any further ill-treatment, and, if the detention is unlawful or unnecessary, order the prisoner's immediate release under safe conditions.[26]

Sri Lanka: Torture victim helped by court appearances

For several years in Vavuniya district, Sri Lanka, there had been frequent reports of torture, particularly by officers of the Counter Subversive Unit (CSU) of the police. But when detainees brought before a judge were asked whether they had any complaints, they were almost always afraid to say they had been tortured, especially because the security legislation under which they were held did not give the judge the power to release detainees, so they were inevitably returned to the custody of CSU officers.

In early 2000 a newly-appointed district judge began asking detainees who were brought to court to take off their shirt and lift up their trousers or *sarong* above their knees. If there were marks on their bodies, the judge required the detainees to explain them; encouraged by their lawyers, they were more willing to respond to the judge's specific questions than to provide information on their own initiative.

Following the introduction of this practice there was a marked decline in the frequency of reports of torture by CSU officers in Vavuniya district and in the severity of the abuses they were alleged to have committed. The new practice also helped victims of torture to obtain compensation and gain release from custody through fundamental rights petitions to the Supreme Court, which accepted as corroborating evidence the judge's detailed notes of the injuries he had observed. During 2000, 32 suspects detained in Vavuniya district and tortured were released on the order of the Supreme Court after the Court found that reports by judicial medical doctors who had examined the victim were consistent with notes taken earlier by the district judge.

4.5 Access to the outside world

Access of prisoners to the outside world and access from the outside to them is a key safeguard against torture and ill-treatment. Alongside the other measures described in this chapter, it helps to break down the isolation in which the abuses are committed. By visiting prisoners, relatives and others concerned about their well-being can see where they are held and learn about their condition so as to be able to intervene on their behalf if there is reason to believe they are being ill-treated. It is also a safeguard against "disappearances" and extrajudicial executions: once a prisoner is seen by concerned people from outside, there is less chance that he or she will "disappear" or be killed.

The Human Rights Committee has stated: "The protection of the detainee... requires that prompt and regular access be given to doctors and lawyers and, under appropriate supervision when the investigation so requires, to family members."[27] The Committee against Torture has stated that "[c]ounsel, family members and the doctor of their own choice must be guaranteed immediate access to persons deprived of liberty"[28] and has recommended "the free access of a person deprived of his liberty to a lawyer and to a doctor of his choice and to his relatives at all stages of detention".[29]

Because of its urgency as a safeguard against torture, Amnesty International holds that relatives, lawyers and doctors should have access to prisoners **without delay** and regularly thereafter. Specific safeguards on access to lawyers and doctors are described in the next two sections. Access by others such as representatives of human rights organizations and (in armed conflicts and other applicable situations) the ICRC is also of great importance.

Sometimes prisoners are held for days, weeks or months without contact with the outside world. This **incommunicado detention** facilitates torture.

The UN Commission on Human Rights has stated that "prolonged incommunicado detention may facilitate the perpetration of torture and can in itself constitute a form of cruel, inhuman or degrading treatment" or even torture.[30]

The Human Rights Committee has stated: "Provisions should... be made against incommunicado detention."[31] The Committee against Torture has called for the elimination of incommunicado detention[32] and has criticized its prolonged use in particular countries.[33]

The Inter-American Commission on Human Rights has held that the use of a confession obtained while the accused was detained incommunicado and without access to counsel violated the accused's right against self-incrimination under Article 8 of the American Convention on Human Rights and the provision in that article that a confession of guilt shall be valid only if made without coercion of any kind.[34]

The Special Rapporteur on torture has stated:

"Torture is most frequently practised during incommunicado detention. Incommunicado detention should be made illegal, and persons held incommunicado should be released without delay."[35]

4.6 Access to legal counsel

Principle 17 of the Body of Principles on Detention states:

> "A detained person shall be entitled to have the assistance of a legal counsel. He shall be informed of his right by the competent authority promptly after arrest and shall be provided with reasonable facilities for exercising it."

The Human Rights Committee has stated that detained persons should have "immediate access to counsel and contact with their families".[36] The Committee against Torture has recommended "unrestricted access to counsel immediately after arrest".[37]

The CPT has stated that the right of access to a lawyer is a "fundamental safeguard" against ill-treatment and that this right should apply from the outset of custody (see section 4.1).[38]

The Special Rapporteur on torture has stated:

> "Legal provisions should ensure that detainees are given access to legal counsel within 24 hours of detention. Security personnel who do not honour such provisions should be punished. In exceptional circumstances, under which it is contended that prompt contact with a detainee's lawyer might raise genuine security concerns and where restriction of such contact is judicially approved, it should at least be possible to allow a meeting with an independent lawyer, such as one recommended by a bar association."[39]

The UN Commission on Human Rights has stressed the recommendation of the Special Rapporteur on torture "[t]hat the right to have access to a lawyer is one of the basic rights of a person who is deprived of his liberty and that restrictions on this right should therefore be exceptional and always subject to judicial control".[40]

The right to legal counsel is one of the key norms for a fair trial under international human rights standards. Under Article 14(3) of the ICCPR, it includes the right of accused people to defend themselves through counsel of their own choosing, the right of an accused person "[t]o have adequate time and facilities... to communicate with counsel of his own choosing", the right to confidential communication with counsel[41] and the right to free legal assistance for those who lack the means to pay for it. There are similar provisions in other international and regional instruments.

4.7 Medical examinations and care

The Standard Minimum Rules (Rule 24) and the Body of Principles on Detention (Principle 24) call for prisoners to be given or offered a medical examination as promptly as possible after admission to a place of detention (see section 5.4.2 of this manual). International human rights bodies and mechanisms have gone further by developing the notion of a medical examination as a safeguard against torture and stating that the examination should be independent. Thus, the Human Rights Committee has emphasized the need "to have suspects examined by an independent doctor as soon as they are arrested, after each period of questioning and before they are brought before the examining magistrate or released".[42] Furthermore, prisoners should have a right to be examined by a doctor of their own choice.

The Special Rapporteur on torture has stated: "At the time of arrest, a person should undergo a medical inspection, and medical inspections should be repeated regularly and should be compulsory upon transfer to another place of detention."[43] He has proposed detailed safeguards to ensure that medical personnel making such examinations can operate independently and that the findings of doctors chosen by the prisoners themselves are given due weight as evidence.[44]

The CPT has identified the right to a medical examination by a doctor of one's choice as a "fundamental safeguard" against ill-treatment which should apply from the outset of police custody (see section 4.1). The CPT's recommendations on access to a doctor have been formulated as follows:

> "The CPT recommends that specific legal provisions be adopted on the subject of the right of persons in police custody to have access to a doctor. Those provisions should stipulate *inter alia* that:
>
> • a person taken into police custody has the right to be examined, if he so wishes, by a doctor of his own choice, in addition to any medical examination carried out by a doctor called by the police authorities;[45]
>
> • all medical examinations of persons in custody are to be conducted out of the hearing and – unless the doctor concerned expressly requests otherwise in a given case – out of the sight of police officers;
>
> • the results of every examination, as well as any relevant statements by the person in custody and the doctor's conclusions, are to be recorded in writing by the doctor and made available to the person in custody and his lawyer;
>
> • the confidentiality of medical data is to be strictly observed."[46]

Steps should be taken to ensure the ability of doctors employed by the state to act independently in recording and reporting signs of ill-treatment in accordance with medical ethics.

When there is reason to believe that a prisoner has been ill-treated, the prisoner should be given an immediate medical examination by a doctor who is able to make an accurate report without interference from the authorities.[47]

Medical personnel who see signs of ill-treatment should take steps to protect the prisoner against further ill-treatment. Such steps could include approaching the person responsible for medical care in the place of detention.

International standards also call for medical assistance to be given to prisoners when necessary (see section 5.4.2). In particular, Article 6 of the UN Code of Conduct for Law Enforcement Officials states: "Law enforcement officials shall ensure the full protection of the health of persons in their custody and, in particular, shall take immediate action to secure medical attention whenever required." A person injured in the course of arrest should be given medical assistance immediately. In a case in which a person injured during arrest was seen by a medical doctor only eight days later, the European Commission of Human Rights held that the failure by the authorities to provide adequate medical treatment constituted inhuman treatment in violation of Article 3 of the European Convention on Human Rights.[48]

Where it becomes evident that a prisoner has an underlying medical problem or displays signs of serious mental illness, appropriate medical care should be organized in a manner reflecting the urgency of the problem, including where necessary transfer to a specialist clinic.

Doctors, whether working permanently within the prison system or carrying out regular or occasional sessions with prisoners, must be guaranteed clinical freedom and, in particular, not be subjected to pressure to modify their findings to conform to the wishes of the police or prison officials. Professional associations should make efforts to ensure that the interests of prison medical staff are adequately represented.[49]

4.8 Habeas corpus and other judicial remedies for protecting prisoners

A key safeguard against torture is for prisoners or others acting on their behalf to be able to invoke the power of the courts to challenge the legality of the detention and otherwise ensure the prisoner's safety. It can also serve as a safeguard against "disappearances" by invoking the courts to locate a person who has "disappeared".

This safeguard is derived from the ancient legal notion of habeas corpus. Habeas corpus (literally, "that you have the body") is a remedy in national law under which a person can petition a court to determine whether a detention is legal and order the person's release if it proves not to be. Although its purpose is to test the legality of a detention, habeas corpus can also serve to ensure the prisoner's safety: as stated by the Inter-American Commission on Human Rights, "the immediate aim of this remedy is to bring the detainee before a judge, thus enabling the latter to verify whether the detainee is still alive and whether or not he or she has been subjected to torture or physical or psychological abuse".[50]

Another relevant legal device is *amparo* (protection), provided under the laws of many Latin American countries. Its scope is broader than that of habeas corpus, as it affords protection not only of the right to liberty but also of other constitutional rights such as the prohibition of torture and ill-treatment.

The right of habeas corpus is set out in Article 9(4) of the ICCPR: "Anyone who is deprived of his liberty by arrest or detention shall be entitled to take proceedings before a court, in order that that court may decide without delay on the lawfulness of his detention and order his release if the detention is not lawful."[51] The European Convention on Human Rights (Article 5) contains a similar provision, as does the Body of Principles on Detention (Principle 32), while the American Convention on Human Rights provides for both habeas corpus (Article 7) and *amparo* (Article 25(1)).

The Inter-American Court of Human Rights has ruled that because they are judicial guarantees essential for the protection of rights (including the right not to be tortured or ill-treated) which themselves cannot be suspended under the provisions for derogation in the American Convention on Human Rights, the rights of habeas corpus and *amparo* under the Convention also can never be suspended.[52] Similarly, the Human Rights Committee has stated that the right of habeas corpus is a non-derogable guarantee under the ICCPR.[53] The Declaration on Enforced Disappearance also sets out the right to a judicial remedy to protect prisoners and states that this right must never be suspended.[54]

The role of the judge in responding to petitions intended to protect prisoners from ill-treatment should be as wide as possible. The Special Rapporteur on torture has stated: "Judges should make full use of the possibilities provided for in the law regarding the proceedings of habeas corpus (*procedimiento de amparo*). They should, in particular, seek access to the detainee and verify his/her physical condition."[55]

Relatives and others acting on behalf of prisoners need to be genuinely able to use judicial remedies for protecting prisoners, especially when prisoners themselves are unable to do so.[56] They must have easy access to the courts, where they must be able to file petitions quickly and without intimidation or undue or prohibitive expense. The process of applying for the remedy should be as simple as possible. Relatives and others should be able to apply directly to the courts without having to use the services of a lawyer.[57]

Because of the serious risk to prisoners' lives and well-being, the courts should act immediately on receiving a petition.[58] Moreover, if the courts themselves learn that a person may be undergoing torture or ill-treatment, they must be able to act even if they have not received a petition on the prisoner's behalf.

4.9 Safeguards during interrogation

One of the common purposes of torture is to force people to "confess" or to give information, and interrogation remains one of the commonest settings in which torture is inflicted. A series of standards and safeguards have been developed to combat this use of torture.

Principle 21 of the Body of Principles on Detention states:

> "1. It shall be prohibited to take undue advantage of the situation of a detained or imprisoned person for the purpose of compelling him to confess, to incriminate himself otherwise or to testify against any other person.

> "2. No detained person while being interrogated shall be subject to violence, threats or methods of interrogation which impair his capacity of decision or his judgement."

As stated in section 4.2.2, prisoners should be informed at the time of their arrest of the reasons for their arrest, and of their rights. Before being interrogated, prisoners should also be informed of their rights during interrogation, including the rights set out in Principle 21 of the Body of Principles on Detention, quoted above, as well as the **right against self-incrimination**[59] and the **right to remain silent**.[60]

Other safeguards during interrogation include:

- **Separation of the authorities responsible for detention from those in charge of interrogation.** The Special Rapporteur on torture has stated: "Those legally arrested should not be held in facilities under the control of their interrogators or investigators for more than the time required by law to obtain a judicial warrant of pre-trial detention which, in any case, should not exceed a period of 48 hours. They should accordingly be transferred to a pre-trial facility under a different authority at once, after which no further unsupervised contact with the interrogators or investigators should be permitted".[61] The Committee against Torture has stated that it "expects that the detention and interrogation functions will be separated".[62]

- **Presence of a lawyer during interrogation**. The Committee against Torture has recommended "that counsel be permitted to be present during interrogation, especially since such presence would be in furtherance of the implementation of article 15 of the Convention [against Torture]".[63] The CPT has stated: "Access to a lawyer for persons in police custody should include... in principle, the right for the person concerned to have the lawyer present during interrogation."[64] The right to have counsel present during questioning is stipulated in the rules of procedure of the international criminal tribunals for the former Yugoslavia and Rwanda and in the Rome Statute of the International Criminal Court (Rome Statute).[65] The Special Rapporteur on torture has stated: "No statement or confession made by a person deprived of liberty, other than one made in [the] presence of a judge or a lawyer, should have a probative value in court, except as evidence against those who are accused of having obtained the confession by unlawful means."[66]

- **Right to an interpreter**. Principle 14 of the Body of Principles on Detention sets out the right of a detainee to an interpreter "in connection with legal proceedings subsequent to his arrest", a phrase which encompasses interrogation. Article 55(1)(c) of the Rome Statute states with respect to an investigation under the Statute that a person "[s]hall, if questioned in a language other than a language the person fully understands and speaks, have, free of any cost, the assistance of a competent interpreter and such translations as are necessary to meet the requirements of fairness".

- **Identification of everyone present during interrogations**. The Special Rapporteur on torture has stated: "Each interrogation should be initiated with the identification of all persons present."[67]

- **Prohibition of blindfolding and hooding**. The Special Rapporteur on torture has stated: "The practice of blindfolding and hooding often makes the prosecution of torture virtually impossible, as victims are rendered incapable of identifying their torturers. Thus, blindfolding or hooding should be forbidden".[68] The Committee against Torture has made a similar recommendation.[69] Amnesty International has recommended that the practice of blindfolding in police custody be outlawed and that officers who engage in the practice be prosecuted.[70]

- **Medical examinations.** The Human Rights Committee has recommended having "suspects examined by an independent doctor... after each period of questioning".[71]

Proper **records** of all interrogations must be kept, and the audio or video recording of interrogations is an additional valuable safeguard. Principle 23 of the Body of Principles on Detention states:

> "1. The duration of any interrogation of a detained or imprisoned person and of the intervals between interrogations as well as the identity of the officials who conducted the interrogations and other persons present shall be recorded and certified in such form as may be prescribed by law.

> "2. A detained or imprisoned person, or his counsel when provided by law, shall have access to the information described in paragraph 1 of the present principle."

The Special Rapporteur on torture has stated: "All interrogation sessions should be recorded and preferably video-recorded, and the identity of all persons present should be included in the records. Evidence from non-recorded interrogations should be excluded from court proceedings."[72]

Articles 11 and 16 of the Convention against Torture oblige states parties to "keep under systematic review interrogation rules, instructions, methods and practices" with a view to preventing torture and ill-treatment. The same requirement is stated in the Declaration against Torture (Article 6) and has been referred to by the Human Rights Committee as an effective means of preventing torture or ill-treatment.[73] Citing these provisions, individuals and organizations should press their governments to disclose what rules, instructions, methods and practices of interrogation are in effect and what is being done to keep them under regular review.[74]

An excuse sometimes offered for torture during interrogation is that a country's police forces are poorly trained and lacking in resources. It is important that law enforcement agencies have the scientific and technical equipment necessary to investigate crimes effectively and lawfully. While the extent to which they are provided with these means is frequently dependent on the material resources available to governments, a lack of resources is not a justification for torture or other unprofessional behaviour. Law enforcement officials should be trained and encouraged to operate as effectively as they can within the resources available to them without breaching legal, ethical or professional standards.

In particular, law enforcement officials should be trained in the skills of interviewing victims, witnesses and those suspected of crime. In relation to suspects, these skills include the abilities to:

- gather all available evidence in a case before interviewing a suspect;

- plan an interview based on that evidence so that an effective interview can be conducted;

- treat an interview as a means of gathering more information or evidence rather than as a means of securing a confession;

- conduct an interview in a manner that respects the suspect's rights;

- analyse information obtained during the interview, and carry out any further investigation into the case suggested by that analysis;

- check any admission or confession made by the suspect against available evidence; and

- evaluate each interview with a view to learning from each experience and developing interviewing and investigative skills further.

4.10 Safeguards for particular groups

As discussed in section 5.7 below, the Standard Minimum Rules and other international standards contain special provisions relating to the treatment of particular groups of imprisoned people. Certain provisions are especially important in preventing torture and ill-treatment in the initial stages of custody and during interrogation, when (for example) there may be a risk of **women** suffering rape and sexual abuse by male security agents, or **children** being subjected to abuse because of their inability to defend themselves in comparison with older prisoners. Thus:

- International standards relating to the separation of prisoners should be observed from the outset of custody. Female prisoners should be separated from male prisoners and should only be attended and supervised by female guards. There should be no contact between male guards and female prisoners without the presence of a female guard.

- Detained children should be separated from detained adults, and untried prisoners from convicted prisoners (see section 5.3.2). Other groups of prisoners also may need to be segregated if there is a risk of violence between groups.

- The CPT has emphasized "that persons deprived of their liberty should only be searched by staff of the same gender and that any search which requires an inmate to undress should be conducted out of the sight of custodial staff of the opposite gender."[75]

- The police training manual, *To Serve and to Protect*, published by the ICRC, recommends "ensuring that the arrest of a woman is carried out by a female official (whenever practicable)".[76]

Law enforcement officials should be clearly informed of the prohibition of rape and other sexual abuse and of the penalties that will be imposed on any public official who commits them. Any female prisoner who alleges that she has been raped or sexually assaulted should be given an immediate medical examination, preferably by a female doctor, or at least in the presence of female personnel.*

Amnesty International believes that practices such as allowing male staff to search women prisoners, or allowing male staff to patrol areas where women may be viewed in their cells while dressing, washing or taking showers, constitute inhuman and degrading treatment.

---

* Male prisoners alleging rape or sexual assault should likewise be given an immediate medical examination.

International standards relating to the arrest and custody of **children** set out special requirements in addition to those which apply to adults. Thus, alongside the right of prisoners to notify family members of their arrest, detention, imprisonment and transfer from one place of custody to another, set out in Principle 16(1) of the Body of Principles on Detention, Principle 16(3) states:

> "If a detained or imprisoned person is a juvenile or is incapable of understanding his entitlement, the competent authority shall *on its own initiative* undertake the notification referred to in the present principle. Special attention shall be given to notifying parents or guardians."[77] (Emphasis added)

Rule 10.1 of the United Nations Standard Minimum Rules for the Administration of Juvenile Justice (Beijing Rules) requires the *immediate* notification of family members: "Upon the apprehension of a juvenile, her or his parents or guardian shall be immediately notified of such apprehension, and, where such immediate notification is not possible, the parents or guardian shall be notified within the shortest possible time thereafter." Rule 10.2 states: "A judge or other competent official or body shall, *without delay*, consider the issue of release [of an apprehended juvenile]."[78] (Emphasis added)

In a similar vein, the CPT has noted that:

> "[C]ertain jurisdictions recognise that the inherent vulnerability of juveniles requires that additional precautions be taken. These include placing police officers under a formal obligation themselves to ensure that an appropriate person is notified of the fact that a juvenile has been detained (regardless of whether the juvenile requests that this be done). It may also be the case that police officers are not entitled to interview a juvenile unless such an appropriate person and/or a lawyer is present. The CPT welcomes this approach."[79]

As regards **foreign prisoners,** Article 36(1)(b) of the Vienna Convention on Consular Relations provides that "if he so requests, the competent authorities of the receiving State shall, without delay, inform the consular post of the sending State if, within its consular district, a national of that State is arrested or committed to prison or to custody pending trial or is detained in any other manner. Any communication addressed to the consular post by the person arrested, in prison, custody or detention shall also be forwarded by the said authorities without delay. The said authorities shall inform the person concerned without delay of his rights under this sub-paragraph."

Principle 16(2) of the Body of Principles on Detention provides for a foreign prisoner to be informed promptly of their right to communicate with their country's diplomatic representatives or "with the representative of the competent international organization, if he is a refugee or is otherwise under the protection of an intergovernmental organization".[80] The CPT has stated that "foreign nationals should be provided with the address and telephone number of the consular authorities of their country".[81]

As the Body of Principles on Detention applies to everyone under any form of detention or imprisonment,[82] the safeguards set out in that instrument must be afforded to asylum-seekers and other foreign prisoners.[83]

As noted in section 4.2.2, international standards require that prisoners be informed of the reasons for their arrest and of their rights in a language which they understand. Interpretation and translation facilities should be provided for prisoners throughout the period of detention and imprisonment.[84]

The Third Geneva Convention of 1949 deals with the treatment of **prisoners of war** in international armed conflicts. It contains detailed provisions relating to interrogation,[85] conditions of detention, correspondence, penal and disciplinary sanctions, termination of captivity, and access by delegates of Protecting Powers and the ICRC (Article 126). Additional Protocol II to the Geneva Conventions, relating to non-international armed conflicts, sets out fundamental guarantees for people "who do not take a direct part or who have ceased to take part in hostilities" (Article 4), additional provisions for the humane treatment of people "deprived of their liberty for reasons related to the armed conflict" (Article 5), and provisions including fair trial safeguards for the "prosecution and punishment of criminal offences related to the armed conflict" (Article 6).

Depending on the circumstances in a country, **other groups** may be at particular risk of torture or ill-treatment in custody or have particular difficulty defending themselves against it. Such groups include members of ethnic and religious minorities; indigenous peoples; lesbian, gay, bisexual and transgender people; and people accused of certain crimes. These groups may also be at risk of abuse from other prisoners. Where this is the case, the authorities should take appropriate preventive measures, including special instructions and training for law enforcement officials. Where necessary, they should seek the advice of representatives of the affected groups in setting up such measures.

4.11 Safeguards at release

Release from custody is a moment which can carry further risks. The officers in charge of a prisoner's release may use the opportunity to inflict a final beating. The prisoner may be released into an unsafe environment where he or she will be at risk of violence or even – in some cases – of "disappearance" or extrajudicial execution.

Article 11 of the Declaration on Enforced Disappearance states: "All persons deprived of liberty must be released in a manner permitting reliable verification that they have actually been released and, further, have been released in conditions in which their physical integrity and ability fully to exercise their rights are assured."

To protect prisoners against ill-treatment at the moment of release, governments should ensure adequate surveillance and control of the actions of law enforcement officials during the process of release and the availability of effective complaint mechanisms for prisoners who have been released.

To protect prisoners against release into an unsafe environment, governments should ensure that officials are aware of the environment into which prisoners are released and that they heed whatever fears prisoners may express on that score. Where necessary, special arrangements should be made – for example, to release prisoners in the presence of a relative or another person or organization which can assure their safety.[86]

In accordance with Rule 7(1) of the Standard Minimum Rules, information on the release of prisoners should be included in prisoners' custodial records.

4.12 Blocking the use of evidence obtained through torture

One of the commonest purposes of torture is to obtain confessions or other evidence which can be used in criminal proceedings. If the use of such evidence can be effectively excluded, the motivation for obtaining it will disappear and the use of torture should diminish accordingly.

This reasoning lies behind the elaboration in international standards of a safeguard designed specifically to tackle the problem. It is formulated in Article 15 of the Convention against Torture as follows:

> "Each State Party shall ensure that any statement which is established to have been made as a result of torture shall not be invoked as evidence in any proceedings, except against a person accused of torture as evidence that the statement was made."

The prohibition in Article 15 refers not only to self-incriminating statements introduced in criminal proceedings but also to statements of any kind introduced as evidence in "any proceedings", where such statements are established to have been made under torture. Although Article 15 refers only to torture, Article 12 of the Declaration against Torture also prohibits the use of statements made as a result of ill-treatment other than torture.

The Human Rights Committee has stated that the use or admissibility in judicial proceedings of statements or confessions obtained through torture or "other prohibited treatment" should be prohibited by law[87] and that – as regards self-incriminating statements – the law should prohibit the use of statements obtained through torture, ill-treatment, acts which fail to respect the human dignity of prisoners or "any other form of compulsion":

> "In considering this safeguard [the prohibition of self-incrimination] the provisions of article 7 and article 10, paragraph 1 [of the ICCPR], should be borne in mind. In order to compel the accused to confess or to testify against himself, frequently methods which violate these provisions are used. The law should require that evidence provided by means of such methods or any other form of compulsion is wholly unacceptable."[88]

Similarly, the Committee against Torture has stated that "the existence, in procedural legislation, of detailed provisions on the inadmissibility of unlawfully obtained confessions and other tainted evidence" is "[o]ne of the essential means in preventing torture".[89]

When there is reason to suspect that evidence obtained through torture is being used, what should the officials involved in the proceedings do? This question is beginning to be addressed in international standards. The standards relating to prosecutors are the most explicit. Article 16 of the UN Guidelines on the Role of Prosecutors states:

> "When prosecutors come into possession of evidence against suspects that they know or believe on reasonable grounds was obtained through recourse to unlawful methods, which constitute a grave violation of the suspect's human rights, especially involving

torture or cruel, inhuman or degrading treatment or punishment, or other abuses of human rights, they shall refuse to use such evidence against anyone other than those who used such methods, or inform the Court accordingly, and shall take all necessary steps to ensure that those responsible for using such methods are brought to justice."

More broadly, the Committee against Torture has recommended that "all evidence obtained directly or indirectly by torture be strictly prevented from reaching the cognizance of the deciding judges in all judicial proceedings".[90]

When at any time in the course of a judicial proceeding it is alleged that a statement was made under torture or ill-treatment[91] or when a judge otherwise has reason to suspect that evidence was obtained through torture or ill-treatment, a separate hearing should be held before such evidence is admitted. Amnesty International believes that if the hearing determines that a statement was not made voluntarily, it should be excluded as evidence, except as evidence against those accused of using coercion to obtain the statement.[92]

As recommended by the Special Rapporteur on torture, "Prosecutors and judges should not require conclusive proof of physical torture or ill-treatment (much less final conviction of an accused perpetrator) before deciding not to rely as against the detainee on confessions or information alleged to have been obtained by such treatment; indeed, the burden of proof should be on the State to demonstrate the absence of coercion."[93]

Jordan: Rejecting evidence obtained under torture

Badr Ramadan Sha'th was arrested in Amman, Jordan in June 2000. After being held incommunicado for nine days in the Criminal Investigation Department of the police, he signed a confession to having participated in two murders together with a friend who had since committed suicide. At his trial, he retracted the confession and claimed he had been tortured. He was nevertheless convicted and sentenced to death. Amnesty International members sent Urgent Action appeals to the Prime Minister and the Minister of Justice calling for a retrial and expressing concern at the reports of torture.

On appeal, the Court of Cassation sent the case back for retrial because of procedural irregularities. At the retrial, a police officer testified that he had heard Badr Ramadan Sha'th screaming and had seen him in a state indicating he had been beaten. The officer concluded from this that he had been subjected to physical force during his interrogation which had resulted in his confession. Noting that his confession was inconsistent with other evidence which did not point to his guilt, and taking note of a medical report of bruising resulting from an injury which must have occurred during his initial detention, the court acquitted him in November 2001.

In February 2002, however, Amnesty International learned that the case had been sent for retrial again, and the decision to acquit was upheld. At the time of writing, the case was pending before the Court of Cassation following an appeal made by the prosecution.

If there are reasonable grounds to believe that torture or ill-treatment was inflicted, either during interrogation or in the course of judicial proceedings, the judge should ensure that a prompt and impartial investigation is initiated, in accordance with Articles 12, 13 and 16 of the Convention against Torture and Articles 8 and 9 of the Declaration against Torture.[94] The supposed victim should have access to independent doctors and lawyers for assistance in securing the evidence needed to back up the claim.

Principle 27 of the Body of Principles on Detention states: "Non-compliance with these principles in obtaining evidence shall be taken into account in determining the admissibility of such evidence against a detained or imprisoned person." This principle opens the possibility of challenging the introduction of evidence on grounds that it was obtained in connection with violations of other safeguards set out in the Body of Principles on Detention. Such violations could include irregularities in the course of arrest (Principles 9, 12), failure to inform the prisoner of the reasons for arrest, of the charges against him or her or of his or her rights (Principles 10, 13), failure to give the prisoner an opportunity to be heard promptly by a judicial or other authority (Principle 11), denial of the right to legal assistance (Principles 17-18), denial of contact with the outside world for more than a few days (Principle 15), the use of violence, threats or methods of interrogation which impair the prisoner's judgment or capacity of decision or taking "undue advantage of the situation" to compel statements (Principle 21), and the failure to keep records of interrogation sessions (Principle 23).

© AI

Overcrowding in a Brazilian prison: *Casa de Detenção Dr. José Mário Alves da Silva* (better known as *Urso Branco*), in Porto Velho, Rondônia state, April 2002. An Amnesty International delegation found 23 prisoners confined 24 hours a day in very hot weather in an airless cell measuring 30 square metres. A hose was used to provide brackish water for an hour each day for drinking, washing and cleaning the single open toilet. Rubbish and leftover food were deposited outside the cell.

Chapter 5: Conditions
of detention

5.1 Introduction

"During his visit to Butyrskaya, the Special Rapporteur entered one
of the large cells in which there were 83 persons. Despite having
read critical reports and having received first-hand accounts of the
conditions of detention in Moscow's Butyrskaya and Matrosskaya
Tishina No. 1, the Special Rapporteur was unprepared for the
appalling reality he encountered there. When the door to such a
general cell is opened, one is hit by a blast of hot, dark, stinking
(sweat, urine, faeces) gas that passes for air. These general cells may
have one filthy sink and a tap, from which water does not always
emerge, near a ground-level toilet around which the inmates may
drape some cloth for a minimum of privacy and to conceal the
squalor of the installation. There is virtually no daylight from
covered or barred windows, through which only a small amount of
fresh air can penetrate. Artificial lighting is weak and not always
functioning...

"Due to the overcrowding in the general cells visited at both
Butyrskaya and Matrosskaya Tishina No. 1, there is insufficient
room for everyone to lie down, sit down or even stand up at the same
time. At Matrosskaya Tishina No. 1 the Special Rapporteur saw
some detainees lying on the floor underneath the lowest bunk
(about 50cm above the floor). All the detainees in these cells suffer
from swollen feet and legs due to the fact that they must stand for
extensive periods of time. The inmates tend to be half-clothed and

are even stripped to their undershorts (at least in the summer, when the Special Rapporteur visited). Their bodies are perspiring and nothing can dry due to the humidity. Despite the existence of some medical and even hospital facilities (often without sufficient medicines), the general cells are the obverse of a hospital regime: they are disease incubators. Festering sores and boils abound; most if not all inmates suffer from skin diseases that cause pervasive itching...

"The Special Rapporteur would need the poetic skills of a Dante or the artistic skills of a Bosch adequately to describe the infernal conditions he found in these cells. The senses of smell, touch, taste and sight are repulsively assailed. The conditions are cruel, inhuman and degrading; they are torturous. To the extent that suspects are confined there to facilitate the investigation by breaking their wills with a view to eliciting confessions and information, they can properly be described as being subjected to torture."

Report of the UN Special Rapporteur on torture on a visit to the Russian Federation in 1994[1]

Around the world, great numbers of prisoners are held in conditions which are damaging to their physical and mental well-being and can constitute threats to health and life. Conditions such as overcrowding, poor sanitation, lack of food and medicines and denial of contact with families and friends fall short of UN standards for the treatment of prisoners. Singly or in combination, the worst conditions can constitute ill-treatment or even torture.

Amnesty International's survey of its research files from 1997 to mid-2000 found reports of cruel, inhuman or degrading conditions of detention in 90 countries. Such conditions were widespread in over 50 countries.

Many prisoners are serving sentences imposed by courts as penalties for criminal offences. Many others are held awaiting trial. Others, such as asylum-seekers and political detainees, are held in administrative detention without any charge having been lodged against them. Still others are prisoners of war.

As detailed in this chapter, international standards encourage states to avoid holding people in custody where possible. Despite this, in many countries the current trend is to increase the use of detention and incarceration, often in response to hardening public attitudes towards crime. Pre-trial detention becomes automatic, even where the accused person poses little or no risk to society. Sentences of imprisonment provided by law and imposed by courts become ever longer. Those behind bars are quickly forgotten. Accused prisoners who have not been found guilty of any crime languish for years awaiting trial. Prison services suffer from low budgets, making it difficult to pay adequate salaries to custodial staff or to provide proper facilities. Inadequate funding, staffing, training and administration leads to corruption and to situations where sections of prisons are effectively controlled by violent and dangerous prisoners.[2]

Deprivation of liberty entails curtailing an important human right – the right to personal liberty. This right should not be curtailed except where necessary and justified: arbitrary detention is prohibited under international law (see section

4.2.1 of this manual). Moreover, being deprived of one's liberty does not mean forfeiting other human rights. As stated in the UN Basic Principles for the Treatment of Prisoners (Principle 5):

> "Except for those limitations that are demonstrably necessitated by the fact of incarceration, all prisoners shall retain the human rights and fundamental freedoms set out in the Universal Declaration of Human Rights, and, where the State concerned is a party, the International Covenant on Economic, Social and Cultural Rights, and the International Covenant on Civil and Political Rights and the Optional Protocol thereto, as well as such other rights as are set out in other United Nations covenants."

For prisoners as for everyone, the right to life and the prohibition of torture and ill-treatment must be respected at all times. Furthermore, Article 10(1) of the International Covenant on Civil and Political Rights (ICCPR) states:

> "All persons deprived of their liberty shall be treated with humanity and with respect for the inherent dignity of the human person."[3]

The UN Human Rights Committee has referred to the requirement in Article 10(1) of the ICCPR as "a fundamental and universally applicable rule"[4] and "a norm of general international law not subject to derogation" under the ICCPR.[5] According to the Human Rights Committee,

> "Article 10, paragraph 1, imposes on States parties a positive obligation towards persons who are particularly vulnerable because of their status as persons deprived of liberty, and complements for them the ban on torture or other cruel, inhuman or degrading treatment or punishment contained in article 7 of the Covenant. Thus, not only may persons deprived of their liberty not be subjected to treatment that is contrary to article 7, including medical or scientific experimentation, but neither may they be subjected to any hardship or constraint other than that resulting from the deprivation of liberty; respect for the dignity of such persons must be guaranteed under the same conditions as for that of free persons. Persons deprived of their liberty enjoy all the rights set forth in the Covenant, subject to the restrictions that are unavoidable in a closed environment."[6]

Governments which allow cruel, inhuman or degrading conditions of detention to persist are violating their obligations under international law to prohibit torture and ill-treatment and to ensure respect for human dignity. Yet often such conditions could be improved cost free or at very little expense.

In addition to the broad provisions of general human rights treaties, the UN and other intergovernmental organizations have developed comprehensive standards on conditions of detention over the years. In 1955 the UN **Standard Minimum Rules for the Treatment of Prisoners** (Standard Minimum Rules) were adopted, representing "as a whole, the minimum conditions which are accepted as suitable by the United Nations" (para. 2).[7] Most of the rules apply not only to convicted prisoners but to people in pre-trial detention and people held without charge (para. 4(2) and Rule 95).

Since their adoption, successive UN resolutions have called on states to implement the Standard Minimum Rules.[8] Over the years the Standard Minimum Rules have been supplemented by other standards adopted by the UN, including the **Body of Principles for the Protection of All Persons under Any Form of Detention or Imprisonment** (Body of Principles on Detention), as well as standards for the protection of particular groups such as children (see section 5.7 below). On a regional level, the **European Prison Rules,** adopted by the Committee of Ministers of the Council of Europe in 1987, resemble the Standard Minimum Rules but include some new features. Other standards have been articulated by the UN Special Rapporteur on torture and the European Committee for the Prevention of Torture (CPT). The **Special Rapporteur on Prisons and Conditions of Detention in Africa** of the African Commission on Human and Peoples' Rights has made recommendations regarding prison conditions in several countries.[9] The **Organization of American States** is studying the possibility of elaborating an inter-American declaration on the rights and the care of persons deprived of liberty.[10]

Concerning prisoners held in connection with international armed conflicts, the **Third and Fourth Geneva Conventions of 1949** respectively contain detailed provisions on the treatment of prisoners of war, and of interned civilians in occupied territories and aliens in the territory of a party to the

---

Haiti: Improving the treatment of prisoners

Prisons in Haiti were the scene of egregious human rights violations under the dictatorship of the Duvalier family and in the succeeding years of alternating civilian and military rule. Following the restoration of civilian rule in 1994, the authorities removed the prisons from military control and set about creating a prison guard corps in collaboration with the United Nations Development Programme. While improvements to physical facilities have been limited, there has been considerable progress in the administration of prisons and relations with inmates. Prison guards now receive human rights training during their induction, and subsequently their conduct towards detainees is regulated on several levels. Since 1999 a commission of three inspectors with special training in penal matters has been in place to investigate allegations of misconduct by prison guards. In 1999 regulations were published, covering such matters as the provision of food, sanitary conditions, visiting rights, body and cell searches, and dealing with cases where detainees arriving at prisons appear to have been ill-treated while in police custody. New internal disciplinary regulations for prison guards were introduced in 2000. Both these texts have been released in pocket-sized format so that guards can refer to them in their day-to-day work with detainees. Haitian NGOs have been consulted during the process of change, and, at times, in connection with their own investigations of alleged abuses against prisoners. Despite some serious ongoing human rights violations, these measures have resulted in an overall reduction in ill-treatment since the prisons passed from military to civilian control. This reduction is particularly remarkable given that the prison population has nearly tripled since 1995 while the basic budget for prisons has remained unchanged.

conflict. These provisions cover many of the same matters as the Standard Minimum Rules.[11]

Under international standards, a key aim in the treatment of convicted prisoners is rehabilitation. Article 10(3) of the ICCPR states: "The penitentiary system shall comprise treatment of prisoners the essential aim of which shall be their reformation and social rehabilitation." According to the Human Rights Committee, "No penitentiary system should be only retributory; it should essentially seek the reformation and social rehabilitation of the prisoner."[12]

In the 1990s a questionnaire was sent to UN member states on the implementation of the Standard Minimum Rules. The results were reported to the UN Commission on Crime Prevention and Criminal Justice in 1996.[13] The survey (referred to in this chapter as the "1996 UN survey") does not give a comprehensive picture – only 72 countries replied – but its findings give some indication of the extent to which the Standard Minimum Rules were being applied some 40 years after their adoption.

The Human Rights Committee has stated that as the requirement to treat prisoners with humanity and respect for their dignity is a fundamental and universally applicable rule, "the application of this rule, as a minimum, cannot be dependent on the material resources available in the State party".[14] Whatever the resource constraints, it is essential that governments afford people certain basic requirements when they put them behind bars. According to the Human Rights Committee,

> "[C]ertain minimum standards regarding the conditions of detention must be observed regardless of a State party's level of development. These include, in accordance with rules 10, 12, 17, 19 and 20 of the Standard Minimum Rules for the Treatment of Prisoners, minimum floor space and cubic content of air for each prisoner, adequate sanitary facilities, clothing which shall be in no manner degrading or humiliating, provision of a separate bed and provision of food of nutritional value adequate for health and strength. It should be noted that these are minimum requirements which the Committee considers should always be observed, even if economic or budgetary considerations may make compliance with these obligations difficult."[15]

The Special Rapporteur on torture has proposed a radical change in approach to deprivation of liberty, both as a safeguard against torture and as a means of promoting the improvement of conditions of detention:

> "The Special Rapporteur is convinced that there needs to be a radical transformation of assumptions in international society about the nature of deprivation of liberty. The basic paradigm, taken for granted over at least a century, is that prisons, police stations and the like are closed and secret places, with activities inside hidden from public view. The international standards referred to are conceived of as often unwelcome exceptions to the general norm of opacity, merely the occasional ray of light piercing the pervasive darkness. What is needed is to replace the paradigm of opacity by one of transparency. The assumption should be one of open access to all places of deprivation of liberty. Of course, there will have to be regulations to safeguard the security of the institution and

individuals within it, and measures to safeguard their privacy and dignity. But those regulations and measures will be the exception, having to be justified as such; the rule will be openness."[16]

This chapter brings together the main standards on conditions of detention which have been adopted or articulated to date.

Further reading

The Penal Reform International publication *Making Standards Work: An International Handbook on Good Prison Practice* (1995, cited in this chapter as the *"PRI Handbook"*) contains detailed discussions of the provisions of the Standard Minimum Rules and other international standards on the treatment of prisoners. The forthcoming UN manual *Human Rights and Prisons*[17] gives many practical recommendations for ensuring the humane treatment of convicted prisoners and other detainees.

5.2 Reducing the use of custody and imprisonment

"Member States shall develop non-custodial measures within their legal systems to provide other options, thus reducing the use of imprisonment."

United Nations Standard Minimum Rules for Non-custodial Measures (Tokyo Rules), Rule 1.5

Overcrowding is one of the most serious problems in prisons and other places of detention today. In many countries, reducing the number of people held in custody or imprisonment would be the simplest and most economical way of reducing overcrowding and improving conditions of detention.

International standards encourage governments to avoid holding people in custody where possible and to develop alternatives to imprisonment. Pre-trial detention (see below) and the detention of children, asylum-seekers and refugees (see section 5.7) are especially to be avoided.

Article 9(1) of the ICCPR states that no one shall be deprived of liberty "except on such grounds... as are established by law". Detention in the absence of such grounds constitutes arbitrary detention in violation of international law.

As regards pre-trial detention, Article 9(3) of the ICCPR states:

"It shall not be the general rule that persons awaiting trial shall be detained in custody, but release may be subject to guarantees to appear for trial, at any other stage of the judicial proceedings, and, should occasion arise, for execution of the judgement."[18]

The Human Rights Committee has stated: "Pre-trial detention should be an exception and as short as possible."[19] The European Court of Human Rights has stated that pre-trial detention "can be justified in a given case only if there are specific indications of a genuine requirement of public interest which, notwith-standing the presumption of innocence, outweighs the rule of respect for individual liberty".[20] The UN Committee against Torture has stated that holding pre-trial detainees and convicted prisoners for long periods in police stations and other places not adequately equipped for long periods of detention could violate the prohibition of cruel, inhuman or degrading treatment or punishment under the Convention against Torture.[21]

Principle 36 of the Body of Principles on Detention states that the arrest or detention of a person suspected of or charged with a criminal offence pending investigation "shall be carried out only for the purposes of the administration of justice on grounds and under conditions and procedures specified by law". Principle 39 states that except in special cases provided for by law, a person detained on a criminal charge shall be entitled to release pending trial "subject to the conditions that may be imposed in accordance with the law", "unless a judicial or other authority decides otherwise in the interest of the administration of justice".

Rule 6.1 of the **United Nations Standard Minimum Rules for Non-custodial Measures** (Tokyo Rules) states: "Pre-trial detention shall be used as a means of last resort in criminal proceedings, with due regard for the investigation of the alleged offence and for the protection of society and the victim."

The Tokyo Rules contain many other provisions on alternatives to impris-onment. Under Rule 2.5, "[c]onsideration shall be given to dealing with offenders in the community avoiding as far as possible resort to formal proceedings or trial by a court, in accordance with legal safeguards and the rule of law". The Tokyo Rules contain provisions relating to discharging suspected offenders rather than bringing them to trial (Rule 5), providing the courts with a range of sentencing options besides imprisonment (Rule 8) and providing a range of post-sentencing alternatives including work or education release, "half-way houses", parole, remission and pardon (Rule 9). They also cover such matters as the involvement of the community, the supervision of offenders subjected to non-custodial measures and the conditions to be observed by such offenders.

In a similar vein, Article 18 of the UN Guidelines on the Role of Prosecutors states:

> "In accordance with national law, prosecutors shall give due con-sideration to waiving prosecution, discontinuing proceedings conditionally or unconditionally, or diverting criminal cases from the formal justice system, with full respect for the rights of suspect(s) and the victim(s). For this purpose, States should fully explore the possibility of adopting diversion schemes not only to alleviate excessive court loads, but also to avoid the stigmatization of pre-trial detention, indictment and conviction, as well as the possible adverse effects of imprisonment."

The Special Rapporteur on torture has recommended reducing the number of pre-trial detainees to reduce overcrowding in specific situations.[22] The Special Rapporteur on Prisons and Conditions of Detention in Africa also has made specific recommendations to reduce the number of people held behind bars.[23] Many of these ideas are reflected also in a 1999 recommendation of the Council of Europe on prison overcrowding.[24]

5.3 Accommodation

5.3.1 Physical conditions

Rule 10 of the Standard Minimum Rules states: "All accommodation provided for the use of prisoners and in particular all sleeping accommodation shall meet all requirements of health, due regard being paid to climatic conditions and particularly to cubic content of air, minimum floor space, lighting, heating and ventilation." Rule 11 states:

"In all places where prisoners are required to live or work,

"(a) The windows shall be large enough to enable the prisoners to read or work by natural light, and shall be so constructed that they can allow the entrance of fresh air whether or not there is artificial ventilation;

"(b) Artificial light shall be provided sufficient for the prisoners to read or work without injury to eyesight."[25]

Rules 9(1) and 86 of the Standard Minimum Rules provide for prisoners to sleep singly in separate rooms. Rule 9(2) states that "[w]here dormitories are used, they shall be occupied by prisoners carefully selected as being suitable to associate with one another in those conditions". The CPT has, in contrast, acknowledged that "various factors – including those of a cultural nature – can make it preferable in certain countries to provide multi-occupancy accommodation for prisoners rather than individual cells" but has warned that the use of large-capacity dormitories can entail problems such as insufficient facilities, inter-prisoner violence and the difficulty of maintaining control.[26]

The CPT has held that certain levels of overcrowding can amount to inhuman or degrading treatment, either in their own right[27] or in combination with other oppressive aspects of custody. It has recommended that the basic standard of living space for both male and female prisoners should be not less than four square metres per prisoner.[28] It has recommended that prison cells of less than six square metres should be taken out of service[29] and has stated that a dormitory of 60 square metres should never hold more than 12 prisoners.[30] The Committee against Torture has used the word "torture" in referring to solitary confinement in small cells with poor conditions (see section 5.5.5).

In the interest of prisoners' well-being, the authorities should in general try to increase the amount of space in which prisoners can move. There is no agreed universal standard for cell size, and the CPT recommendations may be difficult for some countries to meet.[31] What is essential is that prisoners are never kept in severely overcrowded conditions, or subjected to extremes of heat or cold.[32] Prisoners should also be protected from the damp and from the risk of fires, floods and earthquakes.

5.3.2 Separation of categories of prisoners

Article 10(2)(a) of the ICCPR states: "Accused persons shall, save in exceptional circumstances, be segregated from convicted persons..." According to the Human

Rights Committee, the segregation of accused people "is required in order to emphasize their status as unconvicted persons who at the same time enjoy the right to be presumed innocent as stated in article 14, paragraph 2 [of the ICCPR]".[33] The same requirement is stated in the Standard Minimum Rules (Rules 8, 85) and the Body of Principles on Detention (Principle 8). The European Prison Rules state that untried prisoners "shall not be put in contact with convicted prisoners against their will" (Rules 7, 85).

Female prisoners should be kept separate from male prisoners, and in most cases children should be kept separate from adults (see section 5.7.2). Political prisoners, prisoners of war in international armed conflicts,[34] detained asylum-seekers and other immigration detainees should be kept separate from people held in criminal cases. Other classes of prisoners also should be held separately where this is necessary to prevent violence and the spread of infectious disease, to maintain discipline and to facilitate rehabilitation.

Rule 8 of the Standard Minimum Rules states: "The different categories of prisoners shall be kept in separate institutions or parts of institutions taking account of their sex, age, criminal record, the legal reason for their detention and the necessities of their treatment." It provides for the separation of civil prisoners from people imprisoned for a criminal offence.

Rules 67 and 68 of the Standard Minimum Rules provide for the classification of prisoners and the separation of different classes. Under Rule 67, the purposes of classification are:

> "(a) To separate from others those prisoners who, by reason of their criminal records or bad characters, are likely to exercise a bad influence;

> "(b) To divide the prisoners into classes in order to facilitate their treatment with a view to their social rehabilitation."

In addition to the criteria specified in the Standard Minimum Rules, Rule 7 of the European Prison Rules recommends, when separating prisoners, taking into account whether they are sick, their mental condition, whether they are first offenders or habitual offenders, and whether they are serving short or long sentences.

5.3.3 Location

Prisoners should normally be held near their homes if possible. Proximity makes it easier for people outside to take steps to protect a prisoner from ill-treatment. Separations of long distances make it hard for prisoners to maintain contact with their families.[35]

Principle 20 of the Body of Principles on Detention states: "If a detained or imprisoned person so requests, he shall if possible be kept in a place of detention or imprisonment reasonably near his usual place of residence."

5.3.4 Sanitation, hygiene, clothing and beds

Places of custody need to maintain proper standards of sanitation and hygiene to avoid disease. Inadequate sanitary facilities can constitute ill-treatment in some circumstances.[36]

Standards for sanitation, hygiene, clothing and beds are set out in the Standard Minimum Rules. Rule 12 states: "The sanitary installations shall be adequate to enable every prisoner to comply with the needs of nature when necessary and in a clean and decent manner."[37] Rule 14 states: "All parts of an institution regularly used by prisoners shall be properly maintained and kept scrupulously clean at all times." Rule 13 calls for the provision of adequate bathing and shower installations.[38] Rule 15 calls for the provision of water for washing and of toilet articles.

Rule 17(1) calls for the provision of suitable clothing, which "shall in no manner be degrading or humiliating". Rule 17(2) states that clothing shall be "clean and kept in proper condition". Rule 19 states that prisoners shall be provided with separate beds and clean bedding.

Rwanda: Urgent action to relieve conditions of detention

The government which took power in Rwanda in July 1994 announced its intention to bring to justice all those who had ordered or taken part in the recent genocide. Suspects detained by the authorities began pouring into prisons and other places of detention which lacked the space or facilities to cope with such large numbers. By the end of 1994 some 16,000 people had been detained in connection with the conflict, and by the end of 1995 there were more than 63,000 detainees. This led to severe overcrowding of up to five people per square metre and major health problems such as dysentery, oedema (swelling) and respiratory problems, placing the lives of thousands of prisoners at risk. As the authorities could not ensure proper hygiene, the International Committee of the Red Cross (ICRC), which had been present in the country throughout the crisis, organized the prisoners into hygiene brigades, providing brooms, detergent and rubber boots and impressing on the prisoners that they must take strict responsibility for their hygiene if they were to survive. The ICRC also repaired prison water supplies, improved sanitary installations, and provided food to the extent that the authorities were unable to feed the prisoners. Contrary to fears, the outbreak of epidemics was avoided. By late 1995 the prison mortality rate had dropped to about that of the rest of the population and all detainees had regular access to food and water, although overcrowding remains a serious problem.[39]

5.4 Other aspects of treatment

5.4.1 Food and drink

Rule 20(1) of the Standard Minimum Rules states:

> "Every prisoner shall be provided by the administration at the usual hours with food of nutritional value adequate for health and strength, of wholesome quality and well prepared and served."

The standards for food in the European Prison Rules are more detailed. Rule 25(1) of the European Prison Rules states:

> "In accordance with the standards laid down by the health authorities, the administration shall provide the prisoners at the normal times with food which is suitably prepared and presented, and which satisfies in quality and quantity the standards of dietetics and modern hygiene and takes into account their age, health, the nature of their work, and, so far as possible, religious or cultural requirements."

Rule 20(2) of the Standard Minimum Rules states:

> "Drinking water shall be available to every prisoner whenever he needs it."[40]

The European Commission of Human Rights has held that lack of access to food and water can constitute inhuman or degrading treatment.[41]

In practice, many countries do not provide prisoners with adequate food and drinking water. It is often the case that prisoners are expected to be fed by their families, posing great difficulties for those who have no family or none nearby, and placing a strain on families' time and resources.[42] In some places there is no provision for feeding people held in police stations.

5.4.2 Medical care and the role of health professionals

The European Court of Human Rights has stated that "the authorities are under an obligation to protect the health of persons deprived of liberty" and that "[t]he lack of appropriate medical treatment" may amount to ill-treatment.[43]

Standards for the provision of medical care are set out in the Standard Minimum Rules. Rule 22 states: "At every institution there shall be available the services of at least one qualified medical officer who should have some knowledge of psychiatry." It also states: "The services of a qualified dental officer shall be available to every prisoner." Rule 22 also provides for the transfer of sick prisoners who require specialist treatment to specialized institutions or civil hospitals.[44] Rule 52 provides for a medical officer to reside at the place of detention or to visit it daily and to live near enough to be able to attend without delay in emergencies. Rule 82 provides for the medical treatment of mentally ill prisoners.[45]

Rule 24 states: "The medical officer shall see and examine every prisoner as soon as possible after his admission and thereafter as necessary, with a view particularly to the discovery of physical or mental illness and the taking of all necessary measures; the segregation of prisoners suspected of infectious or contagious conditions; the noting of physical or mental defects which might hamper rehabilitation, and the determination of the physical capacity of every prisoner for work." (See section 4.7.)

Rule 25 states:

> "(1) The medical officer shall have the care of the physical and mental health of the prisoners and should daily see all sick prisoners, all who complain of illness, and any prisoner to whom his attention is specially directed.[46]
>
> "(2) The medical officer shall report to the director whenever he considers that a prisoner's physical or mental health has been or will

be injuriously affected by continued imprisonment or by any condition of imprisonment."

Rule 26 provides for the medical officer to inspect and advise the director on food, hygiene, sanitation, heating, lighting and ventilation and for the director to act on the medical officer's recommendations.

Principle 24 of the Body of Principles on Detention states that "medical care and treatment shall be provided whenever necessary [to detained or imprisoned people]. This care and treatment shall be provided free of charge."

The CPT, in its 3rd General Report, has developed detailed criteria for health care in prisons. They cover such matters as access to medical care, the provision of psychiatric care, patients' consent and confidentiality, the prevention of transmissible diseases, and the professional competence and independence of medical staff. In the CPT's view, "prisoners are entitled to the same level of medical care as persons living in the community at large. This principle is inherent in the fundamental rights of the individual."[47]

The evolution of international standards relating to the medical care of prisoners has been paralleled by the elaboration of ethical principles for health professionals in their relations with prisoners (see section 8.6). The **Declaration of Tokyo**, adopted by the World Medical Association in 1975, states that doctors shall not "countenance, condone or participate in" torture or ill-treatment, while the UN **Principles of Medical Ethics relevant to the Role of Health Personnel, particularly Physicians, in the Protection of Prisoners and Detainees against Torture and Other Cruel, Inhuman or Degrading Treatment or Punishment**, adopted by the UN General Assembly in 1982, states: "It is a gross contravention of medical ethics, as well as an offence under applicable international instruments, for health personnel, particularly physicians, to engage, actively or passively, in acts which constitute participation in, complicity in, incitement to or attempts to commit torture or other cruel, inhuman or degrading treatment or punishment." Under the latter instrument, it is also a contravention of medical ethics for health personnel, including physicians, to apply their knowledge and skills in order to assist in the interrogation of prisoners and detainees in a manner that may adversely affect "the physical or mental health or condition" of such prisoners; to certify the fitness of prisoners for any form of treatment or punishment that may adversely affect their physical or mental health; or to participate in any procedure for restraining a prisoner unless the procedure is determined "in accordance with purely medical criteria" to be necessary for the protection of the physical or mental health or the safety of the prisoner or others "and presents no hazard to his physical or mental health" (Principles 4, 5). Statements precluding participation in torture or ill-treatment have also been adopted by professional associations of psychiatrists[48] and nurses.[49]

There is no UN standard concerning the forcible feeding of prisoners who are on a hunger strike. According to the Declaration of Tokyo, a prisoner who refuses nourishment should not be artificially fed if a doctor judges that he or she is capable of forming an unimpaired and rational judgment concerning the consequences of refusal of nourishment (Article 4). A more elaborate set of guidelines for doctors responsible for the health of hunger-strikers can be found in the **Declaration of Malta on Hunger Strikers**, adopted by the World Medical Association in 1991 and editorially revised in 1992.

In addition to the standards described above, every prisoner should have a medical file which follows them throughout their time in custody.

Further reading

Amnesty International, 2000, *Ethical Codes and Declarations Relevant to the Health Professions...* is a compilation of UN and professional codes and statements, including those cited above, many of which are relevant to the role of health professionals in places where people are deprived of their liberty.

5.4.3 Exercise, recreation and other facilities

Standards regarding exercise, recreation, education and other features of life in detention are set out in the Standard Minimum Rules and other instruments. In particular, Rule 21(2) of the Standard Minimum Rules states: "Every prisoner who is not employed in outdoor work shall have at least one hour of suitable exercise in the open air daily if the weather permits."[50]

Rule 40 of the Standard Minimum Rules provides for libraries. Rules 41 and 42 provide for religious services, pastoral visits and the possession by prisoners of religious books. Rule 90 states that untried prisoners shall be able to procure books, newspapers, writing materials and other means of occupation at their own expense or at the expense of a third party.

Rule 66 provides for programs for rehabilitating convicted offenders and preparing them for reintegration into society, including "education, vocational guidance and training, social casework, employment counselling, physical development and strengthening of moral character". Rules 71-76 concern work by convicted prisoners and remuneration for work. Rules 77-78 provide for education and for recreational and cultural activities.

The CPT has cited the standard of at least one hour's exercise in the open air each day and has emphasized that "all prisoners without exception (including those undergoing cellular confinement as a punishment) should be offered the possibility to take outdoor exercise daily". The CPT has also stated that "[a] satisfactory program of activities (work, education, sport, etc.) is of crucial importance for the well-being of prisoners", including both convicted prisoners and those awaiting trial.[51]

5.4.4 Contact with the outside world

As stated in section 4.5, a key measure for the prevention of torture is for prisoners to have access to relatives, lawyers and doctors without delay after being deprived of their liberty and regularly thereafter. Contact with the outside is essential not only as a safeguard against torture but in order to respect prisoners' right to family and private life.[52] Contact with the outside helps to promote prisoners' general well-being and – for convicted prisoners – their rehabilitation and ultimate reintegration into society.[53]

Concerning relatives, Rule 37 of the Standard Minimum Rules states: "Prisoners shall be allowed under necessary supervision to communicate with their family and reputable friends at regular intervals, both by correspondence and by receiving visits." Principle 19 of the Body of Principles on Detention has a similar provision for visits and correspondence with family members and also states that prisoners "shall be given adequate opportunity to communicate with the outside world, subject to reasonable conditions and restrictions as specified by law or lawful regulations".

The responses in the 1996 UN survey cited in section 5.1 indicated wide differences in practice concerning visits to prisoners (para. 58). Some countries allowed more than six visits per month; others allowed one per month and a few allowed less than one per month.

The CPT has deemed a single visit of one hour per month unsatis-factory.[54] It has stated:

> "It is very important for prisoners to be able to maintain reasonably good contact with the outside world. Above all, a prisoner must be given the means of safeguarding his relationships with his family and close friends, in particular with his wife/partner and children. The continuation of such relationships is of critical importance for all the interested parties, and especially for the social rehabilitation of a prisoner. The guiding principle should be the promotion of contact with the outside world...".[55]

The CPT has also spoken in favour of allowing intimate visits. It has stated that "granting prisoners the right to receive extended unsupervised visits in order to maintain family and personal (including sexual) relations would be a

---

Brazil: Practical reforms for prisoners

Some smaller prisons in Brazil, mainly those run by charitable foundations, have instituted practical reforms which show that despite lack of staff and other resources, it is possible to administer a prison based on principles of rehabilitation of the offender and respect for fundamental human rights. One such prison – the *Penitenciária Juiz Plácido de Souza*, in Caruaru, Pernambuco state – was visited by an Amnesty International delegation in 1998 and again in 2002. The delegation found that although the prison was overcrowded, with over 300 inmates in a space built to accommodate 90, the prison administration had managed to reduce tension among the prisoners by introducing programs aimed at rehabilitation and by ensuring that open dialogue was maintained between the director, the staff and the inmates. Most inmates worked in the prison producing goods for sale or to earn remission, and education programs had been established which included basic literacy classes and computer training. Family visits were encouraged, with programs of activities for inmates and their children. Although the prison had no staff doctor, the director, who was himself a doctor, often provided these services where possible, or in extreme cases intervened with the authorities to ensure the provision of medical aid. These improvements resulted in a significant decline in ill-treatment, deaths in custody and inter-prisoner violence.

commendable step, provided that such visits took place in conditions which respected human dignity".[56]

In the interest of enabling prisoners to maintain healthy relationships with their families and close friends, the physical setting for visits should be as relaxed and supervision as unobtrusive as possible, allowing physical contact, except where there is a high security risk. Communication will be much better if prisoners and their visitors are sitting at a table with a guard nearby than if they are separated by bullet-proof glass and can only speak to each other through microphones.[57]

5.5 Discipline and security

Rule 27 of the Standard Minimum Rules states: "Discipline and order shall be maintained with firmness, but with no more restriction than is necessary for safe custody and well-ordered community life." There are also specific standards which apply to various aspects of discipline and the maintenance of order and security in places of detention and imprisonment.

5.5.1 Searches

Searches of prisoners and their visitors should be as unobtrusive as possible, strictly limited to security needs and avoiding humiliation. Sometimes guards search visitors in a deliberately humiliating way or damage their property, causing chagrin to the prisoners, who may feel partly responsible for what has been done to those who have come to see them. Sometimes body searches of prisoners or their visitors are conducted with the deliberate purpose of humiliation. Such practices should be forbidden.

As noted in section 4.10, the CPT has emphasized "that persons deprived of their liberty should only be searched by staff of the same gender and that any search which requires an inmate to undress should be conducted out of the sight of custodial staff of the opposite gender".[58] Guidelines for the involvement of doctors in body searches can be found in the **Statement on Body Searches of Prisoners**, adopted by the World Medical Association in 1993.[59]

5.5.2 Use of force

As discussed in section 6.3, the UN Code of Conduct for Law Enforcement Officials and the UN Basic Principles on the Use of Force and Firearms by Law Enforcement Officials establish that force should be used in law enforcement only when strictly necessary, that the use of force should not be disproportionate to the legitimate objective to be achieved, and that firearms should not be used except as an extreme measure in a restricted range of situations. These standards are applicable to the use of force in places of detention, as any legitimate use of force by guards there would be in connection with a law enforcement function.

The Standard Minimum Rules also contain provisions on the use of force by prison officers. Rule 54 states:

"**(1) Officers of the institutions shall not, in their relations with the prisoners, use force except in self-defence or in cases of attempted escape, or active or passive physical resistance to an order based on** law or regulations. Officers who have recourse to force must use no more than is strictly necessary and must report the incident immediately to the director of the institution.

"(2) Prison officers shall be given special physical training to enable them to restrain aggressive prisoners.

"(3) Except in special circumstances, staff performing duties which bring them into direct contact with prisoners should not be armed. Furthermore, staff should in no circumstances be provided with arms unless they have been trained in their use."[60]

In a case in which prisoners were beaten by prison staff after refusing to submit to a search procedure, the European Court of Human Rights found that the prisoners had been subjected to ill-treatment in violation of Article 3 of the European Convention on Human Rights. The Court reiterated the principle that "in respect of a person deprived of his liberty, any recourse to physical force which has not been made strictly necessary by his own conduct diminishes human dignity and is in principle an infringement of the right set forth in Article 3 of the Convention" (see section 3.4) and stated that it applied to everyone deprived of liberty, including people held in prisons.[61]

Excessive force resulting in loss of life would generally constitute a violation of the right to life.[62]

5.5.3 Restraint techniques and devices

Law enforcement officials frequently need instruments of restraint to control dangerous prisoners or to prevent prisoners escaping while being taken from one place to another. But instruments of restraint are open to abuse. If improperly used they can be painful and can cause injury or even death. Their use can be degrading. They can be used to inflict torture or as an adjunct to torture. Some instruments and techniques of restraint are such that their use is inherently cruel, inhuman or degrading.[63]

Amnesty International has recorded many cases in which instruments of restraint have been used when there was no genuine security need, and where a humane approach to the prisoners would have dictated the removal of the restraint. Dying prisoners have been held in restraints. Women prisoners have been shackled while in labour. Pregnant women have been shackled at their wrists, ankles and waists, risking injury to themselves and their unborn children if they fall, as they cannot use their hands to protect their bodies.[64]

Rule 33 of the Standard Minimum Rules states:

"Instruments of restraint, such as handcuffs, chains, irons and strait-jackets, shall never be applied as a punishment. Furthermore, chains or irons shall not be used as restraints. Other instruments of restraint shall not be used except in the following circumstances:

(a) As a precaution against escape during a transfer, provided that they shall be removed when the prisoner appears before a judicial or administrative authority;[65]

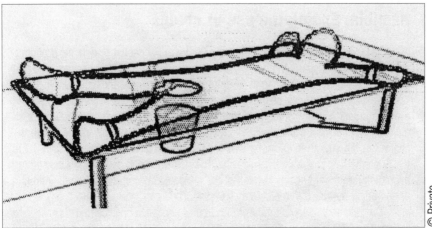

Diagram of a Chinese "tiger bed" or shackle board. Prisoners are attached to the board with their arms and legs spreadeagled. A hole in the centre of the board allows evacuation of urine and excrement. Reports from the early 1990s described how women under sentence of death were kept shackled in this way for months awaiting execution. Fellow prisoners, who had to feed and wash the shackled women and help them defecate, reported that after one week on the board, the women were unable to stand without assistance. Some prisoners kept shackled to the board reportedly became mentally disturbed.

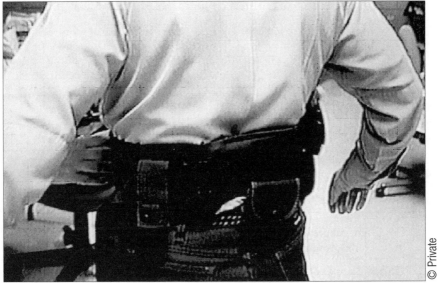

Electro-shock stun belt fitted at a county sheriff's office, USA, 1999. The belt, which is activated by remote control, contains a power pack and electrodes which are attached to the wearer's back near the kidneys. The wearer is under the constant fear of a severe shock being administered at any moment, for reasons over which he or she may have no control. Amnesty International believes that the use of the electro-shock stun belt is inherently cruel, inhuman and degrading (see section 5.5.3).

Namibia: Ending the use of chains

In Namibia, lawyers at the Legal Assistance Centre in the capital, Windhoek, brought a case against the prison authorities on behalf of a group of untried prisoners who had been held in chains for four months or more since their escape and recapture in 1997. Because of the shortness of the chains it was difficult to walk and impossible to exercise properly; one prisoner said that he found it hard to sleep with the chains on and that he could not shower because it was hard to remove one's trousers with the chains on. Shortly after the case was lodged, the chains were removed. In 1999 the Supreme Court of Namibia ruled that the use of chains or leg-irons constituted degrading treatment in contravention of the prohibition of torture and cruel, inhuman or degrading treatment in the country's Constitution.

The judgment stated: "Whatever the circumstances the practice to use chains and leg-irons on human beings is a humiliating experience which reduces the person placed in irons to the level of a hobbled animal whose mobility is limited so that it cannot stray. It is furthermore still a strong reminder of days gone by when people of this continent were carted away in bondage to be sold like chattels. To be continuously in chains or leg-irons and not to be able to properly clean oneself and the clothes one is wearing sets one apart from other fellow beings and is in itself a humiliating and undignified experience."[66] (See also section 2.4, "USA: Federal action to combat local abuses".)

(b) On medical grounds by direction of the medical officer;

(c) By order of the director, if other methods of control fail, in order to prevent a prisoner from injuring himself or others or from damaging property; in such instances the director shall at once consult the medical officer and report to the higher administrative authority."

Rule 34 states that instruments of restraint "must not be applied for any longer time than is strictly necessary".

In accordance with these rules and with the prohibition of torture and ill-treatment, Amnesty International holds that:

- All law enforcement agencies should introduce strict guidelines on restraint techniques and the use of restraint devices, including handcuffs.[67] Such guidelines should seek to eliminate unnecessary use of restraint devices. The guidelines should cover the situations in which the devices are to be used, the techniques of use, and such matters as the issuance of equipment and documentation of its use.[68] Monitoring mechanisms should be set up to keep the guidelines under review and to ensure that they are adhered to.

- Devices whose use is inherently cruel, inhuman or degrading[69] should be banned from use. These include leg irons,[70] sharp or serrated cuffs[71] and electro-shock stun belts.[72] The manufacture and promotion of such devices should be banned. Dangerous restraint holds should also be banned.[73]

- The practice of chain gangs[74] and the shackling of women while in advanced pregnancy or labour and after delivery[75] should be forbidden.

In addition to these recommendations, Amnesty International has called for an independent and rigorous review of instruments of restraint whose use in practice has revealed a substantial risk of abuse or unwarranted injury.[76]

5.5.4 Disciplinary punishments

Rule 31 of the Standard Minimum Rules states:

> "Corporal punishment, punishment by placing in a dark cell, and all cruel, inhuman or degrading punishments shall be completely prohibited as punishments for disciplinary offences."[77]

Rule 32 sets out medical safeguards that must surround the infliction of punishment by close confinement or reduction of diet or any other punishment that may be prejudicial to the physical or mental health of a prisoner.

The CPT has stated that prisons should have "clear disciplinary procedures" which include prisoners having "a right to be heard on the subject of the offences it is alleged they have committed, and to appeal to a higher authority against any sanctions imposed".[78]

Special considerations may apply to disciplinary punishments imposed on mentally ill prisoners. In the case of *Keenan v. UK,* involving a prisoner known to be a suicide risk who later committed suicide in prison, the European Court of Human Rights held that "[t]he belated imposition on him in those circumstances of a serious disciplinary punishment – seven days' segregation in the punishment block and an additional 28 days to his sentence imposed two weeks after the event and only nine days before his expected date of release – which may well have threatened his physical and moral resistance, is not compatible with the standard of treatment required in respect of a mentally ill person" and that it constituted inhuman and degrading treatment and punishment.[79]

5.5.5 Solitary confinement

Solitary confinement can be cruel, unnecessary and damaging to the physical and mental health of a prisoner. International standards increasingly favour its restriction or elimination.

Article 7 of the UN Basic Principles for the Treatment of Prisoners states: "Efforts addressed to the abolition of solitary confinement as a punishment, or to the restriction of its use, should be undertaken and encouraged."

The Human Rights Committee has stated that "prolonged solitary confinement... may amount to acts prohibited by article 7 [of the ICCPR]".[80] The Human Rights Committee has found violations of the prohibition of torture and ill-treatment and of the obligation to respect human dignity in cases where prisoners had been held in solitary confinement.[81]

The Inter-American Court of Human Rights has held that "prolonged isolation and deprivation of communication" amounts to cruel and inhuman treatment.[82] In the case of *Castillo Petruzzi and others v. Peru*, the Court held that a sentence beginning with a year of continuous solitary confinement constituted cruel, inhuman or degrading treatment in violation of Article 5 of the American Convention on Human Rights.[83] The Committee against Torture, which visited a maximum security detention centre in Peru where leaders of an armed opposition movement were serving long sentences in complete solitary confinement, found that the sensory deprivation and almost total prohibition of communication amounted to torture.[84] The Committee has also used the word "torture" in referring to solitary confinement in small cells with poor conditions.[85]

The Special Rapporteur on torture has stated: "Judges should not have the power to order solitary confinement, other than as a measure in cases of breach of institutional discipline, for more than two days."[86]

The CPT has stated that "a solitary confinement-type regime... can have very harmful consequences for the person concerned. Solitary confinement can, in certain circumstances, amount to inhuman and degrading treatment; in any event, all forms of solitary confinement should be as short as possible."[87] In one instance the CPT found that maximum security prisoners held for periods of as much as a year or more and subject to a regime of isolation in "austere material conditions of detention with little or nothing by way of activity" were subjected to "inhuman treatment".[88]

5.5.6 Preventing inter-prisoner violence

The Special Rapporteur on torture has stated:

> "Countries should take effective measures to prevent prisoner-on-prisoner violence by investigating reports of such violence, prosecuting and punishing those responsible, and offering protective custody to vulnerable individuals, without marginalizing them from the prison population more than necessitated by the needs of protection and without rendering them at further risk of ill-treatment. Training programmes should be considered to sensitize prison officials as to the importance of taking effective steps to prevent and remedy prisoner-on-prisoner abuse and to provide them with the means to do so."[89]

Certain groups of prisoners may be especially at risk of violence from others. These include members of particular racial, ethnic or national groups, lesbian, gay, bisexual and transgender people and prisoners convicted or suspected of sexual crimes. Where necessary, prisoners especially vulnerable to attack or intimidation should be separated from those likely to attack them, in accordance with the principles on separation of prisoners described above (section 5.3.2). Perpetrators of violence should be punished.

The CPT has stated: "The duty of care which is owed by custodial staff to those in their charge includes the responsibility to protect them from other inmates who wish to cause them harm." According to the CPT,

> "Tackling the phenomenon of inter-prisoner violence requires that prison staff be placed in a position, including in terms of staffing levels, to exercise their authority and their supervisory tasks in an appropriate manner. Prison staff must be alert to signs of trouble and be both resolved and properly trained to intervene when necessary. The existence of positive relations between staff and prisoners... is a decisive factor in this context; this will depend in large measure on staff possessing appropriate interpersonal communication skills."[90]

As recommended by the CPT, any signs of violence noted when a prisoner is medically examined following a violent episode within a prison "should be fully recorded, together with any relevant statements by the prisoner and the doctor's conclusions. Further, this information should be made available to the prisoner".[91]

5.6 Record-keeping

Accurate record-keeping is an essential element of the proper administration of prisons and other places of detention, including police stations and military bases. Official records establish where prisoners are held and who is responsible for them. The existence of official records that are open to review helps to ensure that proper procedures are followed when people are deprived of their liberty and that public officials involved in the treatment of people deprived of liberty can be held accountable for their actions.

The maintenance of records on the admission and release of prisoners is required under Rule 7 of the Standard Minimum Rules. Under Rules 4 and 95, this requirement applies to all categories of prisoners, untried or convicted, including people arrested or imprisoned without charge. Rule 7(1) states:

> "In every place where persons are imprisoned there shall be kept a bound registration book with numbered pages in which shall be entered in respect of each prisoner received:
>
> (a) Information concerning his identity;
>
> (b) The reasons for his commitment and the authority therefor;
>
> (c) The day and hour of his admission and release."[92]

To avoid any tampering with the information, records should be kept in a permanent form such as a bound book with numbered pages, as required under the Standard Minimum Rules. In addition to the items specified above, other information to be kept in prisoners' records should include requests and complaints made by prisoners or on their behalf, and key information about risks to particular prisoners such as serious mental health problems or life-threatening illnesses requiring attention. Instances of legitimate use of force against prisoners or violence by prisoners against guards, interrogators or other prisoners should also be recorded. Evidence of injuries sustained in custody in the absence of any such record would be an indication that these injuries were more likely to be   the result of illegal violence used by officials than of any above-mentioned (but unrecorded) causes.

The requirement of keeping and preserving accurate and complete custodial records and making the information available when required should be incorporated in national laws and regulations. Any breach of these requirements should be punished by appropriate sanctions. (See also section 4.2.5.)

5.7 Standards for particular groups

Alongside the safeguards against torture and ill-treatment in custody for particular groups described in section 4.10, special measures are needed in relation to their conditions of detention. These measures respond to the special situations and needs of such groups.[93]

5.7.1 Women

As stated in section 5.3.2, Rule 8 of the Standard Minimum Rules provides for male and female prisoners to be held in separate premises, while Rule 53 provides for female officers to control the premises for female prisoners and to accompany any male officers who enter there. Rule 23(1) calls for "special accommodation for all necessary pre-natal and post-natal care and treatment" in women's institutions. These rules apply to all prisoners, including people held without charge.

The CPT has developed criteria concerning "Women deprived of their liberty" in its 10th General Report.[94] While emphasizing that "[a]s a matter of principle, women deprived of their liberty should be held in accommodation which is physically separate from that occupied by any men being held at the same establishment", the CPT has welcomed "arrangements for couples (both of whom are deprived of their liberty) to be accommodated together, and/or for some degree of mixed gender association in prisons", "provided that the prisoners involved agree to participate, and are carefully selected and adequately supervised" (para. 24).

The CPT has noted, "Women deprived of their liberty should enjoy access to meaningful activities (work, training, education, sport, etc.) on an equal footing with their male counterparts." It has stated that "depending upon the circumstances, denying women equal access to regime activities could be qualified as degrading treatment" (para. 25).

The CPT has stated that "[t]he specific hygiene needs of women should be addressed in an adequate manner" and that "[t]he failure to provide such basic necessities can amount, in itself, to degrading treatment" (para. 31). Health care should be of an equivalent standard to that in the outside community (para. 32). Also, "Every effort should be made to meet the specific dietary needs of pregnant women prisoners, who should be offered a high protein diet, rich in fresh fruit and vegetables" (para. 26).[95]

5.7.2 Children

Article 37(c) of the Convention on the Rights of the Child states: "Every child deprived of liberty shall be treated with humanity and respect for the inherent dignity of the human person, and in a manner which takes into account the needs of persons of his or her age..."

International standards particularly encourage states to avoid holding children in custody, including pre-trial detention. The older standards also provide for the separation of children from adult prisoners. More recently, the standards have been developed to accommodate the possibility of holding children together with their parents or certain other adults where this is in the child's best interest. This could for example be to help protect them against violence from other children.[96]

Under Article 37(b) of the Convention on the Rights of the Child, "The arrest, detention or imprisonment of a child... shall be used only as a measure of last resort and for the shortest appropriate period of time". Rule 5(2) of the Standard Minimum Rules states that young people should as a rule "not be sentenced to imprisonment". Under Article 2 of the **United Nations Rules for the Protection of Juveniles Deprived of their Liberty**, "Deprivation of the liberty of a juvenile should be a disposition of last resort and for the minimum necessary period and should be limited to exceptional cases", while Article 70 states that "all efforts shall be made to apply alternative measures" to pre-trial detention. Rule 13.2 of the **United Nations Standard Minimum Rules for the Administration of Juvenile Justice** (Beijing Rules) states: "Whenever possible, detention pending trial shall be replaced by alternative measures, such as close supervision, intensive care or placement with a family or in an educational setting or home."

Under Article 10 of the ICCPR, "Accused juvenile persons shall be separated from adults and brought as speedily as possible for adjudication", and "Juvenile offenders shall be segregated from adults and be accorded treatment appropriate to their age and legal status." The Standard Minimum Rules state that young untried prisoners "shall in principle be detained in separate institutions" from adults (Rule 85; see also Rule 8(d)).[97] The Convention on the Rights of the Child states that "every child deprived of liberty shall be separated from adults unless it is considered in the child's best interest not to do so and shall have the right to maintain contact with his or her family through correspondence and visits, save in exceptional circumstances" (Article 37(c)).[98]

Detailed standards for the treatment of children deprived of their liberty have been set out in the United Nations Rules for the Protection of Juveniles Deprived of their Liberty. These rules apply to people under the age of 18 under "any form of detention or imprisonment or the placement of a person in a public or private custodial setting, from which this person is not permitted to leave at will, by order of any judicial, administrative or other public authority" (Rule 11). They cover such matters as accommodation, activities, medical care, contact with the outside, staffing, discipline, inspection and complaints. Among other things, they state that "closed or solitary confinement or any other punishment that may compromise the physical or mental health of the juvenile concerned" shall be strictly prohibited and that "The reduction of diet and the restriction or denial of contact with family members should be prohibited for any purpose." Also, "Collective sanctions should be prohibited" (Rule 67).

The CPT, in its 9th General Report, has developed criteria for the treatment of "Juveniles deprived of their liberty" (children under the age of 18). They cover safeguards against deliberate ill-treatment and a range of other matters similar to those covered under the United Nations Rules for the Protection of Juveniles Deprived of their Liberty.[99]

5.7.3 Lesbian, gay, bisexual and transgender people

Amnesty International has reported on a range of abuses concerning lesbian, gay, bisexual and transgender prisoners. Guards have tortured or ill-treated them because of their sexual orientation. Lesbian, gay, bisexual and transgender prisoners are at risk of violence from other inmates as well as from prison officials. Guards have encouraged violence against them by other prisoners as a way of regulating the prison environment.[100]

To prevent such abuses, guards should be clearly informed that they must not ill-treat lesbian, gay, bisexual and transgender prisoners or allow other prisoners to do so. Transgender prisoners should normally be held in accommodation based on their preferred gender identity. Rights to intimate visits should be granted on an equal basis to all prisoners, regardless of the sex of their partners. Segregation of prisoners should avoid further marginalizing lesbian, gay, bisexual and transgender people within the prison community or rendering them at further risk of torture or ill-treatment.

5.7.4 Pre-trial detainees

As described above, international standards encourage governments to avoid pre-trial detention (section 5.2) and state that, if detained, accused people shall be separated from convicted prisoners (section 5.3.2). In addition, Article 10(2)(a) of the ICCPR states that accused people deprived of their liberty "shall be subject to separate treatment appropriate to their status as unconvicted persons".

Rules 84-93 of the Standard Minimum Rules contain special provisions for pre-trial detainees. They provide, among other things, that pre-trial detainees shall be allowed to wear their own clothing if it is clean and suitable (Rule 88), to procure reading and writing materials and other suitable means of occupation at their own expense (Rule 90), and to be visited and treated by their own doctor or dentist at their own expense (Rule 91).

Principle 36 of the Body of Principles on Detention refers to detainees suspected of or charged with a criminal offence. It states: "The imposition of restrictions upon such a person which are not strictly required for the purpose of the detention or to prevent hindrance to the process of investigation or the administration of justice, or for the maintenance of security and good order in the place of detention shall be forbidden."[101]

The CPT has recognized that it is not possible to offer as developed a program of activities for remand prisoners as for sentenced prisoners. Nevertheless, the CPT considers that they should be provided with "[a] satisfactory program of activities (work, education, sport, etc.)" in which they can positively spend their time during the "eight hours or more" that they should daily be outside their cells.[102]

5.7.5 Asylum-seekers and other immigration detainees

Asylum-seekers are entitled to protection under international human rights law and international refugee law. Detention of asylum-seekers should be seen primarily as a human rights issue, governed by international human rights standards such as the ICCPR and the Body of Principles on Detention. Detention of asylum-seekers is prohibited unless it can be justified in the individual case and is subject to periodic review by an independent body.[103]

The UN High Commissioner for Refugees (UNHCR) has also made statements on the undesirability of detaining asylum-seekers. In its Conclusion 44 on the detention of refugees and asylum-seekers, adopted in 1986, the Executive Committee of the UNHCR stated that the detention of refugees and asylum-seekers "should normally be avoided" and that "[i]f necessary, detention may be resorted to only on grounds prescribed by law" for one or another of certain specified purposes. The Executive Committee also stressed that

> "[C]onditions of detention of refugees and asylum-seekers must be humane. In particular, refugees and asylum-seekers shall, whenever possible, not be accommodated with persons detained as common

Japan: Action for detained asylum-seekers

In a crack-down beginning in the early 1990s, many foreigners living in Japan were arrested for overstaying and held in detention centres pending deportation. Ill-treatment was rife, but the secrecy surrounding detention and imprisonment in Japan meant that little information reached the public. In two cases which came to light when the victims sought redress, Tao Yaping, a Chinese woman, and Amjadi Khorasani Muhammad Meshdi, an Iranian man, suffered serious injuries as a result of severe beatings. Amjadi Khorasani Muhammad Meshdi had also been held in solitary confinement for two weeks with his arms handcuffed behind his back, and compelled to eat like an animal using only his mouth.

Other abuses reported since then have included sexual harassment, the punitive and excessive use of measures such as special "protection cells", other humiliating treatment such as handcuffing at all times, even during mealtimes and defecation, and numerous cases of injuries resulting from beatings, in some instances resulting in death.

In 1994 a young guard in an immigration detention centre near Tokyo was so disturbed by the brutality of the guards that he quit his job after four months and reported what he had seen to his former teacher, Takahashi Tohru, who was a member of a small group of people concerned about the plight of refugees and migrants in Japan. The information provided by his former student motivated Takahashi Tohru and his associates to develop their group into a network, the Immigration Review Task Force (IRTF), to coordinate research and action by lawyers, academics, concerned members of the *Diet* (Japan's parliament), NGOs, and ordinary citizens. By 2000 it comprised more than 90 organizations, including community groups of refugees and immigrants, and 350 individuals.

Since the mid-1990s, when the IRTF began sustained and coordinated work, it has worked with sympathetic journalists to obtain exposure of the issue in the media. This has raised public awareness and increased pressure on the authorities to take action. Lawyers from the network are now allowed access to immigration detention centres to provide legal advice to their clients, which has on occasion enabled them also to become aware of other detainees in need of advice and assistance. The network's lawyers also travel abroad to assist deportees who were ill-treated in detention to seek compensation in the Japanese courts.

There also appears to have been a significant improvement in the treatment of detainees. Despite the improved availability of means to lodge complaints, there are now fewer reports of beatings, excessive handcuffings and other abuses, although the general regime of detention continues to be severe. Where complaints have been made, some former detainees have been awarded compensation in the courts, and a few guards have been subjected to disciplinary sanctions, although to date there have been no known prosecutions.

criminals, and shall not be located in areas where their physical safety is endangered."[104]

In 1999 the UNHCR issued Revised Guidelines on Applicable Criteria and Standards relating to the Detention of Asylum-Seekers. The Guidelines state that the detention of asylum-seekers is "inherently undesirable".[105] They elaborate on permissible reasons for detention and set out a series of alternatives to detention, with special provisions concerning the detention of women, children, unaccompanied elderly people, people with mental or physical disabilities and trauma or torture victims. They state that, if detained, asylum-seekers should be entitled to minimum procedural guarantees including being informed of the right to legal counsel and being able to contact and be contacted by the local UNHCR office, available national refugee bodies or other agencies and an advocate, and being able to communicate with them in private. The Guidelines also set out standards for conditions of detention, including provisions for contact with the outside and screening to identify trauma or torture victims, who should have access to treatment.[106]

The Guidelines state:

> "Separate detention facilities should be used to accommodate asylum-seekers. The use of prisons should be avoided. If separate detention facilities are not used, asylum-seekers should be accommodated separately from convicted criminals or prisoners on remand. There should be no co-mingling of the two groups."[107]

With respect to the detention of immigrants generally, as well as of asylum-seekers, the UN Working Group on Arbitrary Detention has developed a set of principles, including procedural requirements, for determining whether situations of detention of asylum-seekers and immigrants are arbitrary. The decision on detention "must be taken by a duly empowered authority with a sufficient level of responsibility and must be founded on criteria of legality established by the law". Also, "[a] maximum period should be set by law and the custody may in no case be unlimited or of excessive length". Detention "must be effected in a public establishment specifically intended for this purpose"; when this is not practical, "the asylum-seeker or immigrant must be placed in premises separate from those for persons imprisoned under criminal law".[108]

The CPT, in its 7th General Report, has developed criteria for the treatment of detained asylum-seekers and other foreign nationals deprived of their liberty under aliens legislation[109] which are similar to the UNHCR Guidelines cited above. According to the CPT, "Immigration detainees should – in the same way as other categories of persons deprived of their liberty – be entitled, as from the outset of their detention, to inform a person of their choice of their situation and to have access to a lawyer and a doctor" (para. 30). The right of access to a lawyer should apply throughout the detention (para. 31). If they are held for an extended period, the accommodation should be designed "to avoid as far as possible any impression of a carceral environment" (para. 29). The period of time spent in police stations "should be kept to the absolute minimum" (para. 27), while the practice of holding immigration detainees in prisons is "fundamentally flawed", as they are neither convicted nor suspected of a criminal offence. If in exceptional cases immigration detainees are kept in a prison, they "should be held quite separately from prisoners, whether on remand or convicted" (para. 28).[110]

Further reading

For further information on problems surrounding the treatment of particular groups of people deprived of their liberty, along with recommendations, see Amnesty International, *Broken bodies, shattered minds: Torture and ill-treatment of women*; *Hidden scandal, secret shame: Torture and ill-treatment of children*; *Crimes of hate, conspiracy of silence: Torture and ill-treatment based on sexual identity*; *Racism and the administration of justice.*

5.8 Visits of inspection

There should be official systems of visits of inspection to all places where people are deprived of their liberty by a public authority. Such visits may uncover evidence of torture; such exposure can contribute to prevention.[111] The visits also serve to monitor conditions of detention.

Rule 55 of the Standard Minimum Rules calls for "a regular inspection of penal institutions and services by qualified and experienced inspectors appointed by a competent authority".[112] Principle 29(1) of the Body of Principles on Detention states:

> "In order to supervise the strict observance of relevant laws and regulations, places of detention shall be visited regularly by qualified and experienced persons appointed by, and responsible to, a competent authority distinct from the authority directly in charge of the administration of the place of detention or imprisonment."

Two such systems now operate at the international and regional levels respectively. One is that of the ICRC, which visits prisoners of war[113] and civilian detainees[114] in international armed conflicts, people deprived of their liberty as a result of non-international armed conflicts and people arrested for offences with political connotations in other situations of violence. The other is the system operated by the CPT, which is empowered to visit "any place... where persons are deprived of their liberty by a public authority" within the jurisdiction of a state party to the European Convention for the Prevention of Torture with a view to "strengthening, if necessary, the protection of such persons from torture and from inhuman or degrading treatment or punishment".[115]

From the experiences of these two bodies and other sources it is possible to derive a number of principles which should apply to national systems of visits:

- The inspectors must be independent of the authorities in charge of the places to be visited.

- Official bodies of inspectors should be composed of "members of the judiciary, law enforcement officials, defence lawyers and physicians, as

Bhutan: Gaining access for ICRC visits

In January 1992 an Amnesty International delegation visited Bhutan but was refused permission to visit prisons in order to meet political prisoners. In its report on the visit to the country issued in December of that year, Amnesty International recommended that the government allow the ICRC to develop a full program of regular visits to all places of detention.

In January 1993 the ICRC was invited by the government to visit Bhutan, and a memorandum of understanding was signed later that year which gave ICRC delegates permission to visit "persons detained for 'anti-national' activities". By the end of 1997 the ICRC had completed 10 visits to the two main places of detention, in and near the capital, Thimpu. The ICRC has continued to visit political detainees on a twice-yearly basis and on some visits has also visited places of detention in other parts of the country.

Former political prisoners interviewed by Amnesty International shortly after the visits started reported that after the ICRC first visited their detention camp in January 1993 their shackles were removed and conditions of detention improved. The improvements, which included an increase in the quantity and quality of food, and the provision of heating, radio and reading materials, have been sustained since.

Morocco: Prison visits by national NGOs

With the advances in democratic government and the development of civil society in Morocco since the early 1990s, NGOs have come to play an active role in inspecting prisons.

Two independent NGOs, the *Association marocaine des droits humains* (AMDH), Moroccan Human Rights Association, and the *Organisation marocaine des droits humains* (OMDH), Moroccan Human Rights Organization, had for some years been raising concerns about prison conditions with the authorities, whose increasing responsiveness enabled both organizations in 1998 to visit prisons and report publicly on their findings, with recommendations to the authorities. Some of the NGOs' resulting recommendations were taken into account during the final examination of a new law on the organization and administration of penitentiary establishments, promulgated in 1999. Among other things, the law provided for the establishment of separate facilities for the detention of young people under 20, and of mothers and their infants; set standards for hygiene and access to medical care and minimum conditions for family visits; stipulated that those detained should be informed of their rights and obligations; set limits to the use of disciplinary measures such as isolation; provided for procedures of appeal against prison discipline; and established rules enabling qualified NGOs to have access to prisons.

In November 1999 a new NGO, the *Observatoire marocain des prisons* (OMP), Moroccan Prison Observatory, was established to campaign for the improvement of conditions in prisons. It undertook some 15 visits between February and July 2000 and met prison officials, prisoners and prisoners' families.

well as independent experts and other representatives of civil society", as recommended by the Special Rapporteur on torture.[116]

- Inspectors must be able to visit all places where people are deprived of their liberty, including prisons, police stations, detention centres for asylum-seekers, psychiatric institutions and places of detention in military camps.

- Inspectors must be able to make unannounced visits.[117]

- They must have access to all people deprived of their liberty and must be able to interview them freely and without witnesses.[118]

- They must be able to draw up lists of people deprived of their liberty based on official records and on other information they have gathered.

- Where necessary, inspectors should be able to receive information rapidly from the authorities on all transfers of prisoners or other people deprived of their liberty.

- Inspectors should be able to contact and be contacted by relatives of people deprived of their liberty without fear of reprisals against the relatives. Such contacts may yield information that they can compare with what they learn during visits.

- They must be able to make return visits whenever they wish. Return visits can enable the inspectors to monitor progress and to develop programs of protection.

- They must be able to make recommendations to the authorities concerning the treatment of people deprived of their liberty. Such recommendations can contribute to the prevention of torture and ill-treatment.

- They should report publicly on their findings.

There are many ways in which national systems of visits can be organized. In some countries there are separate institutional bodies for visiting police stations, prisons or other places where people are deprived of their liberty. In some countries human rights ombudspersons, national human rights commissions or other official bodies may have visiting powers. Judges also should have the power to visit places where people are deprived of their liberty.

As recommended by the UN Special Rapporteur on torture[119] and the Special Rapporteur on Prisons and Conditions of Detention in Africa,[120] NGOs also should be able to make visits of inspection.

The Committee against Torture[121] and the Human Rights Committee[122] have called for the establishment of systems of visits to places of detention. The Special Rapporteur on torture has stated that the regular inspection of places of detention "constitutes one of the most effective preventive measures against torture"[123] and has called for the establishment of systems of visits of inspection in countries which he has visited.[124]

A proposal for an Optional Protocol to the Convention against Torture, establishing an international system of visits of inspection to places of detention, was accepted by the UN Commission on Human Rights in April 2002 and forwarded for consideration by the UN Economic and Social Council (ECOSOC) and the UN General Assembly. The text adopted by the Commission on Human Rights would provide for the establishment of a Sub-Committee of the Committee against Torture as an expert body mandated to carry out a system of regular visits to places where people are deprived of their liberty in any country which ratifies the Protocol, with a view to making practical recommendations for the prevention of torture and ill-treatment. States would also be obliged to establish national mechanisms to carry out visits, to work in a complementary manner to the Sub-Committee.[125] Amnesty International has called for the adoption of such a system in the strongest possible form.

Further reading

The CPT system of visits is described in Morgan and Evans, 2001, Chapter 2. For an eyewitness account of CPT visits by a former member of the CPT, see Cassese, 1996, *Inhuman States: Imprisonment, Detention and Torture in Europe Today*. On national systems, see the 1995 PRI Handbook, Section VIII, "Inspection"; Association for the Prevention of Torture, 1999, *The Impact of External Visiting of Police Stations on Prevention of Torture and Ill-treatment*. See also Reyes, 2002, "Visits to Prisoners and Documentation of Torture".

5.9 Ensuring prisoners' rights

Prisoners do not forfeit other human rights simply by being deprived of their liberty (see section 5.1). Under international human rights law, states are responsible for respecting and ensuring the human rights of prisoners. Two of the measures which governments should take are to provide prisoners with an adequate explanation of their rights and of the relevant regulations, and to operate an effective complaints machinery to respond to alleged infringements of prisoners' rights. These measures can help to discourage torture and ill-treatment.

5.9.1 Explaining prisoners' rights

Principle 13 of the Body of Principles on Detention requires the authorities to provide people with *information* on their rights at the moment of their arrest and with an *explanation* of their rights "at the commencement of detention or imprisonment, or promptly thereafter" (see section 4.2.2).[126] Under Principle 14, a prisoner is entitled to receive such an explanation in a language which he or she understands.

Rule 35 of the Standard Minimum Rules states:

> "Every prisoner on admission shall be provided with written information about the regulations governing the treatment of prisoners of his category, the disciplinary requirements of the institution, the authorized methods of seeking information and

making complaints, and all such other matters as are necessary to enable him to understand both his rights and his obligations and to adapt himself to the life of the institution."[127]

Although this rule was written with penal institutions in mind, it should be applied as far as possible to all places where prisoners are held.[128] When prisoners are transferred to a new place of detention, they should likewise be given an explanation of the rules and procedures in force there. The explanation should be given orally for the benefit of prisoners who have difficulty understanding a written text.[129]

5.9.2 Complaints

Under the Convention against Torture (Articles 12, 13, 16) and the UN Declaration against Torture (Article 8), states are required to conduct impartial investigations into all complaints of torture or ill-treatment (see section 7.3). For this to happen, there must be mechanisms whereby people can make complaints without fear of reprisals, within places of detention as well as outside.

Principle 33(1) of the Body of Principles on Detention states:

> "A detained or imprisoned person or his counsel shall have the right to make a request or complaint regarding his treatment, in particular in case of torture or other cruel, inhuman or degrading treatment, to the authorities responsible for the administration of the place of detention and to higher authorities and, when necessary, to appropriate authorities vested with reviewing or remedial powers."

Principle 33(2) provides for a complaint to be made by "a member of the family of the detained or imprisoned person or any other person who has knowledge of the case" when neither the prisoner nor his or her counsel has the possibility to do so. Principle 33(3) provides for confidentiality to be maintained if so requested by the complainant. Principle 33(4) provides that neither the prisoner nor any complainant shall suffer prejudice for making a request or complaint.

Rule 36 of the Standard Minimum Rules provides for prisoners to be able to make requests or complaints to the director of the institution, to the inspector of prisons during his inspection and to "the central prison administration, the judicial authority or other proper authorities through approved channels". It states that "[u]nless it is evidently frivolous or groundless, every request or complaint shall be promptly dealt with and replied to without undue delay."

Most of the responding countries in the 1996 UN survey (paras. 52-53) stated that prisoners could make requests or complaints to the director of the institution or a designated officer at least three times a week, and most responding countries stated that prisoners could make a request or complaint without censorship to the central prison administration, the judicial authority or other proper authorities. Prisoners were said to be able to complain to such bodies as the ombudsperson, the ministry of justice, members of parliament, the prosecutor, visiting magistrates, commissions entrusted with controlling prisons and sometimes to the head of state and to international human rights bodies.

© Mental Disability Rights International

© AI

Woman in a seclusion cell at the Social Home for Adults with Mental Disorders in Sanadinovo, Bulgaria, October 2001. Citing ill-treatment and harsh conditions, Amnesty International called for the permanent closure of the facility. The seclusion cell was dismantled following Amnesty International's visit, and in May 2002 the Bulgarian government decided to close the home. People confined in mental institutions and institutions for the mentally retarded in different countries have been ill-treated and held in poor conditions (section 6.2.1).

(*Insert*) Arm of a victim of domestic violence in Hyderabad, Pakistan, February 1999. The prohibition of torture and ill-treatment can extend to instances of violence in the community and the home as well as torture in state custody (section 6.6).

Chapter 6: Other settings

6.1 Introduction

Chapters 4 and 5 dealt with the prevention of torture and the improvement of conditions in police stations, prisons and other places of detention. This chapter focuses on other settings in which the state has particular responsibilities in ensuring freedom from torture and ill-treatment.

6.2 Institutional settings

6.2.1 Mental institutions and institutions for people with developmental difficulties

People in different countries confined in mental institutions and institutions for people with developmental difficulties, including the mentally retarded, have been ill-treated and held in harsh conditions. During the Cold War there was also considerable international concern about the compulsory confinement of political prisoners in mental institutions in the Soviet Union and the forcible administration to them of disorienting and pain-causing drugs.[1] A similar practice has recently been reported in China with regard to political prisoners, labour activists and members of the banned Falun Gong movement.[2]

The UN **Principles for the protection of persons with mental illness and the improvement of mental health care**, adopted by the UN General Assembly in 1991, state that every person with a mental illness shall have the right to exercise all civil, political, economic, social and cultural rights (Principle 1). The Principles set out procedural safeguards for involuntary admission to mental institutions, which may only be permitted where there is "a serious likelihood of immediate or imminent harm to that person or to other persons" or to avoid "a serious deterioration in his or her condition", or to allow the giving of appropriate treatment for people with a severe mental illness whose judgment is impaired (Principle 16). Forcible treatment may be authorized if it is determined to be "urgently necessary in order to prevent immediate or imminent harm to the patient or to other persons", but psychosurgery and other intrusive and irreversible treatments may never be carried out on an involuntary patient in a mental institution, and sterilization may never be carried out as a treatment for mental illness (Principle 11). Medication shall be given "only for therapeutic or diagnostic purposes and shall never be administered as a punishment or for the convenience of others" (Principle 10). The Principles also set out safeguards concerning the physical restraint or involuntary seclusion of mental patients (Principle 11) and safeguards concerning such matters as the availability of legal counsel, access to information, freedom of communication, and the right to make complaints (Principles 18, 19, 13 and 21 respectively). They state that special care shall be given to protect the rights of minors (Principle 2). Explicit reference is made to the Body of Principles for the Protection of All Persons under Any Form of Detention or Imprisonment (Body of Principles on Detention), an indication that the safeguards set out in the latter instrument must apply to mentally ill people deprived of their liberty.

The European Committee for the Prevention of Torture (CPT), in its 8th General Report, has set out criteria concerning "Involuntary placement in psychiatric establishments".[3] They cover such matters as the procedures for involuntary placement,[4] informing patients of their rights, living conditions, psychiatric treatment, selection and supervision of staff to prevent deliberate ill-treatment of patients, and the restraint of violent or agitated patients. They state among other things that the use of instruments of restraint, such as straps and strait-jackets, "shall only very rarely be justified" and "must always be either expressly ordered by a doctor or immediately brought to the attention of a doctor with a view to seeking his approval"; they should be "removed at the earliest opportunity" and "should never be applied, or their application prolonged, as a punishment".[5] Also, "[s]eclusion should never be used as a punishment".[6]

6.2.2 Corporal punishment in schools

Corporal punishment in schools can amount to ill-treatment or torture. International standards increasingly favour its abolition.

The UN Human Rights Committee has stated that the prohibition of torture and ill-treatment under Article 7 of the International Covenant on Civil and Political Rights (ICCPR) "must extend to corporal punishment, including excessive chastisement ordered... as an educative or disciplinary measure" and has emphasized in this regard "that article 7 protects, in particular, children, pupils and patients in teaching and medical institutions".[7] The European Court of Human Rights has held that the obligation of states parties to the European Convention on Human Rights to secure freedom from torture and ill-treatment can extend to acts of corporal punishment in independent as well as state-run schools.[8]

The Convention on the Rights of the Child prohibits torture and other cruel, inhuman or degrading treatment or punishment (Article 37). It enjoins states parties "to ensure that school discipline is administered in a manner consistent with the child's human dignity" (Article 28) and to protect children from "all forms of physical or mental violence" while in the care of any person who has the care of the child (Article 19). The UN Committee on the Rights of the Child, the monitoring body set up under the Convention on the Rights of the Child, has stated that corporal punishment in schools is incompatible with the Convention.[9] The Committee regularly urges states to prohibit corporal punishment in schools and other institutions.[10]

As noted below (section 6.4), the UN Commission on Human Rights has stated that "corporal punishment, *including of children*, can amount to cruel, inhuman or degrading punishment or even to torture" (emphasis added).[11]

Amnesty International believes that the use of corporal punishment in all schools, public and private, should be abolished.

Kenya: Ending corporal punishment in schools

Violent caning has persisted as a disciplinary measure in Kenyan schools, despite its exposure by non-governmental organizations (NGOs) and Kenyan newspapers and in excess of what is permitted under Kenyan law.[12] Pupils have died from caning, and teachers have rarely been prosecuted. In March 2000, following a visit to the country, the UN Special Rapporteur on torture called for "the immediate repeal of the relevant rules and for the diligent prosecution of school personnel" in incidents of excessive use of corporal punishment in schools.[13]

In September 2001, during the consideration of Kenya's initial report under the Convention on the Rights of the Child, the Kenyan government informed the Committee on the Rights of the Child that in March of that year the Minister for Education had issued a legal notice which prohibited corporal punishment in schools. The Committee expressed concern that corporal punishment continued to be used despite the ban; it recommended that the government monitor the ban and that Kenya "take legislative measures to prohibit all forms of physical and mental violence, including corporal punishment, in the juvenile justice system, in schools and care institutions, and in the family".[14]

6.2.3 Orphanages

Children in orphanages and other institutions have been beaten, sexually abused, shackled, locked in freezing rooms, and subjected to conditions of extreme neglect, including lack of food, medical care and human contact.[15] Such conditions violate provisions of the Convention on the Rights of the Child covering such matters as protection from violence (Article 19), health (Article 24), standard of living (Article 27), education (Article 28), and the prohibition of torture and ill-treatment (Article 37). Steps must be taken to ensure that states fulfil their obligations under the Convention. In addition, to the extent that a child placed in an orphanage or other institution is deprived of their liberty, the applicable international standards should apply, including the standards cited in Chapters 4 and 5.

The Committee on the Rights of the Child has made a series of recommendations concerning children placed in institutions, including the use of "small institutions caring for children in home-type settings" and making efforts to ensure contact of children with their families and to avoid isolation from the community. Due attention should be given to ensuring "the capacity of staff to make effective use of non-violent methods of discipline". Institutions "should adopt anti-bullying and anti-violence strategies and policies, and provide training for staff in their implementation".[16]

6.2.4 Forced medical treatment to change sexual orientation or gender identity

In some societies, homosexuality is regarded as a medical or psychological disorder, and lesbians and gay men have been targeted for medical experimentation or forced psychiatric treatment designed to "cure" them of their homosexuality. Amnesty International believes that the medical "treatment" of lesbian, gay, bisexual or transgender people against their will aimed at changing their sexual orientation or gender identity amounts to ill-treatment or torture. It should be prohibited in all circumstances.[17]

6.2.5 Ill-treatment in the armed forces

Military recruits have been subjected to beating, starvation, rape and sexual abuse, confinement under inhuman conditions, and other forms of cruel and humiliating treatment at the hands of officers and fellow soldiers in the course of their initiation into the armed forces. Such treatment has resulted in death and has led to suicides and desertions. The victims have included conscientious objectors to military service in countries where there is no provision for alternative service.[18]

The Human Rights Committee has urged that "stringent measures be adopted to ensure an immediate end to mistreatment and abuse of army recruits by their officers and fellow soldiers".[19] The state should "prosecute offenders" and "take steps by way of education and training in its armed forces to eradicate the negative culture that has encouraged such practices".[20] The UN Committee against Torture also has called for an end to "bullying and hazing... in the armed forces"[21] and has recommended that the authorities investigate allegations of hazing in the military and "institute proceedings in substantiated cases".[22]

6.3   Use of force in law enforcement

The need to avoid excessive use of force during arrest and in custody has been noted in previous chapters (see sections 4.1, 5.5.2). This principle applies also to settings such as public meetings and demonstrations. As noted in section 3.4, the European Court of Human Rights has held that "any recourse to physical force" which has "not been made strictly necessary" by the conduct of a person deprived of their liberty is in principle an infringement of the right not to be subjected to inhuman or degrading treatment.[23] Excessive force resulting in loss of life would generally constitute a violation of the right to life.[24]

Bolivia: Ill-treatment in the armed forces

In Bolivia legislation enacted in 1997 provided for the office of Ombudsperson (defensor del pueblo) to ensure the protection and promotion of human rights, whose work includes taking action in response to individual complaints as well as more general matters such as public education to inform people about their rights. Between April 1999 and March 2000 the office registered 5,378 complaints, around one third of which were related to violations of personal security and physical integrity committed by the police. The Ombudsperson has also received and taken action on complaints about disciplinary sanctions of army conscripts amounting to torture or ill-treatment. In 1996, before the office of Ombudsperson was established, the Human Rights Commission of the Chamber of Deputies had submitted at least 15 such cases to the armed forces, but no investigations were known to have taken place.

In August 1999 a conscript, Roger Candia Vallejos, was severely beaten by a sergeant in punishment for losing some of his kit. After receiving medical treatment, he returned to barracks in November and was similarly punished again. The resulting injuries included an infected wound to the thorax, a fracture of the spine, and probable contusion of the spinal cord. Disciplinary action was taken against the officer who ordered the punishment, but Roger Candia received no further medical treatment until January 2000, after he had complained to the Ombudsperson's Office and to the human rights division of the Ministry of Justice.

After investigating the case, the Ombudsperson's Office found that the Army General Command was institutionally responsible for the inhuman and degrading treatment suffered by Roger Candia and had a duty to provide compensation to the victim. The Ombudsperson called on the Minister of National Defence and the Commander-in-Chief of the Armed Forces to ensure that the human rights of conscripts and other soldiers were protected and that such instances of ill-treatment would not recur. In November 2000 Amnesty International was informed by the authorities that the Ministry of Defence, in compliance with the Ombudsperson's recommendations, "had instructed each force to immediately investigate any allegations of ill-treatment against conscripts as well as, if sufficient evidence was found, to start appropriate criminal proceedings".

Two important instruments restricting the use of force in law enforcement have been adopted at the UN – the **Code of Conduct for Law Enforcement Officials** and the **Basic Principles on the Use of Force and Firearms by Law Enforcement Officials** (Basic Principles on Force and Firearms).[25] These standards establish that force should be used only when strictly necessary, that the use of force should not be disproportionate to the legitimate objective to be achieved, and that firearms should not be used except as an extreme measure in a restricted range of situations.

The guiding principles of **necessity** and **proportionality** are spelled out in the two instruments.

- Article 3 of the Code of Conduct for Law Enforcement Officials states that force should be used "only when strictly necessary". The Commentary to Article 3, included in the text of the Code, states that the use of force should be "exceptional"; that force should be used only "as is reasonably necessary under the circumstances"; and that it should be used for only two purposes: "the prevention of crime" and "effecting or assisting in the lawful arrest of offenders or suspected offenders". In no case should the provision in Article 3 "be interpreted to authorize the use of force which is disproportionate to the legitimate objective to be achieved".

- Principle 4 of the Basic Principles on Force and Firearms states that "Law enforcement officials, in carrying out their duty, shall, as far as possible, apply non-violent means before resorting to the use of force and firearms. They may use force and firearms only if other means remain ineffective or without any promise of achieving the intended result." Principle 5 states that "Whenever the lawful use of force and firearms is unavoidable, law enforcement officials shall (a) Exercise restraint in such use and act in proportion to the seriousness of the offence and the legitimate objective to be achieved; (b) Minimize damage and injury, and respect and preserve human life..."

The restrictions on the use of firearms are particularly stringent. Principle 9 of the Basic Principles on Force and Firearms states:

> "Law enforcement officials shall not use firearms against persons except in self-defence or defence of others against the imminent threat of death or serious injury, to prevent the perpetration of a particularly serious crime involving grave threat to life, to arrest a person presenting such a danger and resisting their authority, or to prevent his or her escape, and only when less extreme means are insufficient to achieve these objectives. In any event, intentional lethal use of firearms may only be made when strictly unavoidable in order to protect life."[26]

Various measures needed to ensure compliance with the UN standards have been set out in the instruments themselves and in UN resolutions, including the **Guidelines for the Effective Implementation of the Code of Conduct for Law Enforcement Officials**, adopted by the UN Economic and Social Council in 1989. They include the following:

- The international standards should be incorporated in national laws and regulations governing the activities of law enforcement officials.[27] The texts should be made available to all law enforcement officials, and their provisions should be made known through training.[28]

- The laws and regulations should cover all officials who perform law enforcement functions – prison guards and military police as well as the regular police.[29]

- Law enforcement officials should be "selected by proper screening procedures" and should have "appropriate moral, psychological and physical qualities for the effective exercise of their functions" (Basic Principles on Force and Firearms, Principle 18). Their training should involve special attention to "issues of police ethics and human rights, especially in the investigative process, to alternatives to the use of force and firearms, including the peaceful settlement of conflicts, the under-standing of crowd behaviour, and the methods of persuasion, negotiation and mediation, as well as to technical means, with a view to limiting the use of force and firearms" (Principle 20). They should plan for the gradual, progressive use of force in various situations, beginning with non-violent means.[30] Officers should be alert to the physical and mental state of their colleagues and intervene where necessary to see that they receive appropriate training, care or counselling (cf. Principle 21).

- Incidents of possible excessive use of force should be effectively investigated.[31]

- People affected by the use of force and firearms by law enforcement officials should be able to have recourse to a judicial authority (Basic Principles on Force and Firearms, Principle 23). Arbitrary or abusive use of force should be punished as a criminal offence (Principle 7).

Some information on compliance with the standards can be gained from a survey submitted to the UN Commission on Crime Prevention and Criminal Justice in 1996, which was based on replies to a questionnaire from 65 states. The survey found, for example, that in 26 countries, law enforcement officials were allowed to use force to disperse assemblies that were unlawful but peaceful, while in other countries, "unlawful but non-violent assemblies should be dispersed without force, even if dispersal of the assembly was easier when resorting to forceful means".[32] Two countries reported that firearms might be used to disperse assemblies that were unlawful but non-violent.[33]

6.3.1 Police weapons

As described above, international standards impose stringent restrictions on the use of firearms in law enforcement and favour alternative means. Many "non-lethal" incapacitating weapons have been developed and are now available for sale to police forces around the world. Some of them in practice have been found to cause unwarranted injury or to be prone to abuse as instruments of torture and ill-treatment; some have allegedly resulted in unlawful deaths, or have been associated with patterns of deaths. Such weapons include pepper gas weapons and electro-shock devices such as shock batons, stun-guns, stun shields and "tasers" (electro-shock darts).[34]

Principle 2 of the Basic Principles on Force and Firearms states:

"Governments and law enforcement agencies should develop a range of means as broad as possible and equip law enforcement officials with various types of weapons and ammunition that would allow for a differentiated use of force and firearms. These should include the development of non-lethal incapacitating weapons for use in appropriate situations, with a view to increasingly restraining the application of means capable of causing death or injury to persons. For the same purpose, it should also be possible for law enforcement officials to be equipped with self-defensive equipment such as shields, helmets, bullet-proof vests and bullet-proof means of transportation, in order to decrease the need to use weapons of any kind."

Principle 3 states:

"The development and deployment of non-lethal incapacitating weapons should be carefully evaluated in order to minimize the risk of endangering uninvolved persons, and the use of such weapons should be carefully controlled."

To minimize harm in law enforcement and reduce the possibility of ill-treatment, Amnesty International holds that governments should:

- Ban the use of weapons and ammunition which cause unwarranted injury or present an unwarranted risk.[35]

- Suspend the use of equipment whose medical effects are not fully known, such as high-voltage electro-shock weapons, pending the outcome of a rigorous and independent inquiry into its effects.

- Conduct an independent and rigorous review of the use of equipment such as pepper gas weapons whose use in practice has revealed a substantial risk of abuse or unwarranted injury.

- Introduce strict guidelines on the use of firearms and other weapons and equipment in conformity with UN standards, bearing in mind the need to use non-violent means as far as possible. The guidelines should cover the situations in which the equipment is to be used, the techniques of use, and such matters as the issuance of equipment and documentation of its uses. Monitoring mechanisms should be set up to keep the guidelines under review and to ensure that they are adhered to.

- Ensure that all relevant research on the safety of new law enforcement equipment and weapons is placed in the public domain before any decisions are taken on their deployment.

6.4 Judicial and administrative corporal punishment

Judicial corporal punishments are corporal punishments provided by law as penalties for crimes. Those mainly used today are amputation (sometimes "cross-amputation" – amputation of a foot on one side of the body and a hand on the other) and flogging (beating) with a wooden cane or other objects. Crimes for which judicial corporal punishments can be imposed today include theft, gambling, consumption of alcohol or banned drugs and sexual relations outside marriage. Sentences are frequently imposed following unfair trials in which the rights of the defendant were severely curtailed.

© Camera Press

Public flogging in Saudi Arabia. Police officers using long canes beat a man in the main square in Riyadh.

Severed hand on public display in Mogadishu, Somalia. The 19-year-old victim had been sentenced to amputation of his right hand and left foot for threatening a woman with a knife and stealing a scarf worth US$1.50. According to Amnesty International's statistics, judicial amputations were carried out in at least seven countries and judicial floggings in at least 15 countries between 1997 and mid-2000.

© Rex Features Ltd/ Dominic Cunningham-Reid/ Sipa Press

Judicial corporal punishments were provided by law in 31 countries as of June 2000, according to Amnesty International's records. Since 1997 amputations have been inflicted in at least seven countries and floggings in at least 15.[36]

All of these punishments can cause long-term or permanent injuries. The victims experience pain, fear and humiliation. Some victims of flogging have been sentenced to hundreds or even thousands of lashes. The victims of amputation, mutilation and branding are not only permanently maimed, they are also stigmatized as criminals for the rest of their lives.

The Human Rights Committee has stated that the prohibition of torture and ill-treatment under the ICCPR "must extend to corporal punishment".[37] Both the Human Rights Committee[38] and the Committee against Torture[39] have called for the abolition of judicial corporal punishment in various countries. The Special Rapporteur on torture has stated that "corporal punishment is inconsistent with the prohibition of torture and other cruel, inhuman or degrading treatment or punishment."[40] The UN Commission on Human Rights has stated that "corporal punishment, including of children, can amount to cruel, inhuman or degrading punishment or even to torture".[41] UN Special Rapporteurs and Special Representatives have condemned the use of judicial corporal punishment in various countries and have appealed for sentences of corporal punishment not to be carried out.[42]

Governments which retain judicial corporal punishments have justified them by claiming that they are a "lawful sanction" under Article 1 of the Convention against Torture and are therefore not covered by the international prohibition of torture. However, the term "lawful sanctions" must be understood to mean sanctions which are lawful under both national and international law. Judicial corporal punishments are unlawful because they entail key elements of torture or ill-treatment, including the deliberate infliction of severe pain and suffering as a punishment.

Some governments have claimed that they are required to inflict corporal punishment as a punishment provided under Islamic law (*Shari'a*). Responding to this objection, the Special Rapporteur on torture has stated: "As there is no exception envisaged in international human rights or humanitarian law for torturous acts that may be part of a scheme of corporal punishment, the Special Rapporteur must consider that those States applying religious law are bound to do so in such a way as to avoid the application of pain-inducing acts of corporal punishment in practice. In this connection, he draws attention to the axiomatic doctrine that a State may not invoke the provisions of its national law to justify non-compliance with international law."[43]

Corporal punishment can also be inflicted as an **administrative** punishment. As noted earlier, the infliction of corporal punishment for disciplinary offences in places of custody is contrary to Rule 31 of the UN Standard Minimum Rules for the Treatment of Prisoners, and international standards increasingly favour the abolition of corporal punishment in schools (sections 5.5.4, 6.2.2). **Extrajudicial** corporal punishments are also regularly inflicted by the police in some countries.[44]

One route to the abolition of judicial and administrative corporal punishments is through national court decisions declaring them unconstitutional.[45] Another route is legislative action which removes them from the law.

All judicial and administrative corporal punishments should be abolished in law, and laws forbidding extrajudicial corporal punishment by public officials should be enforced. Pending abolition, the infliction of these punishments should cease immediately.

Further reading

Bennoune, 1997, "'A Practice which Debases Everyone Involved': Corporal Punishment under International Law" analyses the practice of corporal punishment as a violation of human rights. See also the observations of the Special Rapporteur on torture concerning corporal punishment, reproduced in Appendix 15 of this manual.

6.5 Torture in armed conflict

Contrary to hopes that the end of the Cold War would usher in a new, more peaceful world order, the disintegration of the old order has been accompanied by new wars and with them, outbreaks of torture. Torture has been used in connection with armed conflicts for all of the purposes listed in the Convention against Torture – for obtaining information, for punishment, for intimidation or coercion, for reasons based on discrimination. It has been used by both state institutions and non-state forces.[46] Members of opposing sides and their families and suspected sympathizers have been taken prisoner and tortured in the hope of extracting information. Civilians have been tortured and terrorized in efforts to subjugate whole populations or drive them from their homes. Methods of torture have included rape,[47] cutting off limbs, and other techniques such as electro-shocks, beating, submersion in water and threats to kill. The victims have included men, women, children and members of particular ethnic and national groups.[48]

Post-Cold-War conflicts have been marked by great cruelty, by a willingness to flout international humanitarian law and a callous disregard for the aims underlying it – the aim of mitigating the sufferings of war, the principle that wars should be fought between combatants and civilians should be spared, the principle of treating prisoners of war humanely. In blatant violation of the laws of war, civilians have been deliberately attacked.

An outbreak of armed conflict is often accompanied by a weakening or dismantling of the safeguards and institutions for preventing torture and other human rights violations. Emergency laws are passed, constitutional guarantees are suspended, the judiciary is weakened, the press is muzzled, independent institutions are threatened. A war mentality sets in. Demonization of the "enemy" is encouraged; abuses by one's own side are made to seem acceptable when measured against the reported abuses of the other side, the supposed needs of the war effort or the destruction caused by the war itself. Some conflicts have been marked by a total collapse of state structures. Paramilitary and voluntary forces have been used to commit abuses, obscuring official responsibility. Criminal organizations and private forces have become involved in conflicts, further complicating the picture.

Torture is also common in other violent situations where armed political groups are active. Armed political groups themselves have used torture and ill-treatment against people suspected of collaborating or sympathizing with government forces or rival groups.[49]

In confronting such situations, it is important to dispel the notion that torture is somehow part of the natural order of armed conflict and cannot be controlled. Armed forces are hierarchical organizations where strict obedience is required. Non-state forces also have to operate within a hierarchy of some sort and under tight control. As in other settings, a clear order from the top will do much to stop torture (see section 1.4).

It is important also to remember that torture is universally prohibited, that the applicability of international humanitarian law in situations of armed conflict is universally accepted and that torture is unreservedly prohibited under international humanitarian law. The commanders and authorities of both state and non-state forces engaged in armed conflict are bound to ensure the prohibition of torture under common Article 3 to the Geneva Conventions of 1949. Finally, it is important to remember that as the fight to overcome impunity for violations of international human rights and humanitarian law progresses, there is a real possibility that the perpetrators of torture will some day have to answer for their deeds.

The four Geneva Conventions of 1949, supplemented by the two Additional Protocols of 1977, prohibit torture and inhuman treatment and specify certain roles for the International Committee of the Red Cross (ICRC) in helping to ensure humane treatment. Most of the rules set out in these instruments apply to international armed conflict. But, as a former President of the ICRC has observed, "[t]he majority of present-day armed conflicts are of a non-international character", and "[m]ost of these situations are not formally recognized as non-international armed conflict", to which "certain rules of international humanitarian law legally apply". Moreover, "[c]ontemporary situations of armed violence characterize themselves through a widespread and systematic disregard of fundamental principles of humanity".[50] These developments pose grave challenges for the protection against torture.

International humanitarian law affords practical protection against torture to **prisoners of war** in international armed conflicts. Article 17 of the Third Geneva Convention of 1949 forbids the use of torture or coercion during interrogation and provides that prisoners of war are required to give only their name, rank and serial number.[51] Article 70 of the Third Geneva Convention establishes the prisoner's right to notify his or her family and the Central Prisoners of War Agency (in practice, the ICRC Central Tracing Agency, located in Geneva) immediately upon capture or transfer to another camp. Article 71 establishes the prisoner's right to correspondence, while Article 126 gives the ICRC the right to see prisoners of war from the beginning of their captivity.

Article 143 of the Fourth Geneva Convention gives the ICRC a similar right to visit detained **civilians** who are "protected persons" under that

Senegal: Action to end torture by the armed forces

Torture, "disappearances" and extrajudicial executions were rife for years during the conflict in the Casamance region of southern Senegal, which began in the early 1980s. Exposures of the abuses by lawyers, national human rights organizations and Amnesty International were regularly met with denials by the authorities and with claims that any isolated abuses were the work of undisciplined individuals in the armed forces.

Following presidential elections in March 2000, a new army commander was appointed in Casamance, and the incoming President asked the new Minister of Defence to tour army camps in the region giving clear orders to the security forces that human rights violations would no longer be tolerated. By the end of the year the incidence of human rights violations in Casamance had decreased significantly.

In December 2000 a businessman trading in food products between Senegal and Guinea-Bissau was held in unacknowledged detention in Senegal after he was stopped at a military checkpoint for a routine check. He was taken to a military camp where he was tortured for three days. After local people reported the matter to an army commander, the businessman was taken to a military hospital for treatment. An investigation was ordered by the commander, and the lieutenant responsible was transferred – a clear sign of disapproval – and reportedly held for some days under disciplinary measures pending investigations by the gendarmerie, which is the sole body competent to investigate allegations of abuses committed by the security forces.

No further information on the case was available at the time of writing of this manual, but in June 2001 the commander assured an Amnesty International delegation that similar acts would not go unpunished in future. Amnesty International has continued to press for a complete end to torture in Senegal and has called for past human rights violations to be investigated and for those responsible to be brought to justice.

Convention. As with visits to prisoners of war under the Third Geneva Convention, the obligation to grant access to detainees applies only in international armed conflicts. In other situations of violence, ICRC visits are permitted only as a concession and subject to *ad hoc* agreements with the governments concerned. As a result, some countries refuse to grant the ICRC any access to prisoners, while in others access is often granted only after prisoners have been interrogated – that is, after the period in which torture is often most likely to take place.

The action points which follow are similar in logic to Amnesty International's 12-Point Program for the Prevention of Torture by Agents of the State (see section 1.4). They include such features as the official condemnation of torture, preventive safeguards in detention, bringing those responsible to justice and affording reparation to victims. Many of them are based on recommendations which Amnesty International has made in relation to specific conflicts.

- States and non-state forces must respect at all times the prohibition of torture and ill-treatment under international human rights and humanitarian law. These provisions should be incorporated in the applicable laws and regulations.

- State authorities and the authorities of non-state forces should make clear to all members of their forces that torture will never be tolerated. The prohibition of torture should be enforced through strict chain-of-command control, including the establishment of adequate reporting and monitoring systems. The training of armed forces and the instructions given to them should reflect the prohibition of torture and respect for civilians – particularly the prohibition of rape and other sexual assaults – and for captured members of opposing forces.

- Detainees held by state forces should be afforded safeguards against torture such as those described in Chapter 4. Non-state forces also should afford the strongest possible safeguards to any detainees.

- All detainees should be held in humane conditions. The use of corporal punishment should be absolutely forbidden.

- The ICRC should be given access to prisoners of war and other detainees in armed conflicts in accordance with the provisions and principles of international humanitarian law.[52]

- People wounded in the course of armed operations should be given access to medical care.

- Governments should ensure that all complaints and reports of torture by their forces are promptly and impartially investigated and that those responsible are brought to justice. The authorities of non-state forces should likewise investigate any allegations of torture and hold those responsible accountable. Anyone suspected of committing torture or ill-treatment should be removed from any position or situation in which he or she could repeat such abuses, pending investigation. Mechanisms of universal jurisdiction (see section 7.5) should be used where necessary to bring to justice people responsible for the perpetration of torture in armed conflicts, including non-state forces. However, those found responsible for torture should never themselves be executed or subjected to other cruel, inhuman or degrading punishment.

- State and non-state forces sometimes take hostages in the hope of obtaining some advantage. Regarded as objects rather than human beings, hostages are often at risk of torture or execution. The absolute prohibition of hostage-taking must be respected.[53]

- Child soldiers are often subjected to ill-treatment or induced to commit atrocities.[54] Governments and non-state forces should immediately cease the forcible, compulsory or voluntary recruitment and use of child soldiers under the age of 18 and should disarm, demobilize and reintegrate all child soldiers. All states parties to the Convention on the Rights of the Child should ratify or accede to the **Optional Protocol to the Convention on the Rights of the Child on the involvement of children in armed conflict**, which raises to 18 years the age at which people can be compulsorily recruited into armed forces or groups and participate in hostilities.

- Governments which are in a position to influence state or non-state forces, including governments which provide military aid, should insist that torture, killings and "disappearances" must never be perpetrated. Bilateral military training programs should fully reflect the prohibition of torture.

- NGOs which monitor human rights violations in armed conflicts should be protected against attacks and reprisals.

- The prohibition of torture and the need for reparation for its victims should be reflected in peace agreements and in the activities of international peace-keeping forces.

6.6 Violence in the community and the family

In recent years, abuses such as violence in the family and racially motivated attacks in the community have gained increasing priority on the human rights agenda. Confronting these abuses has involved examining the scope of state responsibility for the actions of individuals or groups not connected to the state ("**non-state actors**"). This section examines the international standards and the approaches developed by the human rights movement to address violence in the community and the family, and how these efforts can intersect with the fight against torture.

The obligation of states to take action against certain forms of violence by non-state actors has been established explicitly in several human rights treaties adopted since the 1960s to address racial discrimination, the rights of the child and discrimination against women. These instruments recognize that discrimination, social disadvantage and other factors may render particular groups in society vulnerable to violence at the hands of private individuals, as well as state officials. Their provisions therefore aim to reinforce the principles of non-discrimination and equal protection of the law in the enjoyment of human rights.

- Under the **International Convention on the Elimination of All Forms of Racial Discrimination**, adopted in 1965, states parties undertake to guarantee the right of everyone, "without distinction as to race, colour, or national or ethnic origin", to equality before the law in the enjoyment of particular rights, including "[t]he right to security of person and protection by the State against violence or bodily harm, whether inflicted by government officials or by any individual, group or institution" (Article 5).

- The **Convention on the Elimination of All Forms of Discrimination against Women**, adopted in 1979, obliges states parties "to pursue by all appropriate means and without delay a policy of eliminating discrimination against women" (Article 2). "Discrimination against women" is defined in Article 1 as "any distinction, exclusion or restriction made on the basis of sex which has the effect or purpose of impairing or nullifying the recognition, enjoyment or exercise by women, irrespective of their marital status, on a basis of equality of men and women, of human rights and fundamental freedoms in the political, economic, social, cultural, civil or any other field". The Committee on the Elimination of Discrimination against Women (CEDAW), the monitoring body established under the Convention, in 1992 issued General Recommendation 19 affirming that gender-based violence, whether by public officials or private individuals, constitutes "discrimination within the meaning of Article 1 of the Convention".* General Recommendation 19 affirms that states parties to the Convention may be "responsible for private acts if they fail to act with due diligence to prevent violations of rights or to investigate and punish acts of violence"; they may also be responsible for providing compensation. General Recommendation 19 lists a range of preventive, protective and remedial measures which states should take "to overcome all forms of gender-based violence, whether by public or private act" (para. 24).

- The **Convention on the Rights of the Child**, adopted in 1989, obliges states parties to take "all appropriate legislative, administrative, social and educational measures to protect the child from all forms of physical or mental violence, injury or abuse, neglect or negligent treatment, maltreatment or exploitation, including sexual abuse, while in the care of parent(s), legal guardian(s) or any other person who has the care of the child" (Article 19). It also explicitly prohibits torture and ill-treatment (Article 37).

In the 1990s, further action was taken at the international and regional levels to define the responsibilities of states regarding **violence against women**, including violence in the family and the broader community. These actions reflect the efforts of the women's movement to ensure that widespread gender-based abuses in these so-called "private" spheres are no longer shielded from international scrutiny, and that states have an obligation to exercise due diligence – to take effective steps to address acts of violence whether committed by state officials or by private individuals.[55]

- The **Declaration on the Elimination of Violence against Women**, adopted by the UN General Assembly in 1993, defines violence against women as "any act of gender-based violence that results in, or is likely to result in, physical, sexual or psychological harm or suffering to women, including threats of such acts, coercion or arbitrary deprivation of liberty, whether occurring in public or in private life" (Article 1). As listed in the Declaration, the definition encompasses physical, sexual and psychological violence occurring in the family such as battering, marital rape, dowry-related violence, female genital mutilation and other

---

* Extracts from General Recommendation 19 are reproduced in Appendix 12 of this manual.

traditional practices harmful to women; violence within the general community, including rape, sexual abuse and trafficking in women; and "physical, sexual and psychological violence perpetrated or condoned by the State, wherever it occurs" (Article 2). The concept of violence against women under the Declaration thus encompasses gender-based torture or ill-treatment carried out or condoned by agents of the state. The Declaration reaffirms the obligation of states to "[e]xercise due diligence to prevent, investigate and... punish acts of violence against women, whether those acts are perpetrated by the State or by private persons" and spells out the legal, political, administrative, educational and cultural measures to be taken to this effect (Article 4).*

- In 1994 the Organization of American States adopted the **Inter-American Convention on the Prevention, Punishment and Eradication of Violence against Women** (Convention of Belém do Pará), to date the only binding human rights treaty to focus exclusively on gender-based violence. Article 3 states: "Every woman has the right to be free from violence in both the public and private spheres". Its definition of violence against women and its substantive provisions largely reflect those of the UN Declaration. The Convention allows for individual complaints to the Inter-American Commission on Human Rights.[56]

- Also in 1994, the UN Commission on Human Rights appointed a **Special Rapporteur on violence against women, its causes and consequences** (Special Rapporteur on violence against women). The Special Rapporteur has issued thematic reports on violence against women in the family, in the community, in custody and armed conflict, in the context of trafficking, and on cultural practices in the family that are violent towards women. These reports analyse the contexts, causes and consequences of different forms of violence against women; they explore the legal framework for holding states accountable for violence against women, including violence by non-state actors, and they make recommendations for action by governments.** The Special Rapporteur has also carried out fact-finding missions to numerous countries and has initiated dialogue with governments, organizations and individuals on specific cases and patterns of violence against women.

- The **Beijing Declaration and Platform for Action**, adopted by the Fourth World Conference on Women in Beijing in September 1995, set strategies for action to prevent and eliminate violence against women, including the enactment and enforcement of legislation against perpetrators, the creation of mechanisms for reporting incidents of violence, education and training, and the provision of counselling and rehabilitation programs. The Platform for Action includes a commitment by governments to develop "a holistic and multidisciplinary approach... to promoting families, communities and

---

* The Declaration on the Elimination of Violence against Women is reproduced in Appendix 13 of this manual.

** In her report to the 1999 session of the UN Commission on Human Rights (E/CN.4/1999/68, para. 25), the Special Rapporteur has developed a series of questions for assessing whether states have adhered to the standard of due diligence in ensuring the right of women not to be subjected to violence by private individuals. They cover such matters as constitutional guarantees, the functioning of the criminal justice system, the availability of redress, the provision of support services such as shelters and specialized assistance, education and public awareness-raising, and the collection of relevant data and statistics.

States that are free of violence against women".[57] These commitments were reviewed and reaffirmed by the UN General Assembly in June 2000.[58]

Other patterns of violence in the community and the family, including violence against children, racially motivated violence and violence against sexual minorities, have also been subjects of particular concern to UN human rights bodies. As with the norms on violence against women, the statements and recommendations of these bodies have focused on the obligations of states to prevent, investigate, punish and provide redress for acts of violence by non-state actors.

- The Committee on the Rights of the Child has made numerous recommendations regarding the prevention of **violence against children** within the family, at school and in society at large when reviewing states' reports on their compliance with the Convention on the Rights of the Child.[59] It has expressed concern about "the acceptance in the legislation of the use of corporal punishment... within the family" and has stressed "the incompatibility of corporal punishment, as well as any other form of violence, injury, neglect, abuse or degrading treatment, with the provisions of the Convention, in particular articles 19, 28, paragraph 2, and 37".[60] In September 2001 the Committee held a day of general discussion on "Violence against children within the family and in schools". On the basis of the discussion, the Committee adopted numerous recommendations, including the enactment of legislation prohibiting "all forms of violence, however slight, within the family and in schools, including as a form of discipline"; the establishment of effective monitoring systems and complaint mechanisms, with legal advice and assistance for children; public awareness-raising campaigns; and training in child rights for relevant professional groups including social workers, health professionals, law enforcement officials and the judiciary.[61]

- The UN Committee on the Elimination of Racial Discrimination has called on governments to take more resolute action to prevent and punish **racially motivated violence** by groups or individuals.[62] The Durban Declaration and Programme of Action adopted at the World Conference against Racism, Racial Discrimination, Xenophobia and Related Intolerance in September 2001 includes commitments to work to reduce all forms of violence motivated by racism through measures such as research, public education, firm enforcement of laws prohibiting violence, prosecution of perpetrators and assistance to victims.[63]

- The prevalence of **violence against lesbian, gay, bisexual and transgender people** at the hands of private individuals as well as state officials has also been noted by several UN Special Rapporteurs.[64] Their reports have drawn attention to the link between discrimination and vulnerability to violence, as well as highlighting the impunity commonly enjoyed by the perpetrators.

What distinguishes violence against women, racially motivated violence and violence against sexual minorities from other criminal acts in the community is its systemic and discriminatory nature (see section 1.3). It is both a manifestation of discrimination and a factor perpetuating it. Furthermore, children may suffer not only from discrimination on the above grounds but from the additional vulnerability associated with their age.[65] The obligation of states to ensure that human rights are enjoyed without discrimination has therefore required the elaboration of specific provisions to protect those particularly vulnerable to violence in the community and the family.

Parallel to the development of these norms, increasing efforts have been made in recent years to address state responsibility for violence in the community and the family through the prohibition of torture and ill-treatment.

Since the early 1990s, legal scholars and experts on gender-based violence have drawn attention to the similarities between certain forms of violence against women perpetrated by private individuals such as family members on the one hand and torture and ill-treatment by state officials on the other.[66] The physical and psychological abuse inflicted in many cases of violence in the family is similar in both nature and severity to acts of torture inflicted in custody. Rape is common in both contexts. Domestic violence is often intentionally inflicted for purposes such as those listed in Article 1 of the Convention against Torture – to punish women for alleged transgressions, to obtain information from them, to intimidate them – and, as with torture, to break their will and enforce their submission.

It has thus been argued that the key elements of torture as defined in the Convention against Torture (see section 3.3.1) are often present in domestic violence. Although the perpetrators may not be state officials, the pervasive impunity surrounding such violence engages the state's responsibility. The "complicity", "consent" or "acquiescence" of public officials could be present where, for example, the so-called "defence of honour" or the defence of marriage in marital rape cases exempts violence against women from legal sanction. The state's failure to exercise due diligence to prevent, to punish and to provide remedies for abuse in the family as set out in international standards on violence against women could also breach the obligation under general human rights treaties to ensure the right not to be subjected to torture or ill-treatment.

The Special Rapporteur on violence against women has stated: "The argument that domestic violence should be understood and treated as a form of torture and, when less severe, ill-treatment, is one that deserves consideration by the rapporteurs and treaty bodies that investigate these violations together perhaps with appropriate NGO experts and jurists."[67]

This approach to the problem of violence by private individuals has found support in judgments of the regional human rights courts. As noted in section 3.8, the European Court of Human Rights has held that states parties to the European Convention on Human Rights are required to take measures designed to ensure that "individuals within their jurisdiction are not subjected to torture or inhuman or degrading treatment, including such ill-treatment administered by private individuals".[68] Such measures should "provide effective protection, in particular, of children and other vulnerable persons" and should include "reasonable steps to prevent ill-treatment of which the authorities had or ought to have had knowledge", and the "framework of the law" must also provide protection.[69] Similarly, the Inter-American Court of Human Rights has stated: "An illegal act which violates human rights and which is initially not directly imputable to a State (for example, because it is the act of a private person or because the person responsible has not been identified) can lead to international responsibility of the State, not because of the act itself, but because of the lack of due diligence to prevent the violation or to respond to it as required by the Convention."[70] According to the Inter-American Court of Human Rights, "The State has a legal duty to take reasonable steps to prevent human rights violations and to use the means at its disposal to carry out a serious investigation of violations committed within its jurisdiction, to identify those responsible, to impose the appropriate punishment and to ensure the victim adequate compensation."[71]

Treaty bodies also have addressed violence in the community and the family under the prohibition of torture and ill-treatment. For example, the Human Rights Committee has raised concerns regarding child abuse[72] and trafficking in children[73] under the heading of Article 7 of the ICCPR (the right not to be subjected to torture or ill-treatment). As noted in section 3.4, the Committee has also implied that forced abortion, forced sterilization, female genital mutilation, domestic violence against women and a lack of access to safe abortion for women who have become pregnant as a result of rape can give rise to violations of the right not to be subjected to torture or ill-treatment. The Committee against Torture has called for the establishment of "programs to prevent and combat violence against women, including domestic violence".[74]

The Special Rapporteur on violence against women also has referred to cultural practices such as female genital mutilation, honour killings, bride-burning and "any other form of cultural practice that brutalizes the female body" as practices which "involve 'severe pain and suffering' and may be considered 'torture like' in their manifestation".[75]

The prohibition of torture and ill-treatment can therefore extend to instances of violence in the community and the family as well as torture in state custody. These points of convergence suggest that the fight against torture and the efforts to combat other forms of violence can be complementary and mutually reinforcing.

For example, those campaigning to end domestic violence against women have pointed to the strategic benefits of applying international standards on torture in their work. It enables binding treaty obligations to be invoked, obligations which are recognized as matters of general international law (see section 3.2.6). It underscores the gravity of violence in the family and helps to invalidate any attempt to justify such abuses in the name of culture, religion or tradition, since under international standards torture can never be justified in any circumstances. It also allows a broader range of international remedies to be brought into play. As with the judgments of the European Court of Human Rights in cases of domestic violence against children, these remedies may result in compensation being paid to the victims.[76]

Conversely, those focusing their efforts on torture and ill-treatment by agents of the state can engage with a range of non-torture-specific mechanisms and draw on insights gained from the fight against related patterns of violence. International instruments such as those on violence against women enable torture or ill-treatment by the state to be viewed as part of a broader continuum of violence. They can aid the analysis of factors underpinning state-perpetrated violence, such as discrimination and social and economic disadvantage.

The international standards and mechanisms developed to tackle violence in state custody and violence in the community and the family are each tailored to their specific purposes.

Common to all is the notion that states have positive obligations concerning prevention, investigation, punishment and reparation for violations of physical and mental integrity committed by private individuals as well as by public officials. Exploring these commonalities may promote the holistic response to violence in society advocated in the Beijing Platform for Action, as well as facilitating closer collaboration between previously disparate efforts.

© AP

Jean-Paul Akayesu, formerly the chief official of a commune in Rwanda, at a hearing of the International Criminal Tribunal for Rwanda in September 1998. The Tribunal convicted him of torture and rape as crimes against humanity and as genocide.

Chapter 7: Overcoming impunity

7.1 Introduction

> "States should abrogate legislation leading to impunity for those responsible for gross violations of human rights such as torture and prosecute such violations thereby providing a firm basis for the rule of law."
>
> World Conference on Human Rights, Vienna Declaration and Programme of Action (1993), Part II, section B.5

Torturers almost always act with impunity. Not only does no one intervene to make them stop the torture: no one acts afterwards to confront them with their crimes. Not only are the victims subjected to terrible suffering: the suffering goes unacknowledged, and the perpetrators walk free.

Torture is a gross violation of human rights. It is one of the most serious crimes. Those responsible should be brought to justice in a court of law. States also should be held responsible when they fail to fulfil their obligations to respect and ensure the right not to be subjected to torture or ill-treatment.

Impunity can arise at any stage: in not investigating the crimes or investigating them inadequately; in not bringing the suspected culprits to trial in fair proceedings; in not prosecuting them effectively; in not reaching a verdict or convicting them, despite convincing evidence that should suffice to establish their guilt beyond a reasonable doubt; in not sentencing those convicted, or sentencing them to derisory punishments out of all proportion to the gravity of their crimes; in not enforcing sentences; in not ensuring that victims and their families are afforded satisfactory reparation.

Impunity arises from laws, decrees, or other official measures providing that certain officials, classes of officials, or others carrying out official duties will not be brought to justice. Some of these preclude prosecution: they include the many indemnity, immunity or amnesty laws in force in different countries. Often these are enacted during states of emergency or other situations where governments claim there is a special threat to law and order; they have also been enacted to avoid bringing prosecutions for acts committed under a previous government, ostensibly to promote national reconciliation. Other measures such as pardons have ensured that officials convicted of torture do not serve their sentences. Justice may also be blocked by placing human rights cases under the jurisdiction of military courts that lack independence and impartiality.

Other sources of impunity include an inadequate framework of law. Torture and other crimes under international law are often not defined as crimes under national law or are defined in a manner that is not consistent with international law. Principles of individual criminal responsibility, such as responsibility of commanders and superiors for their subordinates, are omitted or defined in a manner inconsistent with international law, permitting those responsible to escape justice. Impermissible defences, such as superior orders,* allow torturers to go free. Statutes of limitation bar prosecutions of torturers after a certain number of years. Jurisdiction of courts in the places where people suspected of torture are found may not provide for universal jurisdiction over crimes in other countries, or there may be no legal mechanism in place to extradite these suspects to places seeking to investigate and prosecute. Often there are no effective mechanisms for victims or their families to obtain reparations for torture – compensation, restitution, rehabilitation, satisfaction, and guarantees of non-repetition (see section 7.7).

Impunity can also stem from weaknesses in the criminal justice system, and from actions of officials which obstruct the course of justice and obscure individual and institutional responsibility. In some countries the judiciary is weak, corrupt, or lacking in independence. Where the judiciary is independent, impunity may come from the institutional resistance of the security forces to judicial proceedings against their members. This resistance can take the form of refusal of security force personnel to attend court hearings; falsification of evidence or refusal to provide it; failure to carry out arrests and other court directives; intimidation of judges, lawyers and witnesses.

Impunity contributes to, and is a standard component of, any official policy or established practice of torture or ill-treatment. In the words of the UN Special Rapporteur on torture, it is "a condition of the continuance of the practice" of torture.[1]

Overcoming impunity is a key element in the eradication of torture. A successful prosecution is the clearest possible sign of an official policy that torture will not be tolerated. It strengthens the rule of law by demonstrating that public officials are not above the law. It contributes to the rehabilitation of victims, giving a sense that justice has been done. It helps to promote a public morality based on human rights values by emphasizing that human rights violations must not go unpunished. A conviction or a finding of state responsibility can provide the basis for financial compensation and other forms of reparation. In addition, a formal finding of state responsibility can lead to important reforms.

---

* Article 2(3) of the Convention against Torture states: "An order from a superior officer or a public authority may not be invoked as a justification of torture." (See section 7.2 below.)

One of the most significant recent advances in the field of human rights has been the development of mechanisms for overcoming impunity for gross human rights violations, including torture. Among the key events have been:

- the entry into force of the Convention against Torture, establishing a system for the exercise of universal jurisdiction over torture;

- judgments of regional human rights courts and decisions of the UN Committee against Torture and the UN Human Rights Committee establishing state responsibility for torture and other ill-treatment in individual cases;

- the creation and operation of international tribunals empowered to try people accused of grave crimes in the former Yugoslavia and in Rwanda;

- the entry into force of the Rome Statute of the International Criminal Court (Rome Statute), providing for the establishment of an international court to try people accused of war crimes, crimes against humanity and genocide;

- the initiation in several countries of legal proceedings against alleged torturers from abroad, based on the principle of universal jurisdiction.

Decisions of the Human Rights Committee, the Committee against Torture, the Inter-American Court of Human Rights and the European Court of Human Rights in individual cases have also contributed to a strengthening of standards. At the national level, strengthened laws have facilitated prosecutions for torture.

The UN Special Rapporteur on impunity (civil and political rights) has prepared a draft **Set of principles for the protection and promotion of human rights through action to combat impunity.**[2] The principles set out in this draft instrument are organized under the headings of what are described as three rights of victims of human rights violations: the "right to justice", which "implies that any victim can assert his rights and receive a fair and effective remedy, including seeing that his oppressor stands trial and obtaining reparations" (para. 26); the "right to reparation", similar to that set out in the draft Basic Principles and Guidelines on the Right to a Remedy and Reparation for Victims of Violations of International Human Rights and Humanitarian Law (see section 7.7 of this manual); and the "right to know", described in the following terms (Principle 3):

> "Irrespective of any legal proceedings, victims, their families and dear ones have the right to know the truth about the circumstances in which violations took place and, in the event of death or disappearance, the victim's fate."

The obligation of states to investigate, to afford reparation and to ensure non-repetition of torture is closely linked to the right of victims of human rights violations to an effective remedy, as set out in the Universal Declaration of Human Rights (Article 8), the International Covenant on Civil and Political Rights (ICCPR) and regional human rights treaties. Article 2(3) of the ICCPR states:

"Each State Party to the present Covenant undertakes:

(a) To ensure that any person whose rights or freedoms as herein recognized are violated shall have an effective remedy, notwithstanding that the violation has been committed by persons acting in an official capacity;

(b) To ensure that any person claiming such a remedy shall have his right thereto determined by competent judicial, administrative or legislative authorities, or by any other competent authority provided for by the legal system of the State, and to develop the possibilities of judicial remedy;

(c) To ensure that the competent authorities shall enforce such remedies when granted."

In its General Comment 20 on Article 7 of the ICCPR (para. 14), reproduced in Appendix 11 of this manual, the Human Rights Committee has stated:

"Article 7 should be read in conjunction with article 2, paragraph 3, of the Covenant. In their reports [to the Committee], States parties should indicate how their legal system effectively guarantees the immediate termination of all the acts prohibited by article 7 as well as appropriate redress. The right to lodge complaints against maltreatment prohibited by article 7 must be recognized in the domestic law. Complaints must be investigated promptly and impartially by competent authorities so as to make the remedy effective. The reports of States parties should provide specific information on the remedies available to victims of maltreatment and the procedure that complainants must follow, and statistics on the number of complaints and how they have been dealt with."

The Human Rights Committee has stated that amnesties are "generally incompatible" with the duty of states to investigate acts of torture; "to guarantee freedom from such acts within their jurisdiction; and to ensure that they do not occur in the future".[3] The Committee against Torture has expressed concern about the use of amnesty laws which might extend to the crime of torture and has recommended that such laws "exclude torture from their reach".[4] Amnesty International has consistently opposed amnesties, pardons and similar measures of impunity for human rights violations that prevent the emergence of the truth, a final judicial determination of guilt or innocence and satisfactory reparations to victims and their families.[5]

The importance of overcoming impunity has been emphasized in repeated UN resolutions stressing that "those who encourage, order, tolerate or perpetrate acts of torture must be held responsible and severely punished".[6] The main actions which the authorities must take to overcome impunity are the prohibition of torture in law; ensuring that all complaints and reports of torture are investigated effectively; bringing those responsible to justice; and affording reparation to victims. All these measures are obligations under the Convention against Torture. In accordance with other international treaties and under general international law, they should be considered obligatory for all states.

Further reading

The Amnesty International report *End Impunity: Justice for the victims of torture* (2001) provides an overview of what is needed to overcome impunity for torture, with examples of the efforts that have been made in different countries. For a discussion of the debates about holding perpetrators of mass human rights violations accountable, see Méndez, 1997, "Accountability for Past Abuses".

7.2 Prohibition in law

The absolute prohibition of torture and ill-treatment under international law should be reflected in the national law.

Many national constitutions have provisions stating that no one may be subjected to torture or cruel, inhuman or degrading treatment or punishment. Depending on the constitutional system, one function of such provisions may be to enable the courts to test whether existing laws violate the prohibition. Another function may be to provide the basis for claims under public law proceedings from individuals alleging that their right not to be subjected to torture or ill-treatment has been violated and claiming compensation. Where constitutions lack prohibitions of torture and ill-treatment, these should be added. However, such constitutional provisions are insufficient in themselves.

To enable prosecution, the national law needs to contain a specific crime of torture, with penalties that reflect the grave nature of the crime; they must not contain anything which narrows its scope of application or impedes prosecution and punishment. Certain forms of ill-treatment also should be specified as crimes. Article 4 of the Convention against Torture states:

> "1. Each State Party shall ensure that all acts of torture are offences under its criminal law. The same shall apply to an attempt to commit torture and to an act by any person which constitutes complicity or participation in torture.

> "2. Each State Party shall make these offences punishable by appropriate penalties which take into account their grave nature."

As the term "torture" is defined in Article 1 of the Convention (see section 3.3.1 of this manual), the phrase "all acts of torture" in Article 4 must be understood to imply that the **acts of torture** which are criminalized in the national law must not be narrower than those covered by the definition in Article 1. Thus, any list of purposes must be non-exhaustive and must not exclude any of the purposes listed in Article 1, and the phrase "by or at the instigation of or with the consent or acquiescence of a public official or other person acting in an official capacity" must not be abridged.

Article 4 also requires that:

- **Attempts** to commit torture and **complicity** or **participation** in torture must be criminalized.*[7]

---

* Under the Inter-American Convention to Prevent and Punish Torture, failure to prevent torture is also specified as a crime. Article 3 of this Convention provides that a public servant or employee who acting in that capacity "being able to prevent it, fails to do so" shall be held guilty of torture.

- These crimes must be "punishable by appropriate **penalties** which take into account their grave nature".[8] (Emphasis added)

The national legal framework for the punishment of torture also needs to be consistent with other provisions of the Convention:

- The law must not allow any **exceptional circumstances** whatsoever to be invoked as a justification for torture (Article 2(2)). It follows from this that any emergency regulations giving state officials **immunity** from prosecution for torture must be repealed.

- The law must not allow an **order from a superior officer** or a public authority to be invoked as a justification of torture (Article 2(3)).[9]

- The law should provide for the exercise of **universal jurisdiction** over torture as specified in Articles 5-8 of the Convention (see section 7.5).

In addition to the express requirements of the Convention, under general international law officials have both the **right**[10] and the **duty**[11] to refuse to obey any order to commit torture or ill-treatment. As noted in section 3.2.6, the status of the prohibition of torture as a peremptory norm of general international law suggests that there should be no **statute of limitations** for the crime of torture. Also, the Geneva Conventions of 1949 require that torture be defined as a **war crime** in national law,[12] and the Rome Statute envisages that states parties will make the **crime against humanity** of torture a crime under their national laws.[13]

In examining the reports of states parties to the Convention, the Committee against Torture regularly calls on states to adopt laws which include the crime of torture in accordance with the terms of the Convention.[14] The Committee has criticized laws which do not fully meet the requirements of Articles 1 and 4 and has called on states to correct the shortcomings of those laws.[15]

Other UN bodies and mechanisms also have called for the creation of a specific crime of torture in national laws. The UN Commission on Human Rights has repeatedly stressed that "under article 4 of the Convention [against Torture], acts of torture must be made an offence under domestic criminal law".[16] The Special Rapporteur on torture has stated: "Torture should be designated and defined as a specific crime of the utmost gravity in national legislation."[17]

Like the Convention against Torture, the Inter-American Convention to Prevent and Punish Torture (Article 6) requires states parties to ensure that acts of torture are criminal offences. All countries should ensure that their laws include a specific crime of torture, in the terms described above, whether or not they are parties to these Conventions.[18]

Concerning other ill-treatment, Article 10 of the UN Declaration against Torture states that if an allegation of ill-treatment other than torture is considered to be well founded, the alleged offenders "shall be subject to criminal, disciplinary or other appropriate proceedings". It follows from this that some forms of ill-treatment besides torture should be treated as crimes. Similarly, the Human Rights Committee has requested states to provide information on "the provisions of their criminal law which penalize torture *and cruel, inhuman and degrading treatment or punishment*, specifying the penalties applicable to such acts, whether committed by public officials or other persons acting on behalf of the State, or by private persons" (emphasis added).[19]

7.3 Investigation

Whenever there is reason to believe that torture or ill-treatment may have been inflicted, the case must be investigated. The facts of the case, revealed through investigation, will serve as the basis for prosecution and other remedial actions, including reparation.

International human rights law imposes on states the obligation to investigate all complaints and credible reports of torture. Often others outside the state apparatus will also need to be able to conduct investigations.

International standards covering various aspects of the investigation of human rights abuses can be used in assessing whether an investigation is effective. The UN **Principles on the Effective Investigation and Documentation of Torture and Other Cruel, Inhuman or Degrading Treatment or Punishment** (Principles on the Investigation of Torture),* for example, refer particularly to medical aspects of investigation, while the UN **Principles on the Effective Prevention and Investigation of Extra-legal, Arbitrary and Summary Executions** contain standards on the investigation of deaths in custody and on the operation of commissions of inquiry.[20]

Article 12 of the Convention against Torture states:

> "Each State Party shall ensure that its competent authorities proceed to a prompt and impartial investigation, wherever there is reasonable ground to believe that an act of torture has been committed in any territory under its jurisdiction."

Article 13 states:

> "Each State Party shall ensure that any individual who alleges he has been subjected to torture in any territory under its jurisdiction has the right to complain to, and to have his case promptly and impartially examined by, its competent authorities. Steps shall be taken to ensure that the complainant and witnesses are protected against all ill-treatment or intimidation as a consequence of his complaint or any evidence given."

Under Article 16 of the Convention, the obligations contained in Articles 12 and 13 apply also to other cruel, inhuman or degrading treatment or punishment.

Like the Convention against Torture, the Inter-American Convention to Prevent and Punish Torture (Article 8) requires investigations into complaints and reports of torture.

The obligation to investigate complaints and reports of torture and ill-treatment is not limited to states which are parties to these Conventions. The UN General Assembly has stressed that "all allegations of torture or other cruel, inhuman or degrading treatment or punishment should be promptly and impartially examined by the competent national authority".[21] The European Court of Human Rights has stated:

> "[W]here an individual raises an arguable claim that he has been seriously ill-treated by the police or other such agents of the State unlawfully and in breach of Article 3 [of the European Convention on

---

* The Principles on the Investigation of Torture are reproduced in Appendix 10 of this manual. The UN General Assembly has stated that it "strongly encourages Governments to reflect upon the Principles as a useful tool in efforts to combat torture" (resolution 56/143 of 19 December 2001, para. 3).

Human Rights], that provision, read in conjunction with the State's general duty under Article 1 of the Convention to 'secure to everyone within their jurisdiction the rights and freedoms defined in… [the] Convention', requires by implication that there should be an effective official investigation. This investigation… should be capable of leading to the identification and punishment of those responsible… If this were not the case, the general legal prohibition of torture and inhuman and degrading treatment and punishment, despite its fundamental importance… would be ineffective in practice and it would be possible in some cases for agents of the State to abuse the rights of those within their control with virtual impunity."[22]

Similarly, the Inter-American Court of Human Rights has held that the obligation to investigate violations of rights protected by the American Convention on Human Rights is a consequence of the state's obligation to respect and ensure those rights, including the right not to be subjected to torture or ill-treatment.[23] The Human Rights Committee, in a case brought before it under the first Optional Protocol to the ICCPR, has stated that "the responsibility for investigations [into the complainant's torture] falls under the State party's obligation to grant an effective remedy".[24] The Human Rights Committee has also referred to the **right to lodge complaints** of torture or ill-treatment and has stated that this right must be recognized in the domestic law.[25]

Under the Convention against Torture, investigations must be made into both *complaints* and *reports* of torture and ill-treatment.

- **Complaints**: The Committee against Torture has stated that "in principle, article 13 of the Convention does not require the formal submission of a complaint of torture. It is sufficient for torture only to have been alleged by the victim for the state to be under an obligation promptly and impartially to examine the allegation."[26]

- **Reports**: The Convention against Torture specifies that an investigation must be made wherever there is "reasonable ground" to believe that an act of torture or ill-treatment has been committed, even if there has been no formal complaint. According to the Committee against Torture, such an investigation must be made "whatever the origin of the suspicion".[27] The Committee has held that one of the sources which may trigger such an investigation is information supplied by non-governmental organizations (NGOs).[28] In one country (Spain), which the Committee against Torture later found had violated Articles 12 and 13 of the Convention, the Committee called on the authorities "to institute procedures for the automatic investigation of any case of torture or ill-treatment brought to their attention by any means whatsoever, even when the victims do not lodge complaints through the prescribed legal channels".[29] The Committee has also on occasion called for clarification of legislation "to remove any doubts concerning the obligation on the part of the competent authorities to initiate investigations of their own accord and systematically in all cases where there are reasonable grounds for believing that an act of torture has been committed on any territory within their jurisdiction".[30]

The Convention against Torture also requires that investigations be *prompt* and *impartial*.

- **Promptness**: The Committee against Torture has observed that "promptness [of investigation under Article 12] is essential both to ensure that the victim cannot continue to be subjected to such acts and also because in general, unless the methods employed have permanent or serious effects, the physical traces of torture, and especially of cruel, inhuman or degrading treatment, soon disappear".[31] The requirement of promptness applies both to the time it takes for the authorities to examine the allegations initially, and to the pace of the investigation thereafter. In a case brought before it under Article 22 of the Convention against Torture, the Committee found that the requirement of promptness had not been met, both because more than two weeks had elapsed between the complainant's initial allegations and the initiation of proceedings in a court of criminal investigation, and because the court thereafter did not proceed with the requisite promptness.[32]

- **Impartiality**: The lack of *thoroughness* of an investigation can be evidence of a lack of *impartiality,* in violation of the requirements of Articles 12 and 13 of the Convention. In a case brought before it under Article 22 of the Convention, the Committee against Torture found that the state violated Articles 12 and 13 because the investigation conducted into the alleged torture was not impartial. The examining magistrate, "by failing to investigate more thoroughly, committed a breach of the duty of impartiality imposed on him by his obligation to give equal weight to both accusation and defence during his investigation". He failed to consult custody records or to examine the officials accused of torture. He also failed to order an exhumation of the body of the alleged victim in order to verify the findings of an independent autopsy report which challenged the official claim that the victim had died in an automobile accident. The Committee noted that the Public Prosecutor had failed to appeal against the examining magistrate's decision to dismiss the case and that the Minister of Justice had failed to order the Public Prosecutor to do so.[33]

The ability to conduct an impartial investigation is closely linked to the **independence** of the investigating body. Referring to "the conflict of interest inherent in having the same institutions responsible for the investigation and prosecution of ordinary law-breaking being also responsible for the same functions in respect of law-breaking by members of those very institutions", the Special Rapporteur on torture has stated: "Independent entities are essential for investigating and prosecuting crimes committed by those responsible for law enforcement."[34] The Human Rights Committee regularly calls on states parties to the ICCPR to set up independent bodies to investigate complaints of torture, ill-treatment and other abuses committed by the police or other agents of the state.[35] The Committee against Torture also has called for the creation of independent investigatory machinery.[36]

Promptness and impartiality are two aspects of an **effective** investigation. The European Court of Human Rights has found states to have violated their obligations to secure the right not to be subjected to torture or ill-treatment under Articles 1 and 3 of the European Convention on Human Rights for having failed to conduct effective investigations into complaints of torture and ill-treatment.[37]

Article 13 of the Convention against Torture also requires the **protection of complainants and witnesses**. Because victims of torture or witnesses may fear lodging a complaint as this may expose them to reprisals, Article 13 requires states parties to take steps to eliminate such risks.[38] The Committee against Torture has called on governmental authorities "[t]o ensure the right of victims of torture to lodge a complaint without the fear of being subjected to any kind of reprisal, harassment, harsh treatment or prosecution, even if the outcome of the investigation into his [*sic*] claim does not prove his or her allegation".[39] It has also called for the protection of judges, prosecutors and informers.[40] The Human Rights Committee has emphasized the need to protect detainees who may wish to lodge complaints.[41] The Special Rapporteur on torture has recommended that consideration should "be given to the creation of witness protection programs for witnesses to incidents of torture and similar ill-treatment which ought to extend fully to cover persons with a previous criminal record".[42] The European Court of Human Rights has held states responsible for violations of the European Convention on Human Rights for having interfered with alleged victims of torture and ill-treatment who attempted to bring complaints before the European Commission of Human Rights.[43]

Alongside the requirements arising from the Convention against Torture and other human rights treaties, Amnesty International has repeatedly recommended that officials suspected of committing torture or ill-treatment should be **suspended from active duty** during an official investigation. The Committee against Torture has made recommendations along these lines.[44] According to the UN Principles on the Investigation of Torture, "[t]hose potentially implicated in torture or ill-treatment shall be removed from any position of control or power, whether direct or indirect, over complainants, witnesses and their families, as well as those conducting the investigation" (para. 3). They should also be removed from any position where they could ill-treat anyone else. The suspension should be without prejudice to the outcome of the investigation: suspension does not mean that the official is presumed to be guilty.

Evidence to be gathered in an investigation should include, where possible:

- statements by the alleged victim, by the alleged perpetrators and by witnesses and others having knowledge of the matter;

- medical evidence;

- other physical evidence, such as bloodstains or equipment used to inflict torture;

- circumstantial evidence, such as custody records and records of interrogation sessions.

If there is reason to believe that torture or a criminal form of ill-treatment has been committed, a **criminal investigation** should be launched. The investigator will want to determine whether a crime was in fact committed and, if so, whether enough evidence exists to bring charges against those suspected of being culpable. If charges are brought, the investigator will want to obtain all the evidence needed to secure a conviction. All evidentiary material should be carefully preserved, before and during trial and thereafter for use in any further proceedings.

In criminal proceedings, where the criminal culpability of an individual is at stake, the principle of the presumption of innocence of the accused person must prevail. In some other proceedings, however, where what is at stake is not the culpability of an individual but the responsibility of the state, it has been suggested that there should be a **reversal of the burden of proof**. The European Court of Human Rights has held that "where an individual is taken into police custody in good health but is found to be injured at the time of release, it is incumbent on the State to provide a plausible explanation as to the causing of the injury, failing which a clear issue arises under Article 3 of the [European] Convention [on Human Rights]".[45] Following a similar logic, the Special Rapporteur on torture has recommended that "[w]here allegations of torture or other forms of ill-treatment are raised by a defendant during trial, the burden of proof should shift to the prosecution to prove beyond reasonable doubt that the confession was not obtained by unlawful means, including torture and similar ill-treatment".[46]

In addition to criminal investigations, there are a number of other types of supplementary investigations which may be done by public bodies. They include:

- **Investigations by human rights ombudspersons and national human rights commissions**. These may, for example, be aimed at helping individual victims to invoke remedies, or at formulating general recommendations for prevention.

- **Investigations by parliamentary commissions**. These can be particularly useful in formulating legislative reforms.

- **Investigations of deaths in custody**. All deaths in custody should be investigated by a judicial or other competent authority to determine the cause of death.[47] If there is reason to believe that a prisoner has died as a result of torture or ill-treatment, a criminal investigation should be launched.[48]

- **Internal investigations**. Police forces, for example, often conduct their own investigations into allegations of abuses by members of their forces with an eye to possible disciplinary sanctions.

- **Commissions of inquiry** or similar procedures. As stated in the Principles on the Investigation of Torture (para. 5), these commissions should be established "[i]n cases in which the established investigative procedures are inadequate because of insufficient expertise or suspected bias, or because of the apparent existence of a pattern of abuse, or for other substantial reasons". Attributes of such commissions are set out in the same Principles.[49]

- **Truth commissions**. As exemplified by the South African truth commission described in section 2.7, commissions of inquiry into gross human rights violations under former regimes, often referred to as "truth commissions", have been set up in several countries as part of an intended process of national reconstruction. Criteria for such commissions have been proposed in the draft Set of principles for the protection and promotion of human rights through action to combat impunity, cited in section 7.1.[50]

Each of these types of investigation can have a role in preventing torture, in helping victims obtain reparation or in protecting potential victims. Each of them needs to be done effectively. The investigating body must have the necessary qualifications, powers and resources to carry out its tasks effectively.[51] Where there is a risk of intimidation or reprisals, the investigators should be protected against them. The authorities should respond to the reports produced by the investigations and implement any valid recommendations.

Investigations of these types should be done in ways that do not preclude the possibility of criminal investigation and prosecution. If a crime has been committed, there must be a criminal investigation.

The Principles on the Investigation of Torture (para. 6) also set out criteria for medical investigations of torture and ill-treatment, covering such matters as the facts to be investigated and recorded, the need to behave in conformity with the highest ethical standards, the need to obtain the informed consent of the alleged victim before making an examination, the need to conduct medical examinations away from the presence of security agents or other government officials, and the need for confidentiality. The Principles further state (para. 4): "Alleged victims of torture or ill-treatment and their legal representatives shall be informed of, and have access to any hearing as well as to all information relevant to the investigation, and shall be entitled to present other evidence."[52]

As a supplement to criminal investigations and other investigations by officials, it will often be valuable for people outside the state apparatus to investigate reports of torture. Human rights organizations, for example, may need to collect information on torture in order to assist victims or to document patterns of torture which can be denounced publicly. Lawyers representing victims will need to document their clients' claims. Journalists may be able to expose cases and patterns of torture through well-documented information. Doctors may need to diagnose the physical and mental effects of torture in order to provide therapy or to help asylum-seekers substantiate their claims. Like official investigations, such investigations must be done competently, with a strict respect for the facts and for the needs and wishes of the victims.

Further reading

Two recent publications provide valuable advice on the investigation of torture and ill-treatment.

- The *Torture Reporting Handbook,* published by the Human Rights Centre of the University of Essex, United Kingdom (Giffard, 2000) describes the basic principles of documentation and gives details of the evidence to be collected and how to interview a person alleging torture. It explains how to submit information to intergovernmental bodies and mechanisms dealing with torture, either in the form of individual complaints or in connection with their monitoring and fact-finding procedures.

- The UN manual *Istanbul Protocol: Manual on the Effective Investigation and Documentation of Torture and Other Cruel, Inhuman or Degrading Treatment or Punishment* was drawn up by a group of experts and was published by the Office of the UN High Commissioner for Human Rights in the High Commissioner's Professional Training Series in 2001. It gives details of procedures to be followed in the medical and psychological examination of alleged torture victims, with discussion of such factors as gender issues (use of male or female investigators in interviewing and examining men or women who may have been raped or subjected to sexual abuse) and the examination of children (Chapters V-VI).

Advice on investigation and reporting in international operations involving a local field presence can be found in the UN *Training Manual on Human Rights Monitoring* (2001) and the handbook produced by the Organization for Security and Co-operation in Europe (OSCE), *Preventing Torture* (1999). See also Giffard and Rodley, 2002, "The Approach of International Tribunals to Medical Evidence in Cases Involving Allegations of Torture".

7.4 Bringing those responsible to justice

Bringing those responsible to justice means ensuring that those people responsible for torture and other criminal ill-treatment are formally identified and held accountable, in principle by being brought to court and tried under procedures which must conform to international norms for a fair trial. Punishments should be commensurate with the gravity of the offence, but the death penalty and other cruel, inhuman or degrading punishments must not be imposed.

Under the Convention against Torture, provisions relating to punishment apply to acts of torture inflicted "by or at the instigation of or with the consent or acquiescence of a public official or other person acting in an official capacity" (Article 1). Punishable offences are "all acts of torture" as well as attempts to commit torture and complicity or participation in torture (Article 4). The Inter-American Convention to Prevent and Punish Torture contains similar provisions (Articles 3, 6).

The obligation to bring torturers to justice applies to all states, whether or not they are parties to these Conventions. The Committee against Torture has stated that there exists "a general rule of international law which should oblige all States to take effective measures... to punish acts of torture".[53] Article 10 of the Declaration against Torture, a non-binding standard which applies to all states, provides that criminal proceedings shall be instituted against alleged torturers and that people alleged to have committed other forms of ill-treatment "shall be

Brazil: Action by public prosecutors

Torture is a standard tool of police investigation in Brazil and is also common in prisons. The Special Rapporteur on torture, who visited the country in 2000, found that torture was "meted out on a widespread and systematic basis" in most parts of the country which he visited and probably in most other parts as well.[54] Although torture was defined as a specific crime in April 1997 under law 9455/97 (the torture law), by the end of 2001 fewer than 10 alleged torturers had been convicted with the conviction upheld on appeal.

One reason for the virtual impunity of torturers in Brazil is the weakness of most public prosecutors' offices in prosecuting cases of torture. Prosecutors are often ignorant of the law; many are sympathetic to, or even complicit with, police officers who inflict torture in what is seen as a war against mounting urban crime. When police are prosecuted for abuses, they are usually charged with minor offences which carry much lighter sentences than those provided under the torture law.

However, a few states, most notably Minas Gerais, have sought to address these problems by establishing public prosecutors' offices focusing primarily on cases of abuses by state officials, under a provision of the 1988 Constitution which enables states to set up public prosecutors' offices dealing with citizens' rights. In these specialized offices, public prosecutors trained in the relevant legislation have ensured that prosecutions are taken forward under the appropriate laws. Although staffed by only two prosecutors, the office in Minas Gerais has prosecuted some 2,000 police officers for human rights violations since it was set up in 1993. In the period from the introduction of the torture law to October 2001, 27 prosecutions under the torture law were initiated in Minas Gerais, including of members of the military and civil police. Although not all these prosecutions have led to final convictions, the number contrasts dramatically with the figures for the 25 other states of Brazil, which in total brought only 18 prosecutions under the torture law during the same period.

---

subject to criminal, disciplinary or other appropriate proceedings". Under international humanitarian law, individual criminal responsibility applies to torture committed in armed conflict (see section 3.2.5). Moreover, torture as a war crime and a crime against humanity falls within the jurisdiction of the International Criminal Court and of the International Criminal Tribunals for the former Yugoslavia and Rwanda (see section 7.6).

Bringing those responsible to justice involves, among other things:

- Enacting laws which adequately provide for the crime of torture and other crimes of ill-treatment, as described in section 7.2.

- Eliminating provisions which could prevent successful prosecutions of alleged torturers, including ineffective principles of criminal responsibility, such as the absence of command and superior responsibility; improper defences, such as the defence of superior orders; and other legal obstacles such as statutes of limitation.

Iran: Action by parliament

In the context of changes in the political and social climate in Iran since the mid-1990s, pressure has built up to hold law enforcement officials accountable in the courts for torture and ill-treatment. Although the legal outcome of such actions has to date been limited, the fact that victims of ill-treatment are seeking redress at all, and that the issue is now discussed openly in parliament and the press, represent significant advances.

Several district mayors in Tehran arrested on corruption charges in late 1997 and early 1998 alleged that they had been tortured or ill-treated in detention. More than 160 members of the 290-seat parliament called for an investigation. In May 1999 a senior police commander and 10 officers were brought to trial. In March 2000 the police commander was sentenced to eight months' imprisonment. (The sentence, however, was not implemented.)

In another case, several students filed complaints that they had been severely beaten during a raid on their dormitory building by the security forces and members of the militant group *Ansar-e Hezbollah* during student protests in Tehran in July 1999. Shortly afterwards, the commander of the Tehran Law Enforcement Forces was dismissed from his post by President Hojjatoleslam val Moslemin Sayed Mohammad Khatami, and he and 19 subordinate officers were brought to trial in February 2000. The court ordered the state to pay small amounts of compensation to the students who had lodged complaints but, although at least one officer was convicted on minor charges, the officers were acquitted on charges of assault. Some 159 parliamentarians signed a petition addressed to the Head of the Judiciary expressing their "deep regret and dissatisfaction" with the verdict.

In March 2002 parliament passed a bill aimed at strengthening the constitutional prohibition of torture, particularly during interrogation. (However, in June the bill was rejected on grounds of "vagueness" by the Council of Guardians, a legislative body charged with ensuring that all laws are in keeping with Iran's constitution and religious precepts.)

- Removing any other provisions which give immunity from prosecution to people who would otherwise be subject to prosecution under those laws.

- Conducting full and effective investigations into complaints and reports of torture.

- Having the ability and the willingness to arrest suspects and to prevent them from fleeing.

- Establishing an effective prosecuting authority with the necessary qualifications and resources, free from corruption and interference.[55]

- Guaranteeing an independent and well-qualified judiciary operating effectively in accordance with international norms for a fair trial.[56]

- Trying those accused of torture before regular civilian courts. As stated by the Special Rapporteur on torture, "Military tribunals should not be used to try persons accused of torture."[57]

- Providing protection where necessary to complainants, witnesses and others involved in the proceedings, including lawyers, prosecutors and judges.

- Removing the alleged offenders from any position where they could repeat the alleged crimes, pending the outcome of the proceedings.

- Sentencing those convicted to punishments commensurate with the gravity of the offence, but excluding the death penalty and other cruel, inhuman or degrading punishments.

- Ensuring that those in charge of a place of detention where torture has taken place are held responsible as well as the actual perpetrators.[58]

The need to exercise the **political will** to bring those responsible to justice applies to the various institutions involved. Prosecutors must have the will to bring charges and pursue an effective prosecution. Judges must have the will to convict and sentence the accused person if the evidence against them is sufficiently strong. Other institutions and authorities, including the police, must provide the necessary support and backing and must not impede the process. In addition, courage and persistence are needed on the part of survivors of torture and their lawyers and supporters.

Two UN instruments are particularly relevant to the capacity of prosecutors and judges to carry out their work effectively:

- The **Guidelines on the Role of Prosecutors** provide, among other things, that "States shall ensure that prosecutors are able to perform their professional functions without intimidation, hindrance, harassment, improper interference or unjustified exposure to civil, penal or other liability" (Article 4) and that "[p]rosecutors and their families shall be physically protected by the authorities when their personal safety is threatened as a result of the discharge of prosecutorial functions" (Article 5).

- The **Basic Principles on the Independence of the Judiciary** provide that "[t]he judiciary shall decide matters before them impartially, on the basis of facts and in accordance with the law, without any restrictions, improper influences, inducements, pressures, threats or interferences, direct or indirect, from any quarter or for any reason" (Article 2) and that "[t]here shall not be any inappropriate or unwarranted interference with the judicial process" (Article 4).

Both instruments provide that those appointed to those posts should have the necessary qualifications and training. Both of them have provisions relating to the maintenance of confidentiality of information.

Officials convicted of torture and criminal acts of ill-treatment should be subjected also to disciplinary sanctions, which can include dismissal.[59] To avoid any appearance that the authorities condone their acts, they should not receive rewards such as promotions while they are under investigation, awaiting trial or during the trial. Officials responsible for non-criminal ill-treatment should be subjected to disciplinary sanctions. Disciplinary proceedings should be conducted fairly and without any presumption that the accused official is guilty.

7.5 Justice abroad: universal jurisdiction

Torturers usually escape justice, either because the criminal justice system is unable or unwilling to prosecute them, or – in some cases – by fleeing abroad. Universal jurisdiction complements efforts to bring torturers to justice at home by making it possible to prosecute them abroad.

The idea of universal jurisdiction over a particular crime is that any state can exercise jurisdiction, wherever the crime was committed and whatever the nationality of the perpetrator or the victim and even if there has been no harm to that state's interest. There are some treaties which *require* states, if they do not extradite the suspect, to exercise universal jurisdiction over specified crimes ("compulsory universal jurisdiction"), but international law also recognizes that there are many crimes over which states are *permitted,* although not required, to exercise jurisdiction on a universal basis ("permissive universal jurisdiction"). The fight against torture has been marked by important developments in law and practice in both areas.

As noted in section 3.2.5, the Geneva Conventions of 1949 provide for universal jurisdiction for "grave breaches" of the Conventions, including torture, "inhuman treatment" and "wilfully causing great suffering or serious injury to body or health". States parties are required to enact the necessary penal legislation, to search for persons allegedly responsible for grave breaches and to bring them before their own courts or hand them over to another state party for trial. However, these provisions apply only to acts committed against "protected persons" in inter-national armed conflicts between states parties to the Conventions.

In 1977, two years after the adoption of the Declaration against Torture, the UN General Assembly adopted a resolution requesting the Commission on Human Rights "to draw up a draft convention against torture and other cruel, inhuman or degrading treatment or punishment".[60] As envisaged in the discussions in the General Assembly, the aim of the proposed convention was to give legal form to the principles set out in the Declaration against Torture, but the initial Swedish draft, submitted to the Commission on Human Rights a few months later, went further by including a provision requiring states to extradite suspects found in their territory or to exercise universal jurisdiction. Despite the opposition of some states, the inclusion of universal jurisdiction in the convention was ultimately accepted.[61] The adoption of the Convention against Torture on 10 December 1984 and its entry into force on 26 June 1987 were milestones in the struggle against torture.

Shortly after the adoption of the 1977 General Assembly resolution, the Organization of American States began a parallel process of drawing up a regional convention against torture. The Inter-American Convention to Prevent and Punish Torture was adopted on 9 December 1985 and entered into force on 28 February 1987. Its provisions on universal jurisdiction are similar to those in the UN Convention against Torture.

The Convention against Torture provides that:

- Each state party shall establish jurisdiction over offences of torture "in cases where the alleged offender is present in any territory under its jurisdiction" and it does not extradite the suspect under the provisions of the Convention (Article 5).

- Offences of torture as defined in Article 4 of the Convention shall be crimes for which it is possible to extradite a suspect from one state party to another (Article 8).

- When a person alleged to have committed torture is present in the territory of a state party, the state party shall take the person into custody or take other necessary measures to ensure his or her presence (Article 6) and "if it does not extradite him, submit the case to its competent authorities for the purpose of prosecution" (Article 7).

An alleged offender is to be prosecuted only if there is sufficient evidence.[62] The alleged offender "shall be guaranteed fair treatment at all stages of the proceedings" (Article 7(3)).

The Convention against Torture provides for a worldwide system whereby the states parties – 130 at the time of writing of this manual – are bound together in an agreement to extradite or bring to justice any person present in any territory under their jurisdiction who is alleged to have committed torture. Once all countries have become parties to the Convention, there will be no safe haven for such suspects anywhere.[63] In the mean time, the zones covered by parties to the Convention against Torture and the Inter-American Convention to Prevent and Punish Torture are zones of compulsory universal jurisdiction (or extradition) over torture.

Even without invoking the Convention against Torture or the Inter-American Convention to Prevent and Punish Torture, a state can exercise *permissive* universal jurisdiction to bring people to justice for torture committed outside its borders. As stated in section 3.2.6, the nature of the prohibition of torture as a peremptory norm of general international law implies that any state is entitled to investigate, prosecute and punish or extradite an alleged torturer who is present in a territory subject to its jurisdiction. Amnesty International believes that all states not only can but should do so.

A considerable amount of national legislation is already in place which could at least partly allow this to be done. The legislation needs to be strengthened, but a survey conducted by Amnesty International found that as of September 2001, at least 80 states parties to the Convention against Torture had legislation permitting them to exercise universal jurisdiction over at least some individual cases of conduct amounting to torture, apart from war crimes, crimes against humanity or genocide.[64]

Since the early 1990s there have been criminal investigations in a number of cases involving torture or ill-treatment committed abroad, resulting in trials and convictions in some cases.[65]

As recommended by the Special Rapporteur on torture, governments should enact legislation providing for universal jurisdiction over torture as a matter of priority.[66] They should also make appropriate provision in their laws and treaties regarding extradition. But even when the necessary legislation is in place, the

Chile: The Pinochet case – an attempt to exercise universal jurisdiction

Responding to petitions submitted by Chileans of Spanish descent about a number of their family members who had "disappeared" or been killed or tortured in Chile during the military government from 1973 to 1990 headed by President Augusto Pinochet, the Spanish National Court in February 1997 initiated judicial investigations under Article 23.4 of the Spanish Judicial Power Law. This article provides that Spanish courts have jurisdiction over acts committed outside Spain where the conduct would violate Spanish law if committed in Spain or violates obligations under international treaties.

In October 1998, learning that Augusto Pinochet was in the UK, Spanish judges Manuel García-Castellón and Baltasar Garzón filed an official petition with the UK authorities to question the former Chilean President. On 16 October 1998 Augusto Pinochet was placed under police custody in the UK. Victims then started petitioning the courts in other countries to try the former President. Unsuccessful attempts were made to have investigations opened in Denmark, Italy, Luxembourg, Norway, Sweden and the UK, and extradition requests were filed by the Belgian, French and Swiss governments.

After a series of court hearings, in March 1999 the House of Lords – the highest UK court – ruled that Augusto Pinochet had no immunity for acts of torture committed when he was Head of State after 8 December 1988 (the date when the Convention against Torture was implemented in national legislation in the UK after ratification by Chile, Spain and the UK), thus permitting his extradition to face trial in Spain. However, in March 2000 the UK authorities decided not to order the extradition of Augusto Pinochet to Spain or to allow legal proceedings in response to extradition requests from the three other countries, on the grounds that Augusto Pinochet was unfit to stand trial. Augusto Pinochet left for Chile the same day.

The case revived efforts to bring Augusto Pinochet to trial in Chile, where the courts lifted his parliamentary immunity as Senator for life, and where by the end of 2000 over 200 criminal complaints had been filed. However, the Second Chamber of the Chilean Supreme Court of Justice ruled in July 2002 that the mental problems of Augusto Pinochet made him unfit to stand trial. The ruling related to the case known as the Caravan of Death involving 75 victims of grave human rights violations, including kidnapping and homicide, committed in October 1973.

The action around the case of Augusto Pinochet also stimulated continuing efforts in other countries to use the principles of universal jurisdiction to bring to justice in national courts people accused of human rights violations under previous governments.[67]

exercise of universal jurisdiction, like so many other elements of the fight against torture, often depends in practice on the exercise of political will. In practice, there will often be contrary pressures, such as diplomatic considerations or pressure from politicians claiming that the accused person should not stand trial. The political and judicial authorities must resist these pressures.

Further reading

See Redress, 2000, *Challenging Impunity for Torture* for a detailed example of the legal issues involved in bringing criminal and civil proceedings in the national courts in one country – the UK – for torture committed abroad.

7.6 International criminal tribunals

In addition to the exercise of universal jurisdiction, there now exists a possibility of torturers being convicted abroad by an international criminal court in certain cases. The **International Criminal Tribunal for the Former Yugoslavia** (Yugoslavia Tribunal) and the **International Criminal Tribunal for Rwanda** (Rwanda Tribunal), operating in relation to the situations for which they have been set up, can convict people of *war crimes* (grave breaches of the Geneva Conventions of 1949 or "violations of the laws or customs of war" in the case of the Yugoslavia Tribunal; violations of common Article 3 to the Geneva Conventions or of Additional Protocol II of 1977 in the case of the Rwanda Tribunal), *crimes against humanity* and *genocide* (see section 3.2.5). The International Criminal Court similarly has jurisdiction over war crimes, crimes against humanity and genocide committed on or after 1 July 2002.

By 30 June 2002, 28 defendants had been convicted by the Yugoslavia Tribunal, sitting in The Hague. By the same date, eight defendants had been convicted by the Rwanda Tribunal, sitting in Arusha, Tanzania, including the former Prime Minister of Rwanda.[68] Torture, rape and other ill-treatment have been elements in a number of cases.

Key findings of the judgments have included the following elements:

- *Prosecutor v. Tadić* (Yugoslavia Tribunal) – convictions for **ill-treatment** as *war crimes* and *crimes against humanity*;

- *Prosecutor v. Akayesu* (Rwanda Tribunal) – convictions for **torture, rape** and **other sexual violence** as *crimes against humanity* and as *genocide;*

- *Prosecutor v. Delalić and others* (Yugoslavia Tribunal) – convictions for **torture (including rape)** and **ill-treatment**, including **inhumane conditions of detention**, as *war crimes;*

- *Prosecutor v. Furundžija* (Yugoslavia Tribunal) – convictions for **torture (including rape)** and **rape** as *war crimes.*

- *Prosecutor v. Kunarac and others* (Yugoslavia Tribunal) – convictions for **torture (including rape)** and **rape** as *war crimes* and *crimes against humanity* and for sexual **enslavement** as a *crime against humanity.*

The case of *Prosecutor v. Tadić*, the first judgment handed down by the Yugoslavia Tribunal, concerned a Serb resident of the Prijedor district of Bosnia-Herzegovina.[69] In 1992 the Prijedor district was taken over by the Yugoslav National Army and the Army of the "Serbian Republic of Bosnia-Herzegovina", and thousands of non-Serb civilians were confined in camps as part of the "Greater Serbia" plan to expel non-Serbs from the region. During the confinement, prisoners were subjected to beatings, sexual assaults and executions.

Having heard witnesses, a trial chamber of the Yugoslavia Tribunal was satisfied beyond reasonable doubt that the defendant, Dusko Tadić, had inflicted or participated in the infliction of severe beatings, stabbing and sexual mutilation on non-Serbs at the Omarska camp and elsewhere, leading to several deaths. For these assaults, the court found him guilty of "other inhumane acts" as *crimes against humanity*[70] and of "cruel treatment" as *violations of the laws or customs of war.*[71] The Appeals Chamber of the Yugoslavia Tribunal subsequently found him also guilty of "inhuman treatment"[72] and "wilfully causing great suffering or serious injury to body and health" as *grave breaches* of the Geneva Conventions of 1949.[73] He was sentenced to terms of imprisonment ranging from six to 10 years for the various assaults.[74]

The case of *Prosecutor v. Akayesu* concerned a man who had been the chief official of a commune in Rwanda, who was responsible for the maintenance of public order and had exclusive control over the local police.[75] Between April and June 1994, during the genocide directed against the Tutsi population of Rwanda, many Tutsis and other civilians who sought refuge in the commune offices were murdered, beaten or subjected to sexual violence.

Having heard witnesses, a trial chamber of the Rwanda Tribunal was satisfied beyond reasonable doubt that Jean-Paul Akayesu had committed, implicitly ordered, instigated or aided and abetted acts of torture against five victims[76] and had ordered, instigated, aided and abetted rapes (many of them repeated) and other acts of sexual violence[77] against more than 30 women and girls. These acts were committed as part of a widespread and systematic attack against the civilian Tutsi population, and the acts against Tutsis were committed as part of an effort in Rwanda to destroy the Tutsi population.

The court found the defendant guilty of *crimes against humanity:* of torture, of rape, and of "other inhumane acts" for the other acts of sexual violence.[78] He was also found guilty of "causing serious bodily or mental harm to members of the group" as acts of *genocide* for the same acts of torture, rape and sexual violence inflicted on members of the Tutsi population.[79]

The case of *Prosecutor v. Delalić and others* concerned events in central Bosnia-Herzegovina in 1992 when forces of the Bosnian government and the Croatian Defence Council (HVO) took over a series of villages. People detained during the operations were confined in the Celebici prison camp where they were killed, raped, tortured and otherwise ill-treated. Three of the defendants were the commander, the deputy commander and a guard at the camp.[80]

Having heard witnesses, a trial chamber of the Yugoslavia Tribunal was satisfied beyond reasonable doubt that the three defendants had been involved in a series of acts with multiple victims including beatings (leading to several deaths), rape and other forms of torture and ill-treatment. The guard and the deputy commander had participated directly in these acts, while the commander was responsible for allowing those under his authority to commit them without taking any disciplinary action.

The defendants were found guilty of *grave breaches* of the Geneva Conventions. They were variously found guilty of "wilful killing" for beatings resulting in the death of four men;[81] of torture for repeatedly raping two women,[82] committing acts against three men including beatings, suffocation and burning for the purposes of punishment and intimidation,[83] and imprisoning another man in an unlit manhole for a night and a day with insufficient air and without food or water in order to intimidate him prior to interrogation;[84] and of "wilfully causing great suffering or serious injury to body or health" and "inhuman treatment" for various acts including beatings, burning, administering electric shocks, forcing two men to commit fellatio on each other in full view of other prisoners and forcing a father and son to beat each other.[85] The three defendants were also found guilty of "wilfully causing great suffering or serious injury to body or health" for subjecting the inmates of the prison camp to inhumane conditions of detention involving an "atmosphere of terror" and inadequate drinking water, medical care and other facilities.[86]

The defendants received sentences of between 15 and 20 years' imprisonment for acts of wilful killing, between seven and 15 years for acts of torture and between five and 10 years on the various counts of wilfully causing great suffering or serious injury to body or health and inhuman treatment.[87]

The case of *Prosecutor v. Furundžija* concerned a man who had been a local commander of a special unit of the military police of the HVO in Bosnia-Herzegovina in 1993, when the HVO was fighting against other armed forces in the country.[88] Having heard witnesses, a trial chamber of the Yugoslavia Tribunal was satisfied beyond reasonable doubt that during a series of sessions while "Witness A", a woman, and "Witness D", a man, were under interrogation by Anto Furundžija, another HVO commander, "Accused B", had seriously assaulted Witness D and had raped Witness A in the presence of Witness D, who knew her as a friend. The court found Anto Furundžija guilty of torture as a *violation of the laws or customs of war* as a co-perpetrator of the torture (including rape) of Witness A and the torture of Witness D[89] and of "outrages upon personal dignity including rape" as a violation of the laws or customs of war for aiding and abetting the rape of Witness A.[90] It sentenced Anto Furundžija to 10 years' imprisonment on the first count and eight years on the second count, the two sentences to be served concurrently.[91]

In the case of *Prosecutor v. Kunarac and others*, the three defendants were variously found guilty of rape[92] and rape as torture[93] as *war crimes* and *crimes against humanity* and of outrages upon personal dignity[94] as a *war crime*. Two of the defendants were also found guilty of enslavement[95] as a *crime against humanity*.

The Yugoslavia Tribunal has also convicted defendants of torture, rape and other ill-treatment in a number of other cases. In the case of *Prosecutor v. Blaškić*, the defendant, a military commander, was convicted of "inhuman treatment" as *grave breaches* of the Geneva Conventions and "cruel treatment" as *violations of the laws or customs of war* for having ordered civilians to be used as "human shields" to protect his headquarters against shelling by the opposing force,[96] and for ordering the use of civilian detainees to dig trenches at the front line under dangerous conditions (some were killed or wounded, and while they worked they suffered "physical and mental violence" inflicted by soldiers and military police).[97] Convictions for torture, rape and/or other crimes of ill-treatment have also been handed down by the Yugoslavia Tribunal in the cases of *Prosecutor v. Aleksovski, Prosecutor v. Jelišić, Prosecutor v. Kupreškić and others* and *Prosecutor v. Kvočka and others*.[98]

7.7 Reparation

If state officials are responsible for torture or ill-treatment, the state must be ready to provide reparation[99] to the victims. Victims should be treated at all times with respect, and reparations should take into account their needs and wishes as far as possible.

Article 14 of the Convention against Torture states:

> "1. Each State Party shall ensure in its legal system that the victim of an act of torture obtains redress and has an enforceable right to fair and adequate compensation, including the means for as full rehabilitation as possible. In the event of the death of the victim as a result of an act of torture, his dependants shall be entitled to compensation.

> "2. Nothing in this article shall affect any right of the victim or other persons to compensation which may exist under national law."

The Inter-American Convention to Prevent and Punish Torture (Article 9) similarly requires that states parties enact legal provisions guaranteeing "suitable compensation" for torture victims.

The obligation to afford reparation is not confined to states parties to these Conventions, or to acts of torture alone. The Inter-American Court of Human Rights has held that the obligation to afford reparation for human rights violations is a rule of customary international law which is "one of the fundamental principles of current international law".[100] As noted in section 7.1, this obligation is closely linked to the right of victims of human rights violations to an effective remedy. Under Article 11 of the Declaration against Torture, reparation is to be afforded for both torture and other ill-treatment.

The UN Special Rapporteur on the right to restitution, compensation and rehabilitation for victims* of gross violations of human rights and fundamental freedoms has prepared draft **Basic Principles and Guidelines on the Right to a Remedy and Reparation for Victims of Violations of International Human**

---

* Victims of torture can include others besides those who have themselves been tortured. According to the draft Basic Principles on Reparation:

"A person is 'a victim' where, as a result of acts or omissions that constitute a violation of international human rights or humanitarian law norms, that person, individually or collectively, suffered harm, including physical or mental injury, emotional suffering, economic loss, or impairment of that person's fundamental legal rights. A 'victim' may also be a dependant or a member of the immediate family or household of the direct victim as well as a person who, in intervening to assist a victim or prevent the occurrence of further violations, has suffered physical, mental, or economic harm." (Article 8)

"A person's status as 'a victim' should not depend on any relationship that may exist or may have existed between the victim and the perpetrator, or whether the perpetrator of the violation has been identified, apprehended, prosecuted, or convicted." (Article 9)

Rights and Humanitarian Law (draft Basic Principles on Reparation).[101] This draft instrument distinguishes five forms of reparation: restitution,[102] compensation, rehabilitation, satisfaction[103] and guarantees of non-repetition.[104] Two of these need special discussion here.

Compensation: The notion of a right to financial compensation is derived from the notion of damages in civil law. As the state is responsible for the damage caused by torture and ill-treatment, the state must provide compensation.

In practice, damages are often awarded, if at all, only against individual perpetrators, who are often unable to pay. The perpetrator's inability to pay does not absolve the state of its obligation to afford compensation for torture or ill-treatment inflicted by a public official.

Principle 35 of the UN Body of Principles for the Protection of All Persons under Any Form of Detention or Imprisonment (Body of Principles on Detention) states:

> "1. Damage incurred because of acts or omissions by a public official contrary to the rights contained in these principles shall be compensated according to the applicable rules or liability provided by domestic law.

> "2. Information required to be recorded under these principles shall be available in accordance with procedures provided by domestic law for use in claiming compensation under the present principle."[105]

According to the draft Basic Principles on Reparation (Article 23):

> "Compensation should be provided for any economically assessable damage resulting from violations of international human rights and humanitarian law, such as:

> (a) Physical or mental harm, including pain, suffering and emotional distress;

> (b) Lost opportunities, including education;

> (c) Material damages and loss of earnings, including loss of earning potential;

> (d) Harm to reputation or dignity; and

> (e) Costs required for legal or expert assistance, medicines and medical services, and psychological and social services."

The Committee against Torture has told states in general terms that they should provide compensation to victims of torture[106] and has called for the enactment of legislation to that effect;[107] in one instance it has recommended the establishment of a national compensation fund for that purpose.[108] The Special Rapporteur on torture has stated: "A complaint [of torture] that is determined to be well founded should result in compensation to the victim or relatives."[109] He has called for compensation for torture victims and improvements in the applicable laws in specific countries.[110]

The Human Rights Committee has urged states to grant appropriate compensation in cases where it has found violations of Article 7 of the ICCPR.[111] The European Court of Human Rights has ordered states to pay specific amounts of compensation in cases involving torture or ill-treatment.[112] The Inter-American Court of Human Rights has ordered compensation to be paid to the relatives of a "disappeared" person in that the suffering inflicted on them constituted a violation of the prohibition of torture and ill-treatment.[113]

In practice, it is usually very hard for victims of torture or ill-treatment to obtain compensation. The authorities will not want to admit, even implicitly, that their agents were guilty of serious crimes; they may also be reluctant to spend the money. Victims may suffer harassment, intimidation and reprisals if they pursue their claims. They may be offered *ex gratia* payments without any admission of wrong-doing, or compensation on condition that they drop any attempt to press criminal charges.

Nonetheless, attempts to obtain compensation are an important means of action for torture survivors and their supporters. Compensation should not be a substitute for criminal prosecution, but it may be easier to pursue because in some instances it is less threatening to the authorities.[114] Once awarded, compensation can be important both materially and morally. It is a tangible recognition of the wrong inflicted.[115]

Rehabilitation is another important form of reparation. According to the draft Basic Principles on Reparation (Article 24), rehabilitation "should include medical and psychological care as well as legal and social services". As regards children, Article 39 of the Convention on the Rights of the Child provides that "States Parties shall take all appropriate measures to promote physical and psycho-logical recovery and social reintegration of a child victim of: any form of neglect, exploitation, or abuse; torture or any other form of cruel, inhuman or degrading treatment or punishment; or armed conflicts. Such recovery and reintegration shall take place in an environment which fosters the health, self respect and dignity of the child."

The development of techniques and facilities for the treatment and rehabil-itation of torture survivors has been one of the important achievements of the anti-torture effort. In some places treatment may be given at specialized units in hospitals; elsewhere there are separate centres for the treatment of torture victims. In some places most victims receiving treatment are from the country itself, while in others most of them are from abroad.[116]

Where the state has been responsible for torture or ill-treatment, the authorities should ensure that victims so desiring are afforded medical care and rehabilitation, in accordance with Article 14 of the Convention against Torture and Article 11 of the Declaration against Torture. The authorities should ensure that the necessary facilities can be provided and should be ready to pay for the treatment.

The Committee against Torture has called for the establishment of torture rehabilitation programs in particular countries.[117] The Special Rapporteur on torture also has called for rehabilitation for torture victims in a number of countries.[118]

The obligation of the state to provide reparation relates to acts of torture and ill-treatment for which the state is responsible. Where the government in question is no longer in existence, the obligation to provide reparation passes to the successor government or state.[119]

As regards human rights abuses for which the state is not responsible, according to the draft Basic Principles on Reparation (Articles 17-18):

"**17. In cases where the violation is not attributable to the State, the party responsible for the violation should provide reparation to the victim or to the State if the State has already provided reparation to the victim.**

"**18. In the event that the party responsible for the violation is unable or unwilling to meet these obligations, the State should endeavour to provide reparation to victims who have sustained bodily injury or impairment of physical or mental health as a result of these violations and to the families, in particular dependants of persons who have died or become physically or mentally incapacitated as a result of the violation. To that end, States should endeavour to establish national funds for reparation to victims and seek other sources of funds wherever necessary to supplement these.**"[120]

The **United Nations Voluntary Fund for Victims of Torture** was established in 1981 to receive voluntary contributions "for distribution, through established channels of assistance, as humanitarian, legal and financial aid to individuals whose human rights have been severely violated as a result of torture and to relatives of such victims".[121] Contributions may be made by governments, NGOs and individuals. Distributions are made through NGOs, which may apply to the Fund for grants.[122] Grants are intended, as a priority, to provide direct medical, psychological, social, economic, legal, humanitarian or other forms of assistance to torture survivors and members of their families. Subject to the availability of funds, a limited number of grants can also be given for the training of professionals or for the organization of conferences and seminars with a special focus on the treatment of victims of torture.

At the time of the annual session of its Board of Trustees in May-June 2001, the Fund had received contributions from 38 governments and a number of individuals over the previous year, yielding US$8 million available for distribution. The totality of this amount was allocated to 187 projects covering victims and their relatives in 70 countries.[123]

The UN General Assembly has repeatedly appealed to all governments "to contribute annually to the Fund... if possible with a substantial increase in the level of contributions, so that consideration may be given to the ever-increasing demand for assistance".[124] As the Fund can only contribute one third of the cost of any project, it is important that other donors also provide assistance.

Further reading

In the past two decades there has been a dramatic increase in the literature relating to medical, psychological and social aspects of torture and the therapeutic response. See, for example, Randall and Lutz, 1991, Serving Survivors of Torture: A Practical Manual for Health Professionals and other Service Providers; Başoğlu, ed., 1992, Torture and its Consequences: Current Treatment Approaches; Jaranson awnd Popkin, eds., 1993, Caring for Victims of Torture; van der Veer, 1998, Counselling and Therapy with Refugees and Victims of Trauma: Psychological Problems of Victims of War, Torture and Repression.

© AI (Kazutoshi Murata)

Activists and Myanmar torture victims attempt to surround the Myanmar embassy in Tokyo, Japan, with "Torture Free Zone" tape. In holding demonstrations and publicizing victims' demands for justice, civil society has important roles to play in building a world without torture.

Chapter 8: Building a world without torture

8.1 Introduction

This manual has shown how the prohibition of torture and ill-treatment has come to be seen to entail specific obligations of states, obligations that are binding under international law. Governments must take adequate preventive measures to ensure that their own agents do not commit torture. They must react appropriately to instances of torture by conducting prompt and effective investigations, applying penal and other sanctions, and affording reparation to victims. The prohibition of torture and ill-treatment also entails that governments must take positive measures to protect people against such abuses committed by private individuals.

Chapters 4-6 of this manual described the measures which governments must take at home to provide safeguards in custody, to ensure proper conditions of detention and to combat torture in other settings, including the community and the family. Chapter 7 dealt with the task of overcoming impunity for torture committed both at home and abroad.

This chapter presents additional measures which governments should take to prevent torture abroad. It also describes the contribution of the medical profession and other parts of civil society to the eradication of torture.

8.2 Action towards other governments

In adopting the Charter of the United Nations (UN Charter), UN member states pledged to take "joint and separate action in cooperation with the [UN] Organization" for the achievement of "universal respect for, and observance of, human rights".[1] The many actions which governments have taken together at the

Albania: Action by the government and civil society

Non-governmental organizations (NGOs) can often work alongside governments in combating torture. In Albania, torture and ill-treatment of detainees by police have remained widespread since the end of communist rule in 1991, but certain measures have yielded positive results. Human rights education projects for police have been organized by Albanian NGOs in cooperation with the Danish Centre for Human Rights and the Albanian Ministry of Public Order. NGOs have also provided human rights education for prison staff. NGOs have visited police stations, detention centres and prisons to speak to prisoners and to monitor conditions. Several NGOs have set up call lines where victims of human rights violations can obtain legal advice about bringing complaints.

In March 2001 the Ministry of Public Order placed full-page advertisements in the press to promote public awareness of legal provisions relating to the police, including constitutional provisions such as the right not to be tortured or ill-treated. In September 2001 the same Ministry opened a telephone complaints line; numerous complaints of police ill-treatment were reportedly received, as a result of which some police officers were dismissed or suspended from their duties.

In February 2000 the Albanian parliament elected the first People's Advocate (Ombudsperson). This institution has in response to complaints intervened in a number of cases of alleged police ill-treatment. Its recommendations have led to the dismissal or suspension of police officers and, in some cases, to the initiation of criminal proceedings. In 2001 at least three police officers were reported to have been convicted of the ill-treatment of detainees.

UN, including the annual adoption without a vote of General Assembly resolutions calling for specific measures against torture,[2] imply that governments are and should be concerned about the infliction of torture and ill-treatment in other countries. As shown in section 7.5, the nature of the prohibition of torture as a peremptory norm of general international law implies that any state is entitled to bring to justice an alleged torturer who is present in its territory, and Amnesty International holds that all states not only can but should do so. Governments can and should also take other actions to promote the eradication of torture and ill-treatment in other countries.[3]

Through their bilateral ties, there is much that governments can do. Through their embassies, they can monitor the situation of torture in a country and raise concerns with the government involved. In urgent cases, they can provide shelter in their diplomatic premises for people who would risk being tortured if apprehended by the authorities. Such actions will normally be handled through diplomatic channels, but governments should not hesitate to voice their concerns publicly where this would be beneficial.

Each government should instruct its diplomatic representatives to:

- seek information on any suspected cases of torture or ill-treatment, as well as on any laws or practices which facilitate these abuses;

- meet local human rights organizations to gather information on alleged cases of torture;

China: Exposure by the press

Exposure by the news media can lead to action. In China, for example, the media have played an increasing role in recent years in exposing abuses by public officials in connection with detention and imprisonment. There is still no reporting on politically sensitive cases, but in other cases some newspapers no longer wait for an official investigation into allegations of torture or ill-treatment before reporting a story. Cases where victims and their families have battled for justice against official obstruction or indifference, sometimes for years, have been resolved following media reporting.

In July 2000 the *China Youth Daily* reported the case of a woman who for over a year had failed in her attempts to file a civil suit for damages against the police and hospital authorities. She had been wrongly detained by police as a "vagrant" and held overnight in a psychiatric hospital where she was gang-raped by mentally ill patients. According to her account, she and her husband had immediately reported the rape to the local police who took no record of their complaint, but accompanied them back to the hospital where she identified several suspects; however, the police failed to collect evidence and did not prevent suspects leaving. Her complaints to other local and provincial authorities met initially with denials and inaction. Five months later she was told that she could pursue a civil suit against one of the suspects, who was to be tried for the offence, but that she could not seek compensation from the police or the hospital. Although the suspect was convicted and sentenced to four years' imprisonment, the woman could not present her case for compensation against him because she was not informed of the trial.

The report of these events by the *China Youth Daily* led to a public outcry. The authorities subsequently announced that one police officer had been dismissed and arrested on charges of dereliction of duty, and another one had been demoted. A local deputy party secretary was appointed to head an investigation, and two hospital workers and a forensic doctor who had provided false reports were placed under investigation.*

- express concern with the host government over allegations of torture or ill-treatment, including conditions of detention amounting to ill-treatment and instances of the use of corporal punishment;

- intercede with the host government to protect people at risk of torture, and to protect members of human rights organizations threatened because of their work;

- in urgent cases, offer shelter to people at risk of torture;

- send observers to trials of people allegedly responsible for torture, as a sign of their own government's wish to see those responsible brought to justice;

- report back on these matters so that the home government can take the situation of human rights into account in formulating policy.

---

* No further information about the case was available at the time of writing of this manual.

Action towards other governments for the eradication of torture also includes:

- public criticism of the practice of governments which commit or tolerate torture;

- efforts through the UN Commission on Human Rights and other inter-governmental bodies to act multilaterally against torture;

- technical assistance contributing to the eradication of torture, including expert assistance in investigative techniques which do not involve ill-treatment;

- protecting people fleeing from torture (see section 8.3);

- ensuring that transfers of security equipment and know-how do not facilitate torture (see section 8.4);

- pressure on armed political groups with which they have ties to stop torture.

Action can also be multilateral. On 9 April 2001 the General Affairs Council of the European Union (EU) adopted **Guidelines to EU Policy towards Third Countries on Torture and Other Cruel, Inhuman or Degrading Treatment or Punishment**. These Guidelines state that "[t]o work towards the prevention and the eradication of all forms of torture and ill-treatment within the EU and worldwide is a strongly held policy view of all EU member states" and that "[p]romotion and protection of this right is a priority of the EU's human rights policy". The EU will urge relevant countries to take "effective measures" against torture and ill-treatment. In well-documented individual cases it will urge the authorities of the country concerned "to ensure physical safety, prevent abuses, provide information and apply relevant safeguards". Third countries are to be urged among other things to provide legal safeguards for persons deprived of their liberty; to bring those responsible for torture and ill-treatment to justice, and to provide reparation to victims; to take appropriate measures relating to "women, children, refugees, asylum-seekers, internally displaced persons, migrants and other groups requiring special protection against torture and ill-treatment"; and to improve conditions in places where people are deprived of their liberty, in conformity with international standards. These actions can be taken both through confidential *démarches* (diplomatic approaches) and through public statements. The policy also provides for bilateral and multilateral cooperation in the legal field and the field of training.

8.3 Protecting people fleeing from torture

Many people at risk of torture face difficulties when they try to find safety in another country. The Universal Declaration of Human Rights proclaims the right of everyone to seek and enjoy asylum from persecution (Article 14), but officials in countries where people wish to seek asylum often deny this right by obstructing the entry of people in need of protection, or by ignoring the risk of torture in returning them forcibly to another country (*refoulement*).

One of the obligations of states which follow from the prohibition of torture and ill-treatment is an obligation not to send a person forcibly to another country or territory where he or she would be at risk of torture or ill-treatment.

Article 3 of the Convention against Torture states:

> "1. No State Party shall expel, return (*'refouler'*) or extradite a person to another State where there are substantial grounds for believing that he would be in danger of being subjected to torture.

> "2. For the purpose of determining whether there are such grounds, the competent authorities shall take into account all relevant considerations including, where applicable, the existence in the State concerned of a consistent pattern of gross, flagrant or mass violations of human rights."

Protection against *refoulement* is afforded also under the UN **Convention relating to the Status of Refugees** (Refugee Convention), the leading international treaty governing the protection of refugees and asylum-seekers. Article 33(1) of the Refugee Convention states:

> "No Contracting State shall expel or return (*'refouler'*) a refugee in any manner whatsoever to the frontiers of territories where his life or freedom would be threatened on account of his race, religion, nationality, membership of a particular social group or political opinion."[4]

According to an Opinion on the Scope and Content of the Principle of *Non-refoulement* prepared for an Expert Roundtable organized by the UN High Commissioner for Refugees (UNHCR) which took place in Cambridge, United Kingdom (UK), in July 2001 as part of the UNHCR Global Consultations on International Protection, the phrase "where his life or freedom would be threatened" must be read "to include circumstances in which there is a real risk" of torture or cruel, inhuman or degrading treatment or punishment.[5] The principle of *non-refoulement* under Article 33(1) of the Convention "precludes any act of *refoulement*, of whatever form, including non-admittance at the frontier, that would have the effect of exposing refugees or asylum-seekers"[6] to "a real risk"[7] of persecution, which can include torture or ill-treatment. Not only does it apply to requests by individuals for asylum, but it is also "applicable to situations of mass influx and temporary protection" and "requires a review of individual circumstances as a condition precedent to any denial of protection". Moreover, "it prohibits *refoulement* to *any* territory where the refugee or asylum-seeker would be at risk, including to a territory where the refugee or asylum-seeker may not be at risk directly but from which they would be in danger of being subsequently removed to a territory where they would be at risk" (emphasis in original).[8]

As mentioned in previous chapters, under Article 22 of the Convention against Torture, the Committee against Torture established under the Convention can hear complaints from individuals subject to the jurisdiction of a state party to the Convention if the state has made a declaration accepting the Committee's competence to do so. Most complaints received to date have been from individuals seeking protection under Article 3 of the Convention from being sent forcibly to a country where they claimed they would be at risk of torture.[9]

When it receives a complaint, the Committee can request the state not to expel the complainant while the complaint is under consideration. As of late 2000 all but two states had complied with such requests.[10]

In 1997 the Committee issued a General Comment on its treatment of individual complaints relating to *refoulement*. Among other things, the General Comment states that a person seeking protection against *refoulement* under Article 22 "must establish that he/she would be in danger of being tortured", that "the grounds for so believing are substantial" and that "such danger is personal and present". The risk of torture will be assessed by the Committee "on grounds that go beyond mere theory or suspicion. However, the risk does not have to meet the test of being highly probable".[11]

Faced with inconsistencies in a complainant's account, which had contributed to the rejection of the complainant's asylum claim by the state authorities, the Committee has held that "complete accuracy is seldom to be expected by victims of torture and that such inconsistencies as may exist in the author's presentation of the facts are not material and do not raise doubts about the general veracity of the author's claims".[12] Some contradictions or inconsistencies could be explained by the fact that the complainant "suffers from post-traumatic stress disorder".[13] The Committee has also held in individual cases that forcible return would be unsafe even if it were to a different part of the country from that where the complainant said he or she had been tortured,[14] and that – in the case of a collapsed state – protection under Article 3 extended to a person at risk of torture at the hands of a non-state entity exercising "quasi-governmental" functions.[15]

The obligation of *non-refoulement* where there is a risk of torture or ill-treatment is not limited to states which are parties to the Convention against Torture or the Refugee Convention. The UN Human Rights Committee has stated that "States parties [to the ICCPR] must not expose individuals to the danger of torture or cruel, inhuman or degrading treatment or punishment upon return to another country by way of their extradition, expulsion or *refoulement*".[16] The Special Rapporteur on torture has underlined "the link between the non-derogable nature of the prohibition of torture and other forms of ill-treatment and the principle of *non-refoulement*"; he has stated that the principle contained in the Human Rights Committee's statement quoted above and the prohibition of refoulement in Article 3 of the Convention against Torture "represents an inherent part of the overall fundamental obligation to avoid contributing in any way to a violation of the prohibition of torture and other cruel, inhuman or degrading treatment or punishment", and that "the protection offered by the principle of *non-refoulement* is of an imperative nature".[17]

The European Court of Human Rights has held that it is "well-established" in the Court's case law "that the fundamentally important prohibition against torture and inhuman and degrading treatment under Article 3 [of the European Convention on Human Rights], read in conjunction with Article 1 of the Convention to 'secure to everyone within their jurisdiction the rights and freedoms defined in [the] Convention', imposes an obligation on Contracting States not to expel a person to a country where substantial grounds have been shown for believing that he would face a real risk of being subjected to treatment contrary to Article 3"[18] and that "the activities of the individual in question, however undesirable or dangerous, cannot be a material consideration".[19]

Drawing from these and other sources, the Opinion on the Scope and Content of the Principle of *Non-refoulement* cited above states that *non-refoulement* is a "fundamental component" of the prohibition of torture and ill-treatment under customary international law (see section 3.2.6). In a human rights context, *non-refoulement* under customary international law is "focused on individuals, regardless of either status or conduct", where substantial grounds can be shown for believing that they would face a real risk of being subjected to torture or ill-treatment. It precludes "any measure, regardless of form, which would have the effect of putting an individual at risk by removing them from a place of safety to a place of threat". It precludes "all such measures taken by or on behalf of a State, whether the measures are taken within the territory of that State or elsewhere, in circumstances in which the measures are or would be attributable to the State". It precludes "the expulsion, return or other transfer of an individual both to a territory where they may be at risk directly or to a territory from which they may be subsequently removed to a third territory where they would be at risk". It "is not subject to exception or limitation for any reason whatever".[20]

Zaire: Victim of torture wins protection

Balabou Mutombo fled Zaire (now the Democratic Republic of the Congo) in 1990 and illegally entered Switzerland, where he applied for recognition as a refugee. A member of an opposition party, he had been arrested in Zaire in 1989 and tortured. Medical reports supported his account. After his asylum application and appeal were rejected, his lawyer, supported by Amnesty International, filed a complaint against Switzerland with the Committee against Torture. Switzerland, as a party to the Convention against Torture, had made a declaration under its Article 22 recognizing the competence of the Committee to consider individual complaints.

In 1994 the Committee found that "the expulsion or return of the author [of the complaint] to Zaire in the prevailing circumstances would constitute a violation of article 3" of the Convention against Torture and that "in the prevailing circumstances", Switzerland had "an obligation to refrain from expelling Balabou Mutombo to Zaire, or to any other country where he runs a real risk of being expelled or returned to Zaire or of being subjected to torture". In reaching its decision, the Committee noted "the author's ethnic background, alleged political affiliation and detention history as well as the fact, which has not been disputed by the State party, that he appears to have deserted from the army and to have left Zaire in a clandestine manner and, when formulating an application for asylum, to have adduced arguments which may be considered defamatory towards Zaire", as well as "the existence in the State concerned of a consistent pattern of gross, flagrant or mass violations of human rights" within the meaning of Article 3(2) of the Convention. The Swiss government then annulled the deportation order.[21]

The Opinion summarizes "the scope and content of the customary principle of *non-refoulement* in the context of human rights" as follows:

> "No person shall be rejected, returned or expelled in any manner whatever where this would compel them to remain in or return to a territory where substantial grounds can be shown for believing that they would face a real risk of being subjected to torture, cruel, inhuman or degrading treatment or punishment. This principle allows of no limitation or exception."[22]

The decisions and judgments of the Committee against Torture,[23] the European Court of Human Rights and other international bodies have provided protection for individual complainants and have served to establish important principles in the handling of their claims. The bulk of decisions, however, will continue to be made at the national level. To comply with states' obligations regarding the prohibition of torture and ill-treatment, it is essential that governmental authorities provide access to fair and satisfactory asylum procedures and end practices that seek to prevent or deter asylum-seekers from pursuing claims.

Further reading

A description of the issues surrounding attempts to claim asylum and the relevant procedures can be found in Amnesty International, *Refugees: Human rights have no borders* (1997).

8.4 Stopping the torture trade

Some equipment used for torture is specially designed for that purpose, while other items often used in torture such as truncheons, handcuffs and electric cattle prods can also be used for legitimate purposes. Similarly, there are some instruments of restraint whose use is inherently cruel, inhuman or degrading, while other restraint devices and police weapons have in practice posed serious risks of abuse or unwarranted injury (see sections 5.5.3, 6.3.1). Much of this equipment is not only used domestically but exported to other countries.

The controls which governments should follow regarding equipment used by their own law enforcement forces are described in Chapters 5 and 6. But the responsibility does not end at the country's borders. The UN General Assembly has called on all governments "to take appropriate effective legislative, administrative, judicial or other measures to prevent and prohibit the production, trade, export and use of equipment that is specifically designed to inflict torture or other cruel, inhuman or degrading treatment".[24]

In line with states' obligations to ensure freedom from torture and ill-treatment and their responsibilities to help ensure human rights internationally, governments should:

- Forbid the transfer to law enforcement agencies in other countries of equipment designed for torture, such as thumbscrews, as well as equipment such as leg-irons, sharp or serrated cuffs and electro-shock stun belts whose use is inherently cruel, inhuman or degrading.

- Introduce strict controls on the export of other law enforcement equipment to ensure that it is not used to inflict torture or ill-treatment. Such controls could include the use of "end-user" certificates which are guaranteed by the recipient government, and monitoring by the exporting country's diplomatic representatives to ensure that the guarantees are adhered to.

- Suspend exports of law enforcement equipment whose medical effects are not fully known or whose use in practice has revealed a substantial risk of abuse or unwarranted injury (see section 6.3.1), pending the outcome of a rigorous and independent inquiry into or review of its use.

- Increase public accountability and transparency in the export of law enforcement equipment so that the public can exercise vigilance.

Multilateral action also could contribute to the exercise of controls. In its periodic review of the implementation of the European Union (EU) 1998 Code of Conduct on Arms Exports, the European Parliament (the parliamentary body of the EU) in October 2001 called on another EU organ, the EU Commission, to draw up a similar instrument for controlling exports of non-military security and police equipment. According to the European Parliament resolution, this instrument should include "a ban on the promotion, trade and export of police and security equipment whose use is inherently cruel, inhuman or degrading, including leg irons, electroshock stun belts and inherently painful devices such as serrated thumbcuffs"; the instrument should "suspend the transfer of equipment whose medical effects are not fully known", pending an inquiry into its effects, as well as the transfer of equipment whose "use in practice has revealed a substantial risk of abuse or unwarranted injury". The resolution urged the EU Commission to commit itself to an EU-wide ban or suspension of the manufacture and use of such equipment.[25]

Stopping the international transfer of knowledge of torture techniques is also part of stopping the torture trade. Governments should:

- Ensure that the training of military, security and police personnel of another country does not involve the transfer of skills, knowledge or techniques likely to lend themselves to torture or ill-treatment in the recipient country. The practical application of relevant human rights standards and international humanitarian law should be fully integrated into such training programs.

- Establish procedures to screen potential participants in the training of military, security and police personnel of other countries to ensure that those who have been involved in serious human rights violations are prevented from participating.

- Make public information on government-sponsored training programs for foreign personnel including the individuals and units trained and the nature of the training.

- Establish mechanisms to monitor the human rights impact of the training provided.

- Introduce legislation to control and monitor the activities of private providers of military, security and police services. Companies and individuals providing such services should be required to register and to provide detailed annual reports of their activities. Every proposed international transfer of personnel or training should require prior government approval, which should only be granted in accordance with publicly available criteria based on international human rights standards and international humanitarian law.

Further reading

Amnesty International, *Stopping the torture trade* (2001) gives details of the international trade in equipment and skills used for torture, and recommendations for bringing it to an end.

8.5 Intergovernmental action: the unfinished agenda

As shown in this manual, international and regional human rights bodies and mechanisms have made many valuable contributions to the fight against torture and ill-treatment. With further support from governments, these bodies and mechanisms could become a truly effective worldwide international system for anti-torture action.

- The Convention against Torture is a binding agreement among states to act against torture and to bring those responsible to justice, where necessary through extradition or the exercise of universal jurisdiction. All states should become parties to the Convention. States parties should make declarations under Articles 21 and 22 providing for inter-state and individual complaints.[26] States which have declared that they do not recognize the competence of the Committee against Torture under Article 20 to investigate reports of systematic torture in their country should withdraw these declarations.[27] States which have made reservations should withdraw them.

- States parties to the Convention against Torture should submit their periodic reports to the Committee against Torture in a timely fashion, as required under Article 19 of the Convention (see section 1.5).[28] Reports should be comprehensive, with factual detail as well as legal analysis, and in accordance with the Committee's guidelines.[29] The Committee should ensure that the questions it raises during the examination of states' reports and the recommendations it makes are as clear and strong as possible.[30] It should persist with its important work of examining complaints under Article 22 of the Convention.[31]

- Governments should implement the recommendations of the Committee against Torture,[32] the UN Special Rapporteur on torture, the Human Rights Committee and the relevant regional bodies and mechanisms and comply with the views adopted by the Committee against Torture and the Human Rights Committee in individual cases.

- All UN member states should press for the speedy adoption of the Optional Protocol to the Convention against Torture, providing for a global system of inspection visits to places of detention as a safeguard against torture (see section 5.8).

- NGOs and other human rights defenders should submit well-documented information on torture to the relevant international bodies and mechanisms. Where appropriate, victims of torture and those acting on their behalf should consider submitting individual complaints. NGOs and the news media should publicize the views and recommendations of international bodies and mechanisms in the hope of inducing the authorities to implement them.

- The anti-torture work of the UN is hampered by serious underfunding.[33] The UN Commission on Human Rights has requested the UN Secretary-General "to ensure, within the overall budgetary framework of the United Nations, the provision of an adequate and stable level of staffing, as well as the necessary technical facilities, for the United Nations bodies and mechanisms dealing with torture, in order to ensure their effective performance".[34] UN member states should act to ensure that this happens.

- All governments should contribute, as substantially as they can, to the United Nations Voluntary Fund for Victims of Torture (see section 7.7) so that the Fund can continue its valuable work of providing assistance to victims and members of their families.

8.6 The role of the medical profession

It is an irony that at the same time as Amnesty International was waging its first Campaign for the Abolition of Torture in 1972-1973, reports of medical participation in torture surfaced in several countries on different continents. Thus, the workshop at Amnesty International's Conference for the Abolition of Torture in Paris, France, in 1973 on the medical role in opposing torture was far from a theoretical discussion. At the time, there were reports of doctors assisting in torture in Chile; allegations of medical participation in torture in Brazil; the alleged abuse of psychiatry in the Soviet Union; and the presence of police doctors in places of torture in Greece. The available evidence suggested that doctors were present to contribute to the extraction of information (including by the resuscitation of victims who were at risk of death under torture) as well as to contribute to the cover-up of the effects of torture and the issuing of false medical or death certificates. In addition, they provided routine medical care to prisoners.[35]

The Paris conference adopted a number of recommendations relating to the role of doctors. Some of these have subsequently come to pass (for example, the adoption of codes of ethics aimed at preventing torture) while others remain unfulfilled (such as the recommendation that prison medical personnel be employed by an authority independent of the prison service).[36]

One of the decisions taken by the conference was to establish a team of doctors to examine people claiming to have been tortured. This concept gave rise the following year to the first Amnesty International medical group and, subsequently, to the organization's health professional network. It also underscored the important role of physicians in documenting torture.

The absence of a specific medical declaration against physician participation in torture was remedied by the World Medical Association at its annual assembly in Tokyo, Japan, in 1975. The Declaration of Tokyo (Article 1) states:

> **"The doctor shall not countenance, condone or participate in the practice of torture or other forms of cruel, inhuman or degrading procedures, whatever the offence of which the victim of such procedures is suspected, accused or guilty, and whatever the victim's beliefs or motives, and in all situations, including armed conflict and civil strife."**[37]

This code remains the strongest statement of the organized medical profession against participation in, or tolerance of, torture, although it has not resolved the problems confronted by those doctors who witness torture and are uncertain of how they can act to stop it.

Over the following decade, in the face of continuing reports of abuses, other professional bodies adopted explicit statements opposing professional involvement in or tolerance of torture. In 1975, the International Council of Nurses adopted a statement on the responsibility of nurses in the care of prisoners and detainees which proscribed participation in torture. In 1977, the World Psychiatric Association adopted the Declaration of Hawaii[38] which proscribed participation by psychiatrists in what might be called "political psychiatry" – the use of psychiatry to detain and punish opponents of the state or others who are committed to an institution for non-medical reasons. Both organizations subsequently revised their statements. The International Council of Nurses went on to adopt a number of human rights declarations including revisions of the 1975 declaration as well as statements on the role of nurses in relation to torture and capital punishment. The World Psychiatric Association in 1996 adopted a general statement on ethics – the Declaration of Madrid[39] – with specific paragraphs addressing issues such as torture. A specialist medical body, the International Council of Prison Medical Services, adopted the Oath of Athens in 1979, committing prison medical personnel to behave ethically in relations with prisoners.

The UN also addressed the issue of medical participation in torture. In 1982 it adopted the **Principles of Medical Ethics relevant to the Role of Health Personnel, particularly Physicians, in the Protection of Prisoners and Detainees against Torture and Other Cruel, Inhuman or Degrading Treatment or Punishment** (see section 5.4.2). This instrument sets out the ethics of relations between health personnel, particularly physicans, and prisoners.

The existence of these standards is a significant advance and provides clear guidance on the principles applying to the medical care of those vulnerable to ill-treatment. Less clearly resolved is the problem of what the medical practitioner should do when he or she witnesses torture or sees its after-effects. The implication of the Declaration of Tokyo's injunction not to "countenance" or "condone" torture or ill-treatment is that unethical behaviour by a colleague, or pressure to behave unethically, should be reported to an appropriate person or organization. Specific guidance is lacking, however, and there remains a need to find more effective support for doctors placed in this unenviable position.[40] The declarations of the International Council of Nurses give guidance on what nurses should do when confronted with torture, although the advice to nurses knowing of torture to "take appropriate action including reporting the matter to appropriate national and/or international bodies", present in the 1975 code,[41] was revised in 1998 to urge them simply to "take appropriate action".[42] Nurses confronted by torture are arguably even more vulnerable than doctors to pressure to conform to the wishes of the torturers.

By the mid-1970s there was increasing concern about the effects of torture and about the need for appropriate medical and psychological care to be made available to torture survivors. In Chile, health professionals addressed the effects of torture which had followed the coup of September 1973. Working with political, church and professional groups, doctors and psychologists provided help to those traumatized by detention and torture. Elsewhere in Latin America health professionals organized services for torture survivors. In Europe and North America, the arrival of refugees prompted local health workers to address the needs of those arriving from countries where torture was endemic. In Denmark, France, Canada, the Netherlands and elsewhere, groups of health professionals established services to address the needs of those suffering the effects of torture and exile.[43]

Today there is a large body of literature on torture and health care,[44] reflecting the enormous increase in medical research and health care provision in recent decades. Coincident with this increase in clinical work has been the growth of specialist centres – some 150 to 200 globally – caring for those who have been affected by political violence, torture or related trauma.[45] In addition, health care is provided to torture survivors within the public health system, although anecdotal reports suggest that workers within this setting frequently are unable to comprehend or adequately address the victim's experiences.

An important role in the development of this work has been the financial support from governments committed to funding human rights initiatives, from charitable foundations and from intergovernmental funding agencies such as the United Nations Voluntary Fund for Victims of Torture (see section 7.7).

As specialist centres saw increasing numbers of people alleging torture, they developed expertise in documenting the evidence of torture. Such evidence includes witness testimony, physical and mental signs, photographic evidence and other documentation.[46] However, there was a lack of international standards on what constituted an adequate medical report on alleged torture and in some cases this led to medical evidence being rejected by courts on grounds that it was not sufficiently "scientific". Physicians in Turkey were among those whose expert opinions were sometimes rejected by courts which wanted more concrete evidence than "mere" professional opinion. This stimulated the work of an international group of medical, legal and human rights experts to develop a rigorous protocol for torture investigation. Between 1996 and 1999 this group elaborated a detailed approach to the medical documentation of torture. In August 1999 the resulting manual – the *Istanbul Protocol* – was presented to the UN High Commissioner for Human Rights, and the manual was published in 2001 in the UN Professional Training Series (see section 7.3, "Further reading").[47]

In recent years a number of professional associations have increased their activity in the realm of human rights protection, seeing it as a natural component of concern for public health and well-being. The Turkish Medical Association has conducted conferences on human rights themes with a particular focus on prison health care, ethics and the problem of ill-treatment. The British Medical Association has continued a tradition of concern with the medical role in opposing torture, most recently publishing a major study on doctors and human rights.[48] The World Medical Association has made appeals in cases of doctors at risk and has adopted human rights declarations.

NGOs such as the International Federation of Health and Human Rights Organizations and the International Rehabilitation Council for Torture Victims, as well as many national medical NGOs, have spoken out against torture, ill-treatment and other human rights abuses. The health professional network of Amnesty International continues to campaign against torture and to promote guidelines such as those set out in the Istanbul Protocol and the numerous professional statements against human rights abuses. There is an important role for all these – professional associations, medical human rights organizations and humanitarian organizations – to play in joining with the wider human rights community to build a world free from torture.

8.7 Towards a world without torture: the role of civil society

As cited earlier in this manual, Article 5 of the Universal Declaration of Human Rights states: "No one shall be subjected to torture or to cruel, inhuman or degrading treatment or punishment." Since its adoption in 1948, the Universal Declaration of Human Rights has served both as a source of international law and as an articulation of the aspirations of humanity. The Preamble to the Universal Declaration refers to it as "a common standard of achievement for all peoples and all nations, to the end that every individual and every organ of society, keeping this Declaration constantly in mind, shall strive by teaching and education to promote respect for these rights and freedoms and by progressive measures, national and international, to secure their universal and effective recognition and observance... " The responsibility to ensure freedom from torture and ill-treatment is a responsibility of governments, but the task of building a world free from torture is a task for all of us.

Around the world, people have formed groups to work for human rights. Much of the work is also done by other organizations, such as trade unions, and by individuals in their professions – lawyers, health professionals, journalists, religious leaders and many others. Their efforts combine to exert a constant pressure on governments to fulfil their obligations for the prevention of torture and ill-treatment. A clear understanding of governments' obligations by these groups and individuals will enable them to remind public officials of what those obligations are.

The efforts are in various realms – in medical clinics, in courts, in the reform of laws, in the area of public opinion. These specialized efforts, carried out by professionals and by organizations which themselves are often specialized, complement each other and are mutually reinforcing. The same complementarity exists at the international level, where organizations such as the members of the Coalition of International NGOs against Torture (CINAT)* are working in their often specialized ways to combat torture – through exposure of the abuses, exerting pressure on governments, lobbying at the international level, providing rehabilitation, supporting survivors who are seeking redress, providing human rights education and training for governmental officials and local NGOs and campaigning to mobilize international opinion.

One contribution which NGOs can make in raising public awareness and mobilizing opinion is through campaigning.[49] In a concerted new effort to eradicate torture around the world, Amnesty International launched its third worldwide campaign against torture in October 2000. The painstaking planning and tireless efforts of those involved set a new benchmark for the level of media coverage and attention that a human rights campaign can and should achieve.**

As a way of attracting attention, Amnesty International members wrapped public buildings, former detention centres and other places of symbolic signifi-cance with yellow-and-black-striped "Torture Free Zone" tape. In Nepal, for example, members organized a motorbike rally involving more than 80 riders. They set out from the capital, Kathmandu, in two groups, heading for the eastern and western extremes of the country. On their way the riders went into every police station trying to persuade police officers to declare their police stations "torture free zones" and to show their commitment by displaying "Torture Free Zone" tape. The day after the launch of the campaign, 14 of the country's 15 newspapers carried reports about the campaign, many on the front page. As well as imaginative and effective public events, members organized a workshop for lawyers on the shortcomings of Nepal's Torture Compensation Act and partici-pated in human rights training for more than 700 police personnel.

More than 30,000 people from 188 countries signed up to participate in actions through an Internet website created for the campaign, www.stoptorture.org.

---

* The Coalition of International NGOs against Torture (CINAT) brings together six international NGOs which are committed to ending and preventing torture, bringing torturers to account, providing rehabilitation and obtaining justice and reparation for survivors of torture. One of its activities is the coordination of events around the world for the annual UN International Day in Support of Victims of Torture (26 June), proclaimed in UN General Assembly resolution 52/149 of 12 December 1997. CINAT has also pressed for universal ratification of the Convention against Torture and lobbied for the adoption of an Optional Protocol to that Convention providing for a global system of inspection visits to places of detention. As stated by the UN High Commissioner for Human Rights, the membership of CINAT "reflects the diversity of approaches and expertise that are needed in order to successfully combat torture around the world" (CINAT, 2001, p. 1). CINAT includes organizations with activist membership structures as well as "umbrella" advisory and support bodies and networks of specialized professional agencies. Its members (in addition to Amnesty International), with website addresses, are the **Association for the Prevention of Torture**, www.apt.ch; the **International Federation of ACAT** (Action by Christians for the Abolition of Torture), www.fiacat.org; the **International Rehabilitation Council for Torture Victims**, www.irct.org; **Redress**, www.redress.org; and the **World Organization against Torture**, www.omct.org. The website address of CINAT is www.cinat.org.

** A list of selected reports issued during this campaign can be found in Appendix 2.

The subscribers were notified within hours of Amnesty International learning of a person at risk of being tortured. On a typical case, thousands of subscribers signed an on-line petition to the authorities and hundreds sent individual email messages. The appeals were followed by improvements in many cases.

One objective of the campaign was to press as many countries as possible to become states parties to the Convention against Torture. Between the campaign launch and 30 June 2002, seven states became parties to the Convention and two others signed it, indicating their intention to become parties at a future date.[50] Seven countries made declarations under Article 22 of the Convention providing for individual complaints.[51]

Chapter 1 of this manual described the rise of the international anti-torture movement since the Second World War, including the formation of NGOs to fight torture and the development of the work of existing NGOs. Such NGOs and other human rights defenders have worked courageously and often under great difficulties in countries where torture has become a method of political repression by the state.[52] But even where a government is firmly committed to the prevention of torture, where strong safeguards are in place and international standards are generally respected, one can never preclude the possibility that some public official will some day commit an act of torture or ill-treatment – just as one can never ensure that no public official will ever commit a crime. The eradication of torture by state agents should rather be seen as the achievement of conditions in which:

- torture and ill-treatment are extremely unlikely;

- they will occur, if at all, only in isolated cases; and

- if they do occur, there will be a reaction from the authorities which prevents the perpetrator from repeating the act, which satisfies the conditions of justice and reparation described in Chapter 7, and which condemns the act in such a way that other public officials will not be tempted to do the same.

Civil society needs to be ready to press the authorities to react appropri-ately when cases of torture or ill-treatment come to light. Two staff members of the International Committee of the Red Cross (ICRC) have coined the term "internal regulatory mechanisms" to refer to all the means by which civil society – including human rights groups, the news media, democratic institutions – can make its voice heard in such cases. There are also "external regulatory mechanisms", including international NGOs and other states, through which pressure may come to bear on the authorities from outside the country.[53] Pressure is also needed to ensure that the authorities fulfil their obligations to act with due diligence in preventing torture and ill-treatment by private individuals and combating violence in the community and the family.

Amnesty International's third worldwide campaign against torture was entitled "Take a step to stamp out torture". This slogan was chosen to convey the idea that each of us can join in the effort to eradicate torture and ill-treatment. As this manual has shown, there are many steps to be taken, in many domains and at all levels – local, national and international. We must hope that through these efforts we will some day come as close as humanly possible to eliminating torture from the face of the earth.

Appendix 1

Bibliography: Books, articles and manuals

(Note: United Nations training manuals are listed in Appendix 3.)

Association for the Prevention of Torture, 1997, *20 ans consacrés à la réalisation d'une idée: Recueil d'articles en l'honneur de Jean-Jacques Gautier* (20 Years Dedicated to the Realization of an Idea: Collection of Articles in Honour of Jean-Jacques Gautier), Geneva, Association for the Prevention of Torture

Association for the Prevention of Torture, 1999, *The Impact of External Visiting of Police Stations on Prevention of Torture and Ill-treatment*, Geneva, Association for the Prevention of Torture

B'Tselem, 1997, *Legitimizing Torture: The Israeli High Court of Justice Rulings in the Bilbeisi, Hamdan and Mubarak Cases*, Jerusalem, B'Tselem

Bank, Roland, 1997, "International Efforts to Combat Torture and Inhuman Treatment: Have the New Mechanisms Improved Protection?", *European Journal of International Law*, ISSN 0938-5428, Vol. 8, No. 4, pp. 613-637

Bank, Roland, 2000, "Country-oriented procedures under the Convention against Torture: Towards a new dynamism", in Philip Alston and James Crawford, eds., *The Future of UN Human Rights Treaty Monitoring*, Cambridge, UK, Cambridge University Press, ISBN 0-521-64195-0 (hardcover), 0-521-64574-3 (paperback), pp. 145-174

Başoğlu, Metin, ed., 1992, *Torture and its Consequences: Current Treatment Approaches*, Cambridge, UK, Cambridge University Press, ISBN 0-521-39299-3 (hardcover), 0-521-65954-X (paperback)

Bennoune, Karima, 1997, "'A Practice which Debases Everyone Involved': Corporal Punishment under International Law", in Association for the Prevention of Torture, 1997, pp. 203-228

Boot, Machtheld, Rodney Dixon and Christopher K. Hall, 1999, "Article 7 – Crimes against Humanity", in Otto Triffterer, ed., *Commentary on the Rome Statute of the International Criminal Court: Observers' Notes, Article by Article*, Baden-Baden, Germany, Nomos, ISBN 3-7890-6173-5, pp. 117-172

Boraine, Alex, 2000, *A Country Unmasked: Inside South Africa's Truth and Reconciliation Commission*, Oxford, UK, Oxford University Press, ISBN 0-19-571805-4

Bossuyt, Marc J., 1987, *Guide to the "Travaux Préparatoires" of the International Covenant on Civil and Political Rights*, Dordrecht, The Netherlands, Martinus Nijhoff, ISBN 90-247-3467-3

Boulesbaa, Ahcene, 1999, *The U.N. Convention on Torture and the Prospects for Enforcement*, The Hague, Kluwer, ISBN 90-411-0457-7

Brett, Rachel and Raymond J. Toney, 1997, "Torture in the Military?", in Association for the Prevention of Torture, 1997, pp. 231-237

British Medical Association, 2001, *The Medical Profession and Human Rights: Handbook for a Changing Agenda*, London, Zed Books, ISBN 1-85649-611-2 (hardcover), 1-85649-612-0 (paperback)

Burgers, J. Herman and Hans Danelius, 1988, *The United Nations Convention against Torture: A Handbook on the Convention against Torture and Other Cruel, Inhuman or Degrading Treatment or Punishment*, Dordrecht, The Netherlands, Martinus Nijhoff, ISBN 90-247-3609-9

Cassese, Antonio, 1996, *Inhuman States: Imprisonment, Detention and Torture in Europe Today*, Cambridge, UK, Polity Press, ISBN 0-7456-1721-2 (hardcover), 0-7456-1722-0 (paperback)

Coalition of International Non-Governmental Organisations Against Torture (CINAT), 2001, *Together against Torture* (booklet)

Copelon, Rhonda, 1994, "Intimate Terror: Understanding Domestic Violence as Torture", in Rebecca J. Cook, ed., 1994, *Human Rights of Women: National and International Perspectives*, Philadelphia, University of Pennsylvania Press, ISBN 0-8122-1538-9, pp. 116-152

Crawshaw, Ralph and Leif Holmström, eds., *Essential Texts on Human Rights for the Police: A Compilation of International Instruments*, The Hague, Kluwer, ISBN 90-411-1557-9

de Rover, Cees, 1998, *To Serve and to Protect: Human Rights and Humanitarian Law for Police and Security Forces*, Geneva, International Committee of the Red Cross, ISBN 2-88145-093-8

Evans, Malcolm D., 2002, "Getting to Grips with Torture", *International and Comparative Law Quarterly*, ISSN 0020-5893, Vol. 51, No. 2, pp. 365-383

Evans, Malcolm D. and Rod Morgan, 1998, *Preventing Torture: A Study of the European Convention for the Prevention of Torture and Inhuman or Degrading Treatment or Punishment*, Oxford, UK, Oxford University Press, ISBN 0-19-826257-4

Giffard, Camille, 2000, *The Torture Reporting Handbook: How to document and respond to allegations of torture within the international system for the protection of human rights*, Colchester, UK, Human Rights Centre, University of Essex, ISBN 1-874635-28-5 (available on the website of the University of Essex Human Rights Centre at www.essex.ac.uk/torturehandbook)

Giffard, Camille and Nigel S. Rodley, 2002, "The Approach of International Tribunals to Medical Evidence in Cases Involving Allegations of Torture", in Peel and Iacopino, eds., pp. 19-43

Gorlick, Brian, 1999, "The Convention and the Committee against Torture: A Complementary Protection Regime for Refugees", *International Journal of Refugee Law*, ISSN 0953-8186, Vol. 11, No. 3, pp. 479-495

Hayner, Priscilla B., 2001, *Unspeakable Truths: Confronting State Terror and Atrocity*, New York and London, Routledge, ISBN 0-415-92477-4

Human Rights Watch, 1995, *Children in Confinement in Louisiana*, New York, Human Rights Watch, ISBN 1-56432-159-2 (available on the Human Rights Watch website at www.hrw.org)

Human Rights Watch, 1996, *Modern Capital of Human Rights? Abuses in the State of Georgia*, New York, Human Rights Watch, ISBN 1-56432-169-X (available on the Human Rights Watch website at www.hrw.org)

Human Rights Watch, 1999, *Spare the Child: Corporal Punishment in Kenyan Schools*, New York, Human Rights Watch (available on the Human Rights Watch website at www.hrw.org)

Ingelse, Chris, 2001, *The UN Committee against Torture: An Assessment*, The Hague, Kluwer, ISBN 90-411-1650-8

Jaranson, James M. and M. K. Popkin, eds., 1993, *Caring for Victims of Torture*, Washington, DC, American Psychiatric Press, ISBN 0-88048-774-7

Jenkins, Catherine, 2000, "After the Dry White Season: The Dilemmas of Reparation and Reconstruction in South Africa", *South African Journal on Human Rights*, ISSN 0258-7203, Vol. 16, Part 3, pp. 415-485

Kois, Lisa M., 1998, "Dance, Sister, Dance!", in Bertil Dunér, ed., *An End to Torture: Strategies for its Eradication*, London, Zed Books, ISBN 1-85649-621-X (hardcover), 1-85649-622-8 (paperback), pp. 85-108

MacKinnon, Catharine A., 1993, "On Torture: A Feminist Perspective on Human Rights", in Kathleen E. Mahoney and Paul Mahoney, eds., *Human Rights in the Twenty-first Century: A Global Challenge*, Dordrecht, The Netherlands, Martinus Nijhoff, ISBN 0-7923-1810-2

Man, Nathalie, 2000, *Children, Torture and Power: The torture of children by states and armed opposition groups*, London, Save the Children, ISBN 1-84187-038-2

Méndez, Juan E., 1997, "Accountability for Past Abuses", *Human Rights Quarterly*, ISSN 0275-0392, Vol. 19, No. 2, pp. 255-282

Morgan, Rod and Malcolm D. Evans, eds., 1999, *Protecting Prisoners: The Standards of the European Committee for the Prevention of Torture in Context*, Oxford, UK, Oxford University Press, ISBN 0-19-829821-8

Morgan, Rod and Malcolm D. Evans, 2001, *Combating torture in Europe: The work and standards of the European Committee for the Prevention of Torture (CPT)*, Strasbourg, Council of Europe Publishing, ISBN 92-871-4614-4

Morsink, Johannes, 1999, *The Universal Declaration of Human Rights: Origins, Drafting, and Intent*, Philadelphia, University of Pennsylvania Press, ISBN 0-8122-3474-X (hardcover), 0-8122-1747-0 (paperback)

Murdoch, Jim, 1999, "CPT Standards within the Context of the Council of Europe", in Morgan and Evans, eds., 1999, pp. 103-136

Nowak, Manfred, 1993, *U.N. Covenant on Civil and Political Rights: CCPR Commentary*, Kehl, Germany, N.P. Engel, ISBN 3-88357-106-7

Organization for Security and Co-operation in Europe (OSCE), 1999, *Preventing Torture: A Handbook for OSCE Field Staff*, Warsaw, OSCE Office for Democratic Institutions and Human Rights (ODIHR) (available on the ODIHR website at www.osce.org/odihr)

Peel, Michael, 2002, "Male Sexual Abuse in Detention", in Peel and Iacopino, eds., 2002, pp. 179-190

Peel, Michael and Vincent Iacopino, eds., 2002, *The Medical Documentation of Torture*, London, Greenwich Medical Media, ISBN 1-84110-068-4

Penal Reform International (PRI), 1995, *Making Standards Work: An international handbook on good prison practice*, The Hague, Penal Reform International (available on the website of Penal Reform International at www.penalreform.org)

Peters, Edward, 1996, *Torture*, expanded edition, Philadelphia, University of Pennsylvania Press, ISBN 0-8122-1599-0

Peukert, Wolfgang, 1999, "The European Convention for the Prevention of Torture and the European Convention on Human Rights", in Morgan and Evans, eds., 1999, pp. 85-102

Pictet, Jean S., ed., 1952-1960, *The Geneva Conventions of 12 August 1949: Commentary* (4 vols), Geneva, International Committee of the Red Cross (ICRC) (available online on the ICRC website at www.icrc.org)

Prokosch, Eric, 1999, "Amnesty International's 12-Point Programme for the Prevention of Torture: An Example of NGO Standard Setting", in Morgan and Evans, eds., 1999, pp. 167-177

Randall, Glenn R., and Ellen L. Lutz, 1991, *Serving Survivors of Torture: A Practical Manual for Health Professionals and Other Service Providers*, Washington, DC, American Association for the Advancement of Science, ISBN 0-87168-433-8

Redress, 2000, *Challenging Impunity for Torture: A Manual for bringing criminal and civil proceedings in England and Wales for torture committed abroad*, London, The Redress Trust, ISBN 0-9534892-1-3

Reyes, Hernan, 2002, "Visits to Prisoners and Documentation of Torture", in Peel and Iacopino, eds., 2002, pp. 77-99

Rodley, Nigel S., 1993, "Soft Law, Tough Standards", Interights *Bulletin* 43, ISSN 0268-3709

Rodley, Nigel S., 1999, *The Treatment of Prisoners Under International Law*, 2nd edition, Oxford, UK, Clarendon Press, ISBN 0-19-826564-6 (hardcover), 0-19-826563-8 (paperback)

Schabas, William A., 1996, *The Death Penalty as Cruel Treatment and Torture: Capital Punishment Challenged in the World's Courts*, Boston, USA, Northeastern University Press, ISBN 1-55553-268-3

Seifert, Ruth, 2002, "Rape: The Female Body as a Symbol and a Sign: Gender-Specific Violence and the Cultural Construction of War", in Ilkka Taipale and others, eds., *War or Health?* A Reader, London, Zed Books, ISBN 1-85649-950-2 (hardcover), 1-85649-951-0 (paperback), pp. 280-294

South Africa, Truth and Reconciliation Commission, 1998, *Truth and Reconciliation Commission of South Africa Report* (5 vols), Pretoria, Truth and Reconciliation Commission; distributed for the Truth and Reconciliation Commission by Juta & Co., Cape Town, ISBN 0-6202-3078-9 (unedited version available on the South African government website at www.polity.org.za/govdocs/commissions)

Stroun, Jacques and Pascal Daudin, 1997, "*Une analyse des facteurs qui favorisent l'apparition de la torture*" ("An Analysis of Factors Conducive to the Appearance of Torture") (French only), in Association for the Prevention of Torture, 1997, pp. 117-128

Sullivan, Donna, 1995, "The Public/Private Distinction in International Human Rights Law", in Julie Peters and Andrea Wolper, eds., *Women's Rights, Human Rights: International Feminist Perspectives*, New York and London, Routledge, ISBN 0-415-90994-5 (hardcover), 0-415-90995-3 (paperback), pp. 126-134

Suntinger, Walter, 1999, "CPT and Other International Standards for the Prevention of Torture", in Morgan and Evans, eds., 1999, pp. 137-166

van der Veer, Guus, 1998, *Counselling and Therapy with Refugees and Victims of Trauma: Psychological Problems of Victims of War, Torture and Repression*, 2nd edition, Chichester, UK, John Wiley, ISBN 0-471-98226-1

Van Bueren, Geraldine, ed., 1998, *Childhood Abused: Protecting Children against Torture, Cruel, Inhuman and Degrading Treatment and Punishment*, Aldershot, UK, Ashgate, ISBN 1-85521-918-2

van Willigen, Loes H.M., 1992, "Organization of care and rehabilitation services for victims of torture and other forms of organized violence: a review of current issues" in Başoğlu, ed., 1992, pp. 277-298

Welsh, J., 1996, "Traumatic Stress and the Role of NGOs: The Contribution of Non-Governmental Organizations", in Yael Danieli, Nigel S. Rodley and Lars Weisaeth, eds., *International Responses to Traumatic Stress: Humanitarian, Human Rights, Justice, Peace and Development Contributions, Collaborative Actions and Future Initiatives*, Amityville, NY, USA, Baywood, ISBN 0-89503-132-9, pp. 131-159

Appendix 2

Bibliography: Amnesty International documents

Amnesty International documents are cited by title and AI Index, except for some early reports which were not given AI Index numbers. The first element of the AI Index (e.g. ACT 40, AMR 51) denotes the subject matter or the region and country; the final element denotes the year of publication (years prior to 2001 are abbreviated, e.g. 99, for 1999, 00 for 2000). Documents denoted by an ISBN have been published for sale as Amnesty International Publications.

Amnesty International documents can be obtained from Amnesty International section offices or, in countries where there is no Amnesty International office, from Amnesty International's International Secretariat at 1 Easton Street, London WC1X 0DW, United Kingdom. Almost all public documents issued since 1996 can be found on the Amnesty International website at www.amnesty.org, which also includes contact details for Amnesty International section offices.

The document *Universal jurisdiction: The duty of states to enact and implement legislation* is available as a CD-ROM from the International Justice Project at Amnesty International's International Secretariat (e-mail address: ijp@amnesty.org).

Documents cited in this manual

Title and bibliographic details	AI Index
Amnesty International Conference for the Abolition of Torture, Paris, 10-11 December 1973, Final report, London, Amnesty International, undated [1974]	
Broken bodies, shattered minds: Torture and ill-treatment of women, ISBN 0-86210-296-0	ACT 40/001/2001
Campaigning Manual, ISBN 0-86210-271-5	ACT 10/002/2001
Crimes of hate, conspiracy of silence: Torture and ill-treatment based on sexual identity, ISBN 0-86210-302-9	ACT 40/016/2001
"Disappearances" and Political Killings – Human Rights Crisis of the 1990s: A Manual for Action (cited as *"Disappearances" and Political Killings...: A Manual for Action*), Amsterdam, Amnesty International Dutch Section, 1994, ISBN 90-6463-095-X	ACT 33/01/94
Documenting human rights violations: The example of torture	ACT 75/04/00
End impunity: Justice for the victims of torture, ISBN 0-86210-307-X	ACT 40/024/2001

Title and bibliographic details	AI Index
Ethical Codes and Declarations Relevant to the Health Professions: An Amnesty International compilation of selected ethical texts, 3rd revised edition, ISBN 0-86210-233-2	ACT 75/04/94
Ethical Codes and Declarations Relevant to the Health Professions: An Amnesty International compilation of selected ethical and human rights texts, 4th revised edition	ACT 75/05/00
Fair Trials Manual, ISBN 0-86210-277-4	POL 30/02/98
Hidden scandal, secret shame: Torture and ill treatment of children, ISBN 0-86210- 294-4	ACT 40/38/00
India: Words into action – recommendations for the prevention of torture	ASA 20/003/2001
International standards on the death penalty	ACT 50/10/98
Israel and the Occupied Territories: Death by shaking – the case of 'Abd al-Samad Harizat	MDE 15/23/95
Medical and psychosocial services for victims of human rights violations	ACT 75/06/00
Pakistan: "Keep your fetters bright and polished" – the continued use of bar fetters and cross fetters	ASA 33/12/95
People's Republic of China: Torture – a growing scourge in China: time for action	ASA 17/004/2001
Racism and the administration of justice, ISBN 0-86210-305-3	ACT 40/020/2001
Refugees: Human rights have no borders, ISBN 0-86210-265-0	ACT 34/03/97
Report of the Stockholm Conference on Torture	ACT 40/05/97
Report on Torture, London, Duckworth and Amnesty International Publications, 1973	
Report on Torture, 2nd edition, London, Duckworth and Amnesty International Publications, 1975, ISBN 0-7156-0711-1 (hardcover), 0-7156-0712-X (paperback)	
Respect, protect, fulfil – Women's human rights: state responsibility for abuses by "non-state actors"	IOR 50/01/00
Saudi Arabia remains a fertile ground for torture with impunity	MDE 23/004/2002
South Africa: Preserving the gains for human rights in the "war against crime" – Memorandum to the South African Government and South African Law Commission on the draft Anti-Terrorism Bill, 2000	AFR 53/04/00
Stopping the torture trade, ISBN 0-86210-295-2	ACT 40/002/2001
Take a step to stamp out torture, ISBN	ACT 40/13/00
Torture in Russia: "This man-made hell"	EUR 46/04/97
Torture in the Eighties, ISBN 0-86210-066-6	ACT 04/01/84
Turkey: The duty to supervise, investigate and prosecute	EUR 44/24/99
United Kingdom: Political killings in Northern Ireland	EUR 45/01/94
United Kingdom: The Pinochet case - universal jurisidction and the absnce of immunity for crimes against humanity	EUR 45/01/99
Universal jurisdiction: Belgian court has jurisdiction in Sharon case to investigate 1982 Sabra and Chatila killings	IOR 53/001/2002

Title and bibliographical details	AI Index
Universal jurisdiction: The duty of states to enact and implement legislation – Chapter 10, Torture: State practice at the national level	IOR 53/013/2001
Universal jurisdiction: The duty of states to enact and implement legislation – Chapter 14, Overcoming obstacles to implementing universal jurisdiction	IOR 53/017/2001
USA: A briefing for the UN Committee against Torture	AMR 51/56/00
USA: Lost in the labyrinth – detention of asylum-seekers	AMR 51/51/99
USA: Rights for all	AMR 51/35/98
USA: Rights for all – cruelty in control? The stun belt and other electro-shock equipment in law enforcement	AMR 51/54/99
Using the international human rights system to combat racial discrimination: A handbook, ISBN 0-86210-300-2	IOR 80/001/2001

Other selected documents issued in 2000-2001 during Amnesty International's third worldwide Campaign against Torture

Title	AI Index
Albania: Torture and ill-treatment – an end to impunity?	EUR 11/001/2001
Armenia: Conclusions and recommendations of the United Nations Committee against Torture	EUR 54/001/2001
Bahrain: Human rights developments and Amnesty International's continuing concerns	MDE 11/03/00
Bangladesh: Torture and impunity	ASA 13/07/00
Belarus: Briefing for the UN Committee against Torture	EUR 49/002/2001
Bolivia: Torture and ill-treatment – Amnesty International's concerns	AMR 18/008/2001
"They treat us like animals": Torture and ill-treatment in Brazil – dehumanization and impunity within the criminal justice system	AMR 19/022/2001
Czech Republic: Arbitrary detention and police ill-treatment following September 2000 protests	EUR 71/001/2001
Democratic Republic of Congo: Torture – a weapon of war against unarmed civilians	AFR 62/012/2001
Ecuador: Continued torture and ill-treatment of lesbian, gay, bisexual and transgender people	AMR 28/009/2001
Egypt: Torture and imprisonment for actual or perceived sexual orientation	MDE 12/033/2001
Egypt: Torture remains rife as cries for justice go unheeded	MDE 12/001/2001
Failures at Fifty: Impunity for torture and ill-treatment in Europe on the 50th anniversary of the European Convention on Human Rights	EUR 01/04/00

Title	AI Index
Guinea: The Alpha Condé affair – a mockery of a trial	AFR 29/02/00
India: The battle against fear and discrimination – the impact of violence against women in Uttar Pradesh and Rajasthan	ASA 20/016/2001
India: Time to act to stop torture and impunity in West Bengal	ASA 20/033/2001
Iraq: Systematic torture of political prisoners	MDE 14/008/2001
Israel and the Occupied Territories: Mass arrests and police brutality	MDE15/58/00
Italy: G8 Genoa policing operation – a summary of concerns	EUR 30/012/2001
Jamaica: Killings and violence by police – how many more victims?	AMR 38/003/2001
Kenya: Ending the cycle of impunity	AFR 32/11/2001
Kenya: Prisons – death due to torture and cruel, inhuman and degrading conditions	AFR 32/10/00
Lebanon: Torture and ill-treatment of women in pre-trial detention – a culture of acquiescence	MDE 18/009/2001
Liberia: Killings, torture and rape continue in Lofa County	AFR 34/009/2001
Mexico: Justice betrayed – torture in the judicial system	AMR 41/021/2001
Myanmar: The institution of torture	ASA 16/24/00
Nepal: Make torture a crime	ASA 31/002/2001
Peru: Torture continues unabated	AMR 46/40/00
Philippines: Fear, shame and impunity – rape and sexual abuse of women in custody	ASA 35/001/2001
Philippines: The Ronaldo Abadilla murder inquiry – an urgent need for effective investigation of torture	ASA 35/08/00
Portugal: "Small problems..."? A summary of concerns	EUR 38/002/2001
Syria: Torture, despair and dehumanization in Tadmur Military Prison	MDE 24/014/2001
Turkey: "F-type" prisons – isolation and allegations of torture or ill-treatment	EUR 44/025/2001
Turkey: An end to torture and impunity is overdue!	EUR 44/072/2001
Ukraine: Ukraine before the United Nations Human Rights Committee	EUR 50/001/2001
USA: Abuses continue unabated? Cruel and inhumane treatment at Virginia supermaximum security prisons	AMR 51/065/2001
USA: Allegations of homophobic abuse by Chicago police officers	AMR 51/022/2001
USA: "I'm not an inmate – why should I be treated as one?" – women asylum-seekers punished for state's failure to protect them	AMR 51/028/2001

Appendix 3

Bibliography: United Nations documents and publications

Appendix 3 gives details of **documents** emanating from the *UN Committee against Torture*, the *Human Rights Committee*, the *Committee on the Elimination of Discrimination against Women* (CEDAW), the *Special Rapporteur on torture* and the *Special Rapporteur on violence against women, its causes and consequences* (Special Rapporteur on violence against women) which are cited in this manual. It also includes full bibliographic details of all UN **publications** referred to in this manual. (Not included in this appendix are decisions of the Committee against Torture and the Human Rights Committee on individual cases, which are listed in Appendix 4.)

Citation of UN documents: UN document symbols include an indication of the organ to whose body of documentation the document belongs, e.g.

A/...	General Assembly
E/CN.4/...	Commission on Human Rights

and an indication of the session or year, e.g.

A/56/...	a document of the 56th session of the General Assembly
E/CN.4/2001/...	a document of the 2001 session of the Commission on Human Rights

The UN document symbol is the same for all language versions of a particular document.

Reports of the **treaty bodies** to the UN General Assembly are published in the General Assembly Official Records (GAOR) and have UN document symbols (A/.../...) in which A refers to the UN General Assembly, the first number refers to the session of the General Assembly to which the report was submitted and the second number refers to the treaty body (38 stands for CEDAW, 40 for the Human Rights Committee, 44 for the Committee against Torture). (The most recent documents had not yet been included in a report to the General Assembly at the time of writing this manual and are cited in the endnotes by the UN document symbol under which they originally appeared. CAT/... stands for documents from the Committee against Torture, CCPR/... for documents from the Human Rights Committee.

UN documents, UN resolutions and some UN publications relating to human rights can be found on the UN human rights website at www.unhchr.ch. Most documents on that website are available in English, French and Spanish. General Comments adopted before April 2001 are also reproduced in *Compilation of General Comments and General Recommendations Adopted by Human Rights Treaty Bodies*, UN Doc. HRI/GEN/1/Rev.5, issued in April 2001. Resolutions of the UN Economic and Social Council (ECOSOC) (since 1982), the General Assembly (since 1977) and the Security Council (since 1946) can be found on the UN website at www.un.org.

Obtaining UN publications: The Human Rights Fact Sheets are distributed free of charge. They can be obtained from:

Office of the UN High Commissioner
    for Human Rights
UN Office at Geneva
CH-1211 Geneva 10, Switzerland

UN High Commissioner for Human Rights –
    New York Office
United Nations
New York, NY 10017, USA

UN sales publications can be purchased from bookstores and distributors or from:

(for orders from North America, Latin America, Asia and the Pacific Islands)

(for orders from Europe, Africa, Middle East)

UN Publications
Sales Section, 2 United Nations Plaza
Room DC2-853, Dept. I010
New York, NY 10017, USA

UN Publications
Sales Office and Bookshop
CH-1211 Geneva 10,
Switzerland

Tel: 1 (212) 963-8302; 1 (800) 253-9646
Fax: 1 (212) 963-3489
e-mail: publications@un.org

Tel: 41 (22) 917-2613, 41 (22) 917-2614
Fax: 41 (22) 917-0027

An order form can be downloaded from the UN human rights website. Most human rights publications are available in the six UN official languages – Arabic, Chinese, English, French, Russian and Spanish.

Committee against Torture

Annual reports to the UN General Assembly

A/48/44/Add.1 Report to 48th session of the General Assembly (1993),
                Inquiry under Article 20: Turkey
A/49/44   Report to 49th session of the General Assembly (1994)
A/50/44   Report to 50th session of the General Assembly (1995)
A/51/44   Report to 51st session of the General Assembly (1996)
A/52/44   Report to 52nd session of the General Assembly (1997)
A/53/44   Report to 53rd session of the General Assembly (1998)
A/54/44   Report to 54th session of the General Assembly (1999)
A/55/44   Report to 55th session of the General Assembly (2000)
A/56/44   Report to 56th session of the General Assembly (2001)

General Comment on the Convention against Torture

General Comment 1 on Article 3 in the context of article 22 (1997), A/53/44, Annex IX

Human Rights Committee

Annual reports to the UN General Assembly

A/50/40   Report to 50th session of the General Assembly (1995)
A/51/40   Report to 51st session of the General Assembly (1996)
A/52/40   Report to 52nd session of the General Assembly (1997)
A/54/40   Report to 54th session of the General Assembly (1999)
A/55/40   Report to 55th session of the General Assembly (2000)
A/56/40   Report to 56th session of the General Assembly (2001)

General Comments on the International Covenant on Civil and Political Rights (ICCPR), indicating the article or subject and year of adoption, with bibliographic details

General Comment 7* on Article 7 (1982), A/37/40, Annex V
General Comment 8 on Article 9 (1982), A/37/40, Annex V
General Comment 13 on Article 14 (1984), A/39/40, Annex VI
General Comment 15 on the position of aliens under the Covenant (1986), A/41/40,
          Annex VI
General Comment 16 on Article 17 (1988), A/43/40, Annex VI
General Comment 18 on non-discrimination (1989), A/45/40, Annex VI.A
General Comment 20 on Article 7 (1992), A/47/40, Annex VI.A
General Comment 21 on Article 10 (1992), A/47/40, Annex VI.B
General Comment 24 on issues relating to reservations made upon ratification or accession
          to the Covenant or the Optional Protocols thereto, or in relation to
          declarations under Article 41 of the Covenant (1994), A/50/40, Annex V
General Comment 28 on Article 3 (2000), A/55/40, Annex VI.B
General Comment 29 on Article 4 (2001), A/56/40, Annex VI

Committee on the Elimination of Discrimination against Women

General Recommendations relating to the Convention on the Elimination of All Forms of Discrimination against Women

General Recommendation 14 on female circumcision (1990), Report to the 45th session
of the UN General Assembly, A/45/38, para. 438
General Recommendation 19 on violence against women (1992), Report to the 47th
session of the UN General Assembly, A/47/38, Chapter I

---

* General comment 7 was superseded by General Comment 20, adopted in 1992.

Special Rapporteur on torture

Annual reports to the UN General Assembly and to the UN Commission on Human Rights

A/54/426	Report to 54th session of the General Assembly (1999)
A/55/290	Report to 55th session of the General Assembly (2000)
A/56/156	Report to 56th session of the General Assembly (2001)
E/CN.4/1986/15	Report to 42nd session of the Commission on Human Rights
E/CN.4/1994/31	Report to 50th session of the Commission on Human Rights
E/CN.4/1995/34	Report to 51st session of the Commission on Human Rights
E/CN.4/1996/35	Report to 52nd session of the Commission on Human Rights
E/CN.4/1997/7	Report to 53rd session of the Commission on Human Rights
E/CN.4/1998/38	Report to 54th session of the Commission on Human Rights
E/CN.4/1998/38/ Add.1	Report to 54th session of the Commission on Human Rights, Addendum: Summary of cases transmitted to Governments and replies received
E/CN.4/2001/66	Report to 57th session of the Commission on Human Rights
E/CN.4/2002/76	Report to 58th session of the Commission on Human Rights
E/CN.4/2002/137	Report to 58th session of the Commission on Human Rights of the newly appointed Special Rapporteur on torture, Mr. Theo van Boven

Reports on country visits

E/CN.4/1992/17/Add.1	Visit to **Indonesia and East Timor** (4 to16 November 1991)
E/CN.4/1995/34/Add.1	Visit to the **Russian Federation** (17 to 28 July 1994)
E/CN.4/1995/111	Visit to **Colombia** with the UN Special Rapporteur on extrajudicial, summary or arbitrary executions (17 to 26 October 1994)
E/CN.4/1996/35/Add.2	Visit to **Chile** (21 to 26 August 1995)
E/CN.4/1997/7/Add. 2	Visit to **Pakistan** (23 February to 3 March 1996)
E/CN.4/1997/7/Add.3	Visit to **Venezuela** (7 to 16 June 1996)
E/CN.4/1998/38/Add.2	Visit to **Mexico** (7 to 16 August 1997)
E/CN.4/1999/61/Add.1	Visit to **Turkey** (9 to 19 November 1998)
E/CN.4/2000/9/Add.2	Visit to **Cameroon** (12 to 20 May 1999)
E/CN.4/2000/9/Add.3	Visit to **Romania** (19 to 29 April 1999)
E/CN.4/2000/9/Add.4	Visit to **Kenya** (20 to 29 September 1999)
E/CN.4/2001/66/Add.1	Visit to **Azerbaijan** (7 to 15 May 2000)
E/CN.4/2001/66/Add.2	Visit to **Brazil** (20 August to 12 September 2000)

Special Rapporteur on violence against women, its causes and consequences

Annual reports to the UN Commission on Human Rights

E/CN.4/1996/53 Report to 52nd session of the Commission on Human Rights
E/CN.4/1997/47 Report to 53rd session of the Commission on Human Rights
E/CN.4/1998/54 Report to 54th session of the Commission on Human Rights
E/CN.4/1999/68 Report to 55th session of the Commission on Human Rights
E/CN.4/2002/83 Report to 58th session of the Commission on Human Rights

UN publications

Human Rights Fact Sheet No. 17, *The Committee against Torture,* Centre for Human Rights, United Nations Office at Geneva, 1992, ISSN 1014-5567

Human Rights Fact Sheet No. 27, *Seventeen frequently asked questions about United Nations Special Rapporteurs,* Office of the UN High Commissioner for Human Rights, Geneva, 2001, ISSN 1014 5567

Human Rights and Law Enforcement: A Manual on Human Rights Training for the Police, High Commissioner for Human Rights, Centre for Human Rights, Professional Training Series No. 5, United Nations, New York and Geneva, 1997, Sales No. E.96.XIV.5, ISBN 92-1-154121-2

Human Rights and Pre-trial Detention: A Handbook of International Standards relating to Pre-trial Detention, Centre for Human Rights and Crime Prevention and Criminal Justice Branch, Professional Training Series No. 3, United Nations, New York and Geneva, 1994, Sales No. E.94.XIV.6, ISBN 92-1-154106-9

Istanbul Protocol: Manual on the Effective Investigation and Documentation of Torture and Other Cruel, Inhuman or Degrading Treatment or Punishment, Office of the High Commissioner for Human Rights, Professional Training Series No. 8, United Nations, New York and Geneva, 2001, Sales No. E.01.XIV.1, ISBN 92-1-154136-0

Manual on the Effective Prevention and Investigation of Extra-legal, Arbitrary and Summary Executions, United Nations Office at Vienna, Centre for Social Development and Humanitarian Affairs, United Nations, New York, 1991, Sales No. E.91.IV.1, ISBN 92-1-130142-2

"These Rights and Freedoms...", United Nations, Department of Public Information, 1950, United Nations, New York, Sales No. 1950.I.6

Training Manual on Human Rights Monitoring, Office of the High Commissioner for Human Rights, Professional Training Series No. 7, United Nations, New York and Geneva, 2001, Sales No. E.01.XIV.2, ISBN 92-1-154137-9

United Nations Action in the Field of Human Rights, United Nations, New York and Geneva, 4th edition, 1994, Sales No. E.94.XIV.11, ISBN 92-1-154107-7

Appendix 4

Cases and judicial rulings

Appendix 4 lists cases and judicial rulings emanating from *United Nations treaty bodies*, the *International Court of Justice*, the *International Criminal Tribunals* for the former Yugoslavia and Rwanda, *regional commissions and courts* and *national courts*. An explanation appears at the beginning of each section, with information on how cases can be found on the Internet and in printed sources.

UN treaty bodies

Each case listing gives the full title with the communication number in parentheses, followed by the date of adoption of the decision and bibliographic details. Bibliographic citations are to the treaty body's annual report to the UN General Assembly, published in the General Assembly Official Records (A/.../...) (see Appendix 3 for an explanation of UN document symbols). Some earlier cases considered by the Human Rights Committee can also be found in *Human Rights Committee: Selected Decisions under the Optional Protocol* (cited as Selected Decisions), UN Docs. CCPR/C/OP/1 (Vol. 1) and CCPR/C/OP/2 (Vol. 2), issued in 1985 and 1990 respectively. Most cases are also available as individual documents on the UN human rights website at www.unhchr.ch.

Cases are listed alphabetically by the complainant's surname.

Committee against Torture

Ismail Alan v. Switzerland (21/1995), 8 May 1996, A/51/44, Annex V
Khaled Ben M'Barek v. Tunisia (60/1996), 10 November 1999, A/55/44, Annex VIII.A.1
Encarnación Blanco Abad v. Spain (59/1996), 14 May 1998, A/53/44, Annex X.A.3
Sadiq Shek Elmi v. Australia (120/1998), 14 May 1999, A/54/44, Annex VII.A.11
G.R.B. v. Sweden (83/1997), 15 May 1998, A/53/44, Annex X.A.6
Pauline Muzonzo Paku Kisoki v. Sweden (41/1996), 8 May 1996, A/51/44, Annex V
Balabou Mutombo v. Switzerland (13/1993), 27 April 1994, A/49/44, Annex V.B
O.R., M.M. and M.S. v. Argentina (1/1988, 2/1988 and 3/1988), 23 November 1989, A/45/44, Annex V
Irène Ursoa Parot v. Spain (6/1990), 2 May 1995, A/50/44, Annex V
Kaveh Yaragh Tala v. Sweden (43/1996), 15 November 1996, A/52/44, Annex V.A.1

Human Rights Committee

A v. Australia (560/1993), 3 April 1997, A/52/40, Annex VI.L

Celis Laureano v. Peru (540/1993), 25 March 1996, A/51/40, Annex VIII.P

Rosa Espinoza de Polay v. Peru (577/1994), 6 November 1997, A/53/40, Annex XI.F

Alberto Grille Motta v. Uruguay (11/1977), 29 July 1980, A/35/40, Annex X

Paul Kelly v. Jamaica (253/1987), 8 April 1991, A/46/40, Annex XI.D

Sergio Rubén López Burgos v. Uruguay (52/1979), 29 July 1981, A/36/40, Annex XIX;
also reported in Selected Decisions (Vol. 1)

Albert Womah Mukong v. Cameroon (458/1991), 21 July 1994, A/49/40, Annex IX.AA

Charles Chitat Ng v. Canada (469/1991), 5 November 1993, A/49/90, Annex IX.CC

Csaba Párkányi v. Hungary (410/1990), 27 July 1992, A/47/40, Annex IX.Q

Elena Quinteros Almeida and María del Carmen Almeida de Quinteros v. Uruguay (107/1981),
21 July 1983, A/38/40, Annex XXII; also reported in Selected Decisions (Vol. 2)

Hugo Rodríguez v. Uruguay (322/1988), 19 July 1994, A/49/40, Annex IX.B

Rafael Armando Rojas García v. Colombia (687/1996), 3 April 2001, A/56/40, Annex X.D

Antti Vuolanne v. Finland (265/1987), 7 April 1989, A/44/40, Annex X.J

International Court of Justice (ICJ)

Cases are published in *International Court of Justice: Reports of Judgments, Advisory Opinions and Orders* (ICJ Reports). Summaries are available on the ICJ website at www.icj-cij.org.

Barcelona Traction, Light and Power Company, Limited (Belgium v. Spain), 1970 ICJ Reports, pp. 3-51

Democratic Republic of the Congo v. Belgium, 14 February 2002, General List No. 121 (not yet reported)

Military and Paramilitary Activities in and against Nicaragua (Nicaragua v. United States of America), 1986 ICJ Reports, pp. 14-150

International Criminal Tribunals

The listings here give the title with the case number in parentheses, followed by the date when the Trial Chamber or the Appeals Chamber issued its judgment. The judgments can be found on the websites of the Yugoslavia Tribunal at www.un.org/icty and the Rwanda Tribunal at www.ictr.org. Judgments of the Yugoslavia and Rwanda tribunals are also published, with summaries and annotations, in André Klip and Göran Sluiter, eds., *Annotated Leading Cases of International Criminal Tribunals*, published by Intersentia, Antwerp, Belgium. Three volumes have been published to date:

Vol. I, 1999, *The International Criminal Tribunal for the former Yugoslavia 1993-1998*, ISBN 90-5095-076-0

Vol. II, 2000, *The International Criminal Tribunal for Rwanda 1994-1999*, ISBN 90-5095-135-X

Vol. III, 2001, *The International Criminal Tribunal for the former Yugoslavia 1997-1999*, ISBN 90-5095-141-4

International Criminal Tribunal for the former Yugoslavia

Prosecutor v. Aleksovski (IT-95-14/1), 25 June 1999 (Trial Chamber)

Prosecutor v. Blaškić (IT-95-14), 3 March 2000 (Trial Chamber)

Prosecutor v. Delalić and others (IT-96-21), 16 November 1998 (Trial Chamber)

Prosecutor v. Furundžija (IT-95-17/1), 10 December 1998 (Trial Chamber)

Prosecutor v. Jelišić (IT-95-10), 14 December 1999 (Trial Chamber); 5 July 2001 (Appeals Chamber)

Prosecutor v. Kunarac and others (IT-96-23 and IT-96-23/1), 22 February 2001 (Trial Chamber)

Prosecutor v. Kupreškić and others (IT-95-16), 14 January 2000 (Trial Chamber) ; 23 October 2001 (Appeals Chamber)

Prosecutor v. Kvočka and others (IT-98-30/1), 2 November 2001 (Trial Chamber)

Prosecutor v. Tadić (IT-94-1), Decision on the Defence Motion for Interlocutory Appeal on Jurisdiction, 2 October 1995 (Appeals Chamber); 7 May 1997 (Trial Chamber); sentencing judgment of 14 July 1997 (Trial Chamber); sentencing judgment of 11 November 1999 (Appeals Chamber)

International Criminal Tribunal for Rwanda

Prosecutor v. Akayesu (ICTR-96-4), 2 September 1998 (Trial Chamber)

Regional commissions and courts

Inter-American Commission and Court of Human Rights

For cases considered by the Inter-American Commission, the listing below gives the title, the case number or report number, the date of the decision, and a citation to where the decision is published in the *Annual Report of the Inter-American Commission on Human Rights*. For cases considered by the Inter-American Court, the listing gives the title, the date of the judgment, and a citation to the Court's reports of cases, as well as the report of the judgment in the *Annual Report of the Inter-American Court of Human Rights*. Most cases can also be found on the websites of the Inter-American Commission on Human Rights at www.cidh.org and the Inter-American Court of Human Rights at www.corteidh.org.cr respectively.

Aguado v. Nicaragua, Commission case 10.198, Resolution No. 29/89, 29 September 1989, Annual Report of the Inter-American Commission on Human Rights 1989-90, pp. 73-96

Aloeboetoe and others v. Suriname, Reparations, 10 September 1993 (Court), Series C, No. 15, Annual Report of the Inter-American Court of Human Rights 1993, Appx. VIII

Blake v. Guatemala, 24 January 1998 (Court), Series C, No. 36, Annual Report of the Inter-American Court of Human Rights 1998, Appx. V; *Reparations*, 22 January 1999 (Court), Series C, No. 48, Annual Report of the Inter-American Court of Human Rights 1999, Appx. II

Carandirú case (Brazil), Commission report 34/00, 13 April 2000, Annual Report of the Inter-American Commission on Human Rights 1999, Vol. I, pp. 370-398

Castillo Petruzzi and others v. Peru, 30 May 1999 (Court), Series C, No. 52, Annual Report of the Inter-American Court of Human Rights 1999, Appx. IX

Habeas Corpus in Emergency Situations, Advisory Opinion OC-8/87 of 30 January 1987 (Court), Series A, No. 8, Annual Report of the Inter-American Court of Human Rights 1987, Appx. II

Heredia Miranda v. Bolivia, Commission case 2721, 6 March 1979, Annual Report of the Inter-American Commission on Human Rights 1978, pp. 58-60

Leonor La Rosa Bustamante v. Peru, Commission report 54/98, 8 December 1998, Annual Report of the Inter-American Commission on Human Rights 1998, Vol. I, pp. 198-201

Mejía v. Peru, Commission report 5/96, 1 March 1996, Annual Report of the Inter-American Commission on Human Rights 1995, pp. 157-200

Neira Alegría and others v. Peru, 19 January 1995 (Court), Series C, No. 20, Annual Report of the Inter-American Court of Human Rights 1995, Appx. IV

Velásquez Rodríguez v. Honduras, 29 July 1988 (Court), Series C, No. 4, Annual Report of the Inter-American Court of Human Rights 1988, Appx. VI

European Commission and Court of Human Rights

The listing below gives the title, the application number and the date of the report of the Commission or of the judgment of the Court, followed in most cases by a citation to *Reports of Judgments and Decisions,* published by Carl Heymanns Verlag, Cologne, Germany. Earlier cases can also be found in the *Yearbook of the European Convention on Human Rights* (Yearbook), published by Martinus Nijhoff in the Netherlands. In addition, most cases are published in *European Human Rights Reports* (EHRR), published by Sweet & Maxwell in the United Kingdom. Cases not yet published in *Reports of Judgments and Decisions* can be found on the European Court website at www.echr.coe.int, as can most earlier cases.

A v. UK (25599/94), Court, 23 September 1998, Reports of Judgments and Decisions 1998-VI

Ahmed v. Austria (25964/94), Court, 17 December 1996, Reports of Judgments and Decisions 1996-VI

Aksoy v. Turkey (21987/93), Court, 18 December 1996, Reports of Judgments and Decisions 1996-VI

Al-Adsani v. UK (35763/97), Court, 21 November 2001

Assenov and others v. Bulgaria (24760/94), Court, 28 October 1998, Reports of Judgments and Decisions 1988-VIII

Aydın v. Turkey (Şükran Aydın, 23178/94), Court, 25 September 1997, Reports of Judgments and Decisions 1997-VI

Aydın v. Turkey (28293/95, 29494/95 and 30219/96), Court, 10 July 2001 (friendly settlement)

Çakıcı v. Turkey (23657/94), Court, 8 July 1999, Reports of Judgments and Decisions 1999-IV

Chahal v. UK (22414/93), Court, 15 November 1996, Reports of Judgments and Decisions 1996-V

Costello-Roberts v. UK (13134/87), Court, 25 March 1993

Cyprus v. Turkey (6780/74 and 6950/75), Report of the Commission 10 July 1976, 4
EHRR 482

Cyprus v. Turkey (25781/94), Court, 10 May 2001

D v. UK, (30240/96), Court, 2 May 1997, Reports of Judgments and Decisions 1997-III

Dougoz v. Greece (40907/98), Court, 6 March 2001

East African Asians v. UK (4403/70-4419/70, 4422/70, 4423/70, 4434/70, 4443/70,
4476/70-4478/70, 4486/70, 4501/70 and 4526/70-4530/70), Report of the
Commission 14 December 1973, (1994) 78-A DR pp. 5-70*

Fox, Campbell and Hartley v. UK (12244/86, 12245/86 and 12383/86), Court, 30 August
1990, Series A, No. 182

Greek Case (3321/67, 3322/67, 3323/67, and 3344/67), Report of the Commission 18
November 1969, Yearbook Vol. 12 (1969) *"The Greek Case"*

Güleç v. Turkey (21593/93), Court, 27 July 1998, Reports of Judgments and Decisions
1998-IV

H.L.R. v. France (24573/94), Court, 29 April 1997, Reports of Judgments and Decisions
1997-III

Hurtado v. Switzerland (17549/90), Opinion of the Commission 8 July 1993, annexed to
Judgment of the Court, Series A, No. 280-A

Ilhan v. Turkey (22277/93), Court, 27 June 2000

Ireland v. UK (5310/71), Extracts of the Report of the Commission, 25 January 1976,
Yearbook Vol. 19 (1976) pp. 512-948; Judgment of the Court, 18 January 1978,
Series A, No. 25

Mahmut Kaya v. Turkey (22535/93), Court, 28 March 2000

Keenan v. UK (27229/95), Court, 3 April 2001

Kelly and others v. UK (30054/96), Court, 4 May 2001

Kudła v. Poland (30210/96), Court, 26 October 2000

Kurt v. Turkey (24276/94), 25 May 1998, Reports of Judgments and Decisions 1998-III

McCann and others v. UK (18984/91), Court, 27 September 1995, Series A, No. 324

John Murray v. UK (18731/91), Court, 8 February 1996, Reports of Judgments and
Decisions 1996-I

Peers v. Greece (28524/95), Court, 19 April 2001

Raninen v. Finland (20972/92), 16 December 1997, Reports of Judgments and Decisions
1997-VIII

Ribitsch v. Austria (18896/91), Court, 4 December 1995, Series A, No. 336

Salman v. Turkey (21986/93), Court, 27 June 2000

Satık and others v. Turkey (31866/96), Court, 10 October 2000

Selçuk and Asker v. Turkey (23184/94 and 23185/94), 24 April 1998, Reports of
Judgments and Decisions 1998-II

Selmouni v. France (25803/94), Court, 28 July 1999, Reports of Judgments and Decisions
1999-V

Soering v. UK (14038/88), Court, 7 July 1989, Series A, No. 161

T.I. v. UK (43844/98), Court, admissibility decision, 7 March 2000

Tomasi v. France (12850/87), Court, 27 August 1992, Series A, No. 241-A

Tyrer v. UK (5856/72), Court, 25 April 1978, Series A, No. 26

W v. Switzerland (14379/88), Court, 26 January 1993, Series A, No. 254-A

Winterwerp v. The Netherlands (6301/73), Court, 24 October 1979, Series A, No. 33

Z and others v. UK (29392/95), Court, 10 May 2001

---

* The full report was not made public at the time, although extracts were published in *European
Human Rights Reports* (3 EHRR 76). The full report was made public by Committee of Ministers
Resolution DH (94) 30 of 21 March 1994 and published in "Decisions and reports of the European
Commission of Human Rights".

National courts

Where cases are published in Law Reports of the Commonwealth (LRC), that citation is given below. Cases can also be found in national law reports. Judgments of the Constitutional Court of South Africa can be found on the Court's website at www.concourt.gov.za.

Ex Parte Attorney General of Namibia, In re Corporal Punishment by Organs of State, Supreme Court of Namibia, 5 April 1991, [1992] LRC (Const) 515

Azanian Peoples' Organisation (AZAPO) and others v. President of the Republic of South Africa and others, Constitutional Court of South Africa, 25 July 1996, [1997] 4 LRC 40

Basu v. State of West Bengal, Supreme Court of India, 18 December 1996, [1997] 2 LRC 1

Filártiga v. Peña-Irala, US Court of Appeals, 2nd Circuit, 30 June 1980, 630 F.2d 876

Namunjepo and others v. Commanding Officer, Windhoek Prison and another, Supreme Court of Namibia, 9 July 1999, [2000] 3 LRC 360

Ncube and others v. The State, Supreme Court of Zimbabwe, 14 December 1987, [1988] LRC (Const) 442

Public Committee Against Torture in Israel and others v. The State of Israel and others, High Court of Justice of Israel, 6 September 1999 (HCJ 5100/94; 4054/94; 6536/95; 5188/96; 7563/97; 7268/97; 1043/99)

State v. Williams and others, Constitutional Court of South Africa, 9 June 1995, [1995] 2 LRC 103

Appendix 5

Checklist of international and regional instruments

This checklist includes the main international and regional instruments providing for the prohibition and prevention of torture and other cruel, inhuman or degrading treatment or punishment. Some instruments contain explicit prohibitions of torture and ill-treatment; others set out measures which are important for preventing torture.

Some of the instruments are international treaties, binding on all states which become parties to them; this is indicated in the third column by the letter T. Others are in the form of resolutions adopted by bodies of the United Nations and other inter-governmental organizations. Some instruments are of worldwide scope; they apply to all countries, or to all states parties, which can be from any part of the world. Others emanate from regional intergovernmental organizations and apply to states in those regions.

Most of the instruments cited in the checklist are reproduced in the UN publication *Human Rights: A Compilation of International Instruments*. Volume I (First Part) of this publication contains international human rights instruments, including instruments relating to rights of women, rights of the child, and human rights in the administration of justice. Volume I (Second Part) contains instruments relating to refugees, international humanitarian law and genocide. Volume II contains regional instruments. The UN Sales Numbers are E.94.XIV.1 for Volume I (Parts I and II) and E.97.XIV.1 for Volume II. They can be obtained from bookstores and distributors or from the UN publications offices indicated in Appendix 3. Many of the instruments can also be found in Crawshaw and Holmström, eds., 2001, *Essential Texts on Human Rights for the Police: A Compilation of International Instruments,* cited in Appendix 1.

UN human rights instruments are available on-line in English, French and Spanish on the UN human rights website at www.unhchr.ch. The **Rome Statute of the International Criminal Court** and the **Vienna Conventions** on Consular Relations and on the Law of Treaties are available on the international law section of the UN website at www.un.org. The **Statute of the Yugoslavia Tribunal** can be found on that Tribunal's website at www.un.org/icty, and the **Statute of the Rwanda Tribunal** on that Tribunal's website at www.ictr.org.

The **African Charter on Human and Peoples' Rights** and the **African Charter on the Rights and Welfare of the Child** can be found on the website of the African Commission on Human and Peoples' Rights at www.achpr.org. Instruments relating to the **Americas** region are available from the website of the Organization of American States at www.oas.org. **European** treaties are available from the website of the Council of Europe's Treaty Office at www.conventions.coe.int, and the **European Prison Rules** can be obtained from the Committee of Ministers website at www.coe.int/cm; both of these sites are accessible through the main Council of Europe website at www.coe.int.

The **Geneva Conventions** and **Additional Protocols** are available on the UN human rights website (see above) and on the website of the International Committee of the Red Cross (ICRC) at www.icrc.org.

Most of these texts can also be found on the website of the University of Minnesota Human Rights Library www1.umn.edu/humanrts.

UN instruments

Abbreviations:

Crime Congress – (UN) Congress on the Prevention of Crime and the Treatment of Offenders

ECOSOC – (UN) Economic and Social Council

UNGA – (UN) General Assembly

Title (abbreviated titles in parentheses)	Adopted	T= treaty, with date of entry into force	Adopted by
Basic Principles for the Treatment of Prisoners	1990		UNGA
Basic Principles on the Role of Lawyers	1990		Eighth UN Crime Congress (Havana)
Basic Principles on the Independence of the Judiciary	1985		Seventh UN Crime Congress (Milan) (endorsed by UNGA, 1985)
Basic Principles on the Use of Force and Firearms by Law Enforcement Officials (Basic Principles on Force and Firearms)	1990		Eighth UN Crime Congress (Havana)
Beijing Declaration and Platform for Action	1995		Fourth World Conference on Women (Beijing)
Body of Principles for the Protection of All Persons under Any Form of Detention or Imprisonment (Body of Principles on Detention)	1988		United Nations Conference on International Organization (San Francisco)
Charter of the United Nations (UN Charter)	1945	T - 24 October 1945	
Code of Conduct for Law Enforcement Officials	1979		UNGA
Convention against Torture and Other Cruel, Inhuman or Degrading Treatment or Punishment (Convention against Torture)	1984	T - 26 June 1987	UNGA

Title (abbreviated titles in parentheses)	Adopted	T= treaty, with date of entry into force	Adopted by
Convention on the Prevention and Punishment of the Crime of Genocide (Genocide Convention)	1948	T - 12 January 1951	UNGA
Convention on the Elimination of All Forms of Discrimination against Women	1979	T - 3 September 1981	UNGA
Optional Protocol to the Convention on the Elimination of All Forms of Discrimination against Women	1999	T - 22 December 2000	UNGA
Convention on the Non-Applicability of Statutory Limitations to War Crimes and Crimes against Humanity	1968	T - 11 November 1970	UNGA
Convention on the Rights of the Child	1989	T - 2 September 1990	UNGA
Optional Protocol to the Convention on the Rights of the Child on the involvement of children in armed conflict	2000	T - 12 February 2002	UNGA
Convention relating to the Status of Refugees (Refugee Convention)	1951	T - 22 April 1954	UN Conference of Plenipotentiaries on the Status of Refugees and Stateless Persons
Protocol relating to the Status of Refugees	1966	T - 4 October 196	UNGA
Declaration of Basic Principles of Justice for Victims of Crime and Abuse of Power	1985		UNGA
Declaration on the Protection of All Persons from Being Subjected to Torture and Other Cruel, Inhuman or Degrading Treatment or Punishment (Declaration against Torture)	1975		UNGA
Declaration on the Protection of All Persons from Enforced Disappearance (Declaration on Enforced Disappearance)	1992		UNGA
Declaration on the Human Rights of Individuals Who are not Nationals of the Country in which They Live	1985		UNGA
Declaration on the Elimination of Violence against Women	1993		UNGA
Declaration on the Right and Responsibility of Individuals, Groups and Organs of Society to Promote and Protect Universally Recognized Human Rights and Fundamental Freedoms	1998		UNGA

Title (abbreviated titles in parentheses)	Adopted	T= treaty with date of entry into force	Adopted by
Durban Declaration and Programme of Action	2001		World Conference against Racism, Racial Discrimination, Xenophobia and Related Intolerance (Durban)
Guidelines on the Role of Prosecutors	1990		Eighth UN Crime Congress (Havana)
International Convention on the Elimination of All Forms of Racial Discrimination	1965	T - 4 January 1969	UNGA
International Convention on the Protection of the Rights of All Migrant Workers and Members of Their Families	1990	T (not yet in force)	UNGA
International Convention on the Suppression and Punishment of the Crime of *Apartheid*	1973	T - 18 July 1976	UNGA
International Covenant on Civil and Political Rights (ICCPR)	1966	T - 23 March 1976	UNGA
Optional Protocol to the International Covenant on Civil and Political Rights (first Optional Protocol to the ICCPR)	1966	T - 23 March 1976	UNGA
International Covenant on Economic, Social and Cultural Rights	1966	T - 3 January 1976	UNGA
Principles of international co-operation in the detection, arrest, extradition and punishment of persons guilty of war crimes and crimes against humanity	1973		UNGA
Principles of Medical Ethics relevant to the Role of Health Personnel, particularly Physicians, in the Protection of Prisoners and Detainees against Torture and Other Cruel, Inhuman or Degrading Treatment or Punishment	1982		UNGA
Principles on the Effective Investigation and Documentation of Torture and Other Cruel, Inhuman or Degrading Treatment or Punishment (Principles on the Investigation of Torture)	2000		UNGA
Principles on the Effective Prevention and Investigation of Extra-legal, Arbitrary and Summary Executions	1989		ECOSOC

Title (abbreviated titles in parentheses)	Adopted	T= treaty with date of entry into force	Adopted by
Rome Statute of the International Criminal Court (Rome Statute)	1998	T - 1 July 2002	UN Diplomatic Conference of Plenipotentiaries on the Establishment of an International Criminal Court (Rome)
Standard Minimum Rules for the Treatment of Prisoners (Standard Minimum Rules)	1955		First UN Crime Congress (Geneva) (approved by ECOSOC, 1957 and 1977)
Statute of the International Criminal Tribunal for Rwanda (Rwanda Tribunal)	1994		UN Security Council
Statute of the International Court of Justice	1945	T - 24 October 1945	(The Statute of the International Court of Justice is an integral part of the UN Charter)
Statute of the International Criminal Tribunal for the former Yugoslavia (Yugoslavia Tribunal)	1993, amended 1998 & 2000		UN Security Council
Supplementary Convention on the Abolition of Slavery, the Slave Trade, and Institutions and Practices Similar to Slavery	1956	T - 30 April 1957	Conference of Plenipotentiaries
Principles for the protection of persons with mental illness and the improvement of mental health care	1991		UNGA
United Nations Rules for the Protection of Juveniles Deprived of their Liberty	1990		UNGA
United Nations Standard Minimum Rules for the Administration of Juvenile Justice (Beijing Rules)	1985		UNGA
United Nations Standard Minimum Rules for Non-custodial Measures (Tokyo Rules)	1990		UNGA
Universal Declaration of Human Rights	1948		UNGA
Vienna Convention on Consular Relations	1963	T - 19 March 1967	UN Conference on Consular Relations (Vienna)

Title (abbreviated titles in parentheses)	Adopted	T= treaty with date of entry into force	Adopted by
Vienna Convention on the Law of Treaties	1969	T - 27 January 1980	UN Conference on the Law of Treaties
Vienna Declaration and Programme of Action	1993		World Conference on Human Rights (Vienna)

International humanitarian law

Title (abbreviated titles in parentheses)	Adopted	T= treaty with date of entry into force	Adopted by
Geneva Convention for the Amelioration of the Condition of the Wounded and Sick in Armed Forces in the Field (First Geneva Convention)	1949	T - 21 October 1950	Diplomatic Conference for the Establishment of International Conventions for the Protection of Victims of War (Geneva)
Geneva Convention for the Amelioration of the Condition of Wounded, Sick and Shipwrecked Members of Armed Forces at Sea (Second Geneva Convention)			
Geneva Convention relative to the Treatment of Prisoners of War (Third Geneva Convention)			
Geneva Convention relative to the Protection of Civilian Persons in Time of War (Fourth Geneva Convention)	1977	T - 7 December 1978	Diplomatic Conference on the Reaffirmation and Development of International Humanitarian Law applicable in Armed Conflicts
Protocol Additional to the Geneva Conventions of 12 August 1949, and relating to the Protection of Victims of International Armed Conflicts (Additional Protocol I)			
Protocol Additional to the Geneva Conventions of 12 August 1949, and relating to the Protection of Victims of Non-International Armed Conflicts (Additional Protocol II)			

Regional instruments

Africa

Abbreviation: OAU – Organization of African Unity

Title (abbreviated titles in parentheses)	Adopted	T= treaty, with date of entry into force	Adopted by
African Charter on Human and Peoples' Rights	1981	T - 21 October 1986	OAU Assembly
Protocol to the African Charter on Human and Peoples' Rights on the Establishment of an African Court on Human and Peoples' Rights	1998	T (not yet in force)	OAU Assembly
African Charter on the Rights and Welfare of the Child	1990	T - 29 November 1999	OAU Assembly

Americas

Abbreviation: OAS – Organization of American States

Title (abbreviated titles in parentheses)	Adopted	T= treaty, with date of entry into force	Adopted by
American Declaration of the Rights and Duties of Man	1948		Ninth International Conference of American States (Bogotá, Colombia)
American Convention on Human Rights ("Pact of San José, Costa Rica")	1969	T - 18 July 1978	Inter-American Specialized Conference on Human Rights (San José, Costa Rica)
Inter-American Convention to Prevent and Punish Torture	1985	T - 28 February 1987	General Assembly of the OAS
Inter-American Convention on the Prevention, Punishment and Eradication of Violence against Women ("Convention of Belém do Pará")	1994	T - 5 March 1995	General Assembly of the OAS
Inter-American Convention on the Forced Disappearance of Persons	1994	T - 28 March 1996	General Assembly of the OAS

Europe

Title (abbreviated titles in parentheses)	Adopted	T= treaty, with date of entry into force	Adopted by
Convention for the Protection of Human Rights and Fundamental Freedoms (European Convention on Human Rights)	1950	T - 3 September 1953	Council of Europe
Protocol No. 11 to the European Convention on Human Rights and Fundamental Freedoms, restructuring the control machinery established thereby	1994	T - 1 November 1998	Council of Europe
European Convention for the Prevention of Torture and Inhuman or Degrading Treatment or Punishment (European Convention for the Prevention of Torture)	1987	T - 1 February 1989	Council of Europe
Protocol No. 1 to the European Convention for the Prevention of Torture and Inhuman or Degrading Treatment or Punishment	1993	T - 1 March 2001	Council of Europe
Declaration on the Police	1979		Parliamentary Assembly of the Council of Europe
European Prison Rules	1973, amended 1987		Committee of Ministers of the Council of Europe

Middle East and Islamic Conference

Title (abbreviated titles in parentheses)	Adopted	T= treaty, with date of entry into force	Adopted by
Arab Charter on Human Rights	1994	T (not yet in force)	League of Arab States
Cairo Declaration on Human Rights in Islam	1990		Organization of the Islamic Conference

Appendix 6

Prohibitions of torture and ill-treatment in international and regional human rights instruments (extracts)

• Universal Declaration of Human Rights
Article 5

No one shall be subjected to torture or to cruel, inhuman or degrading treatment or punishment.

• International Covenant on Civil and Political Rights
Article 7

No one shall be subjected to torture or to cruel, inhuman or degrading treatment or punishment. In particular, no one shall be subjected without his free consent to medical or scientific experimentation.

Article 10

1. All persons deprived of their liberty shall be treated with humanity and with respect for the inherent dignity of the human person. [...]

• African Charter on Human and Peoples' Rights
Article 5

Every individual shall have the right to the respect of the dignity inherent in a human being and to the recognition of his legal status. All forms of exploitation and degradation of man, particularly slavery, slave trade, torture, cruel, inhuman or degrading punishment and treatment, shall be prohibited.

• American Convention on Human Rights
Article 5   Right to Humane Treatment

1. Every person has the right to have his physical, mental, and moral integrity respected.

2. No one shall be subjected to torture or to cruel, inhuman, or degrading punishment or treatment. All persons deprived of their liberty shall be treated with respect for the inherent dignity of the human person. [...]

• European Convention for the Protection of Human Rights and Fundamental Freedoms
Article 3

No one shall be subjected to torture or to inhuman or degrading treatment or punishment.

• Arab Charter on Human Rights (not yet in force)
Article 13

(a) The States parties shall protect every person in their territory from being subjected to physical or mental torture or cruel, inhuman or degrading treatment. They shall take effective measures to prevent such acts and shall regard the practice thereof, or participation therein, as a punishable offence.

(b) No medical or scientific experimentation shall be carried out on any person without his free consent.

Appendix 7

Convention against Torture and Other Cruel, Inhuman or Degrading Treatment or Punishment (Part I)

Article 1

1. For the purposes of this Convention, the term "torture" means any act by which severe pain or suffering, whether physical or mental, is intentionally inflicted on a person for such purposes as obtaining from him or a third person information or a confession, punishing him for an act he or a third person has committed or is suspected of having committed, or intimidating or coercing him or a third person, or for any reason based on discrimination of any kind, when such pain or suffering is inflicted by or at the instigation of or with the consent or acquiescence of a public official or other person acting in an official capacity. It does not include pain or suffering arising only from, inherent in or incidental to lawful sanctions.

2. This article is without prejudice to any international instrument or national legislation which does or may contain provisions of wider application.

Article 2

1. Each State Party shall take effective legislative, administrative, judicial or other measures to prevent acts of torture in any territory under its jurisdiction.

2. No exceptional circumstances whatsoever, whether a state of war or a threat of war, internal political in stability or any other public emergency, may be invoked as a justification of torture.

3. An order from a superior officer or a public authority may not be invoked as a justification of torture.

Article 3

1. No State Party shall expel, return (*"refouler"*) or extradite a person to another State where there are substantial grounds for believing that he would be in danger of being subjected to torture.

2. For the purpose of determining whether there are such grounds, the competent authorities shall take into account all relevant considerations including, where applicable, the existence in the State concerned of a consistent pattern of gross, flagrant or mass violations of human rights.

Article 4

1. Each State Party shall ensure that all acts of torture are offences under its criminal law. The same shall apply to an attempt to commit torture and to an act by any person which constitutes complicity or participation in torture.

2. Each State Party shall make these offences punishable by appropriate penalties which take into account their grave nature.

Article 5

1. Each State Party shall take such measures as may be necessary to establish its jurisdiction over the offences referred to in article 4 in the following cases:

(a) When the offences are committed in any territory under its jurisdiction or on board a ship or aircraft registered in that State;

(b) When the alleged offender is a national of that State;

(c) When the victim is a national of that State if that State considers it appropriate.

2. Each State Party shall likewise take such measures as may be necessary to establish its jurisdiction over such offences in cases where the alleged offender is present in any territory under its jurisdiction and it does not extradite him pursuant to article 8 to any of the States mentioned in paragraph 1 of this article.

3. This Convention does not exclude any criminal jurisdiction exercised in accordance with internal law.

Article 6

1. Upon being satisfied, after an examination of information available to it, that the circumstances so warrant, any State Party in whose territory a person alleged to have committed any offence referred to in article 4 is present shall take him into custody or take other legal measures to ensure his presence. The custody and other legal measures shall be as provided in the law of that State but may be continued only for such time as is necessary to enable any criminal or extradition proceedings to be instituted.

2. Such State shall immediately make a preliminary inquiry into the facts.

3. Any person in custody pursuant to paragraph 1 of this article shall be assisted in communicating immediately with the nearest appropriate representative of the State of which he is a national, or, if he is a stateless person, with the representative of the State where he usually resides.

4. When a State, pursuant to this article, has taken a person into custody, it shall immediately notify the States referred to in article 5, paragraph 1, of the fact that such person is in custody and of the circumstances which warrant his detention. The State which makes the preliminary inquiry contemplated in paragraph 2 of this article shall promptly report its findings to the said States and shall indicate whether it intends to exercise jurisdiction.

Article 7

1. The State Party in the territory under whose jurisdiction a person alleged to have committed any offence referred to in article 4 is found shall in the cases contemplated in article 5, if it does not extradite him, submit the case to its competent authorities for the purpose of prosecution.

2. These authorities shall take their decision in the same manner as in the case of any ordinary offence of a serious nature under the law of that State. In the cases referred to in article 5, paragraph 2, the standards of evidence required for prosecution and conviction shall in no way be less stringent than those which apply in the cases referred to in article 5, paragraph 1.

3. Any person regarding whom proceedings are brought in connection with any of the offences referred to in article 4 shall be guaranteed fair treatment at all stages of the proceedings.

Article 8

1. The offences referred to in article 4 shall be deemed to be included as extraditable offences in any extradition treaty existing between States Parties. States Parties undertake to include such offences as extraditable offences in every extradition treaty to be concluded between them.

2. If a State Party which makes extradition conditional on the existence of a treaty receives a request for extradition from another State Party with which it has no extradition treaty, it may consider this Convention as the legal basis for extradition in respect of such offences. Extradition shall be subject to the other conditions provided by the law of the requested State.

3. States Parties which do not make extradition conditional on the existence of a treaty shall recognize such offences as extraditable offences between themselves subject to the conditions provided by the law of the requested State.

4. Such offences shall be treated, for the purpose of extradition between States Parties, as if they had been committed not only in the place in which they occurred but also in the territories of the States required to establish their jurisdiction in accordance with article 5, paragraph 1.

Article 9

1. States Parties shall afford one another the greatest measure of assistance in connection with criminal proceedings brought in respect of any of the offences referred to in article 4, including the supply of all evidence at their disposal necessary for the proceedings.

2. States Parties shall carry out their obligations under paragraph 1 of this article in conformity with any treaties on mutual judicial assistance that may exist between them.

Article 10

1. Each State Party shall ensure that education and information regarding the prohibition against torture are fully included in the training of law enforcement personnel, civil or military, medical personnel, public officials and other persons who may be involved in the custody, interrogation or treatment of any individual subjected to any form of arrest, detention or imprisonment.

2. Each State Party shall include this prohibition in the rules or instructions issued in regard to the duties and functions of any such person.

Article 11

Each State Party shall keep under systematic review interrogation rules, instructions, methods and practices as well as arrangements for the custody and treatment of persons subjected to any form of arrest, detention or imprisonment in any territory under its juris-diction, with a view to preventing any cases of torture.

Article 12

Each State Party shall ensure that its competent authorities proceed to a prompt and impartial investigation, wherever there is reasonable ground to believe that an act of torture has been committed in any territory under its jurisdiction.

Article 13

Each State Party shall ensure that any individual who alleges he has been subjected to torture in any territory under its jurisdiction has the right to complain to, and to have his case promptly and impartially examined by, its competent authorities. Steps shall be taken to ensure that the complainant and witnesses are protected against all ill-treatment or intimidation as a consequence of his complaint or any evidence given.

Article 14

1. Each State Party shall ensure in its legal system that the victim of an act of torture obtains redress and has an enforceable right to fair and adequate compensation, including the means for as full rehabilitation as possible. In the event of the death of the victim as a result of an act of torture, his dependants shall be entitled to compensation.

2. Nothing in this article shall affect any right of the victim or other persons to compensation which may exist under national law.

Article 15

Each State Party shall ensure that any statement which is established to have been made as a result of torture shall not be invoked as evidence in any proceedings, except against a person accused of torture as evidence that the statement was made.

Article 16

1. Each State Party shall undertake to prevent in any territory under its jurisdiction other acts of cruel, inhuman or degrading treatment or punishment which do not amount to torture as defined in article I, when such acts are committed by or at the instigation of or with the consent or acquiescence of a public official or other person acting in an official capacity. In particular, the obligations contained in articles 10, 11, 12 and 13 shall apply with the substitution for references to torture of references to other forms of cruel, inhuman or degrading treatment or punishment.

2. The provisions of this Convention are without prejudice to the provisions of any other international instrument or national law which prohibits cruel, inhuman or degrading treatment or punishment or which relates to extradition or expulsion.

Appendix 8

Common Article 3 to the four Geneva Conventions of August 12, 1949 (extract)*

Article 3

In the case of armed conflict not of an international character occurring in the territory of one of the High Contracting Parties, each Party to the conflict shall be bound to apply, as a minimum, the following provisions:

(1) Persons taking no active part in the hostilities, including members of armed forces who have laid down their arms and those placed *hors de combat* by sickness, wounds, detention, or any other cause, shall in all circumstances be treated humanely, without any adverse distinction founded on race, colour, religion or faith, sex, birth or wealth, or any other similar criteria.

To this end, the following acts are and shall remain prohibited at any time and in any place whatsoever with respect to the above-mentioned persons:

(a) violence to life and person, in particular murder of all kinds, mutilation, cruel treatment and torture;

(b) taking of hostages;

(c) outrages upon personal dignity, in particular humiliating and degrading treatment; [...]

---

* The text reproduced in this appendix is from the First Geneva Convention of August 12, 1949.

Appendix 9

Rome Statute of the International Criminal Court (extracts)*

Article 5 – Crimes within the jurisdiction of the Court
1. The jurisdiction of the Court shall be limited to the most serious crimes of concern to the international community as a whole. The Court has jurisdiction in accordance with this Statute with respect to the following crimes:
    (a) The crime of genocide;
    (b) Crimes against humanity;
    (c) War crimes;
    (d) The crime of aggression. [...]

Article 6 – Genocide
For the purpose of this Statute, "genocide" means any of the following acts committed with intent to destroy, in whole or in part, a national, ethnical, racial or religious group, as such: [...]
    (b) Causing serious bodily or mental harm to members of the group; [...]

Article 7 – Crimes against humanity
1. For the purpose of this Statute, "crime against humanity" means any of the following acts when committed as part of a widespread or systematic attack directed against any civilian population, with knowledge of the attack: [...]
    (f) Torture;
    (g) Rape, sexual slavery, enforced prostitution, forced pregnancy, enforced sterilization, or any other form of sexual violence of comparable gravity; [...]
    (i) Enforced disappearance of persons; [...]
    (k) Other inhumane acts of a similar character intentionally causing great suffering, or serious injury to body or to mental or physical health.
2. For the purpose of paragraph 1: [...]
    (e) "Torture" means the intentional infliction of severe pain or suffering, whether physical or mental, upon a person in the custody or under the control of the accused; except that torture shall not include pain or suffering arising only from, inherent in or incidental to, lawful sanctions; [...]
    (i) "Enforced disappearance of persons" means the arrest, detention or abduction of persons by, or with the authorization, support or acquiescence of, a State or a political organization, followed by a refusal to acknowledge that deprivation of freedom or to give information on the fate or whereabouts of those persons, with the intention of removing them from the protection of the law for a prolonged period of time. [...]

Article 8 – War crimes
2. For the purpose of this Statute, "war crimes" means:
    (a) Grave breaches of the Geneva Conventions of 12 August 1949, namely, any of the following acts against persons [...] protected under the provisions of the relevant Geneva Convention: [...]

---

* In addition to those listed in this appendix, many other crimes covered by the Rome Statute can also involve torture or ill-treatment. Readers wishing to examine a more extensive list of crimes are advised to consult the full text of the Rome Statute, available on the international law section of the UN website at www.un.org.

(ii) Torture or inhuman treatment, including biological experiments;

(iii) Wilfully causing great suffering, or serious injury to body or health; [...]

(b) Other serious violations of the laws and customs applicable in international armed conflict, within the established framework of international law, namely, any of the following acts: [...]

(x) Subjecting persons who are in the power of an adverse party to physical mutilation or to medical or scientific experiments of any kind which are neither justified by the medical, dental or hospital treatment of the person concerned nor carried out in his or her interest, and which cause death to or seriously endanger the health of such person or persons; [...]

(xxi) Committing outrages upon personal dignity, in particular humiliating and degrading treatment;

(xxii) Committing rape, sexual slavery, enforced prostitution, forced pregnancy, [...] enforced sterilization, or any other form of sexual violence also constituting a grave breach of the Geneva Conventions; [...]

(c) In the case of an armed conflict not of an international character, serious violations of article 3 common to the four Geneva Conventions of 12 August 1949, namely, any of the following acts committed against persons taking no active part in the hostilities, including members of armed forces who have laid down their arms and those placed *hors de combat* by sickness, wounds, detention or any other cause:

(i) Violence to life and person, in particular murder of all kinds, mutilation, cruel treatment and torture;

(ii) Committing outrages upon personal dignity, in particular humiliating and degrading treatment; [...]

(e) Other serious violations of the laws and customs applicable in armed conflicts not of an international character, within the established framework of international law, namely, any of the following acts: [...]

(vi) Committing rape, sexual slavery, enforced prostitution, forced pregnancy, [...] enforced sterilization, and any other form of sexual violence also constituting a serious violation of article 3 common to the four Geneva Conventions; [...]

(xi) Subjecting persons who are in the power of another party to the conflict to physical mutilation or to medical or scientific experiments of any kind which are neither justified by the medical, dental or hospital treatment of the person concerned nor carried out in his or her interest, and which cause death to or seriously endanger the health of such person or persons; [...]

Appendix 10

Principles on the Effective Investigation and Documentation of Torture and Other Cruel, Inhuman or Degrading Treatment or Punishment, annexed to UN General Assembly resolution 55/89 of 4 December 2000

1.   The purposes of effective investigation and documentation of torture and other cruel, inhuman or degrading treatment or punishment (hereinafter "torture or other ill-treatment") include the following:

    (a)   Clarification of the facts and establishment and acknowledgement of individual and State responsibility for victims and their families;

    (b)   Identification of measures needed to prevent recurrence;

    (c)   Facilitation of prosecution and/or, as appropriate, disciplinary sanctions for those indicated by the investigation as being responsible and demonstration of the need for full reparation and redress from the State, including fair and adequate financial compensation and provision of the means for medical care and rehabilitation.

2.   States shall ensure that complaints and reports of torture or ill-treatment are promptly and effectively investigated. Even in the absence of an express complaint, an investigation shall be undertaken if there are other indications that torture or ill-treatment might have occurred. The investigators, who shall be independent of the suspected perpetrators and the agency they serve, shall be competent and impartial. They shall have access to, or be empowered to commission investigations by, impartial medical or other experts. The methods used to carry out such investigations shall meet the highest professional standards and the findings shall be made public.

3.   (a) The investigative authority shall have the power and obligation to obtain all the information necessary to the inquiry.* The persons conducting the investigation shall have at their disposal all the necessary budgetary and technical resources for effective investigation. They shall also have the authority to oblige all those acting in an official capacity allegedly involved in torture or ill-treatment to appear and testify. The same shall apply to any witness. To this end, the investigative authority shall be entitled to issue summonses to witnesses, including any officials allegedly involved, and to demand the production of evidence.

    (b)   Alleged victims of torture or ill-treatment, witnesses, those conducting the investigation and their families shall be protected from violence, threats of violence or any other form of intimidation that may arise pursuant to the investigation. Those potentially implicated in torture or ill-treatment shall be removed from any position of control or power, whether direct or indirect, over complainants, witnesses and their families, as well as those conducting the investigation.

4.   Alleged victims of torture or ill-treatment and their legal representatives shall be informed of, and have access to, any hearing, as well as to all information relevant to the investigation, and shall be entitled to present other evidence.

5.   (a)   In cases in which the established investigative procedures are inadequate because of insufficient expertise or suspected bias, or because of the apparent existence of a pattern of abuse or for other substantial reasons, States shall ensure that investigations are

---

* Under certain circumstances, professional ethics may require information to be kept confidential. These requirements should be respected.

undertaken through an independent commission of inquiry or similar procedure. Members of such a commission shall be chosen for their recognized impartiality, competence and independence as individuals. In particular, they shall be independent of any suspected perpetrators and the institutions or agencies they may serve. The commission shall have the authority to obtain all information necessary to the inquiry and shall conduct the inquiry as provided for under these Principles.*

(b)   A written report, made within a reasonable time, shall include the scope of the inquiry, procedures and methods used to evaluate evidence as well as conclusions and recommendations based on findings of fact and on applicable law. Upon completion, the report shall be made public. It shall also describe in detail specific events that were found to have occurred and the evidence upon which such findings were based and list the names of witnesses who testified, with the exception of those whose identities have been withheld for their own protection. The State shall, within a reasonable period of time, reply to the report of the investigation and, as appropriate, indicate steps to be taken in response.

6.   (a)   Medical experts involved in the investigation of torture or ill-treatment shall behave at all times in conformity with the highest ethical standards and, in particular, shall obtain informed consent before any examination is undertaken. The examination must conform to established standards of medical practice. In particular, examinations shall be conducted in private under the control of the medical expert and outside the presence of security agents and other government officials.

(b)   The medical expert shall promptly prepare an accurate written report, which shall include at least the following:

(i)   Circumstances of the interview: name of the subject and name and affiliation of those present at the examination; exact time and date; location, nature and address of the institution (including, where appropriate, the room) where the examination is being conducted (e.g., detention centre, clinic or house); circumstances of the subject at the time of the examination (e.g., nature of any restraints on arrival or during the examination, presence of security forces during the examination, demeanour of those accompanying the prisoner or threatening statements to the examiner); and any other relevant factors;

(ii)   History: detailed record of the subject's story as given during the interview, including alleged methods of torture or ill-treatment, times when torture or ill-treatment is alleged to have occurred and all complaints of physical and psychological symptoms;

(iii)   Physical and psychological examination: record of all physical and psychological findings on clinical examination, including appropriate diagnostic tests and, where possible, colour photographs of all injuries;

(iv)   Opinion: interpretation as to the probable relationship of the physical and psychological findings to possible torture or ill-treatment. A recommendation for any necessary medical and psychological treatment and/or further examination shall be given;

(v)   Authorship: the report shall clearly identify those carrying out the examination and shall be signed.

(c)   The report shall be confidential and communicated to the subject or his or her nominated representative. The views of the subject and his or her representative about the examination process shall be solicited and recorded in the report. It shall also be provided in writing, where appropriate, to the authority responsible for investigating the allegation of torture or ill-treatment. It is the responsibility of the State to ensure that it is delivered securely to these persons. The report shall not be made available to any other person, except with the consent of the subject or on the authorization of a court empowered to enforce such a transfer.

---

* See footnote on previous page.

Appendix 11

General Comment 20 on Article 7 of the International Covenant on Civil and Political Rights, adopted by the Human Rights Committee at its 44th session in 1992

1.   This general comment replaces general comment 7 (the sixteenth session, 1982) reflecting and further developing it.

2.   The aim of the provisions of article 7 of the International Covenant on Civil and Political Rights is to protect both the dignity and the physical and mental integrity of the individual. It is the duty of the State party to afford everyone protection through legislative and other measures as may be necessary against the acts prohibited by article 7, whether inflicted by people acting in their official capacity, outside their official capacity or in a private capacity. The prohibition in article 7 is complemented by the positive requirements of article 10, paragraph 1, of the Covenant, which stipulates that "All persons deprived of their liberty shall be treated with humanity and with respect for the inherent dignity of the human person".

3.   The text of article 7 allows of no limitation. The Committee also reaffirms that, even in situations of public emergency such as those referred to in article 4 of the Covenant, no derogation from the provision of article 7 is allowed and its provisions must remain in force. The Committee likewise observes that no justification or extenuating circumstances may be invoked to excuse a violation of article 7 for any reasons, including those based on an order from a superior officer or public authority.

4.   The Covenant does not contain any definition of the concepts covered by article 7, nor does the Committee consider it necessary to draw up a list of prohibited acts or to establish sharp distinctions between the different kinds of punishment or treatment; the distinctions depend on the nature, purpose and severity of the treatment applied.

5.   The prohibition in article 7 relates not only to acts that cause physical pain but also to acts that cause mental suffering to the victim. In the Committee's view, moreover, the prohibition must extend to corporal punishment, including excessive chastisement ordered as punishment for a crime or as an educative or disciplinary measure. It is appropriate to emphasize in this regard that article 7 protects, in particular, children, pupils and patients in teaching and medical institutions.

6.   The Committee notes that prolonged solitary confinement of the detained or imprisoned person may amount to acts prohibited by article 7. As the Committee has stated in its general comment No. 6 (16), article 6 of the Covenant refers generally to abolition of the death penalty in terms that strongly suggest that abolition is desirable. Moreover, when the death penalty is applied by a State party for the most serious crimes, it must not only be strictly limited in accordance with article 6 but it must be carried out in such a way as to cause the least possible physical and mental suffering.

7.   Article 7 expressly prohibits medical or scientific experimentation without the free consent of the person concerned. The Committee notes that the reports of States parties

generally contain little information on this point. More attention should be given to the need and means to ensure observance of this provision. The Committee also observes that special protection in regard to such experiments is necessary in the case of persons not capable of giving valid consent, and in particular those under any form of detention or imprisonment. Such persons should not be subjected to any medical or scientific experimentation that may be detrimental to their health.

8.   The Committee notes that it is not sufficient for the implementation of article 7 to prohibit such treatment or punishment or to make it a crime. States parties should inform the Committee of the legislative, administrative, judicial and other measures they take to prevent and punish acts of torture and cruel, inhuman and degrading treatment in any territory under their jurisdiction.

9.   In the view of the Committee, States parties must not expose individuals to the danger of torture or cruel, inhuman or degrading treatment or punishment upon return to another country by way of their extradition, expulsion or refoulement. States parties should indicate in their reports what measures they have adopted to that end.

10. The Committee should be informed how States parties disseminate, to the population at large, relevant information concerning the ban on torture and the treatment prohibited by article 7. Enforcement personnel, medical personnel, police officers and any other persons involved in the custody or treatment of any individual subjected to any form of arrest, detention or imprisonment must receive appropriate instruction and training. States parties should inform the Committee of the instruction and training given and the way in which the prohibition of article 7 forms an integral part of the operational rules and ethical standards to be followed by such persons.

11. In addition to describing steps to provide the general protection against acts prohibited under article 7 to which anyone is entitled, the State party should provide detailed information on safeguards for the special protection of particularly vulnerable persons. It should be noted that keeping under systematic review interrogation rules, instructions, methods and practices as well as arrangements for the custody and treatment of persons subjected to any form of arrest, detention or imprisonment is an effective means of preventing cases of torture and ill-treatment. To guarantee the effective protection of detained persons, provisions should be made for detainees to be held in places officially recognized as places of detention and for their names and places of detention, as well as for the names of persons responsible for their detention, to be kept in registers readily available and accessible to those concerned, including relatives and friends. To the same effect, the time and place of all interrogations should be recorded, together with the names of all those present and this information should also be available for purposes of judicial or administrative proceedings. Provisions should also be made against incommunicado detention. In that connection, States parties should ensure that any places of detention be free from any equipment liable to be used for inflicting torture or ill-treatment. The protection of the detainee also requires that prompt and regular access be given to doctors and lawyers and, under appropriate supervision when the investigation so requires, to family members.

12. It is important for the discouragement of violations under article 7 that the law must prohibit the use of admissibility in judicial proceedings of statements or confessions obtained through torture or other prohibited treatment.

13.   States parties should indicate when presenting their reports the provisions of their criminal law which penalize torture and cruel, inhuman and degrading treatment or punishment, specifying the penalties applicable to such acts, whether committed by public officials or other persons acting on behalf of the State, or by private persons. Those who violate article 7, whether by encouraging, ordering, tolerating or perpetrating prohibited acts, must be held responsible. Consequently, those who have refused to obey orders must not be punished or subjected to any adverse treatment.

14.   Article 7 should be read in conjunction with article 2, paragraph 3, of the Covenant. In their reports, States parties should indicate how their legal system effectively guarantees the immediate termination of all the acts prohibited by article 7 as well as appropriate redress. The right to lodge complaints against maltreatment prohibited by article 7 must be recognized in the domestic law. Complaints must be investigated promptly and impartially by competent authorities so as to make the remedy effective. The reports of States parties should provide specific information on the remedies available to victims of maltreatment and the procedure that complainants must follow, and statistics on the number of complaints and how they have been dealt with.

15.   The Committee has noted that some States have granted amnesty in respect of acts of torture. Amnesties are generally incompatible with the duty of States to investigate such acts; to guarantee freedom from such acts within their jurisdiction; and to ensure that they do not occur in the future. States may not deprive individuals of the right to an effective remedy, including compensation and such full rehabilitation as may be possible.

Appendix 12

General Recommendation 19 on violence against women, adopted by the Committee on the Elimination of Discrimination against Women in 1992, and referring to the Convention on the Elimination of All Forms of Discrimination against Women (extract)

6.   The Convention in article 1 defines discrimination against women. The definition of discrimination includes gender-based violence, that is, violence that is directed against a woman because she is a woman or that affects women disproportionately. It includes acts that inflict physical, mental or sexual harm or suffering, threats of such acts, coercion and other deprivations of liberty. Gender-based violence may breach specific provisions of the Convention, regardless of whether those provisions expressly mention violence.

7.   Gender-based violence, which impairs or nullifies the enjoyment by women of human rights and fundamental freedoms under general international law or under human rights conventions, is discrimination within the meaning of article 1 of the Convention. These rights and freedoms include:

    (a)   The right to life;

    (b)   The right not to be subject to torture or to cruel, inhuman or degrading treatment or punishment;

    (c)   The right to equal protection according to humanitarian norms in time of international or internal armed conflict;

    (d)   The right to liberty and security of person;

    (e)   The right to equal protection under the law;

    (f)   The right to equality in the family;

    (g)   The right to the highest standard attainable of physical and mental health;

    (h)   The right to just and favourable conditions of work.

8.   The Convention applies to violence perpetrated by public authorities. Such acts of violence may breach that State's obligations under general international human rights law and under other conventions, in addition to breaching this Convention.

9.   It is emphasized, however, that discrimination under the Convention is not restricted to action by or on behalf of Governments (see articles 2(e), 2(f) and 5). For example, under article 2(e) the Convention calls on States parties to take all appropriate measures to eliminate discrimination against women by any person, organization or enterprise. Under general international law and specific human rights covenants, States may also be responsible for private acts if they fail to act with due diligence to prevent violations of rights or to investigate and punish acts of violence, and for providing compensation. [...]

Appendix 13

Declaration on the Elimination of Violence against Women (annexed to UN General Assembly resolution 48/104 of 20 December 1993)

Article 1

For the purposes of this Declaration, the term "violence against women" means any act of gender-based violence that results in, or is likely to result in, physical, sexual or psychological harm or suffering to women, including threats of such acts, coercion or arbitrary deprivation of liberty, whether occurring in public or in private life.

Article 2

Violence against women shall be understood to encompass, but not be limited to, the following:

    (a) Physical, sexual and psychological violence occurring in the family, including battering, sexual abuse of female children in the household, dowry-related violence, marital rape, female genital mutilation and other traditional practices harmful to women, non-spousal violence and violence related to exploitation;

    (b) Physical, sexual and psychological violence occurring within the general community, including rape, sexual abuse, sexual harassment and intimidation at work, in educational institutions and elsewhere, trafficking in women and forced prostitution;

    (c) Physical, sexual and psychological violence perpetrated or condoned by the State, wherever it occurs.

Article 3

Women are entitled to the equal enjoyment and protection of all human rights and fundamental freedoms in the political, economic, social, cultural, civil or any other field. These rights include, *inter alia*:

    (a) The right to life;

    (b) The right to equality;

    (c) The right to liberty and security of person;

    (d) The right to equal protection under the law;

    (e) The right to be free from all forms of discrimination;

    (f) The right to the highest standard attainable of physical and mental health;

    (g) The right to just and favourable conditions of work;

    (h) The right not to be subjected to torture, or other cruel, inhuman or degrading treatment or punishment.

Article 4

States should condemn violence against women and should not invoke any custom, tradition or religious consideration to avoid their obligations with respect to its elimination. States should pursue by all appropriate means and without delay a policy of eliminating violence against women and, to this end, should:

(a) Consider, where they have not yet done so, ratifying or acceding to the Convention on the Elimination of All Forms of Discrimination against Women or withdrawing reservations to that Convention;

(b) Refrain from engaging in violence against women;

(c) Exercise due diligence to prevent, investigate and, in accordance with national legislation, punish acts of violence against women, whether those acts are perpetrated by the State or by private persons;

(d) Develop penal, civil, labour and administrative sanctions in domestic legislation to punish and redress the wrongs caused to women who are subjected to violence; women who are subjected to violence should be provided with access to the mechanisms of justice and, as provided for by national legislation, to just and effective remedies for the harm that they have suffered; States should also inform women of their rights in seeking redress through such mechanisms;

(e) Consider the possibility of developing national plans of action to promote the protection of women against any form of violence, or to include provisions for that purpose in plans already existing, taking into account, as appropriate, such cooperation as can be provided by non-governmental organizations, particularly those concerned with the issue of violence against women;

(f) Develop, in a comprehensive way, preventive approaches and all those measures of a legal, political, administrative and cultural nature that promote the protection of women against any form of violence, and ensure that the re-victimization of women does not occur because of laws insensitive to gender considerations, enforcement practices or other interventions;

(g) Work to ensure, to the maximum extent feasible in the light of their available resources and, where needed, within the framework of international cooperation, that women subjected to violence and, where appropriate, their children have specialized assistance, such as rehabilitation, assistance in child care and maintenance, treatment, counselling, and health and social services, facilities and programmes, as well as support structures, and should take all other appropriate measures to promote their safety and physical and psychological rehabilitation;

(h) Include in government budgets adequate resources for their activities related to the elimination of violence against women;

(i) Take measures to ensure that law enforcement officers and public officials responsible for implementing policies to prevent, investigate and punish violence against women receive training to sensitize them to the needs of women;

(j) Adopt all appropriate measures, especially in the field of education, to modify the social and cultural patterns of conduct of men and women and to eliminate prejudices, customary practices and all other practices based on the idea of the inferiority or superiority of either of the sexes and on stereotyped roles for men and women;

(k) Promote research, collect data and compile statistics, especially concerning domestic violence, relating to the prevalence of different forms of violence against women and encourage research on the causes, nature, seriousness and consequences of violence against women and on the effectiveness of measures implemented to prevent and redress violence against women; those statistics and findings of the research will be made public;

(l) Adopt measures directed towards the elimination of violence against women who are especially vulnerable to violence;

(m) Include, in submitting reports as required under relevant human rights instruments of the United Nations, information pertaining to violence against women and measures taken to implement the present Declaration;

(n) Encourage the development of appropriate guidelines to assist in the implementation of the principles set forth in the present Declaration;

(o) Recognize the important role of the women's movement and non-governmental organizations world wide in raising awareness and alleviating the problem of violence against women;

(p) Facilitate and enhance the work of the women's movement and non-governmental organizations and cooperate with them at local, national and regional levels;

(q) Encourage intergovernmental regional organizations of which they are members to include the elimination of violence against women in their programmes, as appropriate.

Article 5

The organs and specialized agencies of the United Nations system should, within their respective fields of competence, contribute to the recognition and realization of the rights and the principles set forth in the present Declaration and, to this end, should, *inter alia*:

(a) Foster international and regional cooperation with a view to defining regional strategies for combating violence, exchanging experiences and financing programmes relating to the elimination of violence against women;

(b) Promote meetings and seminars with the aim of creating and raising awareness among all persons of the issue of the elimination of violence against women;

(c) Foster coordination and exchange within the United Nations system between human rights treaty bodies to address the issue of violence against women effectively;

(d) Include in analyses prepared by organizations and bodies of the United Nations system of social trends and problems, such as the periodic reports on the world social situation, examination of trends in violence against women;

(e) Encourage coordination between organizations and bodies of the United Nations system to incorporate the issue of violence against women into ongoing programmes, especially with reference to groups of women particularly vulnerable to violence;

(f) Promote the formulation of guidelines or manuals relating to violence against women, taking into account the measures referred to in the present Declaration;

(g) Consider the issue of the elimination of violence against women, as appropriate, in fulfilling their mandates with respect to the implementation of human rights instruments;

(h) Cooperate with non-governmental organizations in addressing the issue of violence against women.

Article 6

Nothing in the present Declaration shall affect any provision that is more conducive to the elimination of violence against women that may be contained in the legislation of a State or in any international convention, treaty or other instrument in force in a State.

Appendix 14

Consolidated recommendations of the Special Rapporteur on torture (from the Special Rapporteur's report to the 56th session of the UN General Assembly, A/56/156, 3 July 2001, para. 39)

39. In his last report to the Commission on Human Rights (E/CN.4/2001/66) the Special Rapporteur revised the recommendations that he had compiled in 1994 (E/CN.4/1995/34) into one global recommendation – an end to de facto or de jure impunity. He would like to encourage States to reflect upon them as a useful tool in efforts to combat torture. A further revised version of the recommendations follows:

(a)   Countries that are not party to the Convention against Torture and Other Cruel, Inhuman or Degrading Treatment or Punishment or the International Covenant on Civil and Political Rights should sign and ratify or accede to these Conventions. Torture should be designated and defined as a specific crime of the utmost gravity in national legislation. In countries where the law does not give the authorities jurisdiction to prosecute and punish torture, wherever the crime has been committed and whatever the nationality of the perpetrator or victim (universal jurisdiction), the enactment of such legislation should be made a priority;

(b)   Countries should sign and ratify or accede to the Rome Statute of the International Criminal Court with a view to bringing to justice perpetrators of torture in the context of genocide, crimes against humanity and war crimes and at the same time ensure that their national courts also have jurisdiction over these crimes on the basis of universal jurisdiction;

(c)   The highest authorities should publicly condemn torture in all its forms whenever it occurs. The highest authorities, in particular those responsible for law enforcement activities, should make public the fact that those in charge of places of detention at the time abuses are perpetrated will be held personally responsible for the abuses. In order to give effect to these recommendations, the authorities should, in particular, make unannounced visits to police stations, pre-trial detention facilities and penitentiaries known for the prevalence of such treatment. Public campaigns aimed at informing the civilian population at large of their rights with respect to arrest and detention, in particular to lodge complaints regarding treatment received at the hands of law enforcement officials, should be undertaken;

(d)   Interrogation should take place only at official centres and the maintenance of secret places of detention should be abolished under law. It should be a punishable offence for any official to hold a person in a secret and/or unofficial place of detention. Any evidence obtained from a detainee in an unofficial place of detention and not confirmed by the detainee during interrogation at official locations should not be admitted as evidence in court. No statement of confession made by a person deprived of liberty, other than one made in [the] presence of a judge or a lawyer, should have a probative value in court, except as evidence against those who are accused of having obtained the confession by unlawful means. Serious consideration should be given to introducing video- and audio-taping of proceedings in interrogation rooms;

(e)   Regular inspection of places of detention, especially when carried out as part of a system of periodic visits, constitutes one of the most effective preventive measures against torture. Independent non-governmental organizations should be authorized to have full access to all places of detention, including police lock-ups, pre-trial detention centres, security service premises, administrative detention areas and prisons, with a view to monitoring the treatment of persons and their conditions of detention. When inspection occurs, members of the inspection team should be afforded an opportunity to speak privately with detainees. The team should also report publicly on its findings. In addition, official bodies should be set up to carry out inspections, such teams being composed of members of the judiciary, law enforcement officials, defence lawyers and physicians, as well as independent experts and other representatives of civil society. Ombudsmen and national or human rights institutions should be granted access to all places of detention with a view to monitoring the conditions of detention. When it so requests, the International Committee of the Red Cross should be granted access to places of detention;

(f)   Torture is most frequently practised during incommunicado detention. Incommunicado detention should be made illegal, and persons held incommunicado should be released without delay. Information regarding the time and place of arrest as well as the identity of the law enforcement officials having carried out the arrest should be scrupulously recorded; similar information should also be recorded regarding the actual detention. Legal provisions should ensure that detainees are given access to legal counsel within 24 hours of detention. Security personnel who do not honour such provisions should be punished. In exceptional circumstances, under which it is contended that prompt contact with a detainee's lawyer might raise genuine security concerns and where restriction of such contact is judicially approved, it should at least be possible to allow a meeting with an independent lawyer, such as one recommended by a bar association. In all circumstances, a relative of the detainee should be informed of the arrest and place of detention within 18 hours. At the time of arrest, a person should undergo a medical inspection, and medical inspections should be repeated regularly and should be compulsory upon transfer to another place of detention. Each interrogation should be initiated with the identification of all persons present. All interrogation sessions should be recorded and preferably video-recorded, and the identity of all persons present should be included in the records. Evidence from non-recorded interrogations should be excluded from court proceedings. The practice of blindfolding and hooding often makes the prosecution of torture virtually impossible, as victims are rendered incapable of identifying their torturers. Thus, blindfolding or hooding should be forbidden. Those legally arrested should not be held in facilities under the control of their interrogators or investigators for more than the time required by law to obtain a judicial warrant of pre-trial detention which, in any case, should not exceed a period of 48 hours. They should accordingly be transferred to a pre-trial facility under a different authority at once, after which no further unsupervised contact with the interrogators or investigators should be permitted;

(g)   Administrative detention often puts detainees beyond judicial control. Persons under administrative detention should be entitled to the same degree of protection as persons under criminal detention. At the same time, countries should consider abolishing, in accordance with relevant international standards, all forms of administrative detention;

(h)   Provisions should give all detained persons the ability to challenge the lawfulness of the detention – e.g., through *habeas corpus* or *amparo*. Such procedures should function expeditiously;

(i) Countries should take effective measures to prevent prisoner-on-prisoner violence by investigating reports of such violence, prosecuting and punishing those responsible, and offering protective custody to vulnerable individuals, without marginalizing them from the prison population more than necessitated by the needs of protection and without rendering them at further risk of ill-treatment. Training programmes should be considered to sensitize prison officials as to the importance of taking effective steps to prevent and remedy prisoner-on-prisoner abuse and to provide them with the means to do so. In accordance with the Body of Principles for the Protection of All Persons under Any Form of Detention or Imprisonment, prisoners should be segregated along the lines of gender, age and seriousness of the crime, as well as first-time/repeat offenders and pre-trial/convicted detainees;

(j) When a detainee or relative or lawyer lodges a torture complaint, an inquiry should always take place and, unless the allegation is manifestly ill-founded, public officials involved should be suspended from their duties pending the outcome of the investigation and any subsequent legal or disciplinary proceedings. Where allegations of torture or other forms of ill-treatment are raised by a defendant during trial, the burden of proof should shift to the prosecution to prove beyond reasonable doubt that the confession was not obtained by unlawful means, including torture and similar ill-treatment. Serious consideration should also be given to the creation of witness protection programmes for witnesses to incidents of torture and similar ill-treatment which ought to extend fully to cover persons with a previous criminal record. In cases where current inmates are at risk, they ought to be transferred to another detention facility where special measures for their security should be taken. A complaint that is determined to be well founded should result in compensation to the victim or relatives. In all cases of death occurring in custody or shortly after release, an inquiry should be held by judicial or other impartial authorities. A person in respect of whom there is credible evidence of responsibility for torture or severe maltreatment should be tried and, if found guilty, punished. Legal provisions granting exemptions from criminal responsibility for torturers, such as amnesties, indemnity laws etc., should be abrogated. If torture has occurred in an official place of detention, the official in charge of that place should be disciplined or punished. Military tribunals should not be used to try persons accused of torture. Independent national authorities, such as a national commission or ombudsman with investigatory and/or prosecutorial powers, should be established to receive and to investigate complaints. Complaints about torture should be dealt with immediately and should be investigated by an independent authority with no relation to that which is investigating or prosecuting the case against the alleged victim. Furthermore, the forensic medical services should be under judicial or other independent authority, not under the same governmental authority as the police and the penitentiary system. Public forensic medical services should not have a monopoly of expert forensic evidence for judicial purposes. In that context, countries should be guided by the Principles on the Effective Investigation and Documentation of Torture and other Cruel, Inhuman or Degrading Treatment or Punishment as a useful tool in the effort to combat torture;

(k) Training courses and training manuals should be provided for police and security personnel and, when requested, assistance should be provided by the United Nations programme of advisory services and technical assistance. Security and law enforcement personnel should be instructed on the Standard Minimum Rules for the Treatment of Prisoners, the Code of Conduct for Law Enforcement Officials, the Basic Principles on the Use of Force and Firearms by Law Enforcement Officials, and the Body of Principles for the Protection of All Persons under Any Form of Detention or Imprisonment, and these instruments should be translated into the relevant national languages. In the course of training, particular stress should be placed upon the principle that the prohibition of torture is absolute and non-derogable and that there exists a duty to disobey orders from a superior to commit torture. Governments should scrupulously translate into national guarantees the international standards they have approved and should familiarize law enforcement personnel with the rules they are expected to apply;

(l)   Health-sector personnel should be instructed on the Principles of Medical Ethics relevant to the Role of Health Personnel, Particularly Physicians, in the Protection of Detainees and Prisoners against Torture and Other Cruel, Inhuman or Degrading Treatment or Punishment. Governments and professional medical associations should take strict measures against medical personnel that play a role, direct or indirect, in torture. Such prohibition should extend to such practices as examining detainees to determine their "fitness for interrogation" and procedures involving ill-treatment or torture, as well as providing medical treatment to ill-treated detainees so as to enable them to withstand further abuse. In other cases, the withholding of appropriate medical treatment by medical personnel should be subject to sanction.

Appendix 15

Corporal punishment: Observations of the Special Rapporteur on torture (from the Special Rapporteur's report to the UN Commission on Human Rights, E/CN.4/1997/7, 10 January 1997, paras. 4-11)

4. [...] [A]s indicated in the addendum to this report (E/CN.4/1997/7/Add.1, para. 435), the Government of Saudi Arabia has contested the basis of the Special Rapporteur's concern with corporal punishment. Informal contacts with Governments and non-governmental organizations have also suggested a more generalized interest in the conceptual issues raised by the relationship of the practice to the mandate of the Special Rapporteur. Accordingly, the following paragraphs aim to address the matter.

5. The Special Rapporteur throughout his tenure has received substantial information on the practice of corporal punishment in a number of countries. The information pertains to a variety of methods of punishment, including flagellation, stoning, amputation of ears, fingers, toes or limbs, and branding or tattooing. With respect to the practice in some countries, the authority for the imposition and execution of the punishment derives from legislation or executive decree having the force of legislation. The legal provisions in question envisage the infliction of corporal punishment as an ordinary criminal sanction, either alternative to or in combination with other sanctions such as fine or imprisonment. In some countries the provisions are to be found in administrative regulation, such as that contained in prison manuals in respect of disciplinary offences. In other instances, informal or quasi-official agencies, such as *ad hoc* village tribunals or religious courts, have pronounced sentences of corporal punishment which appear to be extrinsic to the State's constitutional criminal justice system. In respect of these latter cases, the State must be considered responsible for the consequences of these sentences, if they are carried out with its authorization, consent or acquiescence.

6. The Special Rapporteur takes the view that corporal punishment is inconsistent with the prohibition of torture and other cruel, inhuman or degrading treatment or punishment enshrined, *inter alia*, in the Universal Declaration of Human Rights, the International Covenant on Civil and Political Rights, the Declaration on the Protection of All Persons from Being Subjected to Torture and Other Cruel, Inhuman or Degrading Treatment or Punishment and the Convention against Torture and Other Cruel, Inhuman or Degrading Treatment or Punishment. Accordingly, the Special Rapporteur has made a number of urgent appeals on behalf of persons who had been sentenced to corporal punishment, requesting that the concerned Government not carry out the sentence. He has also brought to the attention of a number of Governments information he received on the general practice of corporal punishment in their respective countries, as well as individual cases in respect of which such punishment had been carried out.

7. The Special Rapporteur is aware of the view held by a small number of Governments and legal experts that corporal punishment should not be considered to constitute torture or cruel, inhuman or degrading treatment or punishment, within the meaning of the

obligation of States under international law to refrain from such conduct. Some proponents of the proposition that corporal punishment is not necessarily a form of torture argue that support for their position may be found in article 1 of the Convention against Torture, wherein torture is defined for the purposes of the Convention. That definition excludes from the ambit of proscribed acts those resulting in "pain or suffering arising only from, inherent in or incidental to lawful sanctions". Thus, the argument proceeds, if corporal punishment is duly prescribed under its national law, a State carrying out such punishment cannot be considered to be in breach of its international obligations to desist from torture.

8.   The Special Rapporteur does not share this interpretation. In his view, the "lawful sanctions" exclusion must necessarily refer to those sanctions that constitute practices widely accepted as legitimate by the international community, such as deprivation of liberty through imprisonment, which is common to almost all penal systems. Deprivation of liberty, however unpleasant, as long as it comports with basic internationally accepted standards, such as those set forth in the United Nations Standard Minimum Rules for the Treatment of Prisoners, is no doubt a lawful sanction. By contrast, the Special Rapporteur cannot accept the notion that the administration of such punishments as stoning to death, flogging and amputation – acts which would be unquestionably unlawful in, say, the context of custodial interrogation – can be deemed lawful simply because the punishment has been authorized in a procedurally legitimate manner, i.e. through the sanction of legislation, administrative rules or judicial order. To accept this view would be to accept that any physical punishment, no matter how torturous and cruel, can be considered lawful, as long as the punishment had been duly promulgated under the domestic law of a State. Punishment is, after all, one of the prohibited purposes of torture. Moreover, regardless of which "lawful sanctions" might be excluded from the definition of torture, the prohibition of cruel, inhuman or degrading punishment remains. The Special Rapporteur would be unable to identify what that prohibition refers to if not the forms of corporal punishment referred to here. Indeed, cruel, inhuman or degrading punishments are, then, by definition unlawful; so they can hardly qualify as "lawful sanctions" within the meaning of article 1 of the Convention against Torture.

9.   As regards corporal punishment used for offences against prison discipline, the Special Rapporteur considers that the peremptory language of rule 31 of the Standard Minimum Rules for the Treatment of Prisoners reflects the international prohibition of cruel, inhuman or degrading punishment: "Corporal punishment, punishment by placing in a dark cell, and all cruel, inhuman or degrading punishments shall be completely prohibited as punishments for disciplinary offences."

10.   The Special Rapporteur cannot ignore the objections advanced by some commentators that certain religious law and custom, such as that arising from Shari'a, as interpreted by some Governments, requires the application of corporal punishment in practice and that this exigency overrides any interpretation of the norm against torture which would effectively outlaw corporal punishment. While the Special Rapporteur cannot claim any competence to deal with questions of religious law, he does take note of the fact that there exists a great divergence of views among Islamic scholars and clerics concerning the obligations of States to implement corporal punishment. In this respect, he notes that the overwhelming majority of member States of the Organization of the Islamic Conference do not have corporal punishment in their domestic laws. He stresses that all States have accepted the principle that human rights are universal, most notably in the

Vienna Declaration and Programme of Action. In part II, paragraph 56 of the Vienna Declaration and Programme of Action, the World Conference on Human Rights authoritatively "... reaffirms that under human rights law and international humanitarian law, freedom from torture is a right which must be protected under all circumstances ...". As there is no exception envisaged in international human rights or humanitarian law for torturous acts that may be part of a scheme of corporal punishment, the Special Rapporteur must consider that those States applying religious law are bound to do so in such a way as to avoid the application of pain-inducing acts of corporal punishment in practice. In this connection, he draws attention to the axiomatic doctrine that a State may not invoke the provisions of its national law to justify non-compliance with international law.

11.   The Special Rapporteur notes support for his view in the position of the Human Rights Committee, which has affirmed on at least two occasions that the prohibition on torture and cruel, inhuman or degrading treatment or punishment contained in article 7 of the International Covenant on Civil and Political Rights extends to corporal punishment.[*] Furthermore, the Sub-Commission on Prevention of Discrimination and Protection of Minorities, in resolution 1984/22, recommended to the Commission on Human Rights to urge Governments of States which maintain the penalty of amputation "to take appropriate measures to provide for other punishment consonant with article 5 [of the Universal Declaration of Human Rights]". The United Nations General Assembly has also addressed the issue with respect to the administration of Trust Territories, recommending in resolutions 440 (V) of 2 December 1950 and 562 (VI) of 18 January 1952 that immediate measures be taken to abolish corporal punishment in the Trust Territories. Corporal punishment is plainly prohibited in the context of international armed conflict by the Third and Fourth Geneva Conventions and Additional Protocol I and, in non-international armed conflict, by Additional Protocol II. Finally, various organs of the Commission on Human Rights have contested resort to corporal punishment, including the previous Special Rapporteur on torture (see E/CN.4/1993/26, para. 593), the Special Rapporteur on the situation of human rights in Afghanistan (see A/51/481, annex, para. 81), the Special Representative on the situation of human rights in the Islamic Republic of Iran (see E/CN.4/1991/35, para. 494), the Special Rapporteur on the situation of human rights in Iraq (E/CN.4/1995/56, para. 32; E/CN.4/1996/61, para. 29; A/51/496, annex, para. 108), and the Special Rapporteur on the situation of human rights in the Sudan (E/CN.4/1994/48, paras. 59-61).

---

[*] General Comments 7 (16) and 20 (44). See *Official Records of the General Assembly, Thirty-seventh Session, Supplement No. 40* (A/37/40) and *Forty-seventh Session, Supplement No. 40* (A/47/40).

Appendix 16

Amnesty International's 12-Point Program for the Prevention of Torture by Agents of the State

Torture is a fundamental violation of human rights, condemned by the international community as an offence to human dignity and prohibited in all circumstances under international law.

Yet torture persists, daily and across the globe. Immediate steps are needed to confront torture and other cruel, inhuman or degrading treatment or punishment wherever they occur and to eradicate them totally.

Amnesty International calls on all governments to implement the following 12-Point Program for the Prevention of Torture by Agents of the State. It invites concerned individuals and organizations to ensure that they do so. Amnesty International believes that the implementation of these measures is a positive indication of a government's commitment to end torture and to work for its eradication worldwide.

1. Condemn torture

The highest authorities of every country should demonstrate their total opposition to torture. They should condemn torture unreservedly whenever it occurs. They should make clear to all members of the police, military and other security forces that torture will never be tolerated.

2. Ensure access to prisoners

Torture often takes place while prisoners are held incommunicado – unable to contact people outside who could help them or find out what is happening to them. The practice of incommunicado detention should be ended. Governments should ensure that all prisoners are brought before an independent judicial authority without delay after being taken into custody. Prisoners should have access to relatives, lawyers and doctors without delay and regularly thereafter.

3. No secret detention

In some countries torture takes place in secret locations, often after the victims are made to "disappear". Governments should ensure that prisoners are held only in officially recognized places of detention and that accurate information about their arrest and whereabouts is made available immediately to relatives, lawyers and the courts. Effective judicial remedies should be available at all times to enable relatives and lawyers to find out immediately where a prisoner is held and under what authority and to ensure the prisoner's safety.

4. Provide safeguards during detention and interrogation

All prisoners should be immediately informed of their rights. These include the right to lodge complaints about their treatment and to have a judge rule without delay on the lawfulness of their detention. Judges should investigate any evidence of torture and order release if the detention is unlawful. A lawyer should be present during interrogations. Governments should ensure that conditions of detention conform to international standards for the treatment of prisoners and take into account the needs of members of particularly vulnerable groups. The authorities responsible for detention should be separate from those in charge of interrogation. There should be regular, independent, unannounced and unrestricted visits of inspection to all places of detention.

5. Prohibit torture in law
Governments should adopt laws for the prohibition and prevention of torture incorporating the main elements of the UN Convention against Torture and Other Cruel, Inhuman or Degrading Treatment or Punishment (Convention against Torture) and other relevant international standards. All judicial and administrative corporal punishments should be abolished. The prohibition of torture and the essential safeguards for its prevention must not be suspended under any circumstances, including states of war or other public emergency.

6. Investigate
All complaints and reports of torture should be promptly, impartially and effectively investigated by a body independent of the alleged perpetrators. The methods and findings of such investigations should be made public. Officials suspected of committing torture should be suspended from active duty during the investigation. Complainants, witnesses and others at risk should be protected from intimidation and reprisals.

7. Prosecute
Those responsible for torture must be brought to justice. This principle should apply wherever alleged torturers happen to be, whatever their nationality or position, regardless of where the crime was committed and the nationality of the victims, and no matter how much time has elapsed since the commission of the crime. Governments must exercise universal jurisdiction over alleged torturers or extradite them, and cooperate with each other in such criminal proceedings. Trials must be fair. An order from a superior officer must never be accepted as a justification for torture.

8. No use of statements extracted under torture
Governments should ensure that statements and other evidence obtained through torture may not be invoked in any proceedings, except against a person accused of torture.

9. Provide effective training
It should be made clear during the training of all officials involved in the custody, interrogation or medical care of prisoners that torture is a criminal act. Officials should be instructed that they have the right and duty to refuse to obey any order to torture.

10. Provide reparation
Victims of torture and their dependants should be entitled to obtain prompt reparation from the state including restitution, fair and adequate financial compensation and appropriate medical care and rehabilitation.

11. Ratify international treaties

All governments should ratify without reservations international treaties containing safeguards against torture, including the UN Convention against Torture with declarations providing for individual and inter-state complaints. Governments should comply with the recommendations of international bodies and experts on the prevention of torture.

12. Exercise international responsibility

Governments should use all available channels to intercede with the governments of countries where torture is reported. They should ensure that transfers of training and equipment for military, security or police use do not facilitate torture. Governments must not forcibly return a person to a country where he or she risks being tortured.

This 12-Point Program was adopted by Amnesty International in October 2000 as a program of measures to prevent the torture and ill-treatment of people who are in governmental custody or otherwise in the hands of agents of the state. Amnesty International holds governments to their international obligations to prevent and punish torture, whether committed by agents of the state or by other individuals. Amnesty International also opposes torture by armed political groups.

Endnotes

A guide to the citation of sources

Books and articles are cited in the endnotes by author and date, e.g. Rodley, 1999. Full bibliographic details are given in Appendix 1.

Amnesty International documents: Reports issued as *Amnesty International Publications* are cited by title and year of publication; *other documents,* by title and AI Index number. Details of Amnesty International documents are given in Appendix 2, with information on how to obtain them.

United Nations documents and publications: Appendix 3 contains details of the regular periodic reports of the *Committee against Torture,* the *Human Rights Committee,* the *Committee on the Elimination of Discrimination against Women (CEDAW),* the *Special Rapporteur on torture* and the *Special Rapporteur on violence against women, its causes and consequences* (Special Rapporteur on violence against women) to the UN General Assembly and/or the UN Commission on Human Rights, cited in this manual, and of General Comments and General Recommendations issued by these bodies. The most recent documents which have not yet appeared in the regular periodic reports are cited in the endnotes only (not in Appendix 3). Appendix 3 also contains bibliographic details of UN training manuals and other UN publications cited in the manual. See Appendix 3 for an explanation of UN document symbols and information on how to obtain UN documents and publications.

Documents issued by the European Committee for the Prevention of Torture (CPT) are cited in the endnotes by their title, date and reference number (CPT.../). Many of the references in this manual are to the substantive sections of the CPT's General Reports; the CPT has issued a compilation *"Substantive" sections of the CPT's General Reports* (CPT/Inf/E (99) 1 (REV. 2)). CPT documents can be found on the CPT website at www.cpt.coe.int.

Cases and judicial rulings are cited in the endnotes by name and date. A table of cases, with full citations, is contained in Appendix 4, which also provides details of how case reports can be found on the Internet or from other sources.

International instruments cited in this manual are listed in Appendix 5, which also gives information about how to obtain the texts. Selected texts are reproduced in Appendices 6-15.

Foreword

1. Amnesty International, 1973, *Report on Torture*, pp. 9-10 (cited in Appendix 2 of this manual).

2. These and other statistics on the worldwide incidence of torture can be found in Amnesty International, *Take a step to stamp out torture*, 2000, pp. 2-3, 10, 16, 23, 25, 33, 62.

3. Intergovernmental organizations are international organizations formed by governments, and through which governments can hold consultations and take joint positions and joint actions.

Chapter 1

1. The Preamble to the Universal Declaration of Human Rights states that "it is essential... that human rights should be protected by the rule of law". Evidently referring to the need to hold public officials accountable for their actions, the British delegate who proposed the phrase "rule of law" during the drafting of the Universal Declaration explained that it would show "that every action had to be justified and that every individual could be called upon to answer for his action" (Morsink, 1999, p. 311).

2. UN, Department of Public Information, 1950, *"These Rights and Freedoms..."*, pp. 3-4.

3. The Universal Declaration of Human Rights, the International Covenant on Economic, Social and Cultural Rights and the ICCPR together form the International Bill of Human Rights.

4. The Code of Conduct for Law Enforcement Officials, adopted in 1979, and the Principles of Medical Ethics relevant to the Role of Health Personnel, particularly Physicians, in the Protection of Prisoners and Detainees against Torture and Other Cruel, Inhuman or Degrading Treatment or Punishment, adopted in 1982.

5. Evans and Morgan, 1998, p. 108.

6. The much larger number of countries from which reports of torture and ill-treatment are received today in comparison with the period covered by Amnesty International's first *Report on Torture* (1970 to mid-1973) cannot be taken as an indication that torture and ill-treatment have increased since then. In some countries state-sponsored torture has declined or ceased when repressive regimes have ended; elsewhere it has appeared in times of political tension or armed conflict. There are more countries in the world today than in the 1970s, and more information is available: problems such as the torture and ill-treatment of common criminal suspects and conditions of detention amounting to ill-treatment existed then but were under-reported. It is fair to say, however, that there is still no clear sign of a decline in torture and ill-treatment worldwide, despite the obligation of governments to end it.

7. Vienna Declaration and Programme of Action, Part II, paras. 55, 57.

8. See Amnesty International, *Report of the Stockholm Conference on Torture* (AI Index: ACT 40/05/97).

9. General Comment 7 on Article 7 of the ICCPR, adopted in 1982, para. 2.

10. General Comment 20 on Article 7 of the ICCPR, para. 5, reproduced in Appendix 11 of this manual.

11. General Comment 20, para. 2.

12. See Amnesty International, *International standards on the death penalty* (AI Index: ACT 50/10/98), pp. 1-2; Schabas, 1996.

13. According to the Human Rights Committee, "the term 'discrimination' as used in the [International] Covenant [on Civil and Political Rights] should be understood to imply any distinction, exclusion, restriction or preference which is based on any ground such as race, colour, sex, language, religion, political or other opinion, national or social origin, property, birth or other status, and which has the purpose or effect of nullifying or impairing the recognition, enjoyment or exercise by all persons, on an equal footing, of all rights and freedoms." (General Comment 18 on non-discrimination, para. 7)

14. Sir Nigel Rodley, who served as UN Special Rapporteur on torture from 1992 to 2001, has written that "man's inhumanity to man can thrive only if the torturer or the executioner can deny the humanity of his victim". When torture and other gross human rights violations are part of an institutionalized practice, "the victim is – must be – dehumanized, seen as an object... Whatever the group, its members must be stripped of their inherent dignity as human beings in order to mobilize the rest against them." (Rodley, 1999, pp. 14-15)

15. Contribution of the Committee against Torture to the preparatory process for the World Conference against Racism, Racial Discrimination, Xenophobia and Related Intolerance, UN Doc. A/CONF.189/PC.2/17, 26 February 2001.

16. For example, Convention on the Rights of the Child, Article 2; American Convention on Human Rights, Article 1; European Convention on Human Rights, Article 14; African Charter on Human and Peoples' Rights, Article 2.

17. For example, UN Standard Minimum Rules for the Treatment of Prisoners, Rule 6(1); Body of Principles on Detention, Principle 5.

18. E/CN.4/1995/34, paras. 15-24; A/55/290, paras. 5-9. For bibliographic details of these and other UN documents cited in this manual, see Appendix 3.

19. E/CN.4/1996/35, paras. 9-17; A/55/290, paras. 10-15.

20. A/56/156, paras. 17-25.

21. A/55/290, paras. 34-37.

22. E/CN.4/1995/34, para. 19.

23. Ibid., paras. 18, 21, 23.

24. E/CN.4/1998/54, para. 130.

25. E/CN.4/1996/35, para. 15.

26. A/55/290, para. 13.

27. A/56/156, para. 17.

28. A/55/290, para. 35.

29. E/CN.4/1995/34, para. 22; A/56/156, para. 20; E/CN.4/1996/35, para. 14.

30. A/CONF.189/PC.2/17, 26 February 2001, cited above (note 15).

31. As the Special Rapporteur on torture has stated, "In the final analysis, the elimination of torture is a matter of political will. Its persistence is testimony to the failure of political will" (E/CN.4/1994/31, para. 670).

32. As stated by the Special Rapporteur on torture, "The highest authorities should publicly condemn torture in all its forms whenever it occurs. The highest authorities, in particular those responsible for law enforcement activities, should make public the fact that those in charge of places of detention at the time abuses are perpetrated will be held personally responsible for the abuses." (A/56/156, para. 39(c), reproduced in Appendix 13 of this manual)

33. The Committee against Torture has recommended that a state party to the Convention against Torture "issue and transmit to the police specific and clear instructions designed to prohibit any act of torture in the future" (A/51/44, para. 222, referring to Egypt). The Special Rapporteur on torture has stated: "Senior law enforcement officials should make it clearly known that the ill-treatment of detained persons is not acceptable and will be dealt with severely" (Report on visit to Cameroon, E/CN.4/2000/9/Add.2, para. 78(a)).

34. There is a similar provision in the UN Principles on the Effective Prevention and Investigation of Extra-legal, Arbitrary and Summary Executions (Article 2). Also, the Council of Europe Declaration on the Police, adopted by the Parliamentary Assembly of the Council of Europe in 1979 (Part A, para. 10), states: "There shall be a clear chain of command. It should always be possible to determine which superior may be ultimately responsible for acts or omissions of a police officer." A footnote to the Declaration indicates that this statement applies also to members of the armed forces performing police duties.

35. The Special Rapporteur on torture has called for "effective procedures for internal monitoring and disciplining" of the behaviour of police agents with a view to eliminating torture and ill-treatment. (Report on visit to Turkey, E/CN.4/1999/61/Add.1, para. 113(i))

36. One way of improving chain-of-command control with a view to preventing torture is to remove police forces from military command. In his report on a visit to Chile, where there were many allegations of torture at the hands of the uniformed police (*carabineros*), who tended to enjoy impunity by being subject to military rather than civilian jurisdiction, the Special Rapporteur on torture recommended that the uniformed police "should be brought under the authority of the Minister of the Interior, rather than the Minister of Defence" and should be subject to ordinary criminal jurisdiction only. (E/CN.4/1996/35/Add.2, para. 76(a))

37. See Prokosch, 1999, for an account of the role of the 12-Point Program.

38. For an example of a detailed set of recommendations concerning a country in which torture and ill-treatment have been endemic for many years, see Amnesty International, *India: Words into action – recommendations for the prevention of torture* (AI Index: ASA 20/003/2001).

39. Normally, each resolution reiterates the provisions of the previous year's, but sometimes there are new features. New elements in the resolution adopted in 2001 included a call to governments to prohibit the production, trade and use of equipment designed for torture or ill-treatment (see section 8.4). The resolutions are normally adopted without a vote. In recent years the UN General Assembly also has adopted (without a vote) resolutions on "Torture and other cruel, inhuman or degrading treatment or punishment". They contain many of the same provisions as in the Commission on Human Rights resolutions, but carry the extra authority of the UN's top political body.

40. A *treaty body* is a body established under a human rights treaty to monitor the implementation of the provisions of the treaty. As noted in this section, some treaty bodies are empowered to hear complaints from individuals alleging violations of their rights under the respective treaties. Unlike the judgments of the regional human rights courts, the decisions adopted by treaty bodies in individual cases are not binding on states, but there is a strong presumption that states will comply with them by virtue of their having accepted the jurisdiction of the treaty body to hear complaints.

41. A *mechanism* established by the Commission on Human Rights is a person or a group designated to examine a specific country situation or theme from a human rights perspective. Examples include the Special Rapporteur on torture and the Special Rapporteur on violence against women. Other intergovernmental mechanisms include the Special Rapporteur on Prisons and Conditions of Detention in Africa of the African Commission on Human and Peoples' Rights (see section 5.1).

42. See section 8.5 on the delays which the Committee has experienced in receiving states' periodic reports. Article 19 of the Convention also provides that states parties shall submit "such other reports as the Committee may request". The use of this provision with regard to Israel is described in section 2.2.

43. The Committee normally holds two sessions each year, in April-May and November, at the UN Office in Geneva.

44. Article 21(1) states: "A State Party to this Convention may at any time declare under this article that it recognizes the competence of the Committee to receive and consider communications to the effect that a State Party claims that another State Party is not fulfilling its obligations under this Convention. Such communications may be received and considered according to the procedures laid down in this article only if submitted by a State Party which has made a declaration recognizing in regard to itself the competence of the Committee. No communication shall be dealt with by the Committee under this article if it concerns a State Party which has not made such a declaration..." No inter-state complaint has yet been submitted under Article 21.

45. Article 22(1) states: "A State Party to this Convention may at any time declare under this article that it recognizes the competence of the Committee to receive and consider communications from or on behalf of individuals subject to its jurisdiction who claim to be victims of a violation by a State Party of the provisions of the Convention. No communication shall be received by the Committee if it concerns a State Party which has not made such a declaration."

46. Complaints from individuals under Article 22 of the Convention against Torture are inadmissible if the same matter has been or is being examined under another procedure of international investigation or if domestic remedies have not been exhausted, except where the application of such remedies is unreasonably prolonged or unlikely to bring effective relief to the victim. Other international and regional complaints procedures, such as those of the Human Rights Committee and the regional courts, have similar restrictions on admissibility. However, anyone can submit information on torture allegations to the Special Rapporteur on torture. See Giffard, 2000, Part III on admissibility requirements for complaints of torture.

As of 18 May 2001, the Committee against Torture had adopted decisions on 56 individual complaints, of which 20 were upheld. Most complaints received to date have concerned alleged violations of Article 3 – the article which forbids the forcible sending of a person to a country where he or she would be at risk of torture. During the year ending on 18 May 2001, for example, the Committee adopted decisions on one complaint in which it found violations of Articles 12 and 13 and on 10 other complaints alleging violations of Article 3, of which one was upheld.

47. Article 20 of the Convention against Torture specifies actions to be taken by the Committee if it "receives reliable information which appears to it to contain well-founded indications that torture is being systematically practised in the territory of a State Party" to the Convention. The Committee has defined the systematic practice of torture as follows: "The Committee considers that torture is practised systematically when it is apparent that the torture cases reported have not occurred fortuitously in a particular place or at a particular time, but are seen to be habitual, widespread and deliberate in at least a considerable part of the territory of the country in question. Torture may in fact be of a systematic character without resulting from the direct intention of a Government. It may be the consequence of factors which the Government has difficulty in controlling, and its existence may indicate a discrepancy between policy as determined by the central Government and its implementation by the local administration. Inadequate legislation which in practice allows room for the use of torture may also add to the systematic nature of this practice." (A/48/44/Add.1, para. 39)

48. At 1 October 2002, nine states had made such declarations (see section 8.5). Amnesty International has called for such declarations to be withdrawn.

The Committee against Torture has thus far issued summary accounts of inquiries conducted under Article 20 on Turkey, Egypt and Peru (A/48/44/Add.1, A/51/44, paras. 180-222 and A/56/44, paras. 144-188 respectively). The three inquiries were instigated following information submitted to the Committee by Amnesty International in the case of Turkey, Amnesty International and the Egyptian Organization for Human Rights in the case of Egypt, and Human Rights Watch in the case of Peru.

49. The position of Special Rapporteur on torture was established in 1985 pursuant to UN Commission on Human Rights resolution 1985/33 of 13 March 1985 in which the Commission decided "to appoint for one year a special rapporteur to examine questions relevant to torture". The position has been renewed periodically since then, most recently in Commission on Human Rights resolution 2001/62 of 25 April 2001. The first Special Rapporteur on torture, Peter Kooijmans, appointed in 1985, retired in 1992 and was succeeded by Nigel S. Rodley (later Sir Nigel Rodley). Sir Nigel Rodley was succeeded by Theo van Boven in November 2001. Since 1999 the Special Rapporteur has also submitted reports annually to the UN General Assembly.

50. A description of the Special Rapporteur's methods of work and a review of his work to date appeared in his first written report to the General Assembly (A/54/426, paras. 13-38). See also Rodley, 1999, pp. 147-150. For a list of the Special Rapporteur's country visits, see Appendix 3 of this manual.

51. The CPT's first visit, to Austria, was in 1990. As of 31 December 2001 the CPT had made 135 visits and had visited each state party to the Convention at least once. For a list of visits and bibliographic details of published reports, see Morgan and Evans, 2001, pp. 172-198, Tables 2-3. The CPT's annual General Reports also contain lists of visits.

52. If a state party fails to cooperate or refuses to improve a situation in light of the Committee's recommendations, the Committee may make a public statement on the matter. It has done so only three times thus far – twice on Turkey and once with regard to the Chechen Republic.

53. See section 3.2.3 on the provisions of these Conventions which relate to the prohibition of torture and ill-treatment.

Chapter 2

1. The use of similar, although less severe, methods of torture against Israeli Jews normally leads to immediate protests. For example, when Oren Edri, an officer in the Israeli Defence Force arrested with other Jewish militants in September 1994, complained that he was hooded for hours, roughly handled, insulted, and confined to a cell with cockroaches and rats, a commission of inquiry was immediately set up.

2. Following a review of the Landau Commission guidelines in 1993, the authorities stated that exposure to extreme temperatures, deprivation of food or denial of access to the toilet were not permitted. However, detainees continue to complain of these interrogation methods.

3. See Amnesty International, *Israel and the Occupied Territories – Death by shaking: the case of 'Abd al-Samad Harizat* (AI Index: MDE 15/23/95).

4. *B'Tselem*, 1997 (cited in Appendix 1 of this manual).

5. A/49/44, para. 170.

6. On the case of Muhammad 'Abd al-'Aziz Hamdan, see *B'Tselem*, 1997.

7. As noted in section 1.5 of this manual, Article 19(1) of the Convention against Torture requires states parties to submit "such other reports as the Committee may request".

8. A/52/44, paras. 257, 260.

9. A/53/44, para. 238.

10. *Public Committee Against Torture in Israel and others v. The State of Israel and others* (HCJ 5100/94; 4054/94; 6536/95; 5188/96; 7563/97; 7628/97; 1043/99).

11. Ibid., paras. 23-31, 39. One of the judges concurred in the ruling but wanted it suspended for a year to give the *Knesset* (the Israeli parliament) time to consider the matter.

12. Conclusions and recommendations on the third periodic report of Israel, CAT/C/XXVII/Concl.5, 23 November 2001, para. 6.

13. A/50/44, para. 73.

14. A/51/40, paras. 347-348, 355, 361.

15. Press communiqué 9/97, 5 June 1997, reproduced in Annual Report of the Inter-American Commission on Human Rights 1997, p. 1094.

16. A/53/44, para. 200(c).

17. A/55/44, paras. 58-61.

18. A/56/40, paras. 76(5), 76(9).

19. A/56/44, paras. 163-175.

20. Human Rights Watch published reports on abuses in juvenile detention centres in Georgia and Louisiana, prior to the Department of Justice investigation (Human Rights Watch, 1995, 1996). At the time of the Department of Justice investigation, a lawsuit seeking damages and other redress regarding conditions in Tallulah Detention Center was being pursued separately by the non-govern-mental Louisiana Juvenile Justice Center. The Department of Justice, however, was able to widen its investigation to include all juvenile facilities in the two states.

21. Torture is not explicitly prohibited by Indian law. India signed the Convention against Torture in 1997 but had not yet ratified it at the time of writing of this manual.

22. D.K. Basu was, in the 1970s, an advocate practising in the West Bengal High Court, where he spent much of his time defending victims of torture. He founded the Legal Aid Services–West Bengal, a state-level social action group based in Calcutta.

23. *Basu v. State of West Bengal*, 18 December 1996, [1997] 2 LRC 1. (References are to the num-bered paragraphs in this case as reported in Law Reports of the Commonwealth (LRC).)

24. Plainclothes police officers have regularly arrested and interrogated people in India, making it difficult for victims to identify their torturers.

25. This is an important safeguard against unacknowledged illegal detention, particularly crucial in areas of armed conflict in India where "disappearances" are common.

26. The practice of keeping a "general diary" of arrests at police stations has fallen into disuse, so there are often no records that people have been detained. Lawyers or judicial authorities depend on these records if there are complaints of ill-treatment or other abuses during detention.

27. Police in India have often claimed that detainees were injured before arrest or were unwell at the time of arrest and that their condition subsequently deteriorated, thereby arguing that deaths in custody were not the result of police violence.

28. In issuing this requirement, the court was seeking to ensure evidence of the medical condition of detainees as a means of guarding against conflicting allegations of torture, etc.

29. Under section 57 of the Code of Criminal Procedure, all detainees in India must be brought before a magistrate within 24 hours of arrest. The magistrate then decides whether to remand them to further police or judicial custody. By requiring that these initial custody records are forwarded to the magistrate at the time of the detainee's appearance before the magistrate, the Supreme Court was attempting to provide checks for the magistrate to ensure that proper legal procedures had been followed. Under normal circumstances the magistrate would only have the word of the detainee or their lawyer against that of the police if there were allegations of illegal detention.

30. Report on initial visit to Austria (1990), CPT/Inf (91) 10, para. 87.

31. Response of Austrian government to report on second periodic visit to Austria, CPT/Inf (96) 29, p. 26.

32. Although the HRAC members are independent and are not bound by external directives, the HRAC does not meet the standards of independence set out in the UN Principles relating to the status and functioning of national institutions for the protection and promotion of human rights (Paris Principles), endorsed by the UN Commission on Human Rights in resolution 1992/54 of 3 March 1992, since its members from the government departments have a voting – as opposed to just an advisory – role in deliberations. In addition, the HRAC's six human rights commissions are directly financed by the Ministry of the Interior.

33. Report on initial visit to Austria, para. 10.

34. Ibid., para. 97.

35. Report on second periodic visit to Austria (1994), CPT/Inf (96) 28, para. 25 (available in French only).

36. Report on third periodic visit to Austria (1999), CPT/Inf (2001) 8, para. 18 (available in French only).

37. South Africa, Truth and Reconciliation Commission, Amnesty Committee, hearing on the application by Jeffrey Benzien for amnesty, July 1997. Transcripts of hearings and decisions of the Amnesty Committee can be found on the website of the Truth and Reconciliation Commission at www.doj.gov.za/trc/.

38. South Africa, Truth and Reconciliation Commission, 1998 (cited below as TRC Report), Vol. 1, p. 56; Hayner, 2001, p. 41. (For bibliographic details of the TRC Report, see Appendix 1 of this manual.)

39. TRC Report, Vol. 1, pp. 48-57.

40. Jenkins, 2000, pp. 459-461.

41. Boraine, 2000, pp. 38-42.

42. Hayner, 2001, p. 41. On 13 January 1995 Amnesty International submitted to the South African parliament and government a *Memorandum to the Select Committee on Justice, Comments and Recommendations by Amnesty International on the Promotion of National Unity and Reconciliation Bill,* and in July 1995 joined South African NGOs in an appeal for an open and credible appointment process for the planned commission (*Amnesty International Supports Call for Public Role in Truth Commission Appointments,* AI Index: AFR 53/10/95, News Service 131/95).

43. *Azanian Peoples' Organisation (AZAPO) and others v. President of the Republic of South Africa and others,* 25 July 1996; Jenkins, 2000, pp. 459-461, 471-475.

44. Hayner, 2001, pp. 142, 156.

45. TRC Report, Vol. 1, pp. 179-190; Hayner, 2001, pp. 125-127.

46. TRC Report, Vol. 3, pp. 444-445.

47. Hayner, 2001, p. 227. The author noted that of the 21,000 statements recorded by Truth and Reconciliation Commission staff from victims of human rights violations, some 2,000 victims and witnesses were involved in giving testimony at about 80 separate public hearings in different parts of the country.

48. TRC Report, Vol. 5, pp. 7-8.

49. TRC Report, Vol. 5, p. 202.

50. Hayner, 2001, pp. 43, 98-100.

51. Amnesty Committee hearing, G. J. Nieuwoudt, September 1997; decision AC/97/0068.

52. Amnesty Committee hearing, Christo Nel, April 2000; decision AC/2000/060.

53. Amnesty Committee hearings, Jeffrey Theodore Benzien, July 1997 and October 1997; decision AC/99/0027.

54. Amnesty Committee decision, Adriaan Pieter van Niekerk and others, AC/2000/059. The notion that torture can be justified as a "proportional" response to an objective, legitimate or otherwise, is contrary to the absolute prohibition of torture (see section 3.5).

55. See the reports of South Africa's Independent Complaints Directorate, which monitors and investigates allegations against the police, on www.icd.gov.za. See also Amnesty International, *South Africa – Preserving the gains for human rights in the "war against crime": Memorandum to the South African Government and South African Law Commission on the draft Anti-Terrorism Bill, 2000* (AI Index: AFR 53/04/00).

Chapter 3

1. For comparisons of the standards emanating from different sources, see, for example, Evans and Morgan, 1998, Chapters 6-8; Ingelse, 2001, Chapters 8-12; Murdoch, 1999; Peukert, 1999; Rodley, 1999, Chapters 2-5; Suntinger, 1999.

2. The four treaties were adopted by the respective regional intergovernmental organizations – the Organization of African Unity (now the African Union), the Organization of American States, the Council of Europe and the League of Arab States. All Council of Europe member states must become parties to the European Convention on Human Rights. Also, Article 20 of the **Cairo Declaration on Human Rights in Islam,** a non-binding instrument adopted by the Organization of the Islamic Conference, states that it is not permitted to subject an individual "to physical or psychological torture or to any form of humiliation, cruelty or indignity".

3. Sir Nigel Rodley has written that the Declaration against Torture "represents a most authoritative interpretation of the UN Charter", as it was adopted by the UN General Assembly without a vote and with no reservations expressed at the time of adoption (Rodley, 1999, p. 64).

4. This Convention does not establish a separate monitoring mechanism analogous to the UN Committee against Torture. Instead, its Article 17 provides that states parties shall inform the Inter-American Commission on Human Rights of the measures they take to apply the Convention.

5. As of 1 October 2002, all 44 member states of the Council of Europe were parties to the Convention. Since 1994 a commitment to become a party to the Convention has been a condition for accession to the Council of Europe.

6. Article 16 of the African Charter on the Rights and Welfare of the Child states: "States Parties to the present Charter shall take specific legislative, administrative, social and educational measures to protect the child from all forms of torture, inhuman or degrading treatment and especially physical or mental injury or abuse, neglect or maltreatment including sexual abuse, while in the care of a parent, legal guardian or school authority or any other person who has the care of the child." Article 10 of the International Convention on the Protection of the Rights of All Migrant Workers and Members of Their Families states: "No migrant worker or member of his or her family shall be subjected to torture or to cruel, inhuman or degrading treatment or punishment."

7. First Geneva Convention, Articles 12, 50; Second Geneva Convention, Articles 12, 51; Third Geneva Convention, Article 130, as well as Article 13 providing for humane treatment; Fourth Geneva Convention, Articles 16, 27, 31, 32, 147.

8. The notion of "non-international" armed conflict typically applies to armed confrontations between governmental armed forces and organized, armed opposition groups that occur within the territory of a particular state. Such conflicts also include those in which two or more armed factions within a country engage in hostilities without the involvement of governmental forces, such as when the established government has dissolved or is too weak to intervene.

9. See Chapter 4, note 85, on safeguards regarding the interrogation of prisoners of war and section 5.1 on standards for the treatment of prisoners of war and of interned civilians in occupied territories and aliens in the territory of a party to a conflict.

10. See, in particular, Third Geneva Convention, Articles 25, 29, 49, 108; Fourth Geneva Convention, Articles 27, 50, 51, 68, 76; Additional Protocol I, Articles 75-78; Additional Protocol II, Articles 4-6.

11. Common Article 3 states that "each Party to the conflict shall be bound to apply, as a minimum", its provisions. This point is discussed in the Commentary to the Geneva Conventions (Pictet, ed., 1952-1960), published by the International Committee of the Red Cross (ICRC) and available on the ICRC website at www.icrc.org.

12. *Military and Paramilitary Activities in and against Nicaragua (Nicaragua v. United States of America)*, 1986, paras. 218-220, cited in Appendix 4 of this manual.

13. Charter of the International Military Tribunal, 8 August 1945, annexed to the Agreement for the Prosecution and Punishment of Major War Criminals of the European Axis (London Agreement), 8 UNTS 279, 59 Stat. 1544.

14. "The fact that the Defendant acted pursuant to order of his Government or of a superior shall not free him from responsibility, but may be considered in mitigation of punishment if the Tribunal determines that justice so requires" (Charter of the International Military Tribunal, Article 8). The UN General Assembly unanimously confirmed the principles of international law recognized by the Charter and the Judgment of the Nuremberg Tribunal in resolution 95(I), adopted on 11 December 1946.

15. The International Law Commission is a body of experts appointed by the UN General Assembly to codify and develop progressively international law.

16. International Law Commission, Report on Principles of the Nuremberg Tribunal, 29 July 1950, 5 UN GAOR Supp. (No. 12) 11, UN Doc. A/1316 (1950).

17. See Additional Protocol I, Article 85(5); Rome Statute of the International Criminal Court, Article 8(2)(a).

18. *Prosecutor v. Tadić*, Decision on the Defence Motion for Interlocutory Appeal on Jurisdiction, Appeals Chamber, 2 October 1995, paras. 134, 137.

19. Convention on the Non-Applicability of Statutory Limitations to War Crimes and Crimes against Humanity, adopted in 1968; Principles of international co-operation in the detection, arrest, extradition and punishment of persons guilty of war crimes and crimes against humanity, adopted in 1973.

20. The *International Tribunal for the Prosecution of Persons Responsible for Serious Violations of International Humanitarian Law Committed in the Territory of the former Yugoslavia since 1991* was established by UN Security Council resolution 827 (1993) of 25 May 1993.

21. The *International Criminal Tribunal for the Prosecution of Persons Responsible for Genocide and Other Serious Violations of International Humanitarian Law Committed in the Territory of Rwanda and Rwandan Citizens Responsible for Genocide and Other Such Violations Committed in the Territory of Neighbouring States, between 1 January 1994 and 31 December 1994* was established by UN Security Council resolution 955 (1994) of 8 November 1994.

22. Unlike grave breaches of the Geneva Conventions, which pertain only to international armed conflicts, this category of war crimes includes acts committed in non-international armed conflicts. The phrase "violations of the laws or customs of war" is from the Charter of the Nuremberg Tribunal.

23. Statute of the Yugoslavia Tribunal, Articles 1-5.

24. Statute of the Rwanda Tribunal, Articles 1-4.

25. The crime of aggression under the Rome Statute had not yet been defined at the time of writing this manual.

26. The Court will have jurisdiction if the crime was committed in the territory of a state party to the Rome Statute or of a state making a declaration accepting the Court's jurisdiction over the crime, or if the crime was committed by a national of either of these states. In addition, the Court will have jurisdiction over a crime in a situation threatening or breaching international peace and security referred to it by the UN Security Council acting under Chapter VII of the Charter of the United Nations (UN Charter).

27. Under Article 7(2) of the Rome Statute, an "attack directed against any civilian population" means "a course of conduct involving the multiple commission of acts referred to in [Article 7] paragraph 1 against any civilian population, pursuant to or in furtherance of a State or organizational policy to commit such attack". An "attack" does not, however, have to involve military action. A civilian population can include people of the same nationality as the perpetrator. It includes members of armed forces who have laid down their arms and people placed *hors de combat* (unable to fight) by sickness, wounds, detention or any other reason. A civilian population does not lose its civilian nature when some individuals within the population are not civilians. (See Boot and others, 1999)

28. The definition of genocide in the Rome Statute is taken from Article II of the Genocide Convention, and most of the ancillary crimes of genocide in Article III of that Convention are included in the Rome Statute.

29. The International Court of Justice was established in 1945 as the "principal judicial organ of the United Nations" (UN Charter, Article 92) to decide disputes between states. Its Statute is an integral part of the UN Charter.

30. Torture is, in fact, widespread, but this does not undermine its prohibition under customary law: according to Sir Nigel Rodley, "human rights violations in the form of torture cannot be offered as evidence of state practice... the best evidence for a customary rule of international law is to be found in what states say they think the rule is *(opinio juris)*, and what they say they are doing (or not doing) in terms of that rule. The fact is that a large number of the governments that proclaim their adherence to the prohibition of torture and their compliance with it, actually commit acts of torture in the dark and secret reaches of their power. But this no more undermines the validity of the prohibition than the covert activities of secret services invalidate international law rules on non-intervention against state sovereignty." (Rodley, 1999, pp. 66-67)

31. General Comment 24 on issues relating to reservations and declarations, paras. 8, 10, cited in Appendix 3 of this manual. One consequence drawn by the Human Rights Committee is that the prohibition of torture and ill-treatment may not be the subject of reservations by states parties to the ICCPR. The Human Rights Committee has noted that some states have entered reservations to Article 7 of the ICCPR but not in terms which reserve a right to torture (ibid.).

32. Yugoslavia Tribunal, *Prosecutor v. Delalić and others*, 16 November 1998, stating that the prohibition of torture constitutes a norm of *jus cogens* (para. 454) and that the prohibition of inhuman treatment is a norm of customary international law (para. 517); European Court of Human Rights, *Al-Adsani v. UK*, 21 November 2001, para. 61, stating that "the prohibition of torture has achieved the status of a peremptory norm in international law".

33. *Barcelona Traction, Light and Power Company, Limited (Belgium v. Spain)*, 1970, para. 34.

34. UN Doc. E/CN.4/1986/15, para. 3, cited in Appendix 3.

35. The Committee against Torture stated in 1989 that there exists "a general rule of international law which should oblige all States to take effective measures to prevent torture and to punish acts of torture" (*O.R., M.M. and M.S. v. Argentina*, 23 November 1989, para. 7.2).

36. *Prosecutor v. Furundžija*, 10 December 1998, para. 156.

37. "...it would seem that other consequences [of the *jus cogens* character of the prohibition of torture] include the fact that torture may not be covered by a statute of limitations, and must not be excluded from extradition under any political offence exemption" (ibid., para 157).

38. Non-binding UN instruments containing express prohibitions of torture or ill-treatment include the **Standard Minimum Rules for the Treatment of Prisoners** (Article 31), the **Body of Principles for the Protection of All Persons under Any Form of Detention or Imprisonment** (Principle 6), the **Code of Conduct for Law Enforcement Officials** (Article 5), the **Principles of Medical Ethics relevant to the Role of Health Personnel, particularly Physicians, in the Protection of Prisoners and Detainees against Torture and Other Cruel, Inhuman or Degrading Treatment or Punishment** (Principle 2), the **Declaration on the Human Rights of Individuals Who are not Nationals of the Country in which They Live** (Article 6), the **United Nations Rules for the Protection of Juveniles Deprived of their Liberty** (Articles 64, 67, 87) and the **Declaration on the Elimination of Violence against Women** (Article 3). See Appendix 5 for details of these and other UN instruments.

39. See Rodley, 1993.

40. Notably the **European Prison Rules** and the **European Declaration on the Police.**

41. The Document of the Copenhagen Meeting of the Conference on the Human Dimension of the Conference on Security and Co-operation in Europe, adopted on 29 June 1990, states that the participating states "reaffirm their commitment to prohibit torture and other cruel, inhuman or degrading treatment or punishment, [and] to take effective legislative, administrative, judicial and other measures to prevent and punish such practices" (para. 16.1).

42. Article 16 of the Convention refers to "other" acts of ill-treatment which "do not amount to torture" as defined in the Convention. The word "other" appears also in the title and text of the Declaration against Torture and in the Code of Conduct for Law Enforcement Officials (Article 5).

43. Rodley, 1999, p. 75.

44. See Rodley, 1999, pp. 86-88, 96-98, 102-103, 287-288.

45. For example, the European Committee for the Prevention of Torture (CPT), which operates with Article 3 of the European Convention on Human Rights as a point of reference, has made many useful recommendations to states without in most cases specifying whether the problems which it has found amount to "torture" or to one or another of the other elements of the formulation in that article.

46. See *Prosecutor v. Delalić and others*, para. 459; *Prosecutor v. Furundžija*, para. 161; *Prosecutor v. Kunarac and others*, 22 February 2001, paras. 482-485, 497.

47. The Committee against Torture has established that a person acting "in an official capacity" does not necessarily have to be acting on behalf of a state. With reference to an area of Somalia, a collapsed state, which was "under the effective control" of a clan which had "established quasi-governmental institutions and provides a number of public services", the Committee has interpreted the phrase "in an official capacity" in Article 1 of the Convention to include the possibility of torture being inflicted by the clan. It held in the case of *Sadiq Shek Elmi v. Australia* that Australia, a party to the Convention, had an obligation under Article 3 of the Convention to refrain from forcibly returning the complainant to Somalia, where there were substantial grounds for believing he would be at risk of torture by the clan, which was in control of the area of the country where he would be likely to reside if returned to the country (*Sadiq Shek Elmi v. Australia*, 14 May 1999, paras. 6, 7). In another case, however, in which the complainant claimed that she would be at risk of torture at the hands of the armed opposition group *Partido Comunista del Perú "Sendero Luminoso"*, Communist Party of Peru "Shining Path", if returned to Peru from Sweden, the Committee held that "the issue whether the State party has an obligation to refrain from expelling a person who might risk pain or suffering inflicted by a non-governmental entity, without the consent or acquiescence of the Government, falls outside the scope of article 3 of the Convention" (*G.R.B. v. Sweden*, 15 May 1998, para. 6.5). (See section 8.3 of this manual for information on rulings by the European Court of Human Rights in analogous cases.)

48. E/CN.4/1997/7, para. 8, reproduced in Appendix 14 of this manual.

49. Complaints can also be submitted by states parties to the Convention.

50. Under Article 46 of the Convention as amended by Protocol No. 11, "The High Contracting Parties undertake to abide by the final judgment of the Court in any case to which they are parties." This article supersedes the previous Article 53 of the Convention, which contained a similar provision.

51. The replacement of the European Commission and Court of Human Rights by a single European Court of Human Rights was effected by Protocol No. 11 to the European Convention on Human Rights, which entered into force on 1 November 1998.

52. Torture in Greece after the 1967 coup had become a prominent human rights issue outside the country. See Amnesty International, *Report on Torture*, 2nd edition, pp. 79-105 for an account of the case.

53. Article 28 of the European Convention on Human Rights authorized the Commission, with a view to ascertaining the facts concerning a petition under examination, to undertake "if need be, an investigation, for the effective conduct of which the States concerned shall furnish all necessary facilities". The same provision applies to the European Court of Human Rights in its examination of petitions since November 1998 under the Convention as amended by Protocol No. 11 (Article 38). The Inter-American Commission on Human Rights has a similar power of investigation under Article 48 of the American Convention on Human Rights.

54. *Greek Case*, Report of the Commission 18 November 1969, Opinion on Article 3, para. 17, Yearbook p. 504.

55. Ibid., Chapter IV, para. 2, Yearbook p. 186. See Rodley, 1999, pp. 77-84 for a discussion of the Commission's treatment of the concept of torture and ill-treatment.

56. The Court stated that "it was the intention that the Convention, with its distinction between 'torture' and 'inhuman or degrading treatment', should by the first of these terms attach a special stigma to deliberate inhuman treatment causing very serious and cruel suffering" (*Ireland v. UK*, 18 January 1978, para. 167).

57. Rodley, 1999, p. 92. The ruling was criticized at the time by Amnesty International (ibid., p. 93).

58. *Ireland v. UK*, 18 January 1978, para. 167. Earlier, the European Commission of Human Rights had found that the five techniques amounted to torture (see section 3.4).

59. *Selmouni v. France*, 28 July 1999, paras. 100, 105. The Court subsequently confirmed that "repeated beatings by prison guards over a period of several days with the aim of extracting a confession... can properly be categorised as torture within the meaning of Article 3 of the Convention" (*Al-Adsani v. UK*, 21 November 2001, para. 58).

60. This doctrine had been articulated by the Court in the case of *Tyrer v. UK*, 25 April 1978 (para. 31).

61. *Selmouni v. France*, para. 101.

62. *Tyrer v. UK*, para. 35.

63. Ibid., para. 30.

64. *Keenan v. UK*, 3 April 2001, para. 108. Similarly, the UN Human Rights Committee has stated that "the assessment of what constitutes inhuman or degrading treatment falling within the meaning of article 7 [of the ICCPR] depends on all the circumstances of the case, such as the duration and manner of the treatment, its physical or mental effects as well as the sex, age and state of health of the victim" (*Vuolanne v. Finland*, 7 April 1989, para. 9.2).

65. *Mahmut Kaya v. Turkey*, 28 March 2000, para. 117.

66. *Selmouni v. France*, para. 100.

67. *Mahmut Kaya v. Turkey*, para. 117. Subsequently, in its finding of torture in the case of *Salman v. Turkey*, the Court took into account the purposive element of obtaining information: it noted "the strong inferences that can be drawn from the evidence" that the torture "occurred during interrogation" about the victim's suspected activities (*Salman v. Turkey*, 27 June 2000, para. 115). However, in other cases the Court has made findings of torture without pointing to a purposive element.

68. *Kudła v. Poland*, 26 October 2000, para. 92.

69. *Keenan v. UK*, para. 109.

70. *Peers v. Greece*, 19 April 2001, para. 74.

71. *Raninen v. Finland*, 16 December 1997, para. 55.

72. *Keenan v. UK*, para. 112. As examples of such circumstances, the Court cited its standard on excessive use of force (see section 6.3) and stated that "treatment of a mentally ill person may be incompatible with the standards imposed by Article 3 in the protection of fundamental human dignity, even though that person may not be able, or capable of, pointing to any specific ill-effects" (loc. cit.). For information on the case, see section 5.5.4.

73. For a recent discussion of the approaches of the European Court of Human Rights and other bodies to the definition of torture and ill-treatment, see Evans, 2002.

74. Report of the Preparatory Commission for the International Criminal Court, Addendum, Part II, Finalized draft text of the Elements of Crimes, UN Doc. PCNICC/2000/1/Add.2. (This and other documents relating to the International Criminal Court are available on the UN website at www.un.org/law/icc.)

75. A footnote attached to the elements of the crime of torture under Article 8(2)(a) states that as the victim or victims "must be 'protected persons' under one or more of the Geneva Conventions of 1949, these elements do not include the custody or control requirement" found in the elements of torture as a crime against humanity under Article 7 of the Rome Statute.

76. The definition of torture as a war crime has also been discussed in several judgments of the Yugoslavia Tribunal. The most recent relevant judgment at the time of writing of this manual was in the case of *Prosecutor v. Kunarac and others* (para. 497).

77. The following descriptions are included in the draft Elements of Crimes:

Crimes specified in the Rome Statute	Draft Elements of Crimes
Inhuman treatment (Article 8(2)(a)) Cruel treatment (Article 8(2)(c))	"The perpetrator inflicted severe physical or mental pain or suffering upon one or more persons."
Wilfully causing great suffering (Article 8(2)(a))	"The perpetrator caused great physical or mental pain or suffering to, or serious injury to body or health of, one or more persons."
Outrages upon personal dignity (Article 8(2)(c))	"1. The perpetrator humiliated, degraded or otherwise violated the dignity of one or more persons." (A footnote states: "For this crime, 'persons' can include dead persons. It is understood that the victim need not personally be aware of the existence of the humiliation or degradation or other violation. This element takes into account relevant aspects of the cultural background of the victim.") "2. The severity of the humiliation, degradation or other violation was of such degree as to be generally recognized as an outrage upon personal dignity."
Mutilation (Article 8(2)(c))	"1. The perpetrator subjected one or more persons to mutilation, in particular by permanently disfiguring the person or persons, or by permanently disabling or removing an organ or appendage. "2. The conduct was neither justified by the medical, dental or hospital treatment of the person or persons concerned nor carried out in such person's or persons' interests."

The draft Elements of Crimes also provide definitions of the war crimes of biological experiments (Article 8(2)(a)) and medical or scientific experiments (Articles 8(2)(b), 8(2)(e)), and of enforced sterilization as a war crime and a crime against humanity.

78. Such sexual abuse includes sexual threats, virginity testing, fondling, and the deliberate use of body searches or sexually explicit language to degrade or humiliate. (See also sections 4.10, 5.7.1)

79. The definition of rape has also been discussed by the Rwanda and Yugoslavia tribunals. See Rwanda Tribunal, *Prosecutor v. Akayesu*, 2 September 1998, paras. 597-598; Yugoslavia Tribunal, *Prosecutor v. Kunarac and others*, paras. 436-464.

80. A footnote is attached to the word "invaded" in the draft Elements of Crimes stating: "The concept of 'invasion' is intended to be broad enough to be gender-neutral."

81. A footnote is attached to the word "consent" stating: "It is understood that a person may be incapable of giving genuine consent if affected by natural, induced or age-related incapacity."

82. The crime of "sexual violence" includes the following element: "The perpetrator committed an act of a sexual nature against one or more persons or caused such person or persons to engage in an act of a sexual nature by force, or by threat of force or coercion, such as that caused by fear of violence, duress, detention, psychological oppression or abuse of power, against such person or persons or another person, or by taking advantage of a coercive environment or such person's or persons' incapacity to give genuine consent." As with the crime of rape, it is understood that "a person may be incapable of giving genuine consent if affected by natural, induced or age-related incapacity". Sexual violence as a war crime must be "of a gravity comparable to that of a grave breach of the Geneva Conventions"; as a crime against humanity, it must be "of a gravity comparable to the other offences" in Article 7(1)(g) of the Rome Statute. The draft Elements of Crimes also provide definitions of sexual slavery, enforced prostitution and forced pregnancy as war crimes and crimes against humanity.

83. E/CN.4/1995/34, para. 19.

84. Oral introduction to the report of the Special Rapporteur to the 1992 session of the Commission on Human Rights, quoted in E/CN.4/1995/34, para. 16.

85. The Commission noted that the victim "was raped with the aim of punishing her personally and intimidating her" (*Mejía v. Peru*, 1 March 1996, Annual Report of the Inter-American Commission on Human Rights 1995, p. 187).

86. *Aydın v. Turkey* (23178/94), 25 September 1997, para. 86. Amnesty International had submitted written comments to the Court supporting the conclusion of the European Commission of Human Rights in the same case that rape of a detained woman by an official or person in authority constitutes torture.

87. *Prosecutor v. Delalić and others,* paras. 943, 965; *Prosecutor v. Furundžija,* para. 269.

88. *Prosecutor v. Furundžija,* para. 275.

89. *Prosecutor v. Akayesu,* paras. 696, 734.

90. *Prosecutor v. Furundžija,* para. 163.

91. Ibid., para. 164.

92. See Peel, 2002.

93. See Amnesty International, *Hidden scandal, secret shame: Torture and ill-treatment of children,* 2000; Man, 2000, pp. 30-32.

94. International humanitarian law also refers to "mental torture" and contains prohibitions of intimidation, including threats of torture or other cruel treatment (Third Geneva Convention of 1949, Articles 13, 17; Additional Protocol II of 1977, Article 4). See also Human Rights Committee, General Comment 20 on Article 7 of the ICCPR, para. 5, reproduced in Appendix 11 of this manual.

95. Report on visit to Azerbaijan, E/CN.4/2001/66/Add.1, para. 115.

96. Ibid., para. 7.

97. Resolution 56/143 of 19 December 2001, para. 1. Police operations conducted in a frightening and unreasonable manner can also amount to ill-treatment. In the case of *Rojas García v. Colombia*, the Human Rights Committee found a violation of Article 7 of the ICCPR where a group of armed men in civilian clothes from the public prosecutor's office had entered a house through the roof and terrified and abused the family while searching the premises. The complainant alleged that these actions resulted in a severe nervous trauma to his sister, an invalid, leading indirectly to her death seven months later. (*Rojas García v. Colombia*, 3 April 2001, para. 10.5)

98. Resolution 2002/38 of 22 April 2002, para. 6.

99. The techniques involved being hooded, forced to stand leaning with only the fingers touching the wall, subjected to continuous noise and deprived of sleep, food and drink. The Commission held that "The combined application of methods which prevent the use of the senses, especially the eyes and the ears, directly affects the personality physically and mentally. The will to resist or to give in cannot, under such conditions, be formed with any degree of independence. Those most firmly resistant might give in at an early stage when subjected to this sophisticated method to break or even eliminate the will." (*Ireland v. UK*, Report of the Commission, 25 January 1976, Yearbook p. 792)

100. A/56/44, para. 186. The prisoners were not allowed to talk among themselves or with the prison guards, and the cells were totally soundproofed against outside noise. The prisoners were allowed to go outside, alone, to a small yard surrounded by high walls for a maximum of one hour per day.

101. *Greek Case*, Report of the Commission, Opinion on Article 3, para. 18, Yearbook p. 505. In a later ruling, the European Court of Human Rights cited the factors behind the Commission's findings in the *Greek Case* as "overcrowding and inadequate facilities for heating, sanitation, sleeping arrangements, food, recreation and contacts with the outside world". The Court added: "When assessing conditions of detention, account has to be taken of the cumulative effects of these conditions, as well as of specific allegations made by the applicant." (*Dougoz v. Greece*, 6 March 2001, para. 46)

102. In the case of *Dougoz v. Greece*, where the complainant had been held for approximately 17 months in police detention, the Court found that the complainant's conditions of detention, "in particular the serious overcrowding and absence of sleeping facilities, combined with the inordinate length of the period during which he was detained in such conditions, amounted to degrading treatment contrary to Article 3" of the European Convention on Human Rights (para. 48). In another case, in which the complainant was confined for much of each day in a prison cell which had no ventilation and was at times "unbearably hot", sharing an open toilet with his cellmate, the Court held that the conditions "diminished the applicant's human dignity and arose [sic] in him feelings of anguish and inferiority capable of humiliating and debasing him and possibly breaking his physical or moral resistance" and amounted to degrading treatment. The Court noted that the authorities had "taken no steps to improve the objectively unacceptable conditions of the applicant's detention" and stated that "this omission denotes lack of respect for the applicant" (*Peers v. Greece*, para. 75).

103. Summary account of inquiry on Peru under Article 20 of the Convention against Torture, A/56/44, paras. 178, 183; also para. 186.

104. Rodley, 1999, pp. 286-295, 304-305.

105. Report on visit to Venezuela, E/CN.4/1997/7/Add. 3, para. 81.

106. Report on visit to the Russian Federation, E/CN.4/1995/34/Add.1, para. 71 (see section 5.1).

107. See Evans and Morgan, 1998, pp. 243-245.

108. *Prosecutor v. Delalić and others*, paras. 1121-1123.

109. See Amnesty International, *"Disappearances" and Political Killings...: A Manual for Action*, 1994, pp. 84-85, "What is a 'disappearance'?". Definitions of "forced disappearance" or "enforced disappearance" can be found in the Inter-American Convention on the Forced Disappearance of Persons, Article II, and the draft Elements of Crimes of the International Criminal Court (Article 7(1)(i) of the Rome Statute).

110. *Celis Laureano v. Peru*, 25 March 1996, para. 8.5.

111. *Velásquez Rodríguez v. Honduras*, 29 July 1988, para. 187.

112. A/56/156, para. 14.

113. *Elena Quinteros Almeida and María del Carmen Almeida de Quinteros v. Uruguay*, 21 July 1983, para. 14.

114. *Kurt v. Turkey*, 25 May 1998, para. 134. Amnesty International had submitted written comments to the Court on the nature of "disappearances" as human rights violations under international law (ibid., paras. 68-71). In a subsequent judgment, however, the Court stated that the case of *Kurt v. Turkey* "does not... establish any general principle that a family member of a 'disappeared person' is thereby a victim of treatment contrary to Article 3" of the European Convention on Human Rights (*Çakıcı v. Turkey*, 8 July 1999, para. 98). In a later case, the Court found that there had been inhuman treatment in violation of Article 3 of the Convention with regard to the failure of the authorities of the Turkish Cypriot-administered area of northern Cyprus to provide information to their relatives on the fate of Greek Cypriots who had gone missing during the conflict in 1974 (*Cyprus v. Turkey* (25781/94), 10 May 2001, paras. 157-158).

115. *Blake v. Guatemala*, 24 January 1998, para. 116.

116. *Selçuk and Asker v. Turkey*, 24 April 1998, para. 78.

117. Conclusions and recommendations on the third periodic report of Israel, CAT/C/XXVII/Concl. 5, 23 November 2001, paras. 6(i), 6(j). The term "closure" refers to the practice of cutting off Palestinian towns and villages from the outside world by army checkpoints or physical barriers.

118. During the early sessions in the process of drafting the Universal Declaration of Human Rights and what later became the ICCPR, delegates had been provided with a special report on the war crimes trials against Nazi leaders, with details of many of their alleged crimes, including the medical experiments (Morsink, 1999, pp. 40, 42). For an account of the drafting history and a discussion of the terms used in this provision of the ICCPR, see Nowak, 1993, pp. 137-139; Bossuyt, 1987, pp. 147-160.

119. The Fourth Geneva Convention prohibits "medical or scientific experiments not necessitated by the medical treatment of a protected person" (Article 32), as does the Third Geneva Convention (Article 13) in similar terms. Additional Protocol I to the Geneva Conventions (Article 11) specifies unwarranted medical or scientific experiments which seriously endanger physical or mental health or integrity as grave breaches of the Protocol, punishable as war crimes. Biological experiments and medical or scientific experiments are also specified as war crimes in the Rome Statute of the International Criminal Court.

120. General Comment 20, para. 5.

121. *Tyrer v. UK*, para. 35; *A v. UK*, 23 September 1998, para. 21.

122. *Ribitsch v. Austria*, 4 December 1995, para. 38.

123. *Soering v. UK*, 7 July 1989, para. 104. Bearing in mind the US "death row phenomenon", a set of circumstances involving a "very long period of time spent on death row" under a stringent custodial regime "with the ever present and mounting anguish of awaiting execution of the death penalty", the Court held that the extradition of the complainant to the USA to face a capital murder charge "would expose him to a real risk of treatment going beyond the threshold set by Article 3" of the European Convention on Human Rights (ibid., paras. 81, 111). In another case involving extradition, the Human Rights Committee found that Canada had violated Article 7 of the ICCPR by extraditing the complainant to the USA to face capital charges and possible execution by gas in California (*Charles Chitat Ng v. Canada*, 5 November 1993, para. 16.3; see also paras. 2.1, 16.4).

124. A/56/44, para. 45(i), referring to Belarus.

125. A/56/44, para. 39(g), referring to Armenia.

126. *East African Asians v. UK*, Report of the Commission, 14 December 1973, para. 207. The complainants, United Kingdom (UK) citizens, faced with expulsion from East Africa, had been denied entry into the UK on racial grounds. The Commission found that the racial discrimination to which they had been publicly subjected constituted "an interference with their human dignity" which, in the circumstances of the case, "amounted to 'degrading treatment' in the sense of Article 3 of the Convention" (para. 208).

127. *Cyprus v. Turkey* (25781/94), 10 May 2001, para. 311. The Greek Cypriots had been compelled to live under severe restrictions to their freedom of movement, affecting their enjoyment of private and family life and their right to practice their religion, conditions which were "debasing" and violated "the very notion of respect for" their human dignity. The treatment to which they were subjected could "only be explained in terms of... their ethnic origin, race and religion" (para. 309).

128. *Prosecutor v. Blaškić*, 3 March 2000, paras. 738, 743 and Disposition.

129. A/55/290, para. 5.

130. Female genital mutilation is recognized in the UN Declaration on the Elimination of Violence against Women (Article 2) as a form of violence against women. The Committee on the Elimination of Discrimination against Women (CEDAW) has referred to female circumcision (female genital mutilation) as a traditional practice "harmful to the health of women" and has recommended that states parties to the Convention on the Elimination of All Forms of Discrimination against Women "take appropriate and effective measures with a view to eradicating" the practice (General Recommendation 14 on female circumcision (1990), preambular para. 1 and operative para. (a). The Special Rapporteur on torture has stated that "traditional practices" such as sexual mutilation "might constitute 'severe pain or suffering' according to international law" and that states "shall provide appropriate protection under law against such treatments, even when the perpetrators are 'private' persons rather than 'public officials'" (E/CN.4/1986/15, para. 49).

131. E/CN.4/2002/83, para. 6.

132. "To assess compliance with article 7 of the Covenant, as well as with article 24, which mandates special protection for children, the Committee needs to be provided information on national laws and practice with regard to domestic and other types of violence against women, including rape. It also needs to know whether the State party gives access to safe abortion to women who have become pregnant as a result of rape. The States parties should also provide the Committee with information on measures to prevent forced abortion or forced sterilization. In States parties where the practice of genital mutilation exists information on its extent and on measures to eliminate it should be provided. The information provided by States parties on all these issues should include measures of protection, including legal remedies, for women whose rights under article 7 have been violated." (General Comment 28 on Article 3 of the ICCPR, para. 11) In line with this statement, the Committee stated in its concluding observations on the fourth periodic report of Peru that the provision of criminal penalties for abortion when pregnancy was the result of rape was incompatible with Article 7 of the ICCPR (A/56/40, para. 20).

133. American Convention on Human Rights, Article 27; European Convention on Human Rights, Article 15; Arab Charter on Human Rights (not yet in force), Article 4.

134. Resolution 2002/38 of 22 April 2002, para. 1, adopted without a vote. The Commission condemned in particular "any action or attempt by States or public officials to legalize or authorize torture under any circumstances, including through judicial decisions" (ibid., para. 2). Similarly, the UN Special Rapporteur on torture has stated that "the legal and moral basis for the prohibition of torture and other cruel, inhuman or degrading treatment or punishment is absolute and imperative and must under no circumstances yield or be subordinated to other interests, policies and practices" (E/CN.4/2002/137, para. 15). See "The non-derogability of the prohibition of torture and cruel, inhuman or degrading treatment or punishment" (ibid., paras. 8-15).

135. *Tomasi v. France*, 27 August 1992, paras. 114-116.

136. One scenario often cited is that of the "ticking bomb", wherein it is argued that a prisoner should be tortured to obtain information about the location of a bomb which would otherwise explode, killing and maiming people. Evoking this scenario, lawyers representing the state of Israel in the case of *Public Committee against Torture in Israel and others v. The Government of Israel and others* (cited in section 2.2) argued that the use of interrogation techniques involving "moderate physical pressure" as a last resort in order to prevent death and injury was legal under the defence of necessity in the Israeli Penal Law, which exempts a person from criminal liability for committing an act immediately necessary to save a person from imminent threat of death or serious injury. The Israeli High Court of Justice, however, ruled that a state interrogator might evoke the defence of necessity if criminally indicted, but that the very nature of this defence, involving an individual reacting to an event in an *ad hoc* way, "does not allow it to serve as the source of a general administrative power". In the words of the Court, "The lifting of criminal responsibility does not imply authorization to infringe upon a human right." (*Public Committee against Torture in Israel and others v. The Government of Israel and others*, 6 September 1999, para. 36)

137. General Comment 20, para. 2.

138. Sir Nigel Rodley has linked dehumanization of the victim to the institutionalized practice of torture against particular groups (see Chapter 1, note 14). International human rights law confronts this "dehumanization of the perceived enemy" by "proscribing the destruction of the inherent dignity of the human person" (Rodley, 1999, p. 15).

139. Declaration against Torture, Article 2.

140. The right to personal integrity is also recognized in Article 4 of the African Charter on Human and Peoples' Rights.

141. In the American Convention on Human Rights, Article 11, "Right to Privacy", begins: "Everyone has the right to have his honor respected and his dignity recognized." In the case of *Mejía v. Peru*, the Inter-American Commission on Human Rights found that the rape of the victim by a member of the security forces constituted torture in violation of Article 5 of the Convention and that the victim had also suffered a violation of Article 11 because the rapes which she suffered "affected both her physical and her moral integrity, including her personal dignity" (*Mejía v. Peru*, Annual Report of the Inter-American Commission on Human Rights 1995, p. 188).

142. For example, in the case of *East African Asians v. UK* (para. 208) the European Commission of Human Rights held that the racial discrimination to which the complainants had been subjected constituted "an interference with their human dignity" amounting to "degrading treatment". In the case of *Tyrer v. UK* (para. 33), the European Court of Human Rights stated that the judicial corporal punishment inflicted on the victim "constituted an assault on precisely that which it is one of the main purposes of Article 3 [of the European Convention on Human Rights] to protect, namely a person's dignity and physical integrity". In its judgments in the cases of *Tomasi v. France* (para. 115) and *Ribitsch v. Austria* (para. 38), in both of which it found that the complainants had been subjected to inhuman and degrading treatment, the same Court referred to the need to protect "the physical integrity of individuals". The Court's judgment in the latter case, quoted in section 3.3, also referred to human dignity.

143. For example, in the case of *Heredia Miranda v. Bolivia*, where the victim had been tortured, the Commission found in 1979 that the government of Bolivia had violated Article I of the American Declaration on the Rights and Duties of Man, which states: "Every human being has the right to life, liberty and the security of his person." The American Declaration on the Rights and Duties of Man was adopted in May 1948 at the international conference in Bogotá which created the Organization of American States. It does not contain an explicit prohibition of torture. The American Convention on Human Rights, which explicitly prohibits torture, did not enter into force until 1978.

144. As noted in section 1.3, the Committee on the Elimination of Discrimination against Women (CEDAW) has stated that gender-based violence against women, which may include torture and ill-treatment, is discrimination within the meaning of the Convention on the Elimination of All Forms of Discrimination against Women (General Recommendation 19, para. 7, reproduced in Appendix 12 of this manual).

145. *Velásquez Rodríguez v. Honduras*, para. 169.

146. Ibid., para. 166.

147. Morsink, 1999, pp. 36-37, 42-43, 48-49.

148. See Amnesty International, *Respect, protect, fulfil – women's human rights: State responsibility for abuses by "non-state actors"* (AI Index: IOR 50/01/00).

149. General Comment 20, para. 2.

150. *A v. UK*, para. 21.

151. Ibid., para. 22.

152. Ibid., para. 24.

153. The Court had referred in that case to protection through "deterrence": "Children and other vulnerable individuals, in particular, are entitled to State protection, in the form of effective deterrence, against such serious breaches of personal integrity" (ibid., para. 22).

154. *Mahmut Kaya v. Turkey*, para. 115. In a subsequent case, the Court held that the state had violated Article 3 of the European Convention on Human Rights through the failure of the social services to protect four children from serious long-term neglect and abuse at the hands of their parents which "reached the threshold of inhuman and degrading treatment" (*Z and others v. UK*, 10 May 2001, paras. 74-75). The authorities had been aware of the ill-treatment and neglect over a period of years but "failed, despite the means reasonably available to them, to take any effective steps to bring it to an end" (ibid., para. 70).

155. *Velásquez Rodríguez v. Honduras*, paras. 166, 172. The case involved a "disappearance" (see section 3.4).

156. In the drafting of the prohibition of torture and ill-treatment in the Universal Declaration of Human Rights, the wording "no one shall be subjected" was chosen in preference to "it shall be unlawful to subject" in order to emphasize the right of the individual rather than the obligation of states (Bossuyt, 1987, pp. 149-150).

157. The Preambles to the ICCPR and the Convention against Torture refer to "the equal and inalienable rights of all members of the human family" and state that these rights "derive from the inherent dignity of the human person". The Preamble to the Universal Declaration of Human Rights similarly refers to "inalienable" rights and to the "inherent" dignity of human beings.

Chapter 4

1. See Amnesty International, *"Disappearances" and Political Killings...: A Manual for Action*, 1994, Chapter 9, on measures for the prevention of "disappearances" and extrajudicial executions.

2. General Comment 20 on Article 7 of the International Covenant on Civil and Political Rights (ICCPR), paras. 11-12, reproduced in Appendix 11 of this manual.

3. The Body of Principles on Detention and the Declaration on Enforced Disappearance were adopted by the UN General Assembly without a vote, a strong sign that the standards set out in them should be regarded as universal norms which all governments should respect.

4. This formulation is from the CPT's report on its second periodic visit to Malta (1995), CPT/Inf (96) 25, paras. 24-25. Evans and Morgan (1998, p. 258) have noted that the essential elements of the formula were first set out in the CPT's 2nd General Report, CPT/Inf (92) 3, published in 1992 (paras. 36-37), but that the precise wording has evolved over time. See Morgan and Evans, 2001, p. 74 for information on further changes in wording.

5. One way of monitoring the treatment of prisoners is through closed-circuit television. The CPT has stated that "as a matter of principle", it "welcomes the use of closed circuit television to monitor custody areas in police establishments" (Report on initial visit to Andorra (1998), CPT/Inf (2000) 11, para. 28).

6. The Committee against Torture has requested states to provide statistical information relevant to the prevention of torture and ill-treatment. For example, after considering the initial report of Indonesia under the Convention against Torture, it recommended that Indonesia "[i]nclude, in its next periodic report, statistical data regarding torture and other forms of cruel, inhuman or degrading treatment or punishment, disaggregated by, inter alia, gender, ethnic group, geographical region, and type and location of detention. In addition, information should be provided regarding complaints and cases heard by domestic bodies, including the results of investigations made and the consequence for the victims in terms of redress and compensation." (CAT/C/XXVII/Concl.3, 22 November 2001, para. 10(p))

7. In the case of *Celis Laureano v. Peru* the victim, a "disappeared" person, had been violently removed from her home by state agents who did not act on the basis of an arrest warrant or on orders of a judge or judicial officer. The Human Rights Committee found that the state had violated Article 9(1) of the ICCPR read together with Article 2(1) (*Celis Laureano v. Peru*, 25 March 1996, para. 8.6).

8. General Comment 8 on Article 9 of the ICCPR, para 1.

9. See section 2.5 for an example of safeguards for arrest and detention set out in the judgment of the Supreme Court of India in the case of *Basu v. State of West Bengal*, 18 December 1996. Among other things, the Supreme Court ordered that police arresting and interrogating suspects should wear "accurate, visible and clear" identification and name tags.

10. Concerning the requirement of promptness, the Human Rights Committee has stated that a period of detention of 72 hours before detainees are informed of the charges being brought against them is "too long and not in compliance with article 9, paragraph 2, of the Covenant" (A/56/40, para. 79(12), referring to Uzbekistan).

11. Similarly, the CPT, in connection with its three "fundamental safeguards" against ill-treatment in police custody, has stated that it "considers it equally fundamental that detained persons be informed without delay of all their rights", including the rights which constitute the three "fundamental safeguards" (see section 4.1). The Special Rapporteur on torture also has recommended that "[a]ll detainees should be provided, immediately after arrest, with information about their rights and how to avail themselves of such rights" (Report on visit to Chile, E/CN.4/1996/35/Add.2, para. 76(d)).

12. Article 5(2) of the European Convention on Human Rights states: "Everyone who is arrested shall be informed promptly, in a language which he understands, of the reasons for his arrest and of any charge against him." The European Court of Human Rights has held that this information covers "the essential legal and factual grounds for his arrest" and that it must be given in "simple, non-technical language" (*Fox, Campbell and Hartley v. UK*, 30 August 1990, para. 40).

13. The Special Rapporteur on torture has recommended: "A statement of detainees' rights... should be readily available at all places of detention for consultation by detained persons and members of the public" (Report on visit to Brazil, E/CN.4/2001/66/Add.2, para. 169(e)). See also the action example on Albania in section 8.1 for an example of efforts by the authorities to publicize the rights of arrested and detained people.

14. Although under Principle 16(4) of the Body of Principles on Detention a notification may be delayed "for a reasonable period where exceptional needs of the investigation so require", Principle 15 states that "communication of the detained or imprisoned person with the outside world, and in particular his family or counsel, shall not be denied for more than a matter of days."

15. A/56/40, para. 86(18), referring to the Democratic People's Republic of Korea.

16. A/52/40, para. 438, referring to India.

17. According to Evans and Morgan, the published responses to CPT reports suggest that in practice prisoners are often not able to exercise the right to have a relative or third party notified of their arrest. The CPT has made clear that the right should be expressly guaranteed, but according to Evans and Morgan "[a] number of states do not accept the need for this procedure to be guaranteed by law whilst others, though not hostile to giving the right a legal basis, seem to think it unnecessary." Where it is necessary to withhold notification for a period of time, "the Committee has stressed the need for further safeguards, namely: that the grounds of restriction are closely defined; that it is for a strictly limited period of time, this being no longer than is absolutely necessary, and that other procedural safeguards are in place. The latter include the provision that 'such delay... be recorded in writing together with the reasons therefor and to require the approval of a senior officer or public prosecutor', subsequent reports referring to the approval of judicial authorities, judges or magistrates, courts or public prosecutors." (Evans and Morgan, 1998, pp. 262-265)

18. "Close family members of persons detained should be immediately informed of their relative's detention and be given access to them" (Report on visit to Kenya, E/CN.4/2000/9/Add.4, para. 92(i); see also the Special Rapporteur's report on his visit to Brazil, E/CN.4/2001/66/Add.2, para. 169(d)).

19. A/56/156, para. 39(f), reproduced in Appendix 14 of this manual. In his report on a visit to Chile, the Special Rapporteur on torture called for people "arrested on suspicion" to be "given the possibility of communicating immediately with relatives and lawyer" (E/CN.4/1996/35/Add.2, para. 76(m)).

20. Report on visit to Pakistan, E/CN.4/1997/7/Add. 2, para. 106.

21. CPT, 2nd General Report, para. 40. See Morgan and Evans, 2001, pp. 77-78 for discussion.

22. General Comment 20, para. 11.

23. A/56/156, para. 39(d).

24. The Inter-American Commission on Human Rights has stated that a person should be brought before a judge or other judicial authority "as soon as it is practicable to do so; delay is unacceptable" (Report on the Situation of Human Rights in Ecuador, OEA/Ser.L/V/II.96, doc.10, rev.1, 24 April 1997, p. 73). The Human Rights Committee has stated that "the period of up to 48 hours before being brought before a court is excessive" (A/56/40, para. 83(17), referring to the Czech Republic; cf. A/55/40, para. 472, referring to Kuwait). A delay of 48 hours is clearly insufficient as a safeguard against torture, which can commence very quickly when a person is apprehended. For additional references, see Amnesty International, *Fair Trials Manual*, 1998, section 5.2, p. 44.

25. The Special Rapporteur on torture has stated: "Magistrates and judges, like prosecutors, should always ask a person brought from police custody how they have been treated and be particularly attentive to their condition" (Report on visit to Kenya, E/CN.4/2000/9/Add.4, para. 93(k)).

26. In Peru, where the Committee against Torture found that torture had been "systematically used as a method of investigation", the Committee recommended that "judges should order an immediate prior [medical] examination of detainees as soon as the latter are brought before them" (A/56/44, para. 169).

27. General Comment 20, para. 11.

28. A/56/44, para. 39(b), referring to Armenia.

29. A/54/44, para. 187, referring to Libya.

30. Resolution 2002/38 of 22 April 2002, para. 14.

31. General Comment 20, para. 11.

32. A/52/44, referring to Georgia, para. 121(d).

33. A/53/44, referring to Spain, para. 135; A/54/44, referring to Libya, para. 182(a).

34. *Aguado v. Nicaragua*, 29 September 1989.

35. A/56/156, para. 39(f).

36. A/55/40, para. 472, referring to Kuwait.

37. A/54/44, para. 51, referring to Yugoslavia.

38. Evans and Morgan have written that "As with third-party notification, the CPT accepts that it may be necessary to withhold access to a lawyer of the detainee's choosing for a period of time, and where this is the case the Committee stresses the need for application of the same range of safeguards: that the grounds of restriction are closely defined; that it is for a strictly limited period of time, this being no longer than is absolutely necessary; that such delay be recorded in writing together with the reasons for the decision; and that approval be given by a senior officer or public prosecutor. Unlike third-party notification, however, the CPT takes the view that there is no justification for totally denying access to a lawyer during this period since it should be possible to arrange access to an independent lawyer 'who can be trusted not to jeopardise the legitimate interests of the police investigation'. If a detainee is being held incommunicado, then the right to legal representation is fulfilled by the presence of an officially appointed lawyer. The right to such assistance should, the Committee believes, be the subject of express guarantee." (Evans and Morgan, 1998, pp. 272-273)

39. A/56/156, para. 39(f).

40. Commission on Human Rights resolution 1994/37 of 4 March 1994.

41. The Human Rights Committee has stated that the provision for communication with counsel in Article 14(3) of the ICCPR "requires counsel to communicate with the accused in conditions giving full respect for the confidentiality of their communications" (General Comment 13 on Article 14 of the ICCPR, para. 9). See Amnesty International, *Fair Trials Manual*, Chapter 3, "The right to legal counsel before trial"; Chapter 20, "The right to defend oneself in person or through counsel".

42. A/52/40, para. 109, referring to Switzerland.

43. A/56/156, para. 39(f).

44. In his report on a visit to Turkey, the Special Rapporteur recommended that medical personnel required to carry out examinations of detainees on entry into or exit from places of detention "should be independent of ministries responsible for law enforcement or the administration of justice and be properly qualified in forensic medical techniques capable of identifying sequelae of physical torture or ill-treatment, as well as psychological trauma potentially attributable to mental torture or ill-treatment". Also, "Examinations of detainees by medical doctors selected by them should be given weight in any court proceedings (relating to the detainees or to officials accused of torture or ill-treatment) equivalent to that accorded to officially employed or selected doctors having comparable qualifications; the police bringing a detainee to a medical examination should never be those involved in the arrest or questioning of the detainees or the investigation of the incident provoking the detention. Police officers should not be present during the medical examination... Medical examinations should not be performed within the State Security Court facilities. Medical certificates should never be handed to the police or to the detainee while in the hands of the police, but should be made available to the detainee once out of their hands and to his or her lawyer immediately." (E/CN.4/1999/61/Add.1, para. 113(d))

45. Where there were grounds for refusing access to a doctor of the prisoner's choice, the CPT has occasionally recommended being able to request an examination by a doctor chosen from a list "drawn up in agreement with the appropriate professional body" (Report on initial visit to Spain (1991), CPT/Inf (96) 9, para. 57; Evans and Morgan, 1998, p. 279).

46. Report on initial visit to the Czech Republic (1997), CPT/Inf (99), para. 32; see Morgan and Evans, 2001, pp. 76-77 for discussion. The CPT has recognized that it may not always be possible to permit such medical examinations to take place, but it has raised questions with governments about provisions which might impede the exercise of this safeguard, such as the practice in one country of denying access to one's own doctor for a period of up to 48 hours (Evans and Morgan, 1998, pp. 277-279).

47. The Human Rights Committee has called for medical examinations to be "automatically provided following allegations of abuse" (A/50/40, para. 94, referring to Tunisia). See the *Istanbul Protocol*, cited in Appendix 3, and the UN Principles on the Effective Investigation and Documentation of Torture and Other Cruel, Inhuman or Degrading Treatment or Punishment (Principles on the Investigation of Torture), reproduced in Appendix 10 of this manual, for information on the medical investigation of torture and ill-treatment.

48. The complainant suffered a broken rib during the arrest. Given the circumstances of the case, the Commission found that the manner of his arrest did not amount to ill-treatment. But "in those circumstances the police officers could not have been unaware that the applicant might have been injured during his arrest". The Commission stated that "in a situation of such gravity, resulting from the use of force by the police, Article 3 of the Convention requires the State authorities to adopt measures to safeguard the physical well-being of a person placed in the charge of the police, judicial or prison authorities" and that "Under Article 3 of the Convention the State has a specific positive obligation to protect the physical well-being of persons deprived of their liberty." (*Hurtado v. Switzerland*, 8 July 1993, paras. 77, 79)

49. The UN Commission on Human Rights has urged governments "to protect medical and other personnel for their role in documenting torture or any other form of cruel, inhuman or degrading treatment or punishment and in treating victims of such acts" (resolution 2002/38 of 22 April 2002, para. 11).

50. Advisory opinion request, quoted in Inter-American Court of Human Rights, *Habeas Corpus in Emergency Situations*, Advisory Opinion OC-8/87 of 30 January 1987, para. 12.

51. The Human Rights Committee has stated that Article 9(4) applies to all persons deprived of their liberty by arrest or detention and that states parties to the ICCPR must also ensure "that an effective remedy is provided in other cases in which an individual claims to be deprived of his liberty in violation of the Covenant" (General Comment 8, para. 1).

52. *Habeas Corpus in Emergency Situations*, para. 44. The Court noted that "habeas corpus performs a vital role in ensuring that a person's life and physical integrity are respected, in preventing his disappearance or the keeping of his whereabouts secret and in protecting him against torture or other cruel, inhumane, or degrading punishment or treatment" (para. 35).

53. "In order to protect non-derogable rights, the right to take proceedings before a court to enable the court to decide without delay on the lawfulness of detention, must not be diminished by a State party's decision to derogate from the Covenant." (General Comment 29 on Article 4 of the ICCPR, para. 16)

54. Article 9(1) of the Declaration states: "The right to a prompt and effective judicial remedy as a means of determining the whereabouts or state of health of persons deprived of their liberty and/or identifying the authority ordering or carry out the deprivation of liberty is required to prevent enforced disappearances under all circumstances, including those referred to in article 7 above." (The circumstances referred to in Article 7 of the Declaration are "a threat of war, a state of war, internal political instability or any other public emergency".) Article 9(2) states: "In such proceedings, competent national authorities shall have access to all places where persons deprived of their liberty are being held and to each part of those places, as well as to any place in which there are grounds to believe that such persons may be found."

55. Report on visit to Chile, E/CN.4/1996/35/Add.2, para. 76(l).

56. Sir Nigel Rodley has pointed out that although Article 9(4) of the ICCPR refers only to proceedings being taken by a person who has been deprived of liberty, "no interpretation aimed at effectiveness would deny to others the power to initiate the proceedings on behalf of that person" (Rodley, 1999, p. 338). Under Article 7(6) of the American Convention on Human Rights, "[t]he interested party or another person on his behalf" is entitled to invoke habeas corpus.

57. Principle 32 of the Body of Principles on Detention, which states that proceedings to challenge the lawfulness of a detention "shall be simple and expeditious and at no cost for detained persons without adequate means".

58. The Human Rights Committee has stated that a delay of "weeks or months" after receipt in hearing applications for habeas corpus is "incompatible with article 9 of the Covenant" (A/56/40, para. 78(13), referring to the Dominican Republic).

59. Article 14(3)(g) of the ICCPR sets out the right of a person "[n]ot to be compelled to testify against himself or to confess guilt" in the determination of any criminal charge against him or her. The Human Rights Committee has stated that the wording of Article 14(3)(g) "must be understood in terms of the absence of any direct or indirect physical or psychological pressure from the investigating authorities on the accused, with a view to obtaining a confession of guilt" (*Paul Kelly v. Jamaica*, 8 April 1991, para. 5.5).

60. Under Article 55(2) of the Rome Statute of the International Criminal Court (Rome Statute), a suspect about to be questioned by the International Criminal Court Prosecutor or by national authorities shall have the right "[t]o remain silent, without such silence being a consideration in the determination of guilt or innocence" and shall be informed of this right prior to being questioned. The right to remain silent during interrogation is also set out in the Rules of Procedure and Evidence of the International Criminal Tribunals for the former Yugoslavia and Rwanda (Rule 42A(iii)). The European Court of Human Rights has stated that "the right to remain silent under police questioning and the privilege against self-incrimination are generally recognized international standards which lie at the heart of the notion of a fair procedure" under Article 6 of the European Convention on Human Rights (*John Murray v. UK*, 8 February 1996, para. 45). The Committee against Torture has recommended "[t]he incorporation into the law of the right of the suspect or detainee to silence at all stages of investigation" (A/53/44, para. 118(c), referring to Cuba). Provisions concerning the interrogation of prisoners of war are set out in the Third Geneva Convention of 1949, Article 17 (see note 85 below).

61. A/56/156, para. 39(f).

62. A/50/44, para. 176, referring to Jordan.

63. A/52/44, para. 68, referring to the Republic of Korea; cf. A/51/44, para. 65(e), referring to the UK.

64. CPT, 2nd General Report, para. 38.

65. Rules of Procedure and Evidence of the Yugoslavia Tribunal, Rule 42B; Rule 42B of the Rwanda Tribunal. Article 55(2)(d) of the Rome Statute provides for the right of a suspect "[t]o be questioned in the presence of counsel unless the person has voluntarily waived his or her right to counsel".

66. A/56/156, para. 39(d).

67. A/56/156, para. 39(f).

68. A/56/156, para. 39(f). The recommendation, as proposed in an earlier report of the Special Rapporteur on torture, was endorsed by the UN Commission on Human Rights in resolution 1994/37 of 4 March 1994.

69. In Turkey, where it found that torture was being systematically practised, the Committee considered it immediately necessary that "[t]he use of a blindfold during questioning should be expressly prohibited". (A/48/44/Add.1, para. 48(a))

70. Amnesty International, *Turkey: The duty to supervise, investigate and prosecute* (AI Index: EUR 44/24/99), p. 35.

71. A/52/40, para. 109, referring to Switzerland.

72. A/56/156, para. 39(f). Also, the CPT has stated that "any request made by a detainee during an interview" should be included in the record of the interrogation. It has also stated that "the electronic recording of police interviews is another useful safeguard against the ill-treatment of detainees (as well as having significant advantages for the police)" (2nd General Report, para. 39). A supplementary safeguard which has been recommended by the CPT is that one electronic tape of an interview be sealed in the presence of the prisoner while another is used as a working copy (Report of initial visit to Sweden (1991), CPT/Inf (92) 4, para. 34). (See Morgan and Evans, 2001, p. 81.) The UN Committee against Torture also has endorsed the electronic recording of interrogations (for example, A/51/44, para. 65(e), referring to the UK). The Rules of Procedure and Evidence of the International Criminal Tribunals for the former Yugoslavia and Rwanda stipulate that whenever the prosecutor questions a suspect, the questioning shall be audio-recorded or video-recorded, and, after making any copies necessary for the purpose of transcription, the tape shall be sealed in the presence of the suspect and signed by the prosecutor and the suspect (Rule 43).

73. General Comment 20, para. 11.

74. The CPT has stated that "clear rules or guidelines should exist on the way in which police interviews are to be conducted. They should address inter alia the following matters: the informing of the detainee of the identity (name and/or number) of those present at the interview; the permissible length of an interview; rest periods between interviews and breaks during an interview; places in which interviews may take place; whether the detainee may be required to stand while being questioned; the interviewing of persons who are under the influence of drugs, alcohol, etc." (2nd General Report, para. 39). The Special Rapporteur on torture has recommended the establishment of a "code of practice for the conduct of interrogations by law enforcement officials" (Report on visit to Venezuela, E/CN.4/1997/7/Add.3, para. 85(j)).

75. CPT, 10th General Report, CPT/Inf (2000) 13, para. 23. The police training manual *To Serve and to Protect* recommends further that women and their clothing be searched by female officials in all circumstances (de Rover, 1998, p. 301). Transgender prisoners should be treated on the basis of their preferred gender identity.

76. de Rover, 1998, p. 301.

77. The term "juvenile" is not defined in the Body of Principles on Detention.

78. Under the Beijing Rules, a juvenile is "a child or young person who, under the respective legal systems, may be dealt with for an offence in a manner which is different from an adult" (Rule 2.2(a)).

79. CPT, 9th General Report, CPT/Inf (99) 12, para. 23.

80. In the case of asylum-seekers and refugees, the "competent international organization" would normally be the Office of the UN High Commissioner for Refugees (UNHCR). Accordingly, they should be informed of their right to contact that body. The UNHCR should normally be informed of such a person in the custody of a state.

81. Report on initial visit to Greece (1993), CPT/Inf (94) 20, para. 37.

82. Body of Principles on Detention, first paragraph, "Scope of the Body of Principles".

83. Minimal procedural guarantees for asylum-seekers are set out in the UNHCR Guidelines on Applicable Criteria and Standards relating to the Detention of Asylum-Seekers, cited in section 5.7.5. The CPT also has stated that "Immigration detainees should – in the same way as other categories of persons deprived of their liberty – be entitled, as from the outset of their detention, to inform a person of their choice of their situation and to have access to a lawyer and a doctor. Further, they should be expressly informed, without delay and in a language they understand, of all their rights and of the procedure applicable to them" (7th General Report, CPT/Inf (97) 10, para. 30); also, "The right of access to a lawyer should apply throughout the detention period and include both the right to speak with the lawyer in private and to have him present during interviews with the authorities concerned" (ibid., para. 31).

On a more general note, the Human Rights Committee has stated that "the rights set forth in the Covenant apply to everyone, irrespective of reciprocity, and irrespective of his or her nationality or statelessness" (General Comment 15 on the position of aliens under the Covenant, para. 1). Thus, aliens may not be subjected to torture or ill-treatment; they "have the full right to liberty and security of the person"; "If lawfully deprived of their liberty, they shall be treated with humanity and with respect for the inherent dignity of their person"; and they "are entitled to recognition before the law" (ibid., para. 7). Foreigners should also be protected from being forcibly returned to a country where they would risk being subjected to torture or ill-treatment (see section 8.3).

84. The availability of free interpretation in court for defendants who need it is required under Article 14(3)(f) of the ICCPR and other relevant standards in connection with the right to a fair trial. See Amnesty International, *Fair Trials Manual*, sections 2.4, 8.4, 9.4 and Chapter 23 for further references to prisoners' rights concerning language.

85. Under the Third Geneva Convention (Article 17), prisoners of war may be questioned, but the only information which a prisoner of war is required to give is "his surname, first names and rank, date of birth, and army, regimental, personal or serial number, or failing this, equivalent information". Furthermore, "No physical or mental torture, nor any other form of coercion, may be inflicted on prisoners of war to secure from them information of any kind whatever. Prisoners of war who refuse to answer may not be threatened, insulted, or exposed to unpleasant or disadvantageous treatment of any kind."

86. Special arrangements which have been devised to prevent prisoners "disappearing" on release are described in Amnesty International, *"Disappearances" and Political Killings...: A Manual for Action*, pp. 133-134.

87. General Comment 20, para. 12.

88. General Comment 13, para. 14.

89. A/54/44, para. 45, referring to Yugoslavia.

90. A/53/44, para. 193, referring to Germany.

91. The Human Rights Committee has stated: "In order to safeguard the rights of the accused under paragraphs 1 and 3 of article 14 [of the ICCPR], judges should have authority to consider any allegations made of violations of the rights of the accused during any stage of the prosecution." (General Comment 13, para. 15)

92. Amnesty International, *Fair Trials Manual*, p. 94.

93. Report on visit to Turkey, E/CN.4/1999/61/Add.1, para. 113(e).

94. In Peru, where the Committee against Torture found that torture had been "systematically used as a method of investigation", the Committee recommended: "Every judge, on learning from the accused's statement that the accused has been subjected to torture in an effort to force him or her to corroborate the police report, without prejudice to the ordering of a medical examination, should immediately order the statement referred to the Public Prosecutor's Office for investigation of the complaint." (A/56/44, para. 172)

Chapter 5

1. E/CN.4/1995/34/Add.1, paras. 43, 44, 71. Butyrskaya prison and Matrosskaya Tishina No. 1 were used for holding prisoners in pre-trial detention, sometimes for up to seven years. The Special Rapporteur noted that "The detention of an individual in a remand centre for several years, regardless of the conditions within the centre, is in and of itself a clear violation of the individual's rights" (para. 40).

2. As the Special Rapporteur on torture has stated, "[c]ontrol of prisons should never be abandoned to its inmates" (Report on visit to Venezuela, E/CN.4/1997/7/Add.3, para. 85(u)).

3. Article 5(1) of the American Convention on Human Rights contains a similar provision.

4. General Comment 21 on Article 10 of the ICCPR, para. 4.

5. General Comment 29 on Article 4 of the ICCPR, para. 13.

6. General Comment 21, para. 3.

7. The Standard Minimum Rules were adopted by the First UN Congress on the Prevention of Crime and the Treatment of Offenders in 1955 and approved by the UN Economic and Social Council in 1957. In 1977 the Economic and Social Council added Rule 95 which extended the scope of the Standard Minimum Rules to people arrested or detained without charge.

8. For example, in resolution 2858(XXVI) of 20 December 1971 the UN General Assembly recommended that the Standard Minimum Rules be effectively implemented in penal and correctional institutions. In 1984 the Economic and Social Council, in resolution 1984/47, adopted the **Procedures for the Effective Implementation of the Standard Minimum Rules for the Treatment of Prisoners**. Among other things, these Procedures state that the Standard Minimum Rules shall be incorporated in national legislation and regulations and made available to all officials concerned.

9. The position of Special Rapporteur on Prisons and Conditions of Detention in Africa was established by the African Commission on Human and Peoples' Rights in 1996 with a mandate to "examine the state of prisons and conditions of detention in Africa and make recommendations with a view to improving them". The first Special Rapporteur, E.V.O. Dankwa, was succeeded by Vera Chirwa in November 2000. Information on the work of the Special Rapporteur can be found on the website of Penal Reform International (PRI) at www.penalreform.org.

10. Organization of American States, General Assembly resolution 1897 (XXXII-O/02) of 4 June 2002.

11. Third Geneva Convention, Parts II and III; Fourth Geneva Convention, Part III, Section IV.

12. General Comment 21, para. 10. Also, Rule 58 of the Standard Minimum Rules states: "The purpose and justification of a sentence of imprisonment or a similar measure deprivative of liberty is ultimately to protect society against crime. This end can only be achieved if the period of imprisonment is used to ensure, so far as possible, that upon his return to society the offender is not only willing but able to lead a law-abiding and self-supporting life." Similarly, Rule 65 calls for treatment which will encourage prisoners' self-respect and develop their sense of responsibility.

13. Use and Application of the Standard Minimum Rules for the Treatment of Prisoners, E/CN.15/1996/16/Add.1. (The text can be found on the website of the UN Crime and Justice Information Network at www.uncjin.org)

14. General Comment 21, para. 4.

15. *Albert Womah Mukong v. Cameroon,* 21 July 1994, para. 9.3. Albert Womah Mukong, a prominent critic of the government, complained that during two periods of detention he had been subjected to severe overcrowding, denial of food, lack of bedding and sanitary facilities and exposure to extreme heat, as well as threats and beating. The Human Rights Committee's statement was in response to the government's assertion that conditions in the country's prisons "must be linked to the state of economic and social development of Cameroon" (para. 6.2).

16. A/56/156, para. 35.

17. *Human Rights and Prisons: A Manual on Human Rights Training for Prison Officials,* Office of the UN High Commissioner for Human Rights, to be issued in the Professional Training Series; pilot edition, 2000.

18. The right of a person detained on a criminal charge to trial within a reasonable time or to release is related to the right of an accused person to be tried without undue delay as set out in Article 14(3)(c) of the ICCPR. As stated by the Human Rights Committee (General Comment 13 on Article 14 of the ICCPR, para. 10), the guarantee in Article 14(3)(c) relates both to "the time by which a trial should commence" and to the time by which it should end and judgment be rendered, both at first instance and on appeal.

19. General Comment 8 on Article 9 of the ICCPR, para. 3. As stated in the UN manual *Human Rights and Pre-trial Detention* (para. 68), the Human Rights Committee has interpreted the necessity for pre-trial detention narrowly.

20. *W v. Switzerland,* 26 January 1993, para. 30.

21. A/56/44, para. 119(b), referring to Brazil.

22. In his report on a visit to the Russian Federation, the Special Rapporteur recommended urgently removing "from confinement in centres of detention on remand (isolators) all 71,000 detained in excess of the officially proclaimed capacity of existing institutions". He suggested that this could be achieved largely "by ordering the release pending trial of all non-violent first-time offenders" and recommended that "[m]uch greater use should be made of existing provisions in the law for release of suspects on bail or on recognizance (signature), especially as regards suspected first time non-violent offenders" (E/CN.4/1995/34/Add.1, paras. 77-79). In Cameroon, where he found "appalling overcrowding" in two penitentiaries, the Special Rapporteur stated: "All non-violent first-time offenders or suspected offenders, especially those under 18, should be released; nor should any such suspected offenders be deprived of liberty until the prison overpopulation problem has been resolved" (E/CN.4/2000/9/Add.2, para. 78(j)). Other recommendations for reducing the number of pre-trial detainees can be found in the Special Rapporteur's reports on visits to Romania (E/CN.4/2000/9/Add.3, para. 57(a,b)) and Venezuela (E/CN.4/1997/7/Add.3, para. 85(q)).

23. The Special Rapporteur has stressed "[t]he importance of reducing the period for which prisoners are remanded" (*Prisons in Zimbabwe,* Series IV No. 1, p. 18, recommendation 3) and suggested early trial as a solution (*Prisons in the Gambia,* Series IV No. 5, p. 39, recommendation 3). He has also suggested granting amnesties to very old, sick or weak prisoners, those who have been on remand for a long time and "those who have served a long sentence, and do not seem to pose any danger to security" (*Prisons in Benin,* Series IV No. 6, p. 49, recommendation 2).

24. Recommendation R(99)22 on prison overcrowding and prison population inflation, adopted by the Committee of Ministers of the Council of Europe on 30 September 1999.

25. The CPT has stated that it "frequently encounters devices, such as metal shutters, slats, or plates fitted to cell windows, which deprive prisoners of access to natural light and prevent fresh air from entering the accommodation". It has recognized the need for specific security measures with regard to certain prisoners but has stated that "the imposition of measures of this kind should be the exception rather than the rule" and that "even when such measures are required, they should never involve depriving the prisoners concerned of natural light and fresh air". It has noted that "removing devices blocking the windows of prisoner accommodation (and fitting, in those exceptional cases where this is necessary, alternative security devices of an appropriate design) should not involve considerable investment and, at the same time, would be of great benefit for all concerned" (11th General Report, CPT/Inf (2001) 16, para. 30).

26. CPT, 11th General Report, para. 29. See also *PRI Handbook*, pp. 60-61.

27. CPT, 2nd General Report, CPT/Inf (92) 3, para. 46.

28. Report on initial visit to Poland (1996), CPT/Inf (98) 13, para. 70.

29. Loc. cit.

30. Report on initial visit to Slovenia (1995), CPT/Inf (96) 18, para. 63. See Morgan and Evans, 2001, pp. 83-84, 99-101 for a discussion of the CPT's standards on cell sizes in police custody and in prisons.

31. Some 23 countries covered in the 1996 UN survey cited in section 5.1 (para. 17 and Table 4) provided less than three square metres of floor space per prisoner. The UN survey also provides information on the cubic content of cells.

32. Five responding countries in the 1996 UN survey (para. 19) reported minimum temperatures of 10°C, and four countries reported temperatures of 5°C. Five countries reported maximum temperatures of 40°C.

33. General Comment 21, para. 9.

34. Third Geneva Convention of 1949, Article 22.

35. In the absence of reasonable grounds, such separations could constitute arbitrary interference with prisoners' right to family life, in violation of Article 17 of the ICCPR.

36. The CPT has characterized as degrading the arrangements in certain European prisons where cells lacked integral sanitation (Report on initial visit to the UK (1990), CPT/Inf (91) 15, para. 57). See also Morgan and Evans, 2001, pp. 101-102.

37. The CPT has stated: "Either a toilet facility should be located in cellular accommodation (preferably in a sanitary annex) or means should exist enabling prisoners who need to use a toilet facility to be released from their cells without undue delay at all times (including at night)." (2nd General Report, para. 49)

38. Rule 13 states that prisoners should be enabled and required to have a bath or shower at least once a week in a temperate climate. The CPT has stated that "access to bathing facilities at least once a week is an absolute minimum requirement... in any prison" (Report on initial visit to the UK, para. 74), and that in particularly hot weather, access more than twice a week is desirable (Report on initial visit to France (1991), CPT/Inf (93) 2 (Part 1), para. 112; available in French only).

39. See *ICRC Annual Report 1994,* Geneva, ICRC, 1995, pp. 59-60; *ICRC Annual Report 1995,* pp. 59-60; *ICRC Annual Report 1996,* pp. 57, 59.

40. Three responding countries in the 1996 UN survey (para. 36) stated that drinking water was not always available, because of resource difficulties.

41. *Cyprus v. Turkey* (6780/74 and 6950/75), Report of the Commission 10 July 1976, para. 405. See Morgan and Evans, 2001, p. 103 on CPT recommendations concerning food and drink.

42. The Special Rapporteur on Prisons and Conditions of Detention in Africa found in one prison that no food had been provided by the prison authorities for seven months; one prisoner was said to have died of hunger and poor hygiene two weeks before the Special Rapporteur's arrival. The Special Rapporteur stated: "Feeding of prisoners is the responsibility of the state, and government should fulfil this obligation." (*Prisons in the Central African Republic,* Series IV No. 7, p. 33, recommendation 12)

43. *Keenan v. UK,* 3 April 2001, para. 110.

44. Two responding countries in the 1996 UN survey (para. 37) stated that less than a quarter of prisoners had medical and dental services available.

45. Detailed standards for the care of mentally ill prisoners are set out in the UN Principles for the protection of persons with mental illness and the improvement of mental health care (see section 6.2.1 of this manual).

46. Five responding countries in the 1996 UN survey (para. 38) stated that daily access to a medical officer was only exceptionally available, for resource reasons.

47. CPT, 3rd General Report, CPT/Inf (93) 12, para. 31. See also Recommendation R(98)7 on the ethical and organizational aspects of health care in prisons, adopted by the Committee of Ministers of the Council of Europe on 8 April 1998.

48. Declaration of Madrid, adopted by the World Psychiatric Association in 1996. (This and similar texts cited in this chapter are reproduced in Amnesty International, *Ethical Codes and Declarations Relevant to the Health Professions...*, 4th revised edition, 2000, and can also be found on Amnesty International's website at www.amnesty.org.

49. Torture, Death Penalty and Participation by Nurses in Executions, adopted by the International Council of Nurses in 1998.

50. The Human Rights Committee has found five minutes per day for personal hygiene and five minutes of exercise in the open air to be incompatible with Article 10 of the ICCPR (*Csaba Párkányi v. Hungary,* 27 July 1992, para. 8.3).

51. CPT, 2nd General Report, paras. 47, 48. See also Morgan and Evans, 2001, pp. 103-104.

52. As stated above (note 35), unreasonable denial of contact with relatives could constitute a violation of Article 17 of the ICCPR, which states: "No one shall be subjected to arbitrary or unlawful interference with his privacy, family, home or correspondence..." The Human Rights Committee has stated that the introduction of the concept of arbitrariness in Article 17 "is intended to guarantee that even interference provided for by law should be in accordance with the provisions, aims and objectives of the Covenant and should be, in any event, reasonable in the particular circumstances" (General Comment 16 on Article 17 of the ICCPR, para. 4).

53. See *PRI Handbook*, section V.

54. Report on initial visit to Hungary (1994), CPT/Inf (96)5 (Part 1), para. 128. The CPT also found unacceptable the situation in one country of remand prisoners who were allowed a single, supervised visit of 15 minutes per week (Report on initial visit to Slovenia, para 79).

55. Report on initial visit to Hungary, CPT/Inf (96) 5 (Part 1), para. 127.

56. Report on initial visit to Ireland (1993), CPT/Inf (95) 14, para. 161. Cf. Cassese, 1996, pp. 53-54, 58 on the need for a suitable environment for intimate visits.

57. See the UN manual *Human Rights and Prisons* (pilot edition, Chapter 23) for additional recommendations on conditions for visits.

58. CPT, 10th General Report, CPT/Inf (2000) 13, para. 23.

59. See note 48 above for bibliographic information.

60. The UN manual *Human Rights and Prisons* (pilot edition, Chapter 3) states: "The use of any instrument which might be used as a weapon by staff should be carefully regulated. In many jurisdictions individual members of staff carry some form of stave or truncheon. The circumstances in which this may be used should be specified quite clearly..." Such use should only be for defensive purposes.

61. *Satık and others v. Turkey,* 10 October 2000, para. 54.

62. In the case of *Neira Alegría and others v. Peru,* involving the use of massive force to quell a prison riot, with many prisoners crushed in the ruins of a demolished building, the Inter-American Court of Human Rights referred to "the disproportionate use of force" and held that the victims were arbitrarily deprived of their lives in violation of Article 4(1) of the American Convention on Human Rights (*Neira*

Alegría and others v. Peru, 19 January 1995, para. 76). In the *Carandirú* case, involving the massacre of over 100 prisoners in the quelling of a prison disturbance in Brazil in October 1992, the Inter-American Commission on Human Rights found violations of Articles 4 (right to life) and 5 (right to personal integrity, including the right not to be subjected to torture or ill-treatment) of the same Convention in the killing or ill-treatment of many prisoners, the lack of planning for dealing with such situations without resort to disproportionate force and the delay in informing relatives of the fate or condition of dead and wounded prisoners (*Carandirú* case, 13 April 2000, paras. 88-91).

63. See Amnesty International, *Stopping the torture trade,* 2001, pp. 3-13, 28-30; *USA: Rights for all,* 1998, pp. 66-70.

64. See Amnesty International, *USA: Rights for all,* p. 70.

65. Contrary to Rule 33(a), accused persons often are routinely kept in handcuffs and shackles when they appear before a court, even though guards are present. Such over-use of restraints can degrade the accused person in their own eyes and the eyes of the court, undermining the presumption of innocence and prejudicing the outcome of the trial.

66. *Namunjepo and others v. Commanding Officer, Windhoek Prison and another,* Supreme Court of Namibia, 9 July 1999.

67. In Austria, the Constitutional Court has qualified the use of handcuffs which was not strictly necessary in the given circumstances as inhuman or degrading treatment, in violation of Article 3 of the European Convention on Human Rights (*Verfassungssammlung,* Judgments and Decisions of the Constitutional Court, Nos. 8146, 9836, 13044).

68. The UN manual *Human Rights and Prisons* (pilot edition, Chapter 3) recommends that instruments of restraint, including handcuffs, "should be held in a central location in the prison and should be issued only on the authority of a senior member of staff. The issue and use of such equipment should be carefully recorded and such records be available for future reference."

69. In its resolution of 3 October 2001 on the Council's Second Annual Report according to Operative Provision 8 of the European Union Code of Conduct on Arms Exports (13177/1/2000 - C5-0111/2001 - 2001/2050(COS)), the European Parliament affirmed that the use of "leg-irons, electro-shock stun-belts and inherently painful devices such as serrated thumb cuffs" is "inherently cruel, inhuman or degrading" (para. 12). (See section 8.4 of this manual)

70. A leg-iron is a fixed bar which holds the legs separated, preventing flexible movement of the limbs and making it difficult for the prisoner to move. The Special Rapporteur on torture has stated that "[t]he use of bar fetters and similar instruments of restraint should be terminated" (Report on visit to Pakistan, E/CN.4/1997/7/Add. 2, para. 104). (See also Amnesty International, *Pakistan: "Keep your fetters bright and polished" – the continued use of bar fetters and cross fetters* (AI Index: ASA 33/12/95).)

71. Sharp or serrated cuffs (handcuffs, thumbcuffs or legcuffs) induce pain when the prisoner moves. Further motion can cause lacerations and swelling.

72. An electro-shock stun belt is attached to a prisoner and activated by a law enforcement official by remote control. The high-pulsed electric current enters the prisoner's body at the site of the electrodes, near the kidneys, and passes through the body, causing severe pain. The person to whom a stun belt is attached is under the constant fear of a severe shock being administered at any moment, without warning, for reasons over which he or she may have no control. The constant subjection to an official who has the power to administer pain at will is degrading, as are the threatened effects of uncontrollable urination and defecation. Lacking the possibility of self-control, the prisoner is deprived of a part of his or her humanity. (See Amnesty International, *USA – Rights for all: Cruelty in control? The stun belt and other electro-shock equipment in law enforcement* (AI Index: AMR 51/54/99))

73. Amnesty International, *USA: A briefing for the UN Committee against Torture* (AI Index: AMR 51/56/00), pp. 13-14.

74. In some US jurisdictions prisoners are made to work outdoors in "chain gangs", shackled together and exposed to public view. This practice contravenes Article 45(1) of the Standard Minimum Rules, which states: "When the prisoners are being removed to or from an institution, they shall be exposed to public view as little as possible, and proper safeguards shall be adopted to protect them from insult, curiosity and publicity in any form." In his 1998 report to the UN Commission on Human Rights, the Special Rapporteur on torture stated with reference to the USA that he was "concerned at the use of practices such as chain gangs, of instruments of restraint in court and of stun belts and stun guns, some of which can only be intended to be afflictive and degrading, others of which have the same effect" (E/CN.4/1998/38, para. 203).

75. The CPT has stated that the practice of shackling pregnant women to beds or other pieces of furniture during gynaecological examinations or delivery "is completely unacceptable, and could certainly be qualified as inhuman and degrading treatment" (10th General Report, para. 27).

76. Amnesty International, *Stopping the torture trade,* pp. 51-2.

77. See section 6.4 for a general discussion of judicial and administrative corporal punishments.

78. CPT, 2nd General Report, para. 55. See Morgan and Evans, 2001, pp. 117-118 for a discussion of the CPT's approach to prison discipline.

79. *Keenan v. UK,* para. 115.

80. General Comment 20 on Article 7 of the ICCPR, para. 6, reproduced in Appendix 11 of this manual.

81. In one case, for example, the Committee found that the "total isolation" of a prisoner for a year, with restrictions on correspondence with his family, was "inhuman treatment" (*Rosa Espinoza de Polay v. Peru,* 6 November 1997, para. 8.6). See, generally, Rodley, 1999, pp. 294-7.

82. *Velásquez Rodríguez v. Honduras,* 29 July 1988, para. 187.

83. *Castillo Petruzzi and others v. Peru,* 30 May 1999, para. 198.

84. A/56/44, para. 186 (see section 3.4 of this manual).

85. In Turkey, where it found torture was practised systematically, the Committee called on the authorities "to demolish immediately and systematically all the solitary confinement cells known as 'coffins', which in themselves constitute a kind of torture. These cells measure approximately 60 by 80 centimetres, they have no light and inadequate ventilation, and the inmate can only stand or crouch" (A/48/44/Add.1, para. 52). With reference to Bolivia, the Committee stated that disciplinary confinement in punishment cells of the kind known as "the can" was "tantamount to torture" (A/56/44, para. 95(g)). The cells in question, used for solitary confinement, measured approximately 1.5 by 2 metres and were cold, damp and without proper bedding or sanitation.

86. Report on visit to Chile, E/CN.4/1996/35/Add.2, para. 76(c).

87. CPT, 2nd General Report, para. 56.

88. Report on initial visit to Spain (1991), CPT/Inf (96) 9, para. 113.

89. A/56/156, para. 39(i), reproduced in Appendix 14 of this manual.

90. CPT, 11th General Report, para. 27.

91. CPT, 3rd General Report, para. 61.

92. Nearly all the 72 countries which replied in the 1996 UN survey (para. 6) claimed that they complied with this requirement. One country reported that they used a card index rather than a registration book, and three countries reported that registration was now computerized. One country reported that its national prisons office kept a central file on every inmate.

93. In addition to the groups discussed in this section, see Morgan and Evans, 2001, on the CPT's work on the treatment of high-security prisoners (pp. 118-121) and prisoners with psychiatric or other medical conditions (pp. 127-130). Also, as noted in the UN manual *Human Rights and Prisons* (pilot edition, Chapter 31), elderly people are emerging as a new minority group in some prisons; they have special needs which should be catered for, as do prisoners with physical disabilities. And concerning prisoners under sentence of death, as stated in *Human Rights and Prisons* (Chapter 32): "Prisoners should not be held in unduly restrictive circumstances purely on the grounds that they have been sentenced to death."

94. CPT, 10th General Report, paras. 21-33.

95. For a discussion of the CPT's work concerning women prisoners, see Morgan and Evans, 2001, pp. 121-124.

96. For example, at Telmond Prison in Israel, which houses both Israeli and Palestinian prisoners, prison authorities used to allow four adult Palestinian prisoners to stay in the cells with Palestinian child detainees, in order to look after them and deal with any problems that might arise. This practice was initiated in 1996, following requests from the children, their parents, and a local human rights organization, but was discontinued by the Israeli Prison Administration in 1999. Since then, Palestinian boys detained at Telmond have complained of being subjected to beatings, threats and bullying from their fellow prisoners.

97. The Special Rapporteur on torture has recommended that "[c]hildren deprived of liberty (as a last resort), even if only for a few days or weeks, should be held exclusively in institutions aimed at protecting them and adapted, from all points of view, to their particular needs. They should be provided with medical, psychological and educational assistance." (Report on visit to Venezuela, E/CN.4/1997/7/Add.3, para. 85(t))

98. The CPT has stated that it "accepts that there may be exceptional situations (e.g. children and parents being held as immigration detainees) in which it is plainly in the best interests of juveniles not to be separated from particular adults. However, to accommodate juveniles and unrelated adults together inevitably brings with it the possibility of domination and exploitation." (9th General Report, CPT/Inf (99) 12, para. 25)

99. CPT, 9th General Report, paras. 20-41. For a discussion of the CPT's work concerning young prisoners, see Morgan and Evans, 2001, pp. 124-127.

100. See Amnesty International, *Crimes of hate, conspiracy of silence: Torture and ill-treatment based on sexual identity,* 2001, Chapter 3.

101. Noting that in many prison systems pre-trial detainees facing relatively minor charges are held in the same conditions of security as those facing serious charges, the UN manual *Human Rights and Prisons* (pilot edition, Chapter 35) recommends: "Consideration should be given to the appropriate degree of security for different groups of pre-trial prisoners."

102. CPT, 2nd General Report, para. 47. See Morgan and Evans, 2001, pp. 89-90 for further information on standards articulated by the CPT concerning pre-trial detainees.

103. See Human Rights Committee, *A v. Australia,* 3 April 1997, para. 9.4.

104. Executive Committee Conclusion 44 (XXXVII), para. (f). The UNHCR's Executive Committee is an intergovernmental body of more than 60 countries. Its conclusions, which are normally adopted by consensus, are regarded as authoritative. (The texts can be found on the UNHCR website at www.unhcr.ch.)

105. The Guidelines state that the UNHCR considers detention as "confinement within a narrowly bounded or restricted location, including prisons, closed camps, detention facilities or airport transit zones, where freedom of movement is substantially curtailed, and where the only opportunity to leave this limited area is to leave the territory". (The text of the Guidelines can be found on the UNHCR website at www.unhcr.ch .)

106. See Amnesty International, *USA: Lost in the labyrinth – detention of asylum-seekers* (AI Index: AMR 51/51/99), Chapter 5 for a discussion of the application of the UNHCR Guidelines and other international standards to the detention of asylum-seekers in the USA.

107. UNHCR Revised Guidelines on Applicable Criteria and Standards relating to the Detention of Asylum-Seekers, Guideline 10(iii).

108. Report of the Working Group on Arbitrary Detention to the 56th session of the UN Commission on Human Rights, E/CN.4/2000/4, Annex II, Deliberation No. 5, "Situation regarding immigrants and asylum-seekers", Principles 6, 7, 9.

109. These can include people held after being refused entry to a country, people who have entered a country illegally and people whose authorization to stay in a country has expired.

110. See Morgan and Evans, 2001, pp. 84-88 for a discussion of the CPT's work concerning immigration detainees, including people held at ports of entry to a country.

111. Sometimes inspectors are able to find torture equipment or other material evidence such as bloodstains. See Cassese, 1996, pp. 73-90 for examples of such discoveries. Refusal of access also can contribute to a finding of torture. During his visit to Pakistan in 1996, the Special Rapporteur on torture made an unannounced visit to a house allegedly used as an unauthorized place of detention, but was refused access by the authorities. Based on the refusal, on his observations while waiting and on detailed allegations by people claiming to have been held there or at an unknown place which matched the description, the Special Rapporteur concluded that the house was indeed being used as a place of unlawful detention and interrogation under torture (E/CN.4/1997/7/Add.2, paras. 20-30).

112. Under the Standard Minimum Rules, this provision is applicable to "all categories of prisoners, criminal or civil, untried or convicted" (Rule 4(1)) and to "persons arrested or imprisoned without charge" (Rule 95).

113. Third Geneva Convention of 1949, Article 126.

114. Fourth Geneva Convention of 1949, Article 143.

115. European Convention for the Prevention of Torture, Articles 1-2. This language gives the CPT the authority to visit not only places of detention but other places such as psychiatric hospitals where people are deprived of their liberty by a public authority. As stated in the Explanatory Report to the European Convention for the Prevention of Torture, "[t]he Convention is... applicable, for example, to places where persons are held in custody, are imprisoned as a result of conviction for an offence, are held in administrative detention, or are interned for medical reasons or where minors are detained by a public authority. Detention by military authorities is also covered by the Convention" (para. 30).

116. A/56/156, para. 39(e).

117. This and other powers of the CPT are set out in Articles 7-14 of the European Convention for the Prevention of Torture. See also the recommendation of the Special Rapporteur on torture (A/56/156, para. 39(c)).

118. Rule 36(2) of the Standard Minimum Rules and Principle 29(2) of the Body of Principles on Detention provide for confidential communications between prisoners and inspectors. Confidential communication is also provided for under Article 126 of the Third Geneva Convention of 1949 and Article 143 of the Fourth Geneva Convention of 1949 with regard to the ICRC, and Article 8(3) of the European Convention for the Prevention of Torture with regard to the CPT.

119. A/56/156, para. 39(e).

120. *Prisons in Mali*, Series IV No. 2, p. 32, recommendation 17.

121. The Committee against Torture has recommended, for example, that "the State party establish a system allowing for inspections of prisons and detention centres by credible impartial monitors, whose findings should be made public" (A/56/44, para. 46(e), referring to Belarus).

122. The Human Rights Committee has recommended, for example, that "The State party should institute a system for independent inspections of detention facilities, which should include elements independent of government, so as to ensure transparency and compliance with article 10 [of the ICCPR]." (Concluding observations on the second periodic report of Azerbaijan, adopted on 1 November 2001, CCPR/CO/73/AZE, para. 13)

123. A/56/156, para. 39(e).

124. The Special Rapporteur made this recommendation in his report on a visit to Indonesia, E/CN.4/1992/17/Add.1, para. 80(i), and has since done so in many reports on other visits.

125. UN Commission on Human Rights resolution 2002/33, adopted on 22 April 2002. The proposal for such a system was originally presented by Costa Rica in 1980. See Burgers and Danelius, 1988, pp. 26-29 on the early history of the proposal.

126. It is clear that the requirement to provide an explanation of rights would apply to arrival at a police station as well as arrival at a prison, since under the Body of Principles on Detention the term "detention" refers generally to the condition of a person deprived of their liberty.

127. Most responding countries in the 1996 UN survey stated that they provided every prisoner on admission with information as required under Rule 35. Six countries reported that prisoners were informed of the regulations governing their treatment but were not always told about the disciplinary requirements and the means of seeking information and making complaints. One country stated that Rule 35 was only applied exceptionally, and one stated that it was never applied but that the prison regimes were not yet clearly established (para. 51). A further recommendation, set out in the Procedures for the Effective Implementation of the Standard Minimum Rules for the Treatment of Prisoners, is that the Standard Minimum Rules themselves, as embodied in national legislation and regulations, be made available and understandable to all prisoners.

128. Under Rule 4(1), the provisions of Rule 35 are "applicable to all categories of prisoners, criminal or civil, untried or convicted".

129. Also, the UN manual *Human Rights and Prisons* (pilot edition, Chapter 4) recommends: "Wherever possible there should be an induction period for all new prisoners during which the relevant legislation, regulations and routine of daily life in prison is explained to them and they are given the opportunity to meet people who are available to help them, such as religious representatives, teachers and others."

Chapter 6

1. See, for example, Amnesty International, *Report on Torture,* 2nd edition, 1975, pp. 188-191; *Torture in the Eighties,* pp. 221-222.

2. Amnesty International, *People's Republic of China: Torture – a growing scourge in China: time for action* (AI Index: ASA 17/004/2001), pp. 20-22.

3. CPT, 8th General Report, CPT/Inf (98) 12, paras. 25-58.

4. The European Court of Human Rights has articulated criteria for determining the lawfulness of the compulsory confinement of "persons of unsound mind" under Article 5 of the European Convention on Human Rights. See, for example, *Winterwerp v. The Netherlands*, 24 October 1979, paras. 39, 45, 60.

5. CPT, 8th General Report, para. 48.

6. Ibid., para. 49. See Morgan and Evans, 2001, Chapter 7, "Patients Detained in Psychiatric Hospitals" for a discussion of the CPT's work in this area.

7. General Comment 20 on Article 7 of the ICCPR, para. 5.

8. *Costello-Roberts v. UK,* 25 March 1993, para. 38. In this case, however, the Court considered that the corporal punishment in question – three blows on the buttocks of a seven-year-old boy through his shorts with a rubber-soled gym shoe, administered by the school headmaster in private – did not attain the "minimum level of severity" to amount to inhuman or degrading treatment (para. 32; see section 3.3.1 on the Court's approach to the definition of ill-treatment).

9. In its concluding observations on the initial report of Zimbabwe, the Committee expressed concern about "the acceptance in the legislation of the use of corporal punishment in school" and stressed "the incompatibility of corporal punishment... with the provisions of the Convention, in particular articles 19, 28, paragraph 2, and 37" (Report to the 53rd session of the UN General Assembly (1998), A/53/41, para. 77).

10. For example, the Committee has recommended that "the use of corporal punishment at home, in schools and other institutions be explicitly prohibited by law" (Report to the 55th session of the UN General Assembly (2000), A/55/41, para. 1390, referring to Peru).

11. Resolution 2002/38 of 22 April 2002, para. 5.

12. See Human Rights Watch, 1999.

13. Report on visit to Kenya, E/CN.4/2000/9/Add.4, para. 56.

14. Concluding observations on the initial report of Kenya, adopted on 12 October 2001, CRC/C/15/Add.160, para. 34.

15. See Amnesty International, *Hidden scandal, secret shame: Torture and ill-treatment of children,* 2000, pp. 80-83.

16. Recommendations adopted during the general day of discussion on State violence suffered by children living in institutions managed, licensed or supervised by the State, 25th session, 18 September - 6 October 2000; Report to the 57th session of the UN General Assembly (2002), A/57/41, para. 83 (recommendations 22, 24).

17. See Amnesty International, *Crimes of hate, conspiracy of silence: Torture and ill-treatment based on sexual identity,* 2001, Chapter 4, "Forced medical treatment in state institutions". The current editions of the World Health Organization's *ICD-10 International Statistical Classification of Diseases and Related Health Problems* (10th Revision, 1992, World Health Organization, Geneva) and the American Psychiatric Association's *Diagnostic and Statistical Manual of Mental Disorders* (DSM-IV, 4th edition, 1994, American Psychiatric Association, Washington, D.C.) do not refer to homosexuality as a pathological condition.

18. See Amnesty International, *Torture in Russia: "This man-made hell"* (AI Index: EUR 46/04/97), pp. 40-43; Brett and Toney, 1997.

19. A/50/40, para. 400, referring to the Russian Federation.

20. Concluding observations on the fifth periodic report of Ukraine, adopted on 24 and 25 October 2001, CCPR/CO/73/UKR, para. 16.

21. Conclusions and recommendations on the fourth periodic report of Ukraine, CAT/C/XXVII/Concl.2, 21 November 2001, para. 5(n).

22. A/56/44, para. 39(d), referring to Armenia.

23. *Ribitsch v. Austria,* 4 December 1995, para. 38; see also *Satık and others v. Turkey,* 10 October 2000, cited in Chapter 5, note 61 of this manual.

24. In the case of *Güleç v. Turkey,* the European Court of Human Rights found that there had been a violation of Article 2 of the European Convention on Human Rights (right to life) because of the use of "disproportionate force" in the quelling of a violent demonstration. The complainant's son, a 15-year-old schoolboy, had apparently been killed by a ricocheting bullet from a machine-gun operated by the security forces. One other person was killed and 12 were wounded in the incident. Stating that "a balance must be struck between the aim pursued and the means employed to achieve it", the Court noted that the security forces "used a very powerful weapon because they apparently did not have truncheons, riot shields, water cannon, rubber bullets or tear gas" and stated that the lack of such equipment was "all the more incomprehensible and unacceptable" because the demonstration occurred in a region under a state of emergency, where "disorder could have been expected" *(Güleç v. Turkey,* 27 July 1998, paras. 71, 73, 83).

25. There is also a Declaration on the Police, adopted by the Parliamentary Assembly of the Council of Europe in 1979, which in some respects is stronger than the Code of Conduct for Law Enforcement Officials. See Rodley, 1999, pp. 368-369.

26. The Basic Principles on Force and Firearms provide for law enforcement officials to give a clear warning of their intent to use firearms (Principle 10). Other provisions in the Basic Principles cover such matters as the control, storage and issuing of firearms (Principle 11).

27. Guidelines for the Effective Implementation of the Code of Conduct for Law Enforcement Officials, para. I; Basic Principles on Force and Firearms, Article 1. (The Guidelines were adopted in UN Economic and Social Council resolution 1989/61, which is available on the UN website, www.un.org; they are also reproduced in the UN manual *Human Rights and Law Enforcement: A Manual on Human Rights Training for the Police.*)

28. Guidelines for the Effective Implementation of the Code of Conduct for Law Enforcement Officials, paras. I, II. In the resolution whereby it adopted the Basic Principles on Force and Firearms, the Eighth UN Congress on the Prevention of Crime and the Treatment of Offenders stated that the Basic Principles should be "brought to the attention of law enforcement officials".

29. Under the Commentary to Article 1 of the Code of Conduct for Law Enforcement Officials, "The term 'law enforcement officials' includes all officers of the law, whether appointed or elected, who exercise police powers, especially the powers of arrest or detention", and "In countries where police powers are exercised by military authorities, whether uniformed or not, or by State security forces, the definition of law enforcement officials shall be regarded as including officers of such services".

30. In cases involving the right to life, the European Court of Human Rights has held that the principle of avoiding excessive use of force applies not only to the immediate situation in which force is used but also to the planning and conduct of the operation, including the use of force in response to demonstrations (*McCann and others v. UK*, 27 September 1995, paras. 202-214; *Güleç v. Turkey*, paras. 71, 73 – see note 24 above.)

31. The Basic Principles on Force and Firearms provide for the reporting and review of incidents involving injury or death caused by the use of force and firearms (Principle 6) and state that "[i]n cases of death and serious injury or other grave consequences, a detailed report shall be sent promptly to the competent authorities responsible for administrative review and judicial control" (Principle 22). In the case of *Güleç v. Turkey,* cited above, the European Court of Human Rights held that there had been a breach of Article 2 of the European Convention on Human Rights because of the "lack of a thorough investigation" into the death of the complainant's son (para. 83).

32. Use and Application of the Code of Conduct for Law Enforcement Officials, together with the Basic Principles on the Use of Force and Firearms by Law Enforcement Officials, E/CN.15/1996/16/Add.2, para. 59. (The text can be found on the website of the UN Crime and Justice Information Network at www.uncjin.org.)

33. Ibid., para. 60.

34. See Amnesty International, *Stopping the torture trade,* 2001, Chapters 3-4 for information on modern weapons and equipment and their uses.

35. Principle 11(c) of the Basic Principles on Force and Firearms calls on governments in their law enforcement rules and regulations to "[p]rohibit the use of those firearms and ammunition that cause unwarranted injury or present an unwarranted risk". This principle should be extended to apply not only to firearms but to all police weapons.

36. Fourteen countries are listed in Amnesty International, *Take a step to stamp out torture,* 2000, p. 25. In addition, floggings have been inflicted in Iran.

37. General Comment 20, para. 5.

38. For example, A/50/40, para. 467, referring to Sri Lanka.

39. The Committee against Torture issued its first clear call for the abolition of corporal punishment in 1997 (A/52/44, para. 250, recommending "the prompt abolition of corporal punishment in so far as it is legally still possible" under the Namibian Prisons and Criminal Procedure Acts). See Ingelse, 2001, pp. 231-236 for a discussion of the Committee's approach to corporal punishment.

40. E/CN.4/1997/7, para. 6, reproduced in Appendix 15 of this manual.

41. Resolution 2002/38 of 22 April 2002, para. 5.

42. See E/CN.4/1997/7, para. 11.

43. Ibid., para. 10.

44. See Amnesty International, *Saudi Arabia remains a fertile ground for torture with impunity* (AI Index: MDE 23/004/2002), p. 17.

45. For examples, see *Ncube and others v. The State* (Zimbabwe), 14 December 1987; *Ex Parte Attorney General of Namibia, In re Corporal Punishment by Organs of State* (Namibia), 5 April 1991; and *State v. Williams and others* (South Africa), 9 June 1995.

46. The term "non-state force" is used in this manual to refer to an armed force belonging to an entity which is not a state, such as a non-state party to a civil war.

47. On rape in war, see Seifert, 2002.

48. See Amnesty International, *Broken bodies, shattered minds: Torture and ill-treatment of women,* 2000, pp. 46-52, "Torture of women in armed conflict"; *Hidden scandal, secret shame...*, Chapter 2, "Torture of children during conflict".

49. See, for example, Amnesty International, *United Kingdom: Political killings in Northern Ireland* (AI Index: EUR 45/01/94), pp. 38-40, 47.

50. Preface by Cornelio Sommaruga of de Rover, 1998, p. 5.

51. See Chapter 4, note 85 of this manual.

52. Third Geneva Convention of 1949, Article 126; Fourth Geneva Convention, Article 143.

53. Hostage-taking in situations of armed conflict is absolutely forbidden under international humanitarian law. See the Geneva Conventions of 1949, common Article 3, reproduced in Appendix 8 of this manual; Fourth Geneva Convention, Article 34; Additional Protocol I of 1977, Article 75(2); Additional Protocol II, Article 4(2). The Human Rights Committee has referred to the prohibition of hostage-taking as a norm of general international law which, as such, is not subject to derogation under the ICCPR (General Comment 29 on Article 4 of the ICCPR, para. 13).

54. See Amnesty International, *Hidden scandal, secret shame...*, pp. 41-48.

55. See Sullivan, 1995.

56. The Commission has declared admissible a complaint under Article 7 of the Convention, which prohibits violence against women by state authorities, by a former intelligence officer alleging that she was tortured by her former colleagues (*Leonor La Rosa Bustamante v. Peru*, 8 December 1998).

57. Beijing Platform for Action, para. 119.

58. Resolutions S-23/2 and S-23/3 of 10 June 2000.

59. For example, the Committee noted that "physical and sexual abuse of children – within and outside the family – is a widespread phenomenon" in Peru. It recommended that "law enforcement should be strengthened with respect to such crimes"; that procedures and mechanisms for dealing with complaints of child abuse be reinforced "in order to provide children with prompt access to justice"; that "multidisciplinary treatment and rehabilitation programs" be set up, and educational programs be established "to combat traditional attitudes within society regarding this issue" (Report to the 55th session of the UN General Assembly (2000), A/55/41, para. 1390).

60. Report to the 53rd session of the UN General Assembly (1998), A/53/41, para. 77, referring to Zimbabwe. (See also notes 9 and 10, above.)

61. Report to the 57th session of the UN General Assembly (2002), A/57/41, para. 87 (recommendations 15, 21, 23, 33).

62. For example, the Committee has recommended that "the activities of organizations of a racist nature be prohibited and the dissemination of ideas based on racial hatred declared punishable by law" (Report to the 48th session of the UN General Assembly (1993), A/48/18, para. 421, referring to the United Kingdom).

63. Durban Declaration and Programme of Action, paras. 74(b), 84.

64. A/56/156, para. 21 (Special Rapporteur on torture); E/CN.4/1997/47, para. 8 (Special Rapporteur on violence against women); Report of the Special Rapporteur on extrajudicial, summary or arbitrary executions to the 57th session of the Commission on Human Rights, E/CN.4/2001/9, paras. 48-50; Report of the Special Representative of the Secretary-General on human rights defenders to the 57th session of the Commission on Human Rights, E/CN.4/2001/94, para. 89(g).

65. See Amnesty International, *Hidden Scandal, Secret Shame...*, pp. 12-13, 21, 23, 59-65.

66. See, for example, Copelon, 1994; Kois, 1998; MacKinnon, 1993.

67. E/CN.4/1996/53, para. 50.

68. *Z and others v. UK,* 10 May 2001, para. 73.

69. *Mahmut Kaya v. Turkey,* 28 March 2000, para. 115.

70. *Velásquez Rodríguez v. Honduras,* 29 July 1988, para. 172.

71 Ibid., para. 174.

72. Concluding observations on the third periodic report of the Netherlands, adopted on 19 and 23 July 2001, CCPR/CO/72/NET, para. 9.

73. Concluding observations on the second periodic report of Guatemala, adopted on 26 July 2001, CCPR/CO/72/GTM, para. 15.

74. Conclusions and recommendations on the initial report of Zambia, CAT/C/XXVII/Concl.4, 23 November 2001, para. 8(h).

75. E/CN.4/2002/83, para. 6.

76. The European Court of Human Rights has awarded non-pecuniary damages to complainants in cases of domestic violence, in addition to pecuniary damages (*A v. UK,* 23 September 1998, para. 34; *Z and others v. UK,* para. 128 – see Chapter 7, note 112 of this manual).

Chapter 7

1. E/CN.4/2001/66, para. 1310.

2. E/CN.4/Sub.2/1997/20/Rev.1, Annex II. This Set of Principles was submitted to the UN Sub-Commission on Prevention of Discrimination and Protection of Minorities in 1997 with the aim of its being approved by the UN Commission on Human Rights and forwarded via the UN Economic and Social Council to the UN General Assembly for adoption. At the time of writing of this manual, the Commission on Human Rights had not yet approved the text. The draft Set of Principles is often referred to as the "Joinet Principles" after the name of the Special Rapporteur, Louis Joinet.

3. General Comment 20, para. 15, reproduced in Appendix 11 of this manual.

4. See, for example, A/55/44, paras. 68, 69, referring to Azerbaijan; A/55/44, paras. 74, 75, referring to Kyrgyzstan; A/55/44, paras. 59, 61, referring to Peru.

5. For a review of recent developments in international law on the compatibility of amnesties with the obligations of states regarding the prohibition of torture, see the section on "Torture and impunity" in the report of the UN Special Rapporteur on torture to the 2001 session of the UN General Assembly, A/56/156, paras. 26-33. See also Amnesty International, *Universal jurisdiction: The duty of states to enact and implement legislation – Chapter 14, Overcoming obstacles to implementing universal jurisdiction* (AI Index: IOR 53/017/2001). This and other chapters of the same work are available as a CD-ROM from ijp@amnesty.org.

6. UN General Assembly resolution 56/143 of 19 December 2001, para. 2, and previous annual resolutions of the General Assembly and the Commission on Human Rights on "Torture and other cruel, inhuman or degrading treatment or punishment". These resolutions have also urged governments "to promote the speedy and full implementation of the Vienna Declaration and Programme of Action", and particularly of its section on overcoming impunity for torture, quoted at the beginning of Chapter 7 of this manual.

7. In their commentary on the Convention, Burgers and Danelius (1988, p. 130) have written that the term "complicity or participation" in Article 4 should be understood to include the "instigation" by or the "consent" or "acquiescence" of a public official under Article 1.

As described in section 3.2.5 of this manual, Article 25 of the Rome Statute includes other forms of ancillary criminal responsibility for torture. Under Article 7(1) of the Statute of the International Criminal Tribunal for the former Yugoslavia (Yugoslavia Tribunal), individual criminal responsibility extends not only to those who commit crimes proscribed in that Statute but also to those who plan, instigate, order or otherwise aid and abet in the planning, preparation or execution of a crime. The question of individual criminal responsibility has been examined in several judgments. In the case of *Prosecutor v. Furundžija,* for example, the Yugoslavia Tribunal held that a perpetrator of torture "must participate in an integral part of the torture and partake of the purpose behind the torture", whereas a person who aids and abets torture need not partake of the purpose behind it but "must assist in some way which has a substantial effect on the perpetration of the crime and with knowledge that torture is taking place" *(Prosecutor v. Furundžija,* 10 December 1998, para. 257). (See also *Prosecutor v. Delalić and others,* 16 November 1998, paras. 326-327.)

8. In their commentary on Article 4 of the Convention, Burgers and Danelius (1988, p. 129) have stated that although criminal penalties in general vary from one country to another, "it seems reasonable to require... that the punishment for torture should be close to the penalties applied to the most serious offences under the domestic legal system. Nevertheless, the Convention, being a human rights instrument, should not be invoked as justification for the application of the death penalty".

9. The Human Rights Committee has stated that "no justification or extenuating circumstances may be invoked to excuse a violation of article 7 [of the ICCPR] for any reasons, including those based on an order from a superior officer or public authority" (General Comment 20, para. 3). Article 5 of the UN Code of Conduct for Law Enforcement Officials states that no law enforcement official may "invoke superior orders... as a justification of torture or other cruel, inhuman or degrading treatment or punishment". The Committee against Torture has repeatedly called for the removal of laws and rules requiring automatic obedience or allowing for a defence of superior orders. In 1997, for example, in considering the second periodic report of Uruguay, the Committee called for "the elimination of obedience to a superior as justification for exculpation from the crime of torture", in conformity with the Convention (A/52/44, para. 93).

10. The Human Rights Committee has stated that "those who have refused to obey orders [to commit torture or ill-treatment] must not be punished or subjected to any adverse treatment" (General Comment 20, para. 13). The UN General Assembly has stressed that "States must not punish personnel... for not obeying orders to commit or conceal acts amounting to torture or other cruel, inhuman or degrading treatment or punishment" (resolution 56/143 of 19 December 2001, para. 10).

11. The Special Rapporteur on torture has stated that "there exists a duty to disobey orders from a superior to commit torture" (A/56/156, para. 39(k), reproduced in Appendix 14 of this manual).

12. First Geneva Convention of 1949, Article 49; Second Geneva Convention, Article 50; Third Geneva Convention, Article 129; Fourth Geneva Convention, Article 146.

13. The Preamble to the Rome Statute states that "it is the duty of every State to exercise its criminal jurisdiction over those responsible for international crimes" (preambular para. 6). As the preambular paragraphs and Articles 1 and 17 of the Statute make clear, the primary responsibility to bring to justice those responsible for crimes under the Statute is with states. To do so, a state will need to provide for these crimes under national law or give its national courts the power to enforce international law directly.

14. The formulation of the recommendation varies. In 1996, for example, in considering the second periodic report of Denmark, the Committee recommended "the enactment of a law in Denmark specifically on the crime of torture in conformity with article 1 of the Convention, so that all the elements of the definition of that offence contained in the said article are fully covered" (A/51/44, para. 40). In 2002 it expressed concern about the continuing lack of a definition of torture as provided in Article 1 of the Convention and "the lack of a specific offence of torture punishable by appropriate penalties, as required by article 4, paragraph 2, of the Convention" (Conclusions and recommendations on the fourth periodic report of Denmark, CAT/C/XXVII/Concl.3, 10 May 2002, para. 6(a)).

15. For example, Guatemala became a party to the Convention against Torture in 1990, and in 1995 the specific crime of torture was created under a new Article 201 *bis* of the Guatemalan Penal Code, a development which was welcomed by the Committee against Torture when it considered Guatemala's initial report under the Convention in late 1995 (A/51/44, para. 46). However, Amnesty International informed the Committee that the language of the new article fell short of the definition in the Convention and contained loopholes under which it could be argued that a public official who committed torture under certain circumstances would not have committed a crime proscribed by Article 201 *bis*. Prosecution might still be possible under the older Article 425, which proscribed the use of "torture" against prisoners and detainees, but the penalties under Article 425 were less than those under Article 201 *bis*. In 1998, after considering Guatemala's second periodic report under the Convention, the Committee against Torture accordingly recommended "[h]armonization of article 201 *bis* of the Penal Code with the definition of torture contained in article 1 of the Convention" (A/53/44, para. 165(f)). When Guatemala appeared before the Committee in 2000 to present its third periodic report, the head of the Guatemalan delegation informed the Committee that the government had decided to propose the amendment of Articles 201 *bis* and 425 in line with the Convention (A/56/44, para. 71(h)). The amendments had not yet been made at the time of writing of this manual.

16. Resolution 2001/62 of 25 April 2001, para. 19. The same statement was included in previous resolutions on torture and ill-treatment.

17. A/56/156, para. 39(a).

18. Data compiled by Amnesty International indicated that as of September 2001, over 20 countries had laws which included a specific crime of torture, although many of these fell short of the requirements of the Convention against Torture. Many other countries which were parties to the Convention had not yet provided for a specific crime of torture in their laws. See Amnesty International, *Universal Jurisdiction: The duty of states to enact and implement legislation – Chapter 10, Torture: State practice at the national level* (AI Index: IOR 53/013/2001).

19. General Comment 20, para. 13.

20. The Principles on the Effective Prevention and Investigation of Extra-legal, Arbitrary and Summary Executions also include other concepts applicable to investigations of torture, such as the involvement of families of victims and the publication of a report of the investigation (Principles 16, 17).

21. Resolution 56/143 of 19 December 2001, para. 2.

22. *Assenov and others v. Bulgaria*, 28 October 1998, para. 102. Amnesty International had submitted written comments to the Court on the obligation under Article 3 of the European Convention on Human Rights to ensure effective investigations into complaints and reports of torture or ill-treatment.

23. *Velásquez Rodríguez v. Honduras*, 29 July 1988, paras. 176, 180, 187. See also *Mejía v. Peru*, 1 March 1996, Annual Report of the Inter-American Commission on Human Rights 1995, p. 192.

24. *Hugo Rodríguez v. Uruguay*, 19 July 1994, para. 12.3.

25. General Comment 20, para. 14.

26. *Irène Ursoa Parot v. Spain*, 2 May 1995, para. 10.4. In a later case, the Committee observed "that article 13 of the Convention does not require either the formal lodging of a complaint of torture under the procedure laid down in national law or an express statement of intent to institute and sustain a criminal action arising from the offence, and that it is enough for the victim simply to bring the facts to the attention of an authority of the State for the latter to be obliged to consider it as a tacit but unequivocal expression of the victim's wish that the facts should be promptly and impartially investigated, as prescribed by this provision of the Convention" *(Encarnación Blanco Abad v. Spain*, 14 May 1998, para. 8.6). When the latter case came before the Committee under Article 22 of the Convention, the authorities maintained that the complainant had not formally reported any mistreatment until more than two years after the events. She had, however, complained several times to the doctor who examined her between interrogation sessions, and when she was brought before a judge shortly thereafter, she repeated the allegations. The Committee held that "these elements should have sufficed for the initiation of an investigation [under Article 12], which did not however take place" (ibid., para. 8.3; see also notes 32 and 33, below).

27. *Blanco Abad v. Spain*, para. 8.2.

28. In the case of *Khaled Ben M'Barek v. Tunisia*, the Committee noted that international NGOs began requesting the authorities to conduct an investigation shortly after the death of the victim in October 1991, but that it was only in September 1992 that an inquiry was ordered into the allegations of torture, "over 10 months after the foreign non-governmental organizations had raised the alarm" and over two months after an official commission suggested that an inquiry be held. The Committee found that Tunisia had violated its obligation to proceed to a prompt investigation of reports of torture under Article 12 of the Convention against Torture *(Khaled Ben M'Barek v. Tunisia*, 10 November 1999, paras. 2.10, 11.4-11.7).

29. A/53/44, para. 136.

30. A/53/44, para. 79, referring to Portugal.

31. *Blanco Abad v. Spain*, para. 8.2.

32. The alleged victim complained of ill-treatment (including hooding, insults, threats, blows, and being forced to remain naked) several times to the doctor who examined her between interrogation sessions while she was held incommunicado between 29 January and 2 February 1992. When she was brought before a judge on 2 February she said that she had been subjected to physical and mental ill-treatment, including the threat of rape. However, preliminary proceedings before the Court of Criminal Investigation were initiated only on 21 February. She was not brought before that Court until 13 March; the report of the doctor who examined her during incommunicado detention was not added to the case file until 13 May, and a statement was not taken from the doctor until 17 November. As noted below, the investigation also failed to meet the requirement of impartiality. The Committee found that Spain had violated its obligations under Articles 12 and 13 of the Convention *(Blanco Abad v. Spain,* paras. 8-9).

33. *Ben M'Barek v. Tunisia*, paras. 11.8-11.10. The Committee found that Tunisia had breached its obligation to proceed to an impartial investigation under Articles 12 and 13 of the Convention (ibid., para. 12). Similarly, in the case of *Blanco Abad v. Spain* the Committee held that the failure of the Court of Criminal Investigation to identify and question any of the officers who might have taken part in the alleged torture was "inexcusable, since a criminal investigation must seek both to determine the nature and circumstances of the alleged acts and to establish the identity of any person who might have been involved therein". This and the refusal of the Court to grant the alleged complainant's request to allow the submission of evidence additional to that of the medical experts were "incompatible with the obligation to proceed to an impartial investigation, as provided for in article 13 of the Convention" (para. 8.8).

34. E/CN.4/2001/66, para. 1310. As stated by Burgers and Danelius (1988, p. 145) in their commentary on Article 12 of the Convention against Torture, "In order to ensure impartiality, it is necessary to avoid entrusting the investigation to persons who have close personal or professional links with the persons suspected of having committed such acts, or who may have an interest in protecting these persons or the particular unit to which they belong."

35. For example: "The State party should ensure that all instances of ill-treatment and of torture and other abuses committed by agents of the State are promptly considered and investigated by an independent body." (A/56/40, para. 86(15), referring to the Democratic People's Republic of Korea)

36. In its inquiry on Egypt under Article 20 of the Convention against Torture, the Committee recommended to the government that "it should set up an independent investigation machinery, including in its composition judges, lawyers and medical doctors, that should efficiently examine all the allegations of torture, in order to bring them expeditiously before the courts" (A/51/44, para. 221).

37. In the case of *Assenov and others v. Bulgaria,* for example, the Court found that the investigation of the alleged ill-treatment was insufficiently thorough and effective because – among other things – the investigating authorities had failed to interview witnesses to one of the key incidents (para. 103).

38. Burgers and Danelius, 1988, pp. 145-146.

39. A/54/44, para. 102, referring to Tunisia.

40. See, for example, A/51/44, para. 57(e), referring to Guatemala; para. 79, referring to Colombia.

41. The Committee has referred in one country to "the many allegations of rape or torture by the security forces of women in detention which the latter are fearful of reporting" and stated that the state "should take effective measures to protect the security of women to ensure that no pressure is brought to bear on them to deter them from reporting such violations" (A/54/40, para. 328, referring to Mexico).

42. A/56/156, para. 39(j).

43. In the case of *Assenov and others v. Bulgaria,* the Court held that the state had violated Article 25(1) of the Convention because the authorities had questioned the parents of one of the complainants about his application to the Commission. The Court stated that "the obligation on States under Article 25(1) of the Convention not to interfere with the right of the individual effectively to present and pursue his or her complaint with the Commission confers upon an applicant a right of a procedural nature which can be asserted in Convention proceedings. It is of the utmost importance for the effective system of individual petition that applicants or potential applicants are able to communicate freely with the Convention organs without being subjected to any form of pressure from the authorities to withdraw or modify their complaints" (para. 169).

44. For example, A/56/44, para 97(d), referring to Bolivia; para. 120(b), referring to Brazil.

45. *Aksoy v. Turkey,* 18 December 1996, para. 61.

46. A/56/156, para. 39(j).

47. Principle 34 of the UN Body of Principles for the Protection of All Persons under Any Form of Detention or Imprisonment (Body of Principles on Detention) states: "Whenever the death or disappearance of a detained or imprisoned person occurs during his detention or imprisonment, an inquiry into the cause of death or disappearance shall be held by a judicial or other authority, either on its own motion or at the instance of a member of the family of such a person or any person who has knowledge of the case."

48. The UN Principles on the Effective Prevention and Investigation of Extra-legal, Arbitrary and Summary Executions, supplemented by the UN *Manual on the Effective Prevention and Investigation of Extra-legal, Arbitrary and Summary Executions,* cited in Appendix 3, should be followed in the investigation of cases where a public official is suspected of responsibility for a death in custody.

49. See also the *Istanbul Protocol,* paras. 106-118, pp. 21-23.

50. Principles 5-12 of this draft instrument concern extrajudicial commissions of inquiry having the role of "establishing the facts so that the truth can be found, and of preventing evidence from disappearing" (Principle 5). They cover such matters as guarantees of independence and impartiality, terms of reference, and guarantees for victims, witnesses and people implicated.

51. Qualifications may include legal expertise and expertise in investigative techniques, including forensic medical investigations. Powers may include the power to conduct on-site investigative visits; to obtain and compel the production of all necessary physical evidence, including government records and medical records; to compel the attendance of alleged perpetrators; to compel the attendance and cooperation of witnesses and ensure their protection; and to receive evidence from witnesses unable to attend in person, including witnesses located outside the country. Resources may include laboratory facilities, clerical equipment such as typewriters and computers, and – where necessary – resources to travel and to hold hearings. The investigative body should have adequate investigative, administrative and clerical staff.

52. In a case involving alleged violations of the right to life, the European Court of Human Rights has stated that "there must be a sufficient element of public scrutiny of the investigation or its results to secure accountability in practice as well as in theory. The degree of public scrutiny required may well vary from case to case. In all cases, however, the next of kin of the victim must be involved in the procedure to the extent necessary to safeguard his or her legitimate interests" (*Kelly and others v. UK,* 4 May 2001, para. 98).

53. *O.R., M.M. and M.S. v. Argentina,* 23 November 1989, para. 7.2.

54. E/CN.4/2001/66/Add.2, para. 166.

55. In some countries the prosecutorial functions of investigation and preparing an indictment are done by an investigating judge. Both these functions and the conduct of prosecutions at trial must be done effectively, with adequate qualifications and resources, free from corruption and interference.

56. The obligation to conduct fair trials is set out in Articles 10 and 11 of the Universal Declaration of Human Rights, Articles 14 and 15 of the ICCPR and regional human rights instruments. Article 7(3) of the Convention against Torture provides for "fair treatment at all stages of the proceedings" for anyone against whom proceedings are brought in connection with the offences specified in the Convention. The Geneva Conventions of 1949 (in the articles concerning repression of grave breaches) provide for "safeguards of proper trial and defence" for persons accused of grave breaches and other acts contrary to the Conventions. For a comprehensive analysis of norms for a fair trial, see Amnesty International, *Fair Trials Manual*, 1998.

57. A/56/156, para. 39(j).

58. The UN Commission on Human Rights has stated that "those who encourage, order, tolerate or perpetrate acts of torture must be held responsible and severely punished, including the officials in charge of the place of detention where the prohibited act is found to have taken place" (resolution 2002/38 of 22 April 2002, para. 8). The Special Rapporteur on torture has stated: "If torture has occurred in an official place of detention, the official in charge of that place should be disciplined or punished." (A/56/156, para. 39(j))

59. In a survey of UN member states whose results were reported to the UN Commission on Crime Prevention and Criminal Justice in 1996, responding countries stated that law enforcement officials who had been found guilty by a court or tribunal of inflicting, instigating or tolerating torture were subject to various sanctions including fines, censure, reduction of rank, reduction of pay, transfer from the law enforcement agency, suspension and dismissal. (Use and Application of the Code of Conduct for Law Enforcement Officials, together with the Basic Principles on the Use of Force and Firearms by Law Enforcement Officials, E/CN.15/1996/16/Add.2, para. 14. The text can be found on the website of the UN Crime and Justice Information Network at www.uncjin.org.)

60. Resolution 32/62 of 8 December 1977, adopted without a vote.

61. Burgers and Danelius, 1988, pp. 35-36, 94-95; Rodley, 1999, pp. 41, 129-130.

62. Article 7(2) states that the authorities to whom a case is submitted for the purpose of prosecution "shall take their decision in the same manner as in the case of any ordinary offence of a serious nature under the law of that State".

63. The International Court of Justice has ruled in the case of *Democratic Republic of the Congo v. Belgium* (14 February 2002) that "the functions of a Minister for Foreign Affairs are such that, throughout the duration of his or her office, he or she when abroad enjoys full immunity from criminal jurisdiction and inviolability" (para. 54). Amnesty International does not believe that the International Court of Justice's judgment on the immunity of government officials from prosecution by another state is a correct statement of customary international law (see Amnesty International, *Universal jurisdiction: Belgian court has jurisdiction in Sharon case to investigate 1982 Sabra and Chatila killings,* AI Index: IOR 53/001/2002, pp. 5-13).

64. Amnesty International, *Universal Jurisdiction: The duty of states to enact and implement legislation – Chapter 10.*

65. For examples, see Amnesty International, *End impunity: Justice for the victims of torture,* pp. 95-99.

66. A/56/156, para. 39(a).

67. See Amnesty International, *United Kingdom: The Pinochet case – universal jurisdiction and the absence of immunity for crimes against humanity* (AI Index: EUR 45/01/99) for an analysis of the legal issues involved in the UK phase of the effort to bring Augusto Pinochet to trial.

68. The figures for the two Tribunals include people whose convictions were under appeal at the time of writing. They do not include convictions overturned on appeal. The figures are based on information available on the websites of the two Tribunals as of July 2002.

69. Dusko Tadić was arrested in 1994 in Germany, where he was then living, on suspicion of having committed offences of torture and genocide in the former Yugoslavia, offences which constitute crimes under German law. In 1995 he was transferred to the Yugoslavia Tribunal after the Tribunal requested Germany to defer to its jurisdiction.

70. *Prosecutor v. Tadić,* Trial Chamber, 7 May 1997, paras. 730, 738, 744, 754, 764. Dusko Tadić was also found guilty of "persecutions on political, racial and religious grounds" as crimes against humanity for a series of killings, beatings and other abuses against Muslim civilians (para. 718).

71. Ibid., paras. 726, 735, 742, 752, 763. The Tribunal found that various beatings and other grievous acts of violence perpetrated by the defendant "were committed in the context of an armed conflict and in close connection to that conflict" (para. 726).

72. He had been charged under Count 8 of the indictment with "torture or inhuman treatment" as a grave breach of the Geneva Conventions, but the Trial Chamber seems to have had "inhuman treatment" in mind when they considered the facts of the case (see *Prosecutor v. Tadić,* judgment of 7 May 1997, para. 244).

73. The appeals chamber found that an international armed conflict existed at the time of the offences and that the jurisdiction of the Yugoslavia Tribunal over grave breaches of the Geneva Conventions therefore applied. As civilians and citizens of the newly independent state of Bosnia-Herzegovina in the hands of Serb forces, the victims were "protected persons" under the Fourth Geneva Convention. *(Prosecutor v. Tadić,* 15 July 1999, paras. 162, 167-171)

74. *Prosecutor v. Tadić,* sentencing judgments of 14 July 1997 (Trial Chamber), para. 74 and 11 November 1999 (Appeals Chamber), para. 32.

75. Jean-Paul Akayesu was arrested in Zambia in 1995 and handed over to the Rwanda Tribunal in 1996.

76. The victims, who were under interrogation, had been beaten, forced to beat each other, or had their lives threatened. As a result of the beatings, one victim sustained a broken rib, another had trouble walking and another had scars and continuing health problems.

77. The other acts of sexual violence committed against five of the women consisted of their being forcibly undressed and being made to march and do exercises naked in public, after which three of the women were raped and allegedly killed.

78. *Prosecutor v. Akayesu,* 2 September 1998, paras. 683-684, 696, 697.

79. Ibid., para. 734. The trial chamber noted that many of the women were raped several times, often in public and often by more than one assailant, and with spoken references to Tutsi women as sexual objects. In most cases the rapes were accompanied with the intention to kill: many rapes were perpetrated near mass graves where the women were taken to be killed (paras. 731-733). "Sexual violence was a step in the process of destruction of the Tutsi group – destruction of the spirit, of the will to live, and of life itself" (para. 732).

80. The fourth defendant, Zejnil Delalić, was the local Bosnian government army commander; he was found not to have had command and control over the prison camp and over the guards who worked there, such as to entail criminal responsibility for their actions, and was therefore acquitted (*Prosecutor v. Delalić and others,* 16 November 1998, para. 721). Two of the defendants had been arrested in Austria and Germany respectively; the other two were handed over to the Tribunal by the government of Bosnia-Herzegovina.

81. Ibid., paras. 824, 834, 845, 856.

82. Ibid., paras. 943, 965. The trial chamber emphasized the severity of the suffering inflicted on the two victims, including the effect of "living in a state of constant fear and depression, suicidal tendencies, and exhaustion, both mental and physical" in the case of the first victim (para. 942) and "the extreme pain of anal penetration and subsequent bleeding, the severe psychological distress evidenced by the victim while being raped under circumstance [*sic*] where Mr Delić [one of the defendants] was armed and threatening her life, and the general depression of the victim, evidenced by her constant crying, the feeling that she was going crazy and the fact that she was treated with tranquilizers" in the case of the second (para. 964). It found that the rapes were committed as a means of punishment, obtaining information, intimidating the victims and others and for reasons based on discrimination.

83. Ibid., paras. 924, 977, 998.

84. Ibid., paras. 1008, 1011.

85. Ibid., paras. 866, 1018, 1047, 1048, 1059, 1066, 1070, 1072.

86. The trial chamber found that "the creation and maintenance of an atmosphere of terror in the Celebici prison-camp, by itself and *a fortiori*, together with the deprivation of adequate food, water, sleeping and toilet facilities and medical care" constituted "wilfully causing great suffering or serious injury to body or health" and "cruel treatment" under the Statute of the Yugoslavia Tribunal (ibid., para. 1119). The guard and the deputy commander were guilty for their direct participation in the creation and maintenance of the atmosphere of terror (paras. 1121-1122), while the commander was guilty for having failed to prevent the acts of terror or punish the perpetrators and – as "the individual with primary responsibility for, and the ability to affect, the conditions in the prison-camp" – for omitting to provide the detainees with adequate food, water, health care and toilet facilities, thereby participating in "the maintenance of the inhumane conditions" that prevailed at the camp (para. 1123).

87. The sentences were under review at the time of writing of this manual.

88. Having been secretly indicted by the Yugoslavia Tribunal in 1995, Anto Furundžija was arrested by members of the multinational Stabilization Force in Bosnia-Herzegovina in 1997 and taken to The Hague for trial.

89. *Prosecutor v. Furundžija,* 10 December 1998, para. 269. The beatings, threats, multiple rapes and sexual assaults inflicted on Witness A caused "severe physical and mental suffering" and were inflicted for the purpose of obtaining information, thereby amounting to torture, and the beatings and forcible witnessing of the rape of his friend inflicted on Witness D in the course of his interrogation also amounted to torture. Anto Furundžija was a co-perpetrator of the torture of Witness A "by virtue of his interrogation of her as an integral part of the torture" (para. 267) and was also a co-perpetrator of the torture of Witness D.

90. Ibid., para. 275. Anto Furundžija had not personally raped Witness A, but his "presence and continued interrogation of Witness A encouraged Accused B and substantially contributed to the criminal acts committed by him" (para. 273).

91. In determining the sentence to be imposed on the first count, the court noted: "Torture is one of the most serious offences known to international criminal law and any sentence imposed must take this into account." In situations such as this where one person tortures someone who is being interrogated by another, "the fellow perpetrator plays a role every bit as grave as the person who actually inflicts the pain and suffering" (ibid., para. 281). In relation to the second count, the court considered that "[t]he circumstances of these attacks were particularly horrifying" and that "[t]he accused, far from preventing these crimes, played a prominent part in their commission" (para. 282).

92. *Prosecutor v. Kunarac and others,* 22 February 2001, paras. 745, 782.

93. Certain rapes were committed by the perpetrator "with the aim of discriminating between the members of his ethnic group and the Muslims, in particular its women and girls" (ibid., para. 654).

94. Ibid., para. 782. This conviction appears to relate to the fact that the defendant forced several women to dance or to stand naked on a table while he and another man watched and pointed weapons at them. Being forced to stand naked while being watched was "a painful and humiliating experience for the three women involved, even more so because of their young age" (para. 773).

95. One defendant and another soldier kept two women as their "personal property" for about six months; the women were raped "continuously and constantly", and the defendant "asserted his exclusivity" over one of the women by forbidding any other soldier to rape her (paras. 741-742, 745). Another defendant kept two women for a week and two others for about four months, exercising a *"de facto* power of ownership" over them; the women were repeatedly raped and were beaten, slapped, threatened and required to do the household chores, and the defendant later sold several of them to other soldiers (paras. 749-751, 759, 778-782). In both instances the defendants were convicted of rape and enslavement (the elements of the crime of enslavement as applied by the Tribunal, involving exercising powers "attaching to the right of ownership over a person", are set out in para. 540).

96. The civilians were placed in front of the headquarters for about two and a half to three hours; they were told that whoever moved would be instantly cut down. The Tribunal concluded: "Quite evidently, this inflicted considerable mental suffering upon the persons involved" *(Prosecutor v. Blaškić,* 3 March 2000, paras. 714-716, 743 and Disposition). In another case, a defendant was convicted of "outrages upon personal dignity" for similar acts *(Prosecutor v. Aleksovski,* 25 June 1999, para. 229).

97. *Prosecutor v. Blaškić,* paras. 693, 699, 735, 738 and Disposition. The defendant was also found guilty of "inhuman treatment" and "cruel treatment" for his responsibility for other ill-treatment of detainees including rape and other violence, poor conditions of detention and an "atmosphere of terror reigning in the detention facilities" (paras. 700, 733-734 and Disposition). The judgment was under appeal at the time of writing of this manual.

98. The case of *Prosecutor v. Kvočka and others* was under appeal at the time of writing.

99. Literally, "reparation" means "repairing". In line with the draft Basic Principles on Reparation (see below), "reparation" is generally used today to refer to the various actions which the state should take to make good the harm inflicted through human rights violations, in place of the older term "redress" (a term derived from the French word *"redresser"*, meaning "to straighten"). According to the Inter-American Court of Human Rights, "[r]eparation involves... measures that are intended to eliminate the effects of the violation that was committed. Their nature and amount depend on the damage done both at the material and moral levels." *(Blake v. Guatemala, Reparations,* 22 January 1999, para. 34)

100. *Aloeboetoe and others v. Suriname, Reparations,* 10 September 1993, para. 43. The Court has also stated: "When a wrongful act occurs that is imputable to a State, the State incurs international responsibility for the violation of international law, with the resulting duty to make reparation, and the duty to put an end to the consequences of the violation." *(Blake v. Guatemala, Reparations,* para. 33)

101. E/CN.4/2000/62, Annex. The draft Basic Principles on Reparation are often referred to as the "van Boven/Bassiouni Principles" after the names of the two Special Rapporteurs – Theo van Boven, who drew up the initial draft as Special Rapporteur of the UN Sub-Commission on Prevention of Discrimination and Protection of Minorities, and M. Cherif Bassiouni, who was appointed Special Rapporteur to the Commission on Human Rights in 1998 to revise the draft prepared by Theo van Boven. At the time of writing of this manual, the draft Basic Principles on Reparation had not yet been adopted by the Commission on Human Rights.

102. According to the draft Basic Principles on Reparation (Article 22), "Restitution should, whenever possible, restore the victim to the original situation before the violations of international human rights or humanitarian law occurred. Restitution includes: restoration of liberty, legal rights, social status, family life and citizenship; return to one's place of residence; and restoration of employment and return of property."

103. Among the measures to be taken for satisfaction under Article 25 of the draft Basic Principles on Reparation are "[a]n official declaration or a judicial decision restoring the dignity, reputation and legal and social rights of the victim and of persons closely connected with the victim" and "[a]pology, including public acknowledgement of the facts and acceptance of responsibility". For an example of the latter, see the statement by the Turkish government in a friendly settlement of a case of "disappearance" in the European Court of Human Rights that it "regret[s] the occurrence of the actions which have led to the bringing of the present applications..." *(Aydın v. Turkey* (28293/95, 29494/95 and 30219/96), 10 July 2001, para. 13).

104. The Human Rights Committee has referred to measures for non-recurrence as an obligation in cases of torture. In 1980, for example, in a case where it found evidence of torture and inhuman treatment along with other human rights violations, the Committee stated that "the State party is under an obligation... to take steps to ensure that similar violations do not occur in the future" *(Alberto Grille Motta v. Uruguay,* 29 July 1980, para. 18). Similarly, in a more recent case involving a violation of Article 7 of the ICCPR, the Committee stated that the state party was "under an obligation to take steps to prevent similar violations occurring in the future" (*Rafael Armando Rojas García v. Colombia,* 3 April 2001, para. 12). Article 25 of the draft Basic Principles on Reparation lists a series of measures to be taken to prevent recurrence of human rights violations.

105. As torture and ill-treatment are prohibited under Principle 6 of the Body of Principles on Detention, the strictures in Principle 35 apply to compensation for these acts. The *information* which the authorities must provide for use in claiming compensation in accordance with Principle 35 would include records on arrest (Principle 12) and interrogation (Principle 23) and information on medical examinations (Principle 26).

106. For example, A/50/44, para. 114, referring to Morocco. See Ingelse, 2001, pp. 370-376 for an analysis of the Committee's views on the obligation to afford compensation and other forms of reparation under Article 14 of the Convention against Torture.

107. For example, A/56/44, para. 66(a), referring to Cameroon.

108. A/53/44, para. 118(h), referring to Cuba. Also, the Rome Statute provides for the establishment of a trust fund for the benefit of victims of crimes under the jurisdiction of the International Criminal Court and the families of such victims (Article 79). This issue was being considered by the Preparatory Commission for the International Criminal Court at the time of writing of this manual.

109. A/56/156, para. 39(j).

110. See, for example, Report on visit to Mexico, E/CN.4/1998/38/Add.2, para. 88(m).

111. In a decision adopted in 1981 concerning a man who had suffered torture and other human rights violations at the hands of the security services, the Committee found that "the State party is under an obligation pursuant to article 2(3) of the Covenant to provide effective remedies to López Burgos [the complainant] including... compensation for the violations which he has suffered" (*Sergio Rubén López Burgos v. Uruguay,* 29 July 1981, para. 14). For a more recent formulation urging the state party to grant compensation, see *Rodríguez v. Uruguay,* para. 14.

112. The Court has awarded non-pecuniary damages with regard to torture or ill-treatment in a number of cases. Factors which the Court has taken into account in deciding on the level of damages have included the fact that the complainant "suffered severe, life-threatening injury at the hands of gendarmes which amounted to torture" and that "there had been a failure to provide an effective remedy" (*Ilhan v. Turkey,* 27 June 2000, para. 112), and "pain and suffering", stemming from "very serious abuse and neglect" and resulting in continuing psychiatric illness (*Z and others v. UK,* 10 May 2001, para. 130).

113. Noting that the "disappearance" of the victim "caused his parents and brothers suffering, intense anguish, and frustration in the face of the Guatemalan authorities' failure to investigate and the cover up of what occurred", and that the "disappearance", which began with the detention of the victim in March 1985, "lasted until 1992 when his mortal remains were located", the Court awarded US$30,000 as moral damages to each of the four family members of the victim, as well as other specific sums for material damages including medical expenses (*Blake v. Guatemala, Reparations,* paras. 57-58, 75).

114. The Human Rights Committee has recommended the establishment of independent bodies with the authority to receive and investigate complaints of police abuses, including ill-treatment, and the power to ensure compensation to the victims (Concluding observations on the second periodic report of Switzerland, adopted on 29 and 30 October 2001, CCPR/CO/73/CH, para. 11).

115. In the celebrated case of *Filártiga v. Peña-Irala,* 30 June 1980, a US court, acting under a rarely invoked provision of the civil law (the Alien Tort Claims Act, Section 1350 of Title 28 of the US Code, providing US courts with jurisdiction over civil actions by foreigners for torts "committed in violation of the law of nations"), awarded two plaintiffs from Paraguay damages in excess of US$10 million for the kidnapping and torturing to death of their respective brother and son by a Paraguayan police official in Paraguay some eight years earlier. A federal Court of Appeals held that "deliberate torture perpetrated under color of official authority violates universally accepted norms of the international law of human rights, regardless of the nationality of the parties. Thus, whenever an alleged torturer is found and served with process by an alien within our borders, [section] 1350 provides federal jurisdiction." The Court of Appeals stated in its judgment that "for purposes of civil liability, the torturer has become – like the pirate and slave trader before him – *hostis humani generis,* an enemy of all mankind". (See Rodley, 1999, pp. 127-129 for an account of the case.) However, in the case of *Al-Adsani v. UK* the European Court of Human Rights held that a state party to the European Convention on Human Rights was not obliged under the Convention to provide a civil remedy for torture for which the authorities of another state, Kuwait, were allegedly responsible (*Al-Adsani v. UK,* 21 November 2001, para. 40).

116. The development of such services is discussed in van Willigen, 1992 and Welsh, 1996.

117. For example, in its conclusions and recommendations on the initial report of Benin, CAT/C/XXVII/Concl.1, 22 November 2001, para. 6(2) (available in French only).

118. With regard to Chile, for example, he recommended that national non-governmental organizations should receive official support to carry out their activities in the rehabilitation of torture victims (E/CN.4/1996/35/Add.2, para. 76).

119. Article 11 of the UN Declaration of Basic Principles of Justice for Victims of Crime and Abuse of Power states: "Where public officials or other agents acting in an official or quasi-official capacity have violated national criminal laws, the victims should receive restitution from the State whose officials or agents were responsible for the harm inflicted. In cases where the Government under whose authority the victimizing act or omission occurred is no longer in existence, the State or Government successor in title should provide restitution to the victims."

120. See also Article 8 of the Declaration of Basic Principles of Justice for Victims of Crime and Abuse of Power, which calls for restitution by offenders to the victims of their crimes. The Declaration also calls on states to endeavour to provide financial compensation to victims of crime when compensation is not fully available from the offender or other sources (Article 12) and encourages the establishment of national funds for compensation to victims (Article 13).

121. UN General Assembly resolution 36/151 of 16 December 1981, para. 1.

122. Applications for grants must be received before 30 November each year for consideration by the Fund's Board of Trustees at its annual session the following May. Guidelines for applicants and application forms can be found on the UN human rights website www.unhchr.ch, under the section relating to the Fund.

123. United Nations Voluntary Fund for Victims of Torture: Report of the Secretary-General to the 56th session of the UN General Assembly (2001), A/56/181, Table 1 and para. 13.

124. Resolution 56/143 of 19 December 2001, para. 25, and previous resolutions.

Chapter 8

1. UN Charter, Articles 55-56.

2. The latest at the time of writing was General Assembly resolution 56/143 of 19 December 2001. As described in section 1.1 of this manual, other key actions at the UN have included the adoption of the Declaration against Torture in 1975, the adoption of the Convention against Torture in 1984, and the statement by the World Conference on Human Rights in 1993 urging all states "to put an immediate end to the practice of torture and eradicate this evil forever" (Vienna Declaration and Programme of Action, Part II, para. 57).

3. The need to act bilaterally to ensure respect for human rights is referred to in the UN Principles on the Effective Prevention and Investigation of Extra-legal, Arbitrary and Summary Executions. Article 8 states: "Governments shall make every effort to prevent extra-legal, arbitrary and summary executions through measures such as diplomatic intercession, improved access of complainants to intergovernmental and judicial bodies, and public denunciation."

4. The Opinion on the Scope and Content of the Principle of *Non-refoulement*, cited below, suggests that in situations where the threat specified in Article 33(1) "is foreseen on account of reasons other than those specified", as in situations of "general violence in the country of origin", it "is appropriate to look at the matter more broadly. It is the facts that matter – that the person concerned is facing some objectively discernible threat of persecution or to life [or] freedom. The precise identification of the cause of that threat is not material" (paras. 138-139). And although Article 33(2) excludes from the protection afforded by Article 33(1) a refugee who can reasonably be regarded as "a danger to the security of the country where he is" or who constitutes "a danger to the community" of that country by virtue of having been convicted in a final judgment of a particularly serious crime, a state "will not be entitled" to rely on these exceptions "if to do so would expose the individual concerned to a danger" of torture or ill-treatment "or a risk coming within the scope of other non-derogable principles of human rights" (ibid., paras. 179, 183).

5. UNHCR, Opinion on the Scope and Content of the Principle of *Non-refoulement,* 20 July 2001, para. 132. (This document can be found on the UNHCR website at www.unhcr.ch.)

6. The term "asylum-seeker" applies to a person who is seeking asylum but whose status as a refugee under the Refugee Convention has not as yet been determined. It is a fundamental principle of international law that an asylum-seeker must be treated as a refugee unless or until they have been finally determined to be otherwise.

7. According to the Opinion, a real risk of torture or ill-treatment in a given case "will be something to be established 'to a reasonable degree' taking account of all the relevant facts. This threshold will require more than mere conjecture concerning a threat but less than proof to a level of probability or certainty" (para. 135).

8. Ibid., para. 144. This last conclusion is based on the word "territories" in Article 33(1). This word carries the meaning of "any territory", including territories from which there is a risk of removal to another territory where the person in question would be at risk. Moreover, the use of the word "territories", rather than "countries" or "states", implies that "the legal status of the place to which the individual may be sent is not material". Thus, the principle of *non-refoulement* applies "in circumstances in which the refugee or asylum-seeker is within their country of origin but is nevertheless under the protection of another Contracting State. This may arise, for example, in circumstances in which a refugee or asylum-seeker takes refuge in the diplomatic mission of another State or comes under the protection of the armed forces of another State engaged in a peace-keeping or other role in the country of origin" (ibid., paras. 113-115).

9. For an analysis of the factors which the Committee has taken into account in deciding on cases, see Gorlick, 1999; Ingelse, 2001, pp. 293-308.

10. Ingelse, 2001, p. 294.

11. General comment on the implementation of article 3 of the Convention in the context of article 22, paras. 6-7, cited in Appendix 3 of this manual. The General comment lists information which would be relevant in assessing the risk of torture, including whether the complainant has been tortured or maltreated in the past, whether a claim of having been tortured or maltreated is supported by medical or other evidence, whether the torture has had after-effects and whether the complainant has engaged in political or other activities which would appear to make him or her particularly vulnerable to a risk of torture if forcibly sent to another state.

12. *Ismail Alan v. Switzerland*, 8 May 1996, para. 11.3; *Pauline Muzonzo Paku Kisoki v. Sweden,* 8 May 1996, para. 9.3.

13. *Kaveh Yaragh Tala v. Sweden,* 15 November 1996, para. 10.3.

14. *Alan v. Switzerland.* The Swiss authorities' rejection of the complainant's asylum claim had been based in part on "the possibility for the author to settle in a part of Turkey where he would not be at risk". The Committee, however, noted that "the author already had to leave his native area, that Izmir did not prove secure for him either, and that, since there are indications that the police are looking for him, it is not likely that a 'safe' area for him exists in Turkey" (paras. 6.2, 11.4). In a similar case before the European Court of Human Rights, the UK authorities had proposed to return the complainant to a different part of India from the Punjab area, where he had been politically active and claimed to have been tortured. The Court, however, noted that the Punjab police had until recently been "fully capable of pursuing their targets into areas of India far away from Punjab" and that "no concrete evidence" had been produced "of any fundamental reform or reorganisation of the Punjab police in recent years" (*Chahal v. UK,* 15 November 1996, paras. 100, 103; see note 19 below).

15. *Sadiq Shek Elmi v. Australia,* 14 May 1999, paras. 6, 7, cited in Chapter 3, note 47. Similarly, in the case of *Ahmed v. Austria* the European Court of Human Rights found that the complainant could not return to Somalia, a collapsed state, without being exposed to the risk of treatment contrary to Article 3 of the European Convention on Human Rights (prohibition of torture and ill-treatment) at the hands of a clan and that owing to the "absolute nature" of Article 3, this conclusion was not invalidated by "the current lack of State authority in Somalia" (*Ahmed v. Austria,* 17 December 1996, paras. 44-46). In the case of *HLR v. France,* where the complainant, a convicted drug trafficker, claimed he would be at risk of ill-treatment if returned to Colombia, the Court held that it did "not rule out the possibility that Article 3 of the Convention may also apply where the danger emanates from persons or groups of persons who are not public officials"; in this case, however, it did not consider that a risk of ill-treatment had been established (*HLR v. France,* 29 April 1997, paras. 40, 44). In another case, the Court held that the removal of a released prisoner dying of AIDS to his own country, where he would face adverse conditions, would expose him to "a real risk of dying under most distressing circumstances" and would therefore amount to inhuman treatment in violation of the Convention (*D v. UK,* 2 May 1997, paras. 51-54).

16. General comment 20 on Article 7 of the ICCPR, para. 9. In the case of *Ng v. Canada,* cited in Chapter 3, note 123, the Committee found that Canada had violated Article 7 of the ICCPR by extraditing the complainant to the USA to face capital charges and possible execution by gas in California (*Charles Chitat Ng v. Canada,* 5 November 1993, para. 16.3).

17. E/CN.4/2002/137, para. 14.

18. *T.I. v. UK,* admissibility decision, 7 March 2000, p. 14.

19. *Chahal v. UK,* para. 80. The Court noted that the UK wished to deport the complainant, a prominent Sikh separatist from India, on the ground that his continued presence in the UK "was unconducive to the public good for reasons of national security, including the fight against terrorism". Citing information submitted by Amnesty International and other evidence, the Court found it to be substantiated that there was "a real risk" of the complainant being subjected to torture or ill-treatment if returned to India; accordingly, "the order for his deportation to India would, if executed, give rise to a violation of Article 3" of the Convention (paras. 75, 107).

20. Opinion, op. cit., para. 251.

21. *Balabou Mutombo v. Switzerland,* 27 April 1994, paras. 9.4, 9.7, 10. This case was the first one in which the Committee found in favour of a rejected asylum-seeker under Article 3 of the Convention.

22. Ibid., para. 252.

23. For analyses of the factors which the Committee against Torture has taken into account in deciding on individual cases, see Gorlick, 1999; Ingelse, 2001, pp. 293-308.

24. Resolution 56/143 of 19 December 2001, para. 11.

25. Resolution of 3 October 2001, cited in Chapter 5, note 68.

26. As of 1 October 2002, 51 states parties to the Convention had made declarations under Article 21 and 50 states had made declarations under Article 22. Of the 130 states parties to the Convention, 76 had not made a declaration under either Article 21 or Article 22.

27. As of 1 October 2002, nine states – Afghanistan, China, Cuba, Israel, Kuwait, Morocco, Poland, Saudi Arabia and Ukraine – had made such declarations. Several states which originally made such declarations have since withdrawn them.

28. The UN General Assembly has urged states parties to the Convention against Torture "to comply strictly with their obligations under the Convention, including, in view of the high number of reports not submitted, their obligation to submit reports in accordance with article 19" (resolution 56/143 of 19 December 2001, para. 8). As of 8 May 2001, 87 states – more than two thirds of the states parties to the Convention – were overdue in submitting one or more of their reports, according to the Committee's annual report to the General Assembly (A/56/44, para. 23). Thirty-five of these states had not submitted their initial reports, including five states whose initial reports were more than 10 years overdue (Guinea, Guyana, Somalia, Togo and Uganda).

29. While the Committee has commended some reports for their thoroughness, it has noted that other reports have lacked important information required under the Committee's guidelines to enable the Committee to assess compliance with states' obligations under the Convention.

30. For a critical examination of the Committee's practice in questioning government delegates on their countries' reports and formulating recommendations, see Bank, 1997, 2000.

31. In a study of the Committee's response to complaints under Article 22 in relation to *refoulement* (see section 8.3), Brian Gorlick has pointed to the risk that the Committee's "increasing workload could lead to a stricter application of its rules of procedure and the adoption of higher evidentiary burdens which may result in the turning away of otherwise meritorious claims" (Gorlick, 1999, p. 495).

32. The UN General Assembly has urged states parties to the Convention against Torture "to take fully into account the conclusions and recommendations made by the Committee after its consideration of their reports" (resolution 56/143 of 19 December 2001, para. 15).

33. In his letter of resignation of 15 October 2001, the Special Rapporteur on torture stated that "the mandate [of the Special Rapporteur] would be much more effective were the Office [of the UN High Commissioner for Human Rights] able to grant resources to permit maximum activity in responding to the enormous amount of information it receives or could obtain. Regrettably, the [UN] organization has still to demonstrate the political will and priority to translate its concerns about torture and other grave human rights problems into more effective action. I hope that the work of my successor will benefit from an allocation of resources commensurate with the scope of the problem." (E/CN.4/2002/76, Annex II)

34. Resolution 2002/38 of 22 April 2002, para. 37.

35. For an example of the involvement of doctors in certifying that prisoners were fit for interrogation methods involving torture, see section 2.2, "Israeli Occupied Territories: Outlawing 'legal' torture".

36. *Amnesty International Conference for the Abolition of Torture, Paris, 10-11 December 1973, Final Report.*

37. World Medical Association, Declaration of Tokyo, available from the World Medical Association website at www.wma.net. (This and similar texts cited in this section are reproduced in Amnesty International, *Ethical Codes and Declarations Relevant to the Health Professions...*, 4th revised edition, 2000, and can be found on Amnesty International's website at www.amnesty.org.)

38. The Declaration of Hawaii, as amended in 1983, is reproduced in Amnesty International, *Ethical Codes and Declarations Relevant to the Health Professions...*, 3rd revised edition, 1994, pp. 18-20. To reflect the impact of changing social attitudes and new medical developments, the World Medical Association examined and revised some of the ethical standards for the practice of psychiatry, which are reflected in the Declaration of Madrid, adopted in 1996 by the World Psychiatric Association (see note below).

39. World Psychiatric Association, Declaration of Madrid, available on-line at www.wpanet.org.

40. Support for doctors who do protest against torture is given, generally, in the Declaration of Tokyo (Article 6) and specifically in the World Medical Association's Declaration Concerning Support for Medical Doctors Refusing to Participate in, or to Condone, the Use of Torture or Other Forms of Cruel, Inhuman or Degrading Treatment (1997). However, as a case study in a recent British Medical Association publication shows, the doctor who protests at ill-treatment cannot expect praise from the prison authorities for his or her action (British Medical Association, 2001, p. 120).

41. International Council of Nurses, The Nurse's Role in the Care of Detainees and Prisoners, 1975, revised 1991 (reproduced in Amnesty International, *Ethical Codes and Declarations Relevant to the Health Professions...*, 3rd revised edition, pp. 24-26).

42. International Council of Nurses, The Nurse's Role in the Care of Prisoners and Detainees, 1998, available on the International Council of Nurses website at www.icn.ch.

43. The evolution of this work is discussed in Welsh, 1996.

44. Amnesty International, 1999, "Publications on health and human rights themes 1982-1998", *Health and Human Rights,* Vol. 4, No. 1, pp. 215-264; this followed an earlier version issued by Amnesty International (AI Index: ACT 75/03/97). The bibliography is available updated online at www.amnesty.org.

45. A list of such centres is contained in Amnesty International, *Medical and psychosocial services for victims of human rights violations* (AI Index: ACT 75/06/00); an updated on-line list can be found on Amnesty International's website at www.amnesty.org. An online list can also be found on the website of the International Rehabilitation Council for Torture Victims at www.irct.org.

46. See Amnesty International, *Documenting human rights violations: The example of torture* (AI Index: ACT 75/04/00).

47. For further discussion of some of the issues addressed in the *Istanbul Protocol,* see Peel and Iacopino, eds., 2002.

48. British Medical Association, 2001. The British Medical Association had previously published reports on medical involvement in human rights abuses and, specifically, in torture. It undertakes appeals in cases of health professionals at risk.

49. For practical information on how to campaign, see Amnesty International, *Campaigning manual,* 2001.

50. The Holy See, Ireland, Lesotho, Mongolia, Nigeria, Saint Vincent and the Grenadines and Sierra Leone became parties to the Convention between 18 October 2000 and 1 October 2002. Madagascar, Nauru and San Marino signed the Convention during the same period.

51. Azerbaijan, Costa Rica, Germany, Ireland, Mexico, Paraguay and the Seychelles made declarations under Article 22 between 18 October 2000 and 1 October 2002.

52. In the **Declaration on the Right and Responsibility of Individuals, Groups and Organs of Society to Promote and Protect Universally Recognized Human Rights and Fundamental Freedoms,** adopted in 1998, the UN General Assembly stated: "The State shall take all necessary measures to ensure the protection by the competent authorities of everyone, individually and in association with others, against any violence, threats, retaliation, *de facto* or *de jure* adverse discrimination, pressure or any other arbitrary action as a consequence of his or her legitimate exercise of the rights referred to in the present Declaration." (Article 12).

53. Stroun and Daudin, 1997.

Index